THE ONE BEST SYSTEM

THE ONE BEST SYSTEM

A History of American Urban Education

DAVID B. TYACK

Harvard University Press
Cambridge, Massachusetts, and London, England

To my students—past, present, and future

ACKNOWLEDGMENTS

Over the course of the seven years that I have spent researching and writing this book so many people have assisted me that thanking each one here would fill many pages. In the notes I have tried to acknowledge my gratitude to a multitude of individual scholars, and the dedication honors those who have most directly shaped this book, my students. To colleagues at the University of Illinois and Stanford University I am most grateful for those extended conversations, exchanges of papers, hallway arguments, and friendships that constitute an essential part of intellectual community. Several historians elsewhere have given me invaluable counsel and criticism: in particular, Lawrence Cremin, David Hammack, Carl Kaestle, Michael Katz, Marvin Lazerson, Robert McCaul, and Selwyn Troen. By naming them I in no way wish to impute guilt to them by association with my errors (indeed, so diverse are their viewpoints that no doubt they would pick different parts of this book to disagree with).

For generous grants underwriting this research I am most grateful to the Carnegie Corporation and to the United States Office of Education. To my research assistants also I owe a special debt: Mobilaji Adenubi, Michael Berkowitz, Paul Chapman, Larry Cuban, Robert Cummings, Deborah Daniels, Toby Edson, Judy Rosenbaum, and Aphrodite Scarato. Dorothy Farana not only typed an early draft of the book but also has been a helpful colleague at Stanford in myriad ways. I am much indebted to Nancy Clemente for her great editorial skill.

It is customary for academic authors to testify about the contributions their wives made to their work. My wife has pursued a career of her own, much to the delight of her family, her students, and her readers.

Three friends, perceptive members of the species "general reader," have given me candid and useful appraisals of the manuscript: Linda Dallin, Ricka Leiderman, and Susan Lloyd.

In this book I have used revised versions of studies I published elsewhere: "Bureaucracy and the Common School: The Example of Portland, Oregon, 1851–1913," *American Quarterly,* 19 (Fall 1967), 475–98. "Catholic Power, Black Power, and the Schools," *Educational Forum,* 32 (Nov. 1967), 27–29. "City Schools: Centralization of Control at the Turn of the Century," in Jerry Israel, ed., *Building the Organizational Society* (New York: Free Press, 1972), 57–72. "From Village School to Urban System: A Political and Social History." Final report of U. S. Office of Education Project no. 0-0809, Sept. 1, 1972. Available through ERIC Document Reproduction Service, order number ED 075 955. "The 'One Best System': A Historical Analysis," in Herbert J. Walberg and Andrew Kopan, eds., *Rethinking Urban Education* (San Francisco: Jossey-Bass, 1972), 231–46. "The Tribe and the Common School: Community Control in Rural Education," *American Quarterly* 24 (Spring 1972), 3–19. "Victims without 'Crimes': Some Historical Perspectives on Black Education," written with Robert G. Newby, *Journal of Negro Education,* 46 (Summer 1971) 192–206.

CONTENTS

Contents

ILLUSTRATIONS

THE ONE BEST SYSTEM

"Lifting American Social and Economic Life"—A School Board Perspective

Prologue

This is an interpretive history of the organizational revolution that took place in American schooling during the last century. It deals with the politics of education: who got what, where, when, and how. It explores some of the changes in institutional structure and ideology in education and what these may have meant in practice to the generations of Americans who passed through classrooms. And it attempts to assess how the schools shaped, and were shaped by, the transformation of the United States into an urban-industrial nation.

I intend this study to be exploratory and tentative. In a sense this synthesis is premature since a new generation of talented scholars is directing its attention to monographic studies of urban schooling and will enrich our knowledge of how schools actually operated. I am deeply indebted to this contemporary scholarship, much of it still in unpublished form. But there is also a mass of earlier empirical investigation of the character of urban education—gathered for purposes other than historical interpretation—that yields useful insights when subjected to new analytic questions and value perspectives. What I am attempting here is a dovetailing of old and new scholarship, together with my own research, into a general interpretive framework. If the book prompts others to contest or refine its explanations, to make its periodization more precise, to describe missing dimensions, so much the better.

I am addressing this study not only to specialists but also to citizens curious and concerned about how we arrived at the present crisis in urban education. We stand at a point in time when we need to examine those educational institutions and values we have taken for granted. We need to turn facts into puzzles in order to perceive alternatives both in the past and in the present. The way we understand that past profoundly shapes how we make choices today.

Any historical writing perforce does violence to the kaleidoscopic surface and hidden dynamics of everyday life. The same "reality" may appear quite different to diverse groups and individuals. That fact alone destroys the possibility of a single objective account of the meaning of events to various people. Much of the written history of schools has revealed the perspective of those at the top of the educational and social system. We need as well to try to examine urban education as students, parents, and teachers saw it and to understand the point of view of clients who were victimized by their poverty, their color, their cultural differences. Accordingly I have tried to look at urban schooling from the varying perspectives of several social groups.[1]

At the same time, I am attempting to analyze a system of schooling that by and large did not operate in haphazard ways. When I began this study I wanted to tell the story of urban education from the point of view of those who were in some sense its victims, the poor and the dispossessed. I soon realized, however, that what was needed was not another tale of classroom horror, for we have a plethora of those, but rather an attempt to interpret the broader political process and the social system of schooling that made such victimization predictable and regular—in short, *systematic*. Behind slogans that mask power—like "keep the schools out of politics"—and myths that rationalize inequality—like the doctrines of ethnic inferiority—lie institutional systems called schools that often reinforced injustice for some at the same time that they offered opportunity to others.

In trying to interpret how these systems operated, what were the patterns of communication and decision-making, what were the various political fields of forces influencing the schools, I have drawn heavily on the work of sociologists and political scientists. Historians, I suppose, have increasingly become cuckoo-

birds who lay their scholarly eggs in the nests of other disciplines. One reason is that some theories in social science lead us
to new sorts of data, to kinds of interpretation that are more
open to proof or disproof than the traditional narrative. While
most historians still enjoy, as I do, the colorful, complex reality
of specific episodes, the explanatory models of social science
theory help us to distinguish what is general and what is particular in historical events—and sometimes even why.[2]

Another way to put particular developments into a broader
frame is through comparison—over time, or place, or social or
economic status. The history of urban education is rich in such
contrasts: of size and location; of the same community at different periods; of different ethnic groups and classes; and of
similar organizations and occupational groups, such as welfare
or police bureaucracies. Some writers imply that urban education is New York or Boston writ large; but any resident of Portland, Oregon, could testify that such is not the case. *The* city
school does not exist, and never did.[3]

Through using a variety of social perspectives and modes of
analysis, I have sought to illuminate the transformation from
village school to urban system. I am using "village" and "urban"
as shorthand labels for the highly complex changes in ways of
thinking and behaving that accompanied revolutions in technology, increasing concentrations of people in cities, and restructuring of economic and political institutions into large bureaucracies. Thoughtful educators—men like Horace Mann, William
T. Harris, John Dewey, among others—were aware that the
functions of schooling were shifting in response to these "modernizing" forces. As village patterns merged into urbanism as a
way of life, factories and counting houses split the place of work
from the home; impersonal and codified roles structured relationships in organizations, replacing diffuse and personal role
relationships familiar in the village; the jack-of-all-trades of the
rural community came to perform specialized tasks in the city;
the older reliance on tradition and folkways as guides to belief
and conduct shifted as mass media provided new sources of information and norms of behavior and as science became a pervasive source of authority; people increasingly defined themselves as members of occupational groups—salesmen, teachers,

engineers—as they became aware of common interests that transcended allegiance to particular communities, thus constituting
what Robert Wiebe calls "the new middle class." [4]

The change from village to urban ways of thinking and acting
was by no means linear or unbroken. Citizens might have one
standard of behavior for the public world of job and interaction
with strangers, quite another for the private world of kinship,
neighborhood, and religious associations. In the midst of large
cities in the mid-twentieth century one might find people whom
Herbert Gans calls "urban villagers," just as in small towns in the
nineteenth century one might encounter cosmopolitan individuals totally unconcerned with local affairs and standards of morality. In the twentieth century, in particular, it became clear to
many observers that small towns were becoming intertwined with
the networks of influence that emanated from the centers of
mass society, the cities, while cities continued to recruit citizens
from isolated rural areas where the traditional folkways were still
strong. The important point is that increasingly the changes in
the means of production, in the forms of human association and
decision-making, and in ways of thinking and acting that I have
labeled "urban" became central in the lives of most Americans.[5]

Schools reflected and shaped these changes in various ways. In
the governance of education, lay community control gave way to
the corporate-bureaucratic model under the guise of "taking the
schools out of politics." Educators developed school systems
whose specialized structures partly reflected the differentiation
of economic roles in the larger social order. As employers and
occupational associations placed ever greater reliance on educational credentials for jobs, schooling acquired a new importance
as the gateway to favored positions. And increasingly the school
developed a curriculum, overt and implicit, that served as a
bridge between the family and the organizational world
beyond—that is, helped to create an urban discipline.[6]

This book begins with an analysis of "community control"
versus "professionalism" in the rural and village school. Why examine rural education in a study which focuses mostly on urban
education? In the first place, during the mid-nineteenth century
the pattern of school governance in many cities followed a village
or rural model. Therefore, understanding the transaction of

school and community in the countryside helps us to look afresh at decentralized decision-making in cities of a century ago. Second, the bureaucratic models developed to reform city schools became educational blueprints for consolidation of rural education in the early twentieth century. Hence the process of consolidation of rural schools illustrates in microcosm many of the shifts occurring in cities and sketches in sharp relief the values underlying the transfer of power to the professionals.

In Parts II and III I trace the complex contest between educational leaders who sought to develop the "one best system" of urban education during the nineteenth century and those dissenters and political interests that often conflicted with their efforts. Gradually schoolmen developed ideological and organizational consensus in their search for educational order, but heterogeneous values among the urban populations and diffusion of power in school governance frequently complicated their task.

Part IV deals with the campaign of reform from the top down that characterized urban education during the years from 1890 to 1920. At that time an interlocking directorate of urban elites—largely business and professional men, university presidents and professors, and some "progressive" superintendents—joined forces to centralize the control of schools. They campaigned to select small boards composed of "successful" people, to employ the corporate board of directors as the model for school committees, and to delegate to "experts" (the superintendent and his staff) the power to make most decisions concerning the schools. Part and parcel of urban "progressivism" generally, this movement glorified expertise, efficiency, and the disinterested public service of elites. Case studies of four cities—New York, Philadelphia, St. Louis, and San Francisco—offer variations on the central theme and analyze the opposition to centralization. Of course, actual political behavior under the new arrangements often departed sharply from the norms justifying the structural reforms.

Part V presents some of the major changes in urban education during the half-century from 1890 to 1940 as perceived by educators and the public they served. During these years the structures of school systems grew complex and often huge, new specializations appeared, conceptions of the nature of "intelligence" and learning shifted, and schools occupied a far larger place in the lives of youth (partly because child labor laws eliminated jobs and more and more employees required certificates and credentials). Schoolmen developed new ways to channel and teach students at the very time when schooling began to matter most in the occupational world. Such transformations of traditional ideas and practices were perceived quite differently by people occupying diverse positions in the social structure. Consequently, in this section of the book I have at times explored these private meanings of education. Reminiscences of an Italian-American about his childhood, for example, shed light on statistics of school drop-outs; descriptions of the job ceiling for black youth point to dilemmas of vocational counselors; a teacher's account of supervision by a principal may contradict progressive rhetoric in the curriculum guide.

Finally, in the Epilogue called "The One Best System under Fire," I look briefly at the present crisis in urban education in the light of the structures, the power relationships, and the ideologies that developed in the last century. If it is wise to be suspicious of historical prescriptions, it is foolish to ignore the storehouse of experience accumulated in the past. Few of the current panaceas or proposals for reform are new—accountability, or community control, or "compensatory education," for example; and contemporary power struggles in urban education are often new forms of past conflicts. If the record of educational reform in city schools is in some respects a discouraging one, it is perhaps because the schools have been asked to do too much or because inadequate solutions were implicit in simplistic definitions of what constituted the problems.

This book focuses, then, on *public* schools in big cities. A generation ago no historian of education would have needed to justify concentrating his attention on public institutions. To writers like Ellwood P. Cubberley and the scholars who preceded and followed him, *the* topic was the evolution of public education. When they talked of urban schools, they told a triumphant "house history" of enlarging enrollments, increasing expenditures, expanding curricula, growing professionalism, and widening opportunities for children. The major purpose of educational history was to give teachers and administrators a greater sense of professional esprit and identity. It was a tale of progress, marred here and there by "politics" or meddling by special interest groups or backward-looking teachers or laymen. It was an insider's view, seen from the top down. From that perspective the narrative was fairly accurate. Most would agree that in comparison with 1900 or 1850, teachers today are better trained, school buildings are more commodious, classes smaller, methods of teaching more varied, and students retained in school far longer.

Today, this inspirational institutional history suffers from two disabilities: it is inspirational, while the tone of much writing on urban schools has become funereal or angry; and it is institutional in focus, while a number of educational historians are now arguing that education is far broader than schooling. In a moment I shall discuss the tone and temper of this book, but now I should like to explain why I believe it is useful to look at institutions. I concede that much "education" takes place outside schools and that it is valuable for historians to examine the family, the church, the media, and many other educative agencies. Still, historians need a familiar place to stand—firm ground whose contours they know—in order to look out on society. Institutions provide just such a standing point. Furthermore, as social scientists remind us, modern America has become an organizational society in which our lives have been increasingly influenced by large institutions. Although these organizations shape and are shaped by the larger social system, they also have an internal momentum and life of their own which influences the behavior of their members. Thus analysis of urban schools can offer a way to ask questions about the whole society while retaining a particular institutional focus. And "institutional history" need not be "house history" but can be broad and multifaceted.

Now the issue of tone and perspective. I endorse neither the euphoric glorification of public education as represented in the traditional historiography nor the current fashion of berating public school people and regarding the common school as a failure. Thoreau once sardonically described a reformer who had written "a book called 'A Kiss for a Blow' " and who "behaved as if there were no alternative between these." That seems to describe many books about schools.[7]

It is fashionable today to impugn the motives of reformers generally, and school leaders have not escaped charges that they were seeking "social control" or "imposing" their views on their victims, the pupils. Such accusations are impossible to deny as long as the epithets remain vague (just as the "failure" of the schools is patent if judged by certain criteria, such as providing genuine equality of opportunity or joyful days for children). "Social control" exists in some form in every organized society from the Bushmen to the Eskimos and in every epoch of recorded history. To announce that schools "impose" on students is hardly news; even the "free school" movement shows signs of recognizing that. The important questions, I believe, are the intent, methods, and effects of the social control or imposition, which can take diverse forms. I would argue that there is quite a moral and educational difference between forcing a Catholic child in a public classroom to read the King James Bible against the teachings of his parents and priest and trying to make him literate; quite a difference between whipping children for not learning their lessons and teaching them to be punctual. One may have legitimate doubts about literacy and punctuality, but they should at least be distinguished from religious bigotry and sadism as forms of "imposition." [8]

In some of the recent polemical literature about the schools—Jonathan Kozol's *Death at an Early Age*, for example, or Edgar Z. Friedenberg's *Coming of Age in America*—there seems to me to be an animus against the lower-middle-class teacher that is uncharitable and insidious. Critics are so intent on exposing the racism and obtuseness of the teacher that it is difficult to understand her view of the world. Like welfare workers and police, teachers in the urban colonies of the poor are part of a social system that shapes *their* behavior, too. It is more important to expose and correct the injustice of the social system than to scold its agents. Indeed, one of the chief reasons for the failures of educational reforms of the past has been precisely that they called for a change of philosophy or tactics on the part of the individual school employee rather than systemic change—and concurrent transformations in the distribution of power and wealth in the society as a whole.

I do not share the view that urban schools have abysmally declined; this is an exaggeration as misleading as the mindless optimism of those who recently saw only progress. Nor do I share the opinion that urban education is some crumbling structure ready to tumble at the blast of a Joshua's trumpet; with its vested interests and crucial role in modern society, urban education is more like the Great Wall of China than like the Walls of Jericho.

Unavoidably a historian's own values influence perceptions of the past. In immersing myself during the last decade in the sources of urban education I have attempted to be open to diverse perspectives as well as systemic regularities, to latent functions as well as explicit aims, to achievements as well as failures. But in this book I shall stress persistent problems and misconceptions, for in my judgment:

The search for the one best system has ill-served the pluralistic character of American society.

Increasing bureaucratization of urban schools has often resulted in a displacement of goals and has often perpetuated positions and outworn practices rather than serving the clients, the children to be taught.

Despite frequent good intentions and abundant rhetoric about "equal educational opportunity," schools have rarely taught the children of the poor effectively—and this failure has been systematic, not idiosyncratic.

Talk about "keeping the schools out of politics" has often served to obscure actual alignments of power and patterns of privilege.

Americans have often perpetuated social injustice by blaming the victim, particularly in the case of institutionalized racism.

There have been important, and heartening, exceptions to these generalizations, and many people have, as I do, genuinely ambivalent feelings about such issues as professional autonomy or politicized schools. Furthermore, it is clear that many educators in the past sought the one best system or centralized control of city schools with the best of conscious motives. Rarely did these developments emerge in covert ways or for purposes which the proponents thought dubious. The search for conspiracies or villains is a fruitless occupation; to the extent that there was deception, it was largely self-deception. But to say that institutionalized racism, or unequal treatment of the poor, or cultural chauvinism were unconscious or unintentional does not erase their effects on children.

Urban schools did not create the injustices of American urban life, although they had a systematic part in perpetuating them. It is an old and idle hope to believe that better education alone can remedy them. Yet in the old goal of a common school, reinterpreted in radically reformed institutions, lies a legacy essential to a quest for social justice.

PART I

The One Best System in Microcosm:
Community and Consolidation in
Rural Education

"Want to be a school-master, do you? Well, what would *you* do in Flat Crick deestrict, I'd like to know? Why, the boys have driv off the last two, and licked the one afore them like blazes." Facing the brawny school trustee, his bulldog, his giggling daughter and muscular son, the young applicant, Ralph Hartsook, felt he had dropped "into a den of wild beasts." In *The Hoosier School-Master,* Edward Eggleston pitted his hero-teacher Hartsook against a tribe of barbarians and hypocrites, ignorant, violent, sinister, in a conflict relieved only by a sentimental love story and a few civilized allies. Across the nation, in Ashland, Oregon, a father named B. Million wrote a letter to his son's teacher, Oliver Cromwell Applegate:

Sir:
I am vary sorry to informe that in my opinion you have Shoed to me that you are unfit to keep a School, if you hit my boy in the face accidentley that will be different but if on purpos Sir you are unfit for the Business, you Seam to punish the Small Scholars to Set a Sample for the big wons that is Rong in the first place Sir Make your big class set the Sample for the little ones Sir is the course you Should do in my opinion Sir

The imaginary Ralph Hartsook and the real Oliver Cromwell Applegate triumphed over their adversaries, but in common with other rural teachers they learned some meanings of "community control." [1]

Community control of schools became anathema to many of the educational reformers of 1900, like other familiar features of the country school: nongraded primary education, instruction of younger children by older, flexible scheduling, and a lack of bureaucratic buffers between teacher and patrons. As advocates of consolidation, bureaucratization, and professionalization of rural education, school leaders in the twentieth century have given the one-room school a bad press, and not without reason. Some farmers were willing to have their children spend their schooldays in buildings not fit for cattle. In all too many neighborhoods it was only ne'er-do-wells or ignoramuses who would teach for a pittance under the eye and thumb of the community. Children suffered blisters from slab seats and welts from birch rods, sweltered near the pot-bellied stove or froze in the drafty corners. And the meagerness of formal schooling in rural areas seriously handicapped youth who migrated to a complex urban-industrial society.

At the turn of the century, leading schoolmen began to argue that a community-dominated and essentially provincial form of education could no longer equip youth to deal either with the changed demands of agriculture itself or with the complex nature of citizenship in a technological, urban society. Formal schooling had to play a much greater part—indeed a compulsory and major part, they believed—in the total education of the country child just as it did for the city pupil. With certain modifications dictated by rural conditions, they wished to create in the countryside the one best system that had been slowly developing in the cities. And while they justified their program as public service, educators also sought greater power and status for themselves.

Because professional educators have dominated writing about rural schools, it is difficult to look at these institutions freshly from other perspectives. Schoolmen saw clearly the deficiencies but not the virtues of the one-room school. Schooling—which farmers usually associated with book learning—was only a small and, to many, an incidental part of the total education the community provided. The child acquired his values and skills from his family and from neighbors of all ages and conditions. The major vocational curriculum was work on the farm or in the craftsman's shop or the corner store; civic and moral instruction came mostly in church or home or around the village where people met to gossip or talk politics. A child growing up in such a community could see work-family-religion-recreation-school as an organically related system of human relationships. Most reminiscences of the rural school are highly favorable, especially in comparison with personal accounts of schooling in the city. But creative writers like Sherwood Anderson, Edgar Lee Masters, Hamlin Garland, and Edward Eggleston have testified that life in the country could be harsh and drab, the tribe tyrannical in its demands for conformity, cultural opportunities sparse, and career options pinched.[2]

Here I shall look at some of the latent functions of the rural school which help to account for the differences in perspective of professional educators and local residents; examine the complex interaction of teacher and community; and inspect the "Rural School Problem" as perceived by educational reformers at the turn of the century. This transformation of rural education into a consolidated and bureaucratized institution reflected, and in microcosm illuminated, a broader change in educational ideology and structure. Beginning in the cities, this organizational revolution set the pattern for public education in the twentieth century, in the countryside and metropolis alike.

1. THE SCHOOL AS A COMMUNITY AND
THE COMMUNITY AS A SCHOOL

During the nineteenth century the country school belonged to the community in more than a legal sense: it was frequently the focus for people's lives outside the home. An early settler of Prairie View, Kansas, wrote that its capitol "was a small white-painted building which was not only the schoolhouse, but the center—educational, social, dramatic, political, and religious—of a pioneer community of the prairie region of the West." In one-room schools all over the nation ministers met their flocks, politicians caucused with the faithful, families gathered for Christmas parties and hoe-downs, the Grange held its baked-bean suppers, Lyceum lecturers spoke, itinerants introduced the wonders of the lantern-slide and the crank-up phonograph, and neighbors gathered to hear spelling bees and declamations.[3]

Daily in school season, children could play with one another at noon, sliding on snowy hills or playing blind man's bluff with the teacher on a bright May day. "The principal allurement of going to schools," said one student, "was the opportunity it afforded for social amusement." For ranch children growing up on the dry plains of western Texas or eastern Wyoming, separated from their neighbors by many miles, school often provided the only social contacts they had outside the family.[4]

Indeed, sometimes the school itself became a kind of young extended family. When Oliver Cromwell Applegate taught in Ashland, four of his pupils were Applegates; when his niece taught thirty years later in Dairy, Oregon, she found that "the majority of children were my own sisters and cousins." Students ranged widely in age. A teacher found on his first day of school in Eastport, Maine, "a company including three men . . . each several years my senior; several young men of about the same age, one of whom seemed to have been more successful than Ponce de Leon in the search for the fountain of perpetual youth, for, according to the records of the school, he had been eighteen years old for five successive years"; and from these giants down to toddlers. Mothers often sent children of three and four years to school with their older sisters or brothers. A young one might play with the counting frame of beads, look at pictures in the readers, or nap on a pine bench, using the teacher's shawl as a pillow. Older boys often split wood and lit the fire; girls might roast apples in the stove at noon.[5]

But unlike the family, the school was a voluntary and incidental institution: attendance varied enormously from day to day and season to season, depending on the weather, the need for labor at home, and the affection or terror inspired by the teacher. During the winter, when older boys attended, usually a man held sway, or tried to. During the summer, when older children worked on the farm, a woman was customarily the teacher.[6]

As one of the few social institutions which rural people encountered daily, the common school both reflected and shaped a sense of community. Families of a neighborhood were usually a loosely organized tribe; social and economic roles were overlapping, unspecialized, familiar. School and community were organically related in a tightly knit group in which people met face to face and knew each others' affairs. If families of a district were amicable, the school expressed their cohesiveness. If they were discordant, the school was often squeezed between warring cliques. Sometimes schooling itself became a source of contention, resulting in factions or even the creation of new districts. A common cause for argument was the location of the school. "To settle the question of where one of the little frame schoolhouses should stand," wrote Clifton Johnson about New England, "has been known to require ten district meetings scattered over a period of two years" and to draw out men from the mountains who never voted in presidential elections. In Iowa, dissident farmers secretly moved a schoolhouse one night to their preferred site a mile away from its old foundation. In tiny Yoncalla, Oregon, feuds split the district into three factions, each of which tried to maintain its own school. Other sources of discord included the selection of the teacher—even that small patronage mattered in rural areas—or the kind of religious instruction offered in the classroom. But more often than not, the rural school integrated rather than disintegrated the community.[7]

Relations between rural communities and teachers depended much on personalities, little on formal status. Most rural patrons had little doubt that the school was theirs to control (whatever state regulations might say) and not the property of the professional educator. Still, a powerful or much-loved teacher in a one-room school might achieve great influence through force of character, persuasion, and sabotage.

A pioneer teacher in Oregon recalled that a school board member instructed her not to teach grammar, so she taught children indirectly through language and literature. Another Oregon teacher followed the state course of study which required her to have the children write their script from the bot-

School and Community—A Rural Transaction

tom of the page up "in order to see the copy at the top of the page." An irate committeeman warned her that "if you don't have the kids write from the top down, I'll have you fired." He won. But when other trustees objected to building two privies— one for boys and one for girls, as the state law said—the same teacher convinced them to comply by showing it would cost only twenty dollars for the two privies together.[8]

Finding his schoolhouse "strewn with bits of paper, whittlings and tobacco" from a community meeting the night before, a young Kansas teacher decided he "would go to that board and demand that the schoolroom be put in sanitary condition, and state the school would not be called till my demands were complied with." He quickly learned that in this village, where three teachers had failed the year before, educational law might be on his side but the patrons could only be managed, not bossed. "Look with suspicion upon the teacher who tells you how he bosses the school board," he observed. "He is either a liar or a one-termer, and the probabilities are that he is both."[9]

Teachers knew to whom they were accountable: the school trustees who hired them, the parents and other taxpayers, the children whose respect—and perhaps even affection—they needed to win. Usually young, inexperienced, and poorly trained, teachers were sometimes no match for the older pupils. When a principal lost a fight with an unruly student in Klamath Falls, Oregon, it was he and not the student who was put on probation by the board—presumably for losing, not for fighting (which was common).[10]

The position of the teacher in the tribal school was tenuous. In isolated communities, residents expected teachers to conform to their folkways. In fact if not in law, local school committeemen were usually free to select instructors. With no bureaucracy to serve as buffer between himself and the patrons, with little sense of being part of a professional establishment, the teacher found himself subordinated to the community. Authority inhered in the person, not the office, of schoolmaster. The roles of teachers were overlapping, familiar, personal, rather than esoteric, strictly defined, and official (the same teacher in a rural school might be brother, suitor, hunting companion, fellow farm worker, boarder, and cousin to different members of the class). The results of his instruction, good or poor, were evident in Friday spelling bees and declamations as neighbors crowded the schoolhouse to see the show. If he "boarded 'round" at the houses of the parents, even his leisure hours were under scrutiny.[11]

If he was a local boy, his faults and virtues were public knowledge, and a rival local aspirant to the office of village schoolmaster might find ways to make his life unpleasant. If he was an outsider, he would have to prove himself, while the patrons waited with ghoulish glee, as in *The Hoosier School-Master*, to see if the big boys would throw him out. Romance was sometimes as threatening as brawn. Matrimony stalked one Yoncalla teacher: "It was not the fault of the Yoncalla 'gals' that the young Gent . . . escaped here in single blessedness. It was a manoeuvre of his own. He was attacked on several occasions mostly in the usually quiet manner but one time furiously, but he artfully overlooked the gauntlet and was not carried away." Against the tyranny of public opinion the teacher had little recourse; against the wiles of the scholars he had as allies only his muscles, his wit, and his charm.[12]

The "curriculum" of the rural school was often whatever textbooks lay at hand. Often these books wedded the dream of worldly success to an absolute morality; cultivation meant proper diction and polite accomplishments. For some children readers such as McGuffey's gave welcome escape from monotony and horse manure, just as play in the schoolyard relieved the loneliness of farm life. A boy in the Duxbury Community School near Lubbock, Texas, discovered a passion for literature and later became a professor. Hamlin Garland recalled that in Iowa "our readers were almost the only counterchecks to the current of vulgarity and baseness which ran through the talk of the older boys, and I wish to acknowledge my deep obligation to Professor McGuffey, whoever he may have been, for the dignity and literary grace of his selections. From the pages of his readers I learned to know and love the poems of Scott, Byron, Southey, Wordsworth and a long line of the English masters. I got my first taste of Shakespeare from the selected scenes which I read in these books." Edgar Lee Masters, by contrast, wrote that his school days "were not happy, they did not have a particle of charm." And a boy in New England wrote in the flyleaf of his textbook: "11 weeks will never go away/ never never never never." [13]

Whether these rites of passage into the world of books were pleasant depended in large part on the teacher. Though usually poorly educated, the rural teacher was sometimes regarded by the community as an intellectual. It didn't take much to convince him that he *was* a man of letters. A friend of Applegate's wrote that he had attended a "State Teachers' Institute, where there was an immense gathering of the literati—no less than eleven men with the title of 'Professor'—and fourteen with the title of Reverend besides about fifty lesser lights." Farmers and pioneers were ambivalent about these literati in their midst. The "old folks" in Yoncalla derided spelling bees and declamations "as a sparking school or some such silly thing." Children often shared their parents' doubts about "all singing schools, Sabbath Schools, Spelling Schools, Grammar Schools and all debating societies." But there lurked in the pioneer a secret bourgeois desire for refinement (at least for the womenfolk). When a teacher could successfully bridge the world of the tribe and the wider world of intellect—as Oliver Cromwell Applegate did, with his fine penmanship and his skill in hunting grizzly bears—the community rejoiced.[14]

2. "THE RURAL SCHOOL PROBLEM" AND POWER TO THE PROFESSIONAL

Beginning in the 1890's and gaining momentum in the early twentieth century, reformers mounted an attack on the Rural School Problem. The "bookish" curriculum, haphazard selection and supervision of teachers, voluntary character of school attendance, discipline problems, diversity of buildings and equipment—these were but symptoms of deeper problems, they believed. What was basically wrong with rural education was that rural folk wanted to run their schools and didn't know what was good for them in the complex new society. Don't underestimate the job of reform, wrote Ellwood P. Cubberley in 1914: "Because the rural school is today in a state of arrested development, burdened by educational traditions, lacking in effective supervision, controlled largely by rural people, who, too often, do not realize either their own needs or the possibilities of rural education, and taught by teachers who, generally speaking, have but little comprehension of the rural-life problem . . . the task of reorganizing and redirecting rural education is difficult, and will necessarily be slow." In their diagnosis and prescription, the rural-school reformers blended economic realism with nostalgia, efficient professionalism with evangelical righteousness.[15]

A large number of the crusaders were themselves once country boys or girls, and their writings portrayed a rural past in which families cooperated in barn raisings and corn huskings, churches and schools flourished, and the yeoman farmer—whom they called the "standard American"—ruled over an industrious, moral, and peaceable republic. A Kansas teacher recalled that President McKinley's train had stopped in the country one September morning next to a field where two barefoot boys had come to milk cows. The boys were warming their feet on the sod where the cows had slept as the President called his Cabinet officers to watch: " 'Gentlemen,' " said McKinley, " 'that sight recalls the happiest days of my life'; and each cabinet officer in turn expressed a like sentiment, and remembered having warmed his feet in the same way. America's great statesmen then gave three cheers in the early morning for the little boys in Iowa who reminded them of their happiest days." [16]

But when it came time for analysis, the more astute reformers saw that industrialization, demographic shifts, and urbanism were altering country life. They argued that now farms were no longer self-sufficient but produced for a world market; agricultural science, the telephone, automobile, Sears Roebuck catalogue, electricity, and farm machinery had profoundly transformed the daily routines of rural families. Fewer people produced more food. The rural educators viewed as ominous the growth of "factories in the field," large commercial, mechanized farms which employed a farm proletariat. And last, in many rural states an increasing proportion of farm tenants and proprietors were "new" immigrants. These southern and eastern Europeans, Cubberley wrote, "are thrifty but ignorant, and usually wretchedly poor; they come from countries where popular education and popular government have as yet made little headway; they are often lacking in initiative and self-reliance; and they lack the Anglo-Teutonic conception of government by popular will." When such foreigners enter agri-business as tenants and field workers, in many communities "there is no longer enough of the older residential class" of "strong, opinionated, virile" native citizens remaining to run things. "Jose Cardoza, Francesco Bertolini, and Petar Petarovich are elected as school directors," Cubberley lamented. "The process is of course educative to these newcomers, though a little hard on local government." In Nebraska, a survey showed that over half of the rural teachers were of foreign extraction, a serious problem to educators from the University of Nebraska. "How can we have national spirit," they asked, "in a Commonwealth where there is an infusion of the language and blood of many nations unless there is a very strong effort made to socialize the different elements and weld them into a unified whole. . . . It therefore becomes evident how important it is that the teacher be an American in sympathy, ideals, training, and loyalty." [17]

Study after study revealed the corruption of the rural Eden as the twentieth century progressed: the old social life disintegrating, talented youth fleeing boredom and mud, schoolhouses falling apart, outhouses reeking, absentee landlords squeezing profit. A Presbyterian survey of 1,764 square miles of Illinois reported that 53 percent of the farms were run by tenants, churches were stagnating, and people were resorting to poolrooms, saloons, and barber shops for recreation. An Oregon teacher complained in 1915 that "at the present time there is little if any, social activity in the rural communities. The days of the husking bees, quilting parties, barn raisings, spelling matches, and literaries, are past. The farmer knows very little of the people about him, and the word 'neighbor' is seldom heard." Crusaders agreed that something must be done to regenerate the countryside now that new social forces had disrupted the community of yeomen. The basic goal, said Cubberley, was "to retain on the farm, as farmers, a class which represents the best type of American manhood," a "standard" which he defined as middle class, public spirited, and owning broad green acres.[18]

After providing a clear analysis of the economic and demographic forces which had disrupted the yeoman ideal, the reformers turned for solution to the school omnipotent. "That the schools, managed as they have been mainly by country people," said Cubberley, "are largely responsible for the condition in which country communities find themselves today, there can be little question." If the country people had botched it, then the only recourse was for the professionals to take over.[19]

Starting with the National Education Association (NEA) Committee of Twelve on Rural Schools in the 1890's, the articulate professionals mostly agreed on the remedies: consolidation of schools and transportation of pupils, expert supervision by county superintendents, "taking the schools out of politics," professionally-trained teachers, and connecting the curriculum "with the everyday life of the community." In the form of a one best system designed by professionals the rural school would teach country children sound values and vocational skills; the result was to be a standardized, modernized "community" in which leadership came from the professionals.[20]

Equality of opportunity for rural youth meant uniform regulation. No detail was unimportant. The Oregon standards for rural schools decreed that an illustration hanging on the wall of a rural school "must be a copy of a picture listed in the State Course of Study, and should contain at least 100 square inches in the body of the picture, or 180 square inches including the frame." Of course graffiti in the privies (that bane of country teachers and subject of so many anguished paragraphs) were strictly forbidden. The duties of the teacher were precise and mundane: "Must maintain good order at all times; supervise play-ground; have her work well prepared; follow State Course of Study; take at least one educational journal; have daily program, approved by county Superintendent, posted in room within first month of school; keep register in good condition; be neat in attire." An angry teacher wrote that the bureaucrats were taking over public education: "By degrees there is being built in our state a machine among the 'aristocratic' element of our profession that . . . will make [teachers] serfs, to be moved about at will of a state superintendent of public instruction through his lieutenants, county superintendents." "The paradox of American education," said another Oregon schoolman in 1926, "is that it asks for education for all, yet urges that control of the educational system be placed in a bureaucracy," as if educated citizens can't be trusted to control their own schools.[21]

Nowhere is this "paradox" more apparent than in the plans to reform the rural school. But on closer examination rural-school reform becomes not so much a paradox as a transfer of power from laymen to professionals. The rural-school reformers talked about democracy and rural needs, but they believed that they had the answers and should run the schools. What they needed was authority: "It is the lack of captains and colonels of larger grasp and insight that is today the greatest single weakness of our rural and village educational army. When matched against the city educational army, with its many captains and colonels, and under generals of large insight and effective personal force, the city army easily outgenerals its opponent." County election of a superintendent and district squabbles must cease, declared one leader: "most questions of educational policy, procedure, and finance . . . are better settled if removed entirely from the control of . . . district officers, and given either to county or state educational authorities for determination." [22]

This movement to take control of the rural common school away from the local community and to turn it over to the professionals was part of a more general organizational revolution in American education in which laymen lost much of their direct control over the schools. In the cities schoolmen pioneered new bureaucratic patterns of educational organization. They sought to "free education from politics" by state laws coercing rural communities to consolidate schools. From 1910 to 1960 the number of one-room schools declined from approximately 200,000 to 20,000. In trying to modernize rural schooling they believed that children as well as teachers would benefit, and indeed the students did gain better school buildings, a broader and more contemporary course of studies, and better qualified teachers and administrators. The new educational standards reflected an increasingly cosmopolitan rather than local scale of values among schoolmen, who sought to blur the differences between district and district, county and county, and even state and state. This in turn gave country youth greater occupational mobility and introduced them to different life-styles.

But patrons continued to resist consolidation and standardization in a battle which made little sense to most educators. Country people may have been dissatisfied with their school buildings and with an archaic curriculum, but they wanted to control their own schools. In a major study of rural schools in New York State in 1921, for example, 65 percent of rural patrons polled wanted to elect their county superintendent; 69 percent opposed consolidation of schools. Subsequent studies showed that rural people in Ohio, Wisconsin, and Idaho also opposed unification. The impetus to consolidate rural schools almost always came from outside the rural community. It was rare to find a local group that "had sponsored or spearheaded the drive for reorganization." [23]

During the twentieth century the consolidation of rural high schools became a major source of controversy. In his study of "Plainville," a midwestern farming community, James West wrote that the small-town high school, like its predecessor the one-room school, became "a new focus of community life and ritual." There residents came to social and athletic events, listened to debates and orations in which the contestants recited speeches which they had bought ready-made for the occasion, and attended graduation ceremonies which became rites of passage into a wider world. As "symbols of community 'modernity,'" the town high schools gave local people the feeling that they had access to a mass society while they still enlisted local loyalties and integrated rural people in social networks. Thus they became institutions valued in themselves, quite apart from the goal of teaching students certain skills and knowledge.[24]

When state educational authorities claimed that unification of districts would produce larger, and hence more educationally effective, high schools, their professional arguments fell largely on hostile ears. In California, for example, state legislative committees had since 1920 attacked small high schools as "inefficient, short-sighted, and unprogressive," but many local districts held out against the Bureau of School District Organization. A case in point was the bitter battle in 1954 over the reorganization of Bret Harte High School (which served as a focus for the towns of Copperopolis, Angels Camp, Murphys, and Avery). Opponents of centralization feared a loss of social identity amid "the creeping menace of unification": "We must fight this thing which is destroying our local autonomy with all our power . . . we of Avery, Murphys, and Copperopolis who are about to disappear behind the iron curtain cry out: 'Carry out the fight.'" Some citizens argued that unification would produce more economical and efficient schools, but they were denounced as "newcomers" and "renegades." Across the country in Maine, E. B. White lamented the loss of a local high school: "The State Board of Education withholds its blessing from high schools that enroll fewer than three hundred students. Under mounting pressure from the state, the town organized a school administration district, usually referred to as SAD. Sad is the word for it. . . . The closing of our high school caused an acute pain in the hearts of most of the townsfolk, to whom the building was a symbol of their own cultural life and a place where one's loyalty was real, lasting, and sustaining." [25]

These mid-century debates over the control of rural high schools echoed earlier developments in cities and their suburbs. In 1960, a leading liberal educator, Myron Lieberman, could indict local control as the chief reason for "the dull parochialism and attenuated totalitarianism" of American education, but today many reformers call for more, not less, "community control" of schools.[26]

As Robert Alford has observed, "systematic analysis of the relation of small communities to the state and the larger society has been hindered by the refusal of some scholars to recognize the conflicts of values involved, or by their tendency to dissolve the conflicts in liberal rhetoric." Thus some commentators have talked of a failure of communication, or defined " 'true' local control as the control exercised by a 'strong' district," or blurred the "division between professional values and community values." Nor has obfuscation been limited to those who wished to enforce state standards on unwilling communities. As Arthur J. Vidich and Joseph Bensman indicate in *Small Town in Mass Society*, rural and small-town dwellers often developed elaborate self-delusions to mask the interconnection of their lives with the institutions of a mass society "that regulate and determine" their existence. "The public enactment of community life and public statements of community values seemed to bear little relationship to the community's operating institutions and the private lives of its members." [27]

If one faces the contest of values and power directly, it is apparent that professional autonomy and community control did often collide, that even the most remote rural community normally did intersect with a complex urban world, that giving students sufficient training to participate in modern society did often diminish diversity of life-styles in the nation even as it opened opportunities to young people. "Imposition" invariably occurred in schools, whether it took the form of the affirmation of local norms of belief and behavior or the substitution of alternate standards from outside the community. In response to a common feeling of powerlessness amid vast bureaucracies, many citizens called for community control, oblivious of possible local tyranny and parochialism, while others carried on the quest for modernization, rarely recognizing how fragile, finally, is a sense of voluntary community in a mass society. The contests we have seen in microcosm in the countryside we will now trace as they developed in villages swelling into vast cities.

PART II

From Village School to Urban System:
Bureaucratization in the Nineteenth Century

Most urban educational systems of the nineteenth century began as loosely-structured village schools. This legacy of village patterns of control and behavior frustrated those who wished to standardize the schools and to adapt them to the demographic, economic, and organizational transformations taking place in the cities. Convinced that there was one best system of education for urban populations, leading educators sought to discover it and implement it. They were impressed with the order and efficiency of the new technology and forms of organization they saw about them. The division of labor in the factory, the punctuality of the railroad, the chain of command and coordination in modern businesses—these aroused a sense of wonder and excitement in men and women seeking to systematize the schools. They sought to replace confused and erratic means of control with careful allocation of powers and functions within hierarchical organizations; to establish networks of communication that would convey information and directives and would provide data for planning for the future; to substitute impersonal rules for informal, individual adjudication of disputes; to regularize procedures so that they would apply uniformly to all in certain categories; and to set objective standards for admission to and performance in each role, whether superintendent or third-grader. Efficiency, rationality, continuity, precision, impartiality became watchwords of the consolidators. In short, they tried to create a more bureaucratic system.[1]

Why did the educational reform impulse in city schools take primarily this form of administrative rationalization? "In all likelihood," writes John Higham about a shift in reform impulses generally, "the principal reason for the trend toward consolidation will be found in the convergence of industrialization and urbanization in the middle decades of the nineteenth century. Certainly the need for a stabler, more distinctly organized environment first arose in the cities." Cities pioneered in systematizing services such as police, public health, charity, and public education, in part in response to needs created by their own chaotic growth, fears aroused by ethnic and class discord, and the adaptation and diffusion of new organizational forms created in conjunction with new technologies.[2]

Although urban school leaders did not abandon entirely the evangelical rhetoric of individual redemption and moral renewal—so abundant during the common school crusade of the 1840's and 1850's—they increasingly turned their attention to perfecting the system and to aggregate economic and social aims. As Michael Katz has observed, schooling became with them more a function than a cause. Strategists of public education like William T. Harris began to argue that bureaucratized schooling was becoming an urban social and economic necessity: "the modern industrial community cannot exist without free popular education carried out in a system of schools ascending from the primary grade to the university." Schooling was essential because it adapted people to the new disciplines and incentives of the urban-industrial order and supplied the "directive intelligence" and specialists required in a complex society. In effect, some saw the school as a critical means of transforming the pre-industrial culture—values and attitudes, work habits, time orientation, even recreations—of citizens in a modernizing society. In 1860 the United States lagged behind England, France, and Germany in its industrial output; by 1894 it led the world and produced almost as much in value as those three nations combined. Schools also expanded in size and complexity in those years to a point where America also surpassed other nations in its educational output.[3]

Although some educational strategists saw the administrative rationalization of schooling as a response to major societal changes, many more advocated bureaucratization mainly to meet pressing internal problems of sheer numbers and chaotic conditions in the schools of swollen villages that were becoming large cities. They struggled with the daily tasks of housing, classifying, teaching, promoting, and keeping records on the thousands of children crowding the classrooms. Such administrative necessities would probably have made some degree of bureaucratization likely even had the school officials had no other organizational models to emulate. But many leaders, both lay and professional, found in the factory, the army, the newly created police departments, and even the railroad attractive organizational schemes to borrow from, although until the turn of the century such analogies were usually only gross and often misunderstood. Career schoolmen like Boston's John Philbrick often believed, however, that educators had most to learn from one another in creating their one best system of schooling; as cosmopolitan borrowers, they garnered new ideas from Europe and across the nation.

As we shall see in Part III, the politics of pluralism in the nineteenth century thoroughly frustrated many of the plans of the bureaucratizers. Instead of being rational, insulated, almost closed systems, urban school systems were often perforated by public demands and sabotaged by internal dissidents. The managers' experience revealed how vulnerable some of the early public bureaucracies could be to "political" influences both inside and outside the organizations.

1. SWOLLEN VILLAGES AND THE NEED FOR COORDINATION

Urbanization proceeded at a faster rate between 1820 and 1860 than in any other period of American history. While the total population grew about 33 percent per decade, the number of people in places of 2,500 or more increased three times as fast. A muddy small town in 1830, Chicago became a metropolis of over 109,000 by 1860. In a single year, 1847, Boston added more than 37,000 Irish immigrants to its population of 114,000.

The following statistics demonstrate the frenetic pace of city-building:

	1820	1860
Places of 5,000 to 10,000	22	136
Places of 10,000 to 25,000	8	58
Places of 25,000 to 50,000	2	19
Places of 50,000 to 100,000	1	7
Places over 100,000	1	9

During the same time the number of people living in urban settlements increased from 693,255 to 6,216,518. From 1839 to 1869, the value added to the economic output of the nation by non-household manufacturing soared from $240,000,000 to $1,630,000,000, while railroad mileage in operation jumped from 23 in 1830 to 52,922 in 1870. Behind the statistics lay massive changes in styles of life and puzzled efforts to control the effects of demographic and technological change.[4]

In a village, each household might have its own well for water, its outhouse, its leather buckets and plans to alert neighbors in case of fire, its horse and carriage for transportation, its kitchen garden. What the family could not do for itself, friends and neighbors or local merchants, craftsmen, or professionals could normally provide. The household was the main unit of production, whether of food or handicrafts. But as established villages grew into crowded urban areas, as new cities mushroomed in the West, residents found that the older self-reliance or voluntary services did not suffice.

Bayrd Still traces the changes that took place in Milwaukee, for example, during the three decades following its incorporation as a city in 1846. The old custom of volunteer services and self-help "was giving way," he wrote, "to a specialization in urban administration which developments in science and increased wealth encouraged and which the growth of population and its attendant problems made inevitable." The marshal and ward constables and night watchmen proved inadequate to quell riots or to prevent the surge of thefts, arson, and murders that struck the city in 1855; consequently, business leaders demanded a regular police force in that year. Likewise, in the 1850's, the traditional volunteer fire companies lost their appeal to recruits, while the task of fighting serious fires with Milwaukee's new steam pump became too complex for amateurs. Thus firefighting became the domain of paid professionals. Able-bodied men were once required to spend two or three days a year building or repairing streets, but this task the city council decided to delegate to a board for public works. Like crime, fire, and bumpy streets, disease threatened all those within the confines of the city: germs did not defer to rank and station. When health became increasingly a public and not an individual or family concern, the city council required vaccination against smallpox, prohibited the accumulation of garbage (as a defense against cholera), and sought to build a sewer system. Private corporations sold stock and secured franchises for public services like street lighting and horse railroads.

As city residents became more interdependent, they increasingly turned to specialized and impersonal agencies to accomplish tasks they and their neighbors had once performed. As the place of work became separated from the home, activities had to be coordinated in time and place, new means of transportation and communication devised, and an urban discipline developed in the city's residents. But the change to bureaucratic specialization of function was gradual and beset with serious problems of group conflict and ambiguity of political authority.[5]

Ambivalent attitudes toward centralized authority shaped the history of the police power in cities like Boston and New York, just as it influenced the politics of urban education. In a study of New York police, James Richardson observed that before the nineteenth century Americans were dubious about the idea of police—and even the word itself, fearing "any quasi-military body that might constitute a threat to civil liberties." Until 1845, New York had night watchmen and officers attached to the courts but no regular police force. The salaried policemen who began work that year were required to live in the ward where they worked. Until 1853 they were untrained and did not wear a uniform.[6]

In Boston, the police force also grew in size and importance during the late 1840's, and for some of the same reasons as in

New York: conservative citizens worried about ethnic and religious riots, feared outbursts of social disorder and crime, and became despondent about traditional methods of social control. As informal mechanisms of shaping behavior broke down, cities created functionaries—men behind badges—to keep disorderly elements in line. The creation of efficient and uniformed police paralleled the movement to standardize schooling. Both were in part responses to the influx of the immigrant poor.[7]

In the 1830's a foreign visitor to Boston observed that "there are no better policemen than the ordinary run of Bostonians. . . . This is by some called the wholesome restraint of public opinion." He echoed earlier comments of both natives and visitors—perhaps idealized—that Boston was a compact, close-knit society in which each person knew that his behavior was an open book to others. When Boston swelled in size in the 1840's, however, its population became increasingly heterogeneous in ethnicity, in religion, and in economic class. Geographical mobility probably also helped to break down the cohesiveness of neighborhoods. Ties of deference, personal acquaintance, and shared religious and moral views became more and more restricted to small voluntary groups.[8]

School reform in Boston illustrates one pattern of educational change at mid-century. To instill common values, to create a new type of public stability, some Bostonians sought to remake public education. But despite attempts to organize the classrooms into a more unified system, public education in Boston in the mid-1840's seemed to reformers more a miscellaneous collection of village schools than a coherent system. Responsibility was diffused, teachers had considerable autonomy in their decentralized domains, and the flow of information was erratic and insufficiently focused for purposes of policy. The primary schools, founded in 1818 to prepare children to enter the grammar schools, were mostly one-room, one-teacher schools scattered across the city. While technically the main Boston school committee appointed the members of the primary school board, in fact the trustees of the primary schools were largely an independent, self-nominating, and self-perpetuating body; by the 1850's their number reached 190, and they supervised that many separate schools. Friends of the arrangement argued that enlisting the help of so many laymen kept the schools close to the people of the neighborhood and fostered interest in education. As Stanley Schultz has found, the twenty-four members of the main school committee that supervised the grammar and writing schools and the high school were mostly representatives of the Boston elite—businessmen, professionals, ministers, leaders of the wealth and opinion of the city—and were elected yearly by wards. Each year subcommittees of this group visited each school (excluding the primary schools) and gave a thumbnail sketch of its virtues and defects after conducting an oral examination of the pupils and monitoring its discipline and mode of instruction. In 1845, for example, a four-man subcommittee simply reported that the Latin School was "in its usual good condition," although the subcommittee on the segregated black school saw fit to report on some of the problems that would subsequently lead members of the Boston Negro community to boycott the school.[9].

Ambiguity of authority and diffusion of control were partially the result of a system of governance that had grown by accretion from village origins and still appealed to some Bostonians. Centralization was a dirty word to many, especially to Democrats, who associated it with King George, Prussian autocaracy, and monopolies. Even though his formal powers were slight as Secretary of the Massachusetts Board of Education, Horace Mann faced bitter attack from foes who portrayed him as a bureaucratic boss who would endanger local autonomy and impose his political and religious views as official doctrine. Many laymen took pride in their work as board members and had no desire to give up their power and influence. And schoolmasters owed their jobs and often a substantial degree of autonomy to the decentralized system; if a subcommittee objected to some defect one year, the next there would be a new group to satisfy, and in the meantime no bureaucrats came around to pester. Rank-and-file Bostonians seemed complacent about the status quo in their schools. An experienced school reformer snorted that "the greatest offence that any citizen can commit is to doubt the perfection of our schools, and any attempt to improve them, on the part of a committee man, is madness, and is instantly visited by official death." [10]

But those who wanted to change the schools found the lack of reliable information about the schools and the absence of lever-age for reform infuriating. Horace Mann, for example, believed that the methods of discipline and teaching employed by the Boston masters were anachronistic at best and sadistic at worst. In Prussian centralized schools he found examples of organiza-tion—supervision, graded classes, well-articulated curricu-lum—and humane methods of instruction which he thought Boston should emulate. As early as 1837 he called for a superin-tendent to improve the schools. But all he succeeded in doing was to provoke a massive rhetorical battle with the masters, one that resembled the conflicts of old Chinese warlords who would assemble their armies to an imaginary line, hurl curses at each other, and leave with bodies intact though tempers super-heated.[11]

Mann's friend and fellow-reformer Samuel Gridley Howe de-cided to take up the battle where Mann left off, but this time with a new weapon: information. Because of the diffusion of au-thority among the large primary board and the school committee and because of the haphazard evaluation of schools by the sub-committees, no one really knew what was going on in the schools as a whole nor was there any way to use such information to determine authoritative policy. When Howe was elected to the school committee in 1844, he decided to revolutionize the collection of data on the performance of children in the gram-mar schools. Clearly his interest was not in the information it-self but in the use of the data as an argument for what he called "radical reform." Accordingly he and his colleagues on the sub-committee devised uniform written tests for the top class in each of the grammar schools—a single standard by which to judge and compare the output of each school, "positive informa-tion, in black and white," to replace the intuitive and often su-perficial written evaluations of oral examinations.

Using required textbooks as a source of questions, they printed a test which they administered in such a way as to ensure its secrecy. In Howe's eyes the results were scandalous. Out of 57,873 possible answers, students answered only 17,216 correctly and accumulated 35,947 errors in punctuation in the process. Bloopers abounded: one child said that rivers in North Carolina and Tennessee run in opposite directions because of "the will of

God." Although the test included abstruse and tricky items, Howe argued that it was fair and showed that children in the Dudley School in Roxbury did much better on the examination than the children in Boston. Students learned facts by rote but not principles, he said: they could give the date of the embargo but not explain what it did.[12]

Howe used the test results as evidence for his charge that the Boston school system "is wrong in the principle of its organization, inefficient in its operation, and productive of little good, in comparison with its expense." To cure these faults required a change in command: employment of a full-time school commissioner (who later would be called superintendent). The school board did adequately "represent all the wants and interests which should be provided for, and all the opinions and feelings which should be consulted." But it was, "necessarily, an uncertain, fluctuating and inexperienced body," and by its very organization it ensured that "no one man, and no Sub-committee is ever required or expected to know the actual condition of all the Grammar Schools in Boston." What the city needed was a professional leader who could offer "permanence, personal responsibility, continued and systematic labor," and who could bridge the information and policy gap between board and individual schools and between the board and the city government. Howe recognized that "many interests will be assailed" by such an office, for under the present system "we have a Board of twenty-four men, not paid for any labor, who share a responsibility, which, thus broken into fragments, presses on no one." An efficient administration would endanger vested interests—those of the masters above all, who enjoyed the immunity afforded by a decentralized power base.[13]

Although Howe's outspoken criticism and use of empirical muckraking offended many people, his more moderate successors as Boston reformers put many of his ideas into practice. They believed that Boston had outgrown the day of amateur village governance in education. The city would become one of the leaders in designing and spreading the one best system.

Philadelphia offered a more extreme example of decentralization and diffusion of authority than Boston. In 1860, the Philadelphia district, a union of the old city with the surrounding county settlements, contained 63,530 students and annually spent over half a million dollars on its ninety-two schools. Real power to make decisions lay with the twenty-four sectional boards which built and repaired schools, hired teachers, and adjusted instruction to the desires of the people. Representatives from each of these ward boards supposedly coordinated civic education through a central board of controllers, but keen rivalry between them often resulted in unequal allocation of funds. Directors felt loyal to their own neighborhoods of Frankford or Passyunk or Kensington or Mantua. Depending on the persuasiveness or influence of the local director, one school might have a full coal bin while another lacked fuel, one might have jammed classrooms while another had empty seats. Members of the central board complained repeatedly that they did not have sufficient information on which to act in disbursing funds or correcting abuses. Edward Steel, a leading businessman and president of the controllers, lamented the inefficiency of the decentralized network of power, but so firmly embedded was it in the political culture of the city that it was not until 1882 that Philadelphia had a superintendent of schools, and not until the twentieth century that the local wards lost their substantial powers. In Pittsburgh, likewise, the old pattern of ward control of schools, stemming from the time when the city was a loose association of neighborhoods, continued past 1900.[14]

A number of new cities passed rapidly through the village stage of organization of schools and early adopted forms of governance pioneered in the East. Chicago was a case in point. In 1854 its first school superintendent, the former master of the Boylston School in Boston, found a lusty city of mud streets and sidewalks plastered over with planks, a large trade with the agricultural hinterlands spurred by the six railroads that served the metropolis, and a set of ambitious plans for development that included dredging the Chicago River and using the dirt to raise the streets twelve feet. But the schools were chaotic, differing "from isolated, primitive, rural schools only in the huge numbers of children each teacher struggled with." Each school had three trustees to select the teacher and keep an eye on the classroom, while the city council appointed seven "inspectors" who tried—largely unsuccessfully—to integrate these schools into a city system. In 1850, twenty-one teachers confronted 1,919 children in their classrooms, almost 100 on the average; the same year there were about 13,500 children of school age in the town.[15]

City promoters sketched plans of overnight metropolises, complete with universities and opera houses, but when actual cities grew as fast as did Chicago, the city fathers had trouble believing their eyes or planning for the actual services citizens would need. The public schools of the 1840's met in the abandoned barracks of Fort Dearborn, in churches, and in rented stores and houses. In 1845 the inspectors persuaded the city council to build a new school, called "Miltimore's Folly" after its chief advocate, much to the consternation of the mayor, who argued that the building would never be filled and might instead "be converted into a factory or an insane asylum for those responsible for its erection." The mayor was wrong: 543 children turned up when it opened, and 843 the next year. Three teachers in that school were expected to instruct all those children in ungraded classrooms, with no uniform textbooks. Like teachers in the other schools, they struggled to maintain order in the vast classes, listened to children recite, and taught the fine art of quill sharpening; as for records, it was hard enough simply to count the scholars as required to receive state aid without bothering to list their names on the register.[16]

So the first superintendent, John Dore, had a big task ahead of him. For two years he struggled to examine each child and to assign him or her to a prticular level in a particular school, to keep records of attendance, to require uniform textbooks, to hire school janitors, and to persuade parents to abandon their "migratory character" and to send their children to school regularly. Dore's successor, William Wells, carried on the battle to transform the haphazard village schools into a graded, standardized city system, but despite Wells's professional skill in inspiring the teachers, in creating a coherent curriculum, and in awakening public interest in education, year after year thousands of children could not attend school for lack of seats. In 1860, 123 teachers faced a staggering total of 14,000 scholars in their classrooms.[17]

Indeed, the pressure of numbers was a main reason for the bureaucratization that gradually replaced the older decentralized village pattern of schooling. "Organization becomes necessary in the crowded schools in congested districts," said Albert Marble, superintendent of schools in Worcester, Massachusetts, "just as hard pavements cover the city street, though the soft turf and the country road are easier for the steed and for the traveller." Like Marble, who argued that an "ideal education would be a small class of children in charge of a thoroughly cultivated man or woman through a series of years," a number of educators glorified the old life-style and broader education of farm or village. "There is no better place to bring up a boy than on a farm," wrote a leading urban educator, William Mowry, in his autobiography, "especially if that farm is located in the midst of an intelligent community with a good rural school." But as the villages grew into congested, heterogeneous cities, as conflicting values and strangers on the streets threatened the old pattern of Protestant socialization, decentralized decision-making and pedagogical variety struck many educational leaders as anarchy. They sought instead to centralize the nerve-centers of information and influence and to standardize the educational process. They tried to design, in short, the one best system.[18]

2. CREATING THE ONE BEST SYSTEM

In 1885, John D. Philbrick wrote a comprehensive survey of *City School Systems in the United States.* His purpose was to hasten that "uniformity of excellence" in urban education which he foresaw as the product of a new expertise and an intensified emulation among American school managers. Now, he believed, the chief task of the educational statesman was not evangelical persuasion but the "perfecting of the system itself. With this end in view, he always has some project in hand: the establishment of a training school for teachers, an evening school, or an industrial school; the adoption of a better method of examining and certificating teachers . . . an improvement in the plan of constructing school-houses; the devising of a more rational program and a more rational system of school examinations." He did not doubt that there was "one best way" of educating urban children everywhere. The French might invent the best primary school, the

Germans the best arrangement of a schoolroom, the Prussians the best way of training teachers. "If America devises the best school desk, it must go to the ends of a civilized world. . . . The really good local thing, the outgrowth of educational laws, that stands the test of experiment, in time becomes general." The New York Commissioner of Education, Andrew S. Draper, told teachers in 1889 that "it is obligatory upon everyone engaged in this work to have full knowledge of all that is being done the wide-world over to diffuse public education, and it is their duty to seize hold of those methods, and put them to use here." Philbrick had only scorn for those "amateur educational reformers" who argued that the machinery of education was "already too perfect," that administrators were putting organization before education. "Modern civilization is rapidly tending to uniformity and unity. . . . The best is the best everywhere." To Philbrick and his fellow schoolmen, the perfecting of urban education was the key to the prosperity and survival of the republic. "The future of our cities will be largely what education makes it and the future of our country will be largely what the cities make it. What but education is to settle the question how far self government is to be practicable in our populous cities?" [19]

In attempting to systematize urban schools, the superintendents of the latter half of the nineteenth century sought to transform structures and decision-making processes in education. From classroom to central office they tried to create new controls over pupils, teachers, principals, and other subordinate members of the school hierarchy. Although they often used the nonpolitical language of social engineers, they were actually trying to replace village forms in which laymen participated in decentralized decision-making with the new bureaucratic model of a closed "nonpolitical" system in which directives flowed from the top down, reports emanated from the bottom, and each step of the educational process was carefully prescribed by professional educators. The purpose of schooling, wrote Philbrick, "is the imposition of tasks; if the pupil likes it, well; if not, the obligation is the same." What was true of the pupils was also true of all the other members of the system, for each person was to be accountable for specific duties as prescribed in detailed rules and regulations.[20]

The goal of a uniform system of education had long been a dream of American educators, although ideas about the precise purpose and structure of schooling differed in successive periods. Many Americans were impressed with Joseph Lancaster's plan to educate poor children by the use of student monitors and a carefully prescribed program of studies, for the Lancasterian system seemed to be a perfectly designed and well-oiled machine. The philanthropic New York Public School Society adopted a modified version of the Lancasterian plan for its schools for poor children. As the population of the city expanded, it simply built additional identical schools under a centralized structure of control. As Carl Kaestle has observed, this blueprint for education not only offered identical small steps of learning for the pupils, but also created a hierarchy of offices which offered a ladder of promotion to the industrious: student, monitor, monitor-general, assistant teacher, teacher, principal, and finally assistant superintendent and superintendent. Lancaster insisted that authority inhered in the office, not the person. Thus, an older or larger student would be expected to obey a precocious monitor just as a private obeys a sergeant.[21]

Although they generally criticized the Lancasterian system, educational leaders in Boston were also fascinated with the thought of applying the factory model to the systematization of schools. Like the manager of a cotton mill, the superintendent of schools could supervise employees, keep the enterprise technically up to date, and monitor the uniformity and quality of the product. The first superintendent of schools in Boston, Nathan Bishop, claimed that "in organizing a system of popular education, the same practical judgment is to be exercised in making special adaptations of means to ends, as in any manufacturing or business enterprise." Using yet another metaphor, a later schoolman would refer to the city superintendent as a conductor on the educational railroad.[22]

In suggesting such analogies to machines and factories, educational publicists were not simply using fashionable jargon to appeal to the prejudices of leading citizens. Just as eighteenth-century theologians could think of God as a clock-maker without derogation, so the social engineers searching for new organizational forms used the words "machine" or "factory" without investing them with the negative associations they evoke today. Furthermore, schoolmen were seeking stable, predictable, reliable structures in which their own role as educational managers would be visible, secure, and prestigious. They believed bureaucracy would provide what Philbrick called "a suitable hierarchical situation for the teacher." Philbrick admiringly quoted a European educator who advocated the bureaucratic ideal of meritocracy: "It is the function of a good administration . . . to ascertain merit and to class individuals according to their aptitudes; then there would be an end of solicitations, of subserviency, of intrigues, of protections, of favors, of injustices." [23]

To those who feared the whims of a decentralized politics of education such a meritocracy had a strong appeal. While it is possible to see in retrospect that school bureaucracy reinforced racial, religious, and class privilege in many cases, its liberal advocates believed that a strong and rational system of education could eliminate corporal punishment, offer new opportunities for women, equalize educational expenditures between rich and poor sections of a city, and provide a system of instruction which was impartially efficient for all classes of the population. As Carl Kaestle said, they worried less than we do today about the depersonalization and alienation which mass education often entails. Indeed, they saw punctuality, order, regularity, and industry as essential features of a uniform urban discipline required for success in later life.[24]

During the latter half of the nineteenth century, there were many channels of communication among the leading urban schoolmen. They met in organizations like the round-table of superintendents in the Ohio Valley or in the Department of Superintendence of the National Education Association (NEA). In 1880 prominent schoolmen formed a prestigious inner sanctum within the NEA called the National Council of Education, which sought to prescribe what was wise and unwise in educational policy for the rest of the nation. Schoolmen read one another's city school reports and wrote for prestigious educational periodicals, most of which were edited in the Northeast but which had nationwide distribution.[25]

New patterns of organization spread rapidly as a result of

these informal and formal networks of communication. Western cities could skip earlier stages of school reform and profit from experience elsewhere. Richard Wade noted that the new cities arising by the banks of the Ohio and the Mississippi—St. Louis, Cincinnati, and the rest—copied the educational systems of "the great cities across the mountains" even though they were "freed from . . . old restraints and traditions." Louisville sent a new principal to study eastern schools to eliminate the need for "expensive errors and fruitless experiments." Denver's cautious superintendent, Aaron Gove, adopted only those changes which had been tested by years of success elsewhere. World fairs and international expositions acquainted Americans with new educational innovations developed elsewhere.[26]

William T. Harris, superintendent of schools in St. Louis and later U.S. Commissioner of Education, was probably the outstanding intellectual leader in American education in the years between the death of Horace Mann in 1859 and the emergence of John Dewey as a spokesman for the new education at the turn of the twentieth century. In 1871, while Harris was still superintendent of schools in St. Louis, he stated succinctly the premises behind the drive to standardize the schools: "The first requisite of the school is *Order:* each pupil must be taught first and foremost to conform his behavior to a general standard." Harris pointed out that in modern industrial society, "conformity to the time of the train, to the starting of work in the manufactory," and to other characteristic activities of the city requires absolute precision and regularity. The corollary was that the school should be a model of bureaucratic punctuality and precision: "The pupil must have his lessons ready at the appointed time, must rise at the tap of the bell, move to the line, return; in short, go through all the evolutions with equal precision." [27]

In order to provide this type of urban discipline for the child in the classroom, urban schoolmen needed to transform village schools into unified city systems. They wanted to divide the cities into attendance districts; calibrate upgraded primary and grammar schools into distinct classes in which children were segregated according to their academic progress; provide adequate schoolhouses and equipment; train and certify teachers for specific tasks within these graded schools; design a sequential curriculum or program of studies that would be uniform throughout the city; devise examinations which would test the achievement of pupils and serve as a basis for promotion (and often as a basis of evaluating the teacher as well); and provide specialized services such as those given in kindergartens, trade schools, evening schools, and institutions for deviant children who did not fit into the regular classroom. At the top of the system was the superintendent of schools, who, in theory at least, was expected to be the architect and overseer of the entire system, the center of communications and directives for the schools as a whole.[28]

Crucial to educational bureaucracy was the objective and efficient classification, or "grading," of pupils. In 1838, Henry Barnard first gave his lecture "Gradation of Public Schools, with Special Reference to Cities and Large Villages," which he would repeat in more than fifty cities across the country during the next two decades. He maintained that a classroom containing students of widely varying ages and attainment was not only inefficient but also inhumane. Methods of discipline, teaching style, school furniture, and intellectual content should be adjusted to the maturity of pupils, and this could be done only where the children were properly classified. In the one-room school, or its inflated urban counterparts containing 200 or more pupils of varying advancement, the instructor hardly had time to teach, so varied were the tasks he faced: "From the number of class and individual recitations . . . exercises are brief, hurried, and of little practical value. They consist, for the most part, of senseless repetitions of the words of a book. . . . *Saying their lessons,* as the operation is significantly described by most teachers." [29]

From Horace Mann in Massachusetts to Calvin Stowe in Ohio to John Pierce in Michigan, leading common school crusaders urged communities to replace the heterogeneous grouping of students with a systematic plan of gradation based on the Prussian model. But it fell to a practical man, John Philbrick, actually to provide a concrete model for his urban colleagues. Philbrick knew that educational function necessarily reflected architectural form. He convinced the Boston school board, therefore, that the proper classification of pupils required a new kind of building— one which has since been dubbed the "egg-crate school." In

1848, the new Quincy School was dedicated and Philbrick became its principal. The building was four stories high, with a large auditorium for 700 pupils and twelve classrooms, each of which would accommodate 56 students. Every teacher had a separate classroom for the one grade she taught, each scholar his own desk. The scholars, he said, should be divided according to their tested proficiency, and "all in the same class [should] attend to precisely the same branches of study. Let the Principal or Superintendent have the general supervision and control of the whole, and let him have one male assistant or sub-principal, and ten female assistants, one for each room." [30]

And thus was stamped on mid-century America not only the graded school, but also the pedagogical harem. This system caught on fast. When the U.S. Commissioner of Education surveyed practices in forty-five cities in 1870, already the pattern of eight years of elementary school had become the norm (although there was considerable variety in the division of schools into primary and grammar categories). A nineteenth-century student of the grading of schools observed that "by 1860 the schools of most of the cities and large towns were graded. By 1870 the pendulum had swung from no system to nothing but system." The "division of labor in educational matters," he wrote, "is but the result of necessary obedience to the universal law of progress. The teacher's time and talents being concentrated upon certain work, it becomes easier by repetition, and, therefore, is likely to be performed more efficiently." [31]

The proper classification of pupils was only the beginning. In order to make the one best system work, the schoolmen also had to design a uniform course of study and standard examinations. Since promotion and grading depended on examinations and examinations upon the curriculum, all learning had to be carefully structured. "A good program for one city would be, in its substance . . . a good program for every other city," Philbrick believed. [32]

The work of William Harvey Wells as superintendent of the Chicago public schools from 1856 to 1864 illustrates the connection between the grading of pupils and the creation of the program of study. Almost single-handedly, Wells divided over 14,000 children into ten grades and assigned 123 teachers to

A Class in the Condemned Essex Market School, New York, early 1890s

these primary and grammar grades. Each teacher was expected to follow a uniform schedule for teaching the subjects of spelling, arithmetic, and reading. In 1862, Wells published *A Graded Course of Instruction with Instructions to Teachers,* which not only outlined specific items to be covered in each subject at each grade level, but also prescribed the proper teaching methods. Children began with the alphabet at the age of five, learned to count to 100 and do simple addition in the next grade, and proceeded in the next years to learn about the mysteries of Roman numerals, the hanging gardens of Babylon, the Crusades, and the Trojan War. Spelling and grammar were the staples of instruction in English. Wells's book was widely adopted in cities of the old Northwest as an official curriculum.[33]

In 1890, eighty-two of the largest cities reported the amount of time devoted during the eight years of elementary education to the various branches of the curriculum. The average amount of total instruction per child was 7,000 hours, meaning that in a given year the typical student spent four and a half hours a day for 200 days in study or recitation during school hours. Of that total amount of time, children averaged 516 hours in spelling; 1,188 in reading; 500 in geography; 1,190 in arithmetic; 300 in grammar or "language lessons"; 150 in history; 169 in physiology (in sixty-six cities); 167 in "morals and manners," largely in oral lessons (in twenty-seven cities); and 176 in natural science (in thirty-nine cities). In addition, singing and physical education normally rounded out the course of study (physical education—probably mostly as "recess"—occupied about 2,000 hours in the average of sixty-three cities reporting it).[34]

Although new subjects and methods of instruction were added to the school curriculum during the latter half of the nineteenth century—such as vocal music, physical training, drawing, physiology, and instruction in science through "object lessons"—textbooks remained the central source of information and authority in the curriculum. One reason for the primacy of the textbook, as we shall see, was the inadequate education of the teacher. But another, perhaps more compelling reason was that both pupils and teachers knew that examinations focused on the information provided in those books.[35]

The use of written examinations in all of the elementary schools in Portland, Oregon, in the 1870's illustrated the hazards of testing for pupils and teachers alike. Portland's first superintendent, Samuel King, developed a uniform curriculum in 1874 and then tested the children at the end of the year to discover if they had been "thoroughly drilled in the work assigned." As a Yankee who believed that "a perfect system of school management is indispensable to the welfare of our Public Schools," King paid examinations the supreme compliment: "System, order, dispatch and promptness have characterized the examinations and exerted a helpful influence over the pupils by stimulating them to be thoroughly prepared to meet their appointments and engagements. Next to a New England climate, these examinations necessitate industry, foster promptness, and encourage pupils to do the right thing *at the right time.*" [36]

The results of the first round of examinations might have dismayed a heart less stout than King's. In seven classrooms out of a total of twenty-one, none of the children passed. Only in six classrooms were more than half of the children promoted. But King maintained that the operation was a great success, though most of the patients died. Not surprisingly, in the next examinations teachers and pupils improved somewhat: this time between 13 percent and 75 percent of the children were promoted (in some of the classes, though, fewer than three fourths of the students got up nerve to take the test). King published the results of the examinations in the newspaper, with the child's score and school next to his name. Parents could draw their own conclusions about the diligence of the child and the competence of the teacher, and they did. Incensed and anxious, the teachers joined irate parents to force King's resignation in 1877.[37]

The new Portland superintendent, Thomas Crawford, promptly abolished the practice of publicizing the test results. He wrote in his report of 1878 that "incalculable injury has been done, both to the teachers and to the pupils of our free schools, resulting from a spirit of rivalry on the part of the teachers." Some teachers had gone to great lengths to protect their reputations, urging children to withdraw from school shortly before the examination and even advising the superintendent to suspend slow students for trivial offenses, so that they would not drag down the percentage of promotions. The system of publicity had led, Crawford said, to cramming, "bitter animosities," and "unpleasant wranglings, over arbitrary standards in marking papers." Yet Crawford was no Paul Goodman; he was a good bureaucrat who wanted harmony in the ranks. He retained the examination system, elaborating it in mandarin detail while softening its rigors, but he kept the examination results the property of the bureaucracy. A later Portland superintendent, Frank Rigler, devoted most of his seventeen years in the office (1896–1913) to perfecting the curriculum and machinery of instruction he had inherited. Lest teachers become too independent in interpreting the course of study, Rigler met with them on Saturdays and went through the textbooks page by page, telling his staff what questions to ask and what answers to accept. It was common knowledge in Portland that Rigler "could sit in his office and know on what page in each book work was being done at the time in every school in the city."[38]

Cities differed in the kinds of tests which they gave to children. Some systems printed uniform city-wide written examinations, some relied on a mixture of written and oral examinations, and in certain cases, children were examined only orally, as had been the practice in rural and village schools. Normally the key figure in the examination process was the principal, although on occasion the superintendent or board members performed the task; the examination or recommendation for promotion of pupils was rarely entrusted to the individual teacher. Uniform tests were sometimes used throughout a state; in Illinois, for example, a professor of pedagogy, Charles DeGarmo, wrote tests which were sent to the schools by the state superintendent. A number of schoolmen criticized such standardized tests. Emerson E. White, a noted school superintendent and leader in the National Education Association, complained that test scores "should not be used to *compare schools and teachers.* A careful observation of this practice for years has convinced me that such comparisons are usually unjust and mischievous." But almost all school leaders agreed with Philbrick that it was essential to find out if students had managed to "acquire a certain amount of positive knowledge." To the extent that the classroom was part of the production line of the school factory, examinations were the means of judging the value added to the raw material, namely the knowledge that the children had acquired during the course of the year.[39]

The acquisition of "positive knowledge" was only part of the purpose of the common school in the city. A number of scholars have recently written about the "hidden curriculum" of the public school, namely the traits of behavior and roles expected of students which are rarely written in curriculum guides or acknowledged in the manifest objectives of the school, but which are nonetheless systematically inculcated and rewarded. These include, for example, competition for extrinsic rewards such as marks, conformity to authority (such as requesting hall passes to go to the toilet), and adaptation to bureaucratic definitions (such as being a part of a group called third-graders). In the view of most urban schoolmen of the late nineteenth century, schools should inculcate obedience to bureaucratic norms *overtly* and with zest. In 1874, William T. Harris and Duane Doty wrote *The Theory of Education in the United States of America,* a pamphlet which was co-signed by seventy-seven college presidents and city and state superintendents of schools. This statement, then, represented not simply the philosophy of the authors, but a consensus of educational leaders. Harris and Doty wrote that "military precision is required in the maneuvering of classes. Great stress is laid upon (1) punctuality, (2) regularity, (3) attention, and (4) silence, as habits necessary through life for successful combination with one's fellow-men in an industrial and commercial civilization." Observers of urban schools, both friendly and critical, reinforced the truth of this statement.[40]

Punctuality was a favorite theme of schoolmen of the time, for it was clear that children's behavior must be precisely controlled, reliable, and predictable. Well into the twentieth century superintendents continued to report attendance and tardiness statistics down to the second and third decimal point. "A school with an enrollment of fifty, daily attendance fifty and none tardy," wrote a lyrical superintendent, "is a grand sight to behold in the morning and afternoon." Clearly punctuality was a very basic part of the curriculum, as were obedience, precision, and silence.[41]

To see how such qualities were taught in the classroom, let us accompany some observers as they visited actual urban schools during the latter half of the nineteenth century. A Scottish writer, David MacRae, reported what he saw in Ward School No. 50 in New York City in the late 1860's. At the morning assembly, the room was filled with 500 to 600 children between the ages of five and twelve. MacRae was impressed with their appearance: "They were neatly (many of them beautifully) dressed, and all scrupulously clean—a point to which great attention is paid in American schools. Any scholar coming with untidy clothes, or with unwashed face or hands, or unbrushed hair, would be sent home at once." The children were perfectly quiet when the principal took her place and conducted the object lesson for the day. "What are you to do when you see any object?" asked the principal. "We are to think of its qualities, parts, uses, colours, and form," replied the pupils in unison. She then showed the children a clay pipe. After the children had said what they knew about pipes and the evils of tobacco, the principal rang a small bell, thereby announcing the close of the lesson. The mass of pupils "rose and moved off with military precision to their various recitation rooms." The principal explained to MacRae that she had achieved such careful order by appealing to the self-respect and sense of shame of the students. As he went with her to the recitation rooms, he found children eagerly competing with one another. After the teacher gave them a problem in arithmetic "everyone dashed into the calculation with a rapidity of an excited terrier chasing a ball" to see which one could come up with the right answer first. In the reading lesson, the teacher stressed an exaggerated articulation of each word so that the students might escape linguistic delinquency. They were no more allowed to be slovenly in their pronunciation than in their appearance.[42]

In 1867, a committee appointed by the Baltimore school board visited the public schools in Philadelphia, New York, Brooklyn, and Boston. Like MacRae, they were impressed by classrooms in New York City. One school contained 507 pupils in the Boys Department, 461 in the Girls Department, and 1,309 in the Primary Department, all in the same building. The children alternated between recitations in the smaller rooms and large group instruction in an assembly hall (which was created by moving aside the partitions that separated two of the largest rooms in the building). Into this single space came all the boys and girls of the Grammar Department: "the movements of the classes from the class rooms to the large assembling room were regulated by pianos, two of which were in each of the large rooms. All the changes were performed in marches, some in the usual step, others in the double quick time of the military development. Calisthenic exercises were performed with great precision under the direction of assistant teachers. The regularity of movement in so large a number of children, all well dressed, and many of them tastefully attired, was truly interesting." The visitors were delighted with the children's "simultaneous enunciation," and the way in which "a thousand little forms are as erect in their seats, as though they were rivetted there by some process of mechanism." In Boston, likewise, the Baltimore visitors applauded the order that they discovered in the operation of the Emerson School: "Every pupil appears to be in anxious waiting for the

A New York School Assembly, c. 1880

A New York School Assembly, c. 1880

word of the teacher, and when issued it is promptly obeyed by the class. The movements and utterances of the class are as nearly simultaneous and similar as they can be." [43]

In 1868, an anonymous author described "Two Representative Schools" of New York City which were "examples of the highest development of the theories now most popular among Boards of Education." Although the article was highly critical, the picture of Public School No. 14 corresponded closely with descriptions by its admirers. Again, there were the hundreds of perfectly silent children, eyes fixed straight ahead, sitting "as regular as rows of machine-planted corn." When the Directress came into the assembly at a given signal "every face turned instantly, as though on a pivot," to greet the principal, all then swinging back again in unison upon the giving of the further signal. Recitations followed a carefully prescribed order. The teacher would propose a problem in arithmetic. "Down would go all the slates and the work of ciphering would proceed, and as the work was completed by different members of the class, the slates would pop up against the breast, one after another; and when a boy was called upon to explain, up he would jump, rattle off his explanation, and then thump down again amidst the perfect stillness of the rest." The faults of such a system, wrote the critic of P.S. 14, were "the inseparable attendance of wholesale schooling. To manage successfully a hundred children, or even half that number, the teacher must reduce them as nearly as possible to a unit." [44]

How did the teachers preserve such order in a school which included members of "many different social classes"? By keeping each child busy at a specific task every minute, by competition for that scarce commodity, praise, and by the "terror of degradation." "Some four hundred pupils cannot, for want of space, be admitted to the assembly-room," explained the author, "and it would be a source of great shame to any pupil in the room to have to give place to one without." As Colin Greer has observed, much of urban schooling was predicated on an economy of scarcity. Not only did many cities fall far behind in providing seats for children in school, but once in school, it was assumed that some children would be losers as children failed or succeeded according to rigid rules of behavior and performance.[45]

In her study of classroom behavior in nineteenth-century schools, Barbara Joan Finkelstein writes that teachers were so committed to discipline that they believed that "the acquisition of knowledge represented a triumph of the will as well as the intellect. Consistently, in every kind of teaching situation, we find that teachers treated academic failure, not as a reflection of their own inabilities as instructors, but as evidence of the students' personal and moral recalcitrance; and this tendency was institutionalized on a grand scale in the village and city schools of the 1850's, 1860's, and 1870's. Indeed the evidence suggests that teachers in every setting only rarely distinguished between the intellectual and the social aspects of student behavior as they meted out rewards and punishments." To many teachers, corporal punishment or humiliation seemed appropriate treatment for children who did not learn their lessons, for academic incompetence was considered a sign of moral laxity. The creative child probably suffered agonies of boredom, since spontaneity was regarded only as a form of naughtiness in such a system. The child whose home and neighborhood background was culturally different from that of the standard curriculum perhaps also suffered. But one result of the classroom's very rigidity and size was that it offered fewer opportunities for educators to separate individuals into preconceived categories based on a shaky and often biased "science." If the pupil conformed to the teacher's set standards of learning and deportment, in other words, if she passed a performance test, she succeeded.[46]

Through an elaborate system of gradation, programmed curriculum, examinations, and rules for "deportment," then, the pupil learned the meaning of obedience, regularity, and precision. He learned to "toe the line"—a phrase that today has lost its literal significance to most people. Joseph Rice, who visited hundreds of urban classrooms in the 1890's, described what it meant in one school. During recitation periods, when students were to demonstrate that they had memorized the text, children were expected, said Rice, "to stand on the line, perfectly motionless, their bodies erect, their knees and feet together, the tips of their shoes touching the edge of a board in the floor." The teacher paid as much attention to the state of their toes and knees as to the words of their mouths: "How can you learn any-

An Arithmetic Class at the Turn of the Century

thing," asked one woman, "with your knees and toes out of order?" [47]

The capstone of the educational arch of city systems was the high school. During the nineteenth century the public high school was predominately urban, for relatively few small towns or villages had the tax base, the desire, or the population density to support a full-fledged secondary school (although sometimes a room or two attached to the grammar school might be called, in the inflationary terminology of educational boosterism, a "high school"). Private academies were common in the countryside and villages, and it was probably not until the 1880's that enrollment in public secondary schools surpassed that in private institutions.

Indeed, the distinction between "public" and "private" secondary schools was very vague, since states or localities often gave scholarship funds or other aid to academies.

In cities, however, the creation of high schools often helped to unify a disparate collection of lower schools into a pedagogical pyramid. Central boards and the superintendent normally controlled high schools even where ward boards persisted, and requirements for admission to the high school gave some degree of control over grammar schools. Schoolmen boasted that competition to get into high school fostered useful emulation in the lower grades. In Chicago the newspapers referred to the annual examinations as the "Olympic Games." [48]

The high school did help to create a hierarchy of schooling, but it is essential to underscore its limited clientele and functions during the nineteenth century. Only a small fraction of students attended public secondary schools before 1900, and of these only a tiny number actually graduated. Although educational statistics need to be interpreted guardedly because of poor returns from local and state officials and the vagueness and shifting character of the classification of "secondary schools," some idea of high school attendance can be gleaned from records of the U.S. Bureau of the Census. It estimates that in 1870 only about 16,000 students graduated from public and private high schools, only 2 percent of the population aged seventeen; by 1890, the comparable statistics were 43,731 and 3.5 percent; and in 1900, 94,883 and 6.4 percent. The 202,926 students in public high schools in 1890 represented 1 percent of the total population, and only 10 percent of that number graduated. Only 732 pupils out of a total enrollment of 185,000 were seniors in high school in Chicago in 1894. [49]

Although schoolmen liked to refer to the high school as "the people's college," they built fancy Gothic structures to compete with the most ornate academies in attracting the attendance of the prosperous. Promoters had a conspicuous edifice complex; men like Philbrick described the "noble edifice" in one city or the "palatial edifice" in another. Yet they were sensitive to the frequent accusation that they were taxing poor people to pay for elegant schooling of the rich or the complaints of self-made men that they were turning out dandies who would scorn manual labor. From the defensive tone of their rhetoric, one suspects that there was some truth in both charges.

Information on the social composition of the high school population is scanty but what there is suggests that the schools probably served mostly the upper reaches of the middle class. Michael Katz found that of 111 families served by the Somerville High School in 1860, 57 percent would so qualify, and no pupils were children of factory operatives, ordinary laborers, or Irish (there were 1,500 Irish immigrants in the city). Selwyn Troen wrote that in 1880 only 31.7 percent of the children of unskilled workers in St. Louis were in school from ages thirteen to sixteen, compared with 64.1 percent for white-collar workers and 80 percent for professional families. The evidence is mixed, however, depending on time and place; in Erie, Pennsylvania, the high school principal reported in 1889 that 200 of the 347 pupils had parents whose property assessment was less than $500, and fifty-four of those had no property assessment.[50]

Whatever the class origins of individual students, it is clear that most schoolmen before 1900 regarded the high school as a minority institution designed for the bright child whose parents were willing and able to forego her or his labor. In 1893 the NEA Committee of Ten declared that the function of high schools was "to prepare for the duties of life that small proportion of all the children in the country . . . who show themselves able to profit by an education prolonged to the eighteenth year, and whose parents are able to support them while they remain so long at school." That committee believed that only a few of those graduates would go on to college but maintained that the rigorous training of the mind through academic subjects would best fit anyone for "the duties of life"—which was another way of saying that the vocational relevance of secondary education was remote at best. One indication that young people and their parents did not regard high school as a necessary step on most career ladders was not only the small size of the graduating classes but also the sex ratio: girls consistently outnumbered boys (in 1890, 57.6 percent of the pupils enrolled were girls, 64.8 percent of the graduates). "Boys are too anxious, perhaps, to take a short cut to business," observed Philbrick. For a minority of the girls, to be sure, high school normal classes did offer a career in

teaching (almost no boys were enrolled in the normal departments that had appeared in twenty-one cities by 1885). But in a
time when few employers required their employees to be high
school graduates, and when entry positions were abundant for
youth with meager schooling, the great majority of the population acted as if the high school was superfluous. For this reason
one cannot judge popular belief in the principle of public education by the criterion of support for the high school. Businessmen
as well as workers often opposed secondary education. The
whole equation would change, of course, when the high school
became a mass institution during the twentieth century.[51]

3. TEACHERS AND THE MALE MYSTIQUE

Like many other segments of the work force, nineteenth-century teachers had minimal formal schooling when judged by the
standards of the 1970's. Nationwide, the typical teacher had only
attended grammar school. Cities and towns with graded schools
claimed the cream of the crop, but only about one fourth of
their instructors had received a normal school diploma. Customarily normal training took place at the secondary level. Thus,
at best, most urban teachers probably had attended high school.
Given the widespread assumption among school superintendents
that teachers should be subordinate—should toe the line, as their
students did—this limited training was an advantage: "such
teachers will almost invariably be in hearty sympathy with
graded-school work," wrote William Payne. "Teachers will teach
chiefly as they have been taught, and will manage pupils as they
themselves were managed during the course of their education."
To Payne, the lesson for the manager and the managed was
clear: "Organization implies subordination. If there is to be a
plan, some one must devise it, while others must execute it. As
the members of the human body execute the behests of the
supreme intelligence, so in human society the many must follow
the direction of the few." One man should control this system,
"vested with sufficient authority to keep all subordinates in their
proper places, and at their assigned tasks." Like most other
school*men* who preceded him, Payne assumed that the boss—the

"supreme intelligence" of the analogy—would be male. Henry Barnard, for example, had tossed many rhetorical bouquets to the underpaid and overworked women teachers—"in whose own hearts, love, hope and patience, have first kept school"—but wrote that the principal in the graded school "may be selected with special reference to *his* ability in arranging the studies, and order of exercises of the school, in administering its discipline, in adapting moral instruction to individual scholars, and superintending the operations of each class-room, so as to secure the harmonious action and progress of every department." [52]

Hierarchical organization of schools and the male chauvinism of the larger society fit as hand to glove. The system required subordination; women were generally subordinate to men; the employment of women as teachers thus augmented the authority of the largely male administrative leadership. An anonymous writer in *Harpers* in 1878 reported that "women teachers are often preferred by superintendents because they are more willing to comply with established regulations and less likely to ride headstrong hobbies." It seemed but an absurd dream to imagine "what would happen if that indefatigable, overworked class, the schoolteachers, should have a 'strike.' " If teachers have advice to give their superior, said the Denver superintendent of schools, "it is to be given as the good daughter talks with the father. . . . The dictation must come from the other end." In 1841, the Boston school committee commended women teachers because they were unambitious, frugal, and filial: "they are less intent on scheming for future honors or emoluments [than men]. As a class, they never look forward, as young men almost invariably do, to a period of legal emancipation from parental control." One reason for the general bias against married teachers appears to be that they were less likely to be acquiescent than unmarried ones. In New York state, a legislator argued that women make better teachers of young children because of their "very weakness," for they taught pupils whose "intellectual faculties" were less developed than the affections. Thus women had more "access to the heart" of little children because of their "peculiar faculties." In return for "complaisant homage," social custom required women to adopt certain roles—to be docile rather than questioning, perceptive of feelings rather than strong of intellect, content with subordination rather than ambitious, timid rather than adventurous—that fit them well to obey superiors in the one best system.[53]

When schoolmen discussed teachers at conventions of the NEA or in official reports, they customarily did so from a supervisor's perspective: how can inefficient teachers *be* improved or dismissed? How should teachers *be* selected? How much responsibility should teachers *be* given? Almost always the passive voice. One superintendent said it was idle for teachers to read professional books since they looked to him for proper methods.[54]

The employment of women appears to correlate highly with the pace of bureaucratization. Early advocates of graded schools claimed that the division of labor and the presence of male principals would enable women to handle their jobs efficiently and to control the older boys (though the presumed superiority of men as executives and disciplinarians seems to rest more on male vanity than on evidence). In 1911, Lotus D. Coffman studied the social composition of the population of teachers, concluding that the vast increase of women in "the teaching force has been due in part to the changed character of the management of the public schools, to the specialization of labor within the school, to the narrowing of the intellectual range or versatility required of teachers, and to the willingness of women to work for less than men." In towns and cities, he observed, almost "all of the graded school positions have been preempted by women; men still survive in public school work as 'managing' or executive officers." [55]

Statistics on teachers are approximations at best, but it appears that the percentages of woman teachers in the United States increased from 59 percent in 1870 to 70 percent in 1900 to 86 percent in 1920. Women teachers clearly predominated in cities. In 1885 in fourteen representative cities, women outnumbered men ten to one. By 1905 only 2 percent of *teachers* in elementary schools were men, as reported in a careful study of 467 cities done for the NEA by Carroll Wright. By contrast, 38 percent of the elementary school *principals* were men. In the high schools, which generally paid more and were more prestigious than the elementary schools, 94 percent of the principals and 38 percent of the teachers were men.[56]

Men not only had a disproportionate share of the higher-paying and high-status jobs, but they were also commonly paid more than women for doing the same work. Indeed, most candid schoolmen agreed that the low salary paid to women was a major reason for their displacing men. Teaching was one of the few large and respectable occupations open to women, and since they were usually willing to work for less than men, school boards eagerly cut costs by employing them. Here are some estimates of the weekly earnings of men and women in city schools:

Year	Men	Women
1870	$35	$12
1880	31	12
1890	33	13
1900	32	14
1910	36	17
1920	61	36

The average salaries of women and men reported in a 1905 NEA study of 467 city systems are as follows:

	Women	Men
Elementary teacher	$650	$1,161
Elementary principal	970	1,542
High School teacher	903	1,303

Sexual discrimination was normally frozen into the official published pay scales rather than achieved through individual bargaining. In 1861–62, for example, St. Louis paid male principals $800 and female principals $400, while in 1904 New York paid a maximum salary of $2,400 to male high school teachers, $1,900 to female.[57]

One reason men continued to earn more money than women was that a number of leading educators began to have doubts about the benefits of the feminization of the profession and held out added pay as an inducement to attract men and to retain them as the managers. The reports of the U.S. Commissioner of Education reveal some of these changing attitudes. In 1873 the Commissioner noted that some educators favored the employment of women as "school-officers," reporting that a "daughter of Ralph Waldo Emerson . . . is said to have done valuable service" as a member of the Concord school committee, while "in the flexible and sometimes impulsive West" women were actually running for state and county superintendent. Cautiously, he said it was too early to judge the wisdom of the experiment. By 1887 the Commissioner still straddled the fence, reporting the opinions of superintendents in Macon, Georgia, and Pawtucket, Rhode Island, that men were needed as principals of elementary schools because they had more executive ability and were firm disciplinarians, but also saying that the substitution of women for men in the higher grades had done no damage. By 1892 the Commissioner was worried, for women not only were monopolizing the assistant teacher slots but in some places had "captured the principalships as well as the minor positions." How to preserve male principalships, he said, "presents new difficulties. The assistants' positions were formerly the training schools of principals, and from them it was always easy to select a man to fill any vacancy; but now it becomes necessary either to employ a new and untried college graduate, to import a rustic schoolmaster, or to transfer a high-school assistant." Confronted with this threat to male supremacy, the Philadelphia schools created a "School of Pedagogy" limited to men and adopted a rule that only men would be hired in the two top grades of the boys' grammar schools. The Commissioner endorsed the "strong stand for the restoration of the element of masculinity" made by the President of the Chicago board of education. Similar fears of the effects of feminine teachers on boys came in crescendo from authorities as disparate as G. Stanley Hall, the flamboyant psychologist, and John Philbrick, the somber bureaucrat.[58]

The doughty feminist Mary Abigail Dodge was outraged by the male mystique and what she called "The Degradation of the Teacher." A former schoolteacher, now free to speak as a freelance writer, she published in 1880 a nineteenth-century version of *Up the Down Staircase*, but with a feminist twist. Here were women teachers, she said, forced to obey, paid less than men for the same work and often barred from advancement because of their sex, bullied by superintendents and school board members who were their intellectual and social inferiors—and now told that they had a bad effect on boys! Superintendents are "taking to themselves the credit of whatever value is in the schools . . . hindering and bothering, discouraging and demoralizing the teachers by giving them so many useless things to do." The men get the money and the credit; the women do all the important work for a mere pittance. "Nothing can more truly and tersely describe the work of school superintendents than 'the form of blanks'—the shape of nothing." All the time writing silly reports and gathering meaningless statistics for administrators, teachers hardly have time to teach. The kind of man who is willing to supervise such a petty system is mediocre by definition. "No man is going to act as nursery governess to female school-teachers who is good for anything else. The men who are capable of doing a man's work in the world will have no time to spend in twitching a woman's apron-strings and hindering her from doing hers." [59]

Yet those very men pompously declaim on how much better male teachers are than female. "Suppose that instead of trying to find out why men are more earnest, devoted, and effective teachers than women," snorted Ms. Dodge, "we spend a little time in ascertaining whether they are such." Her answer was not surprising: "Reflecting on sundry male teachers we have known, to whom the greatest boon that justice could grant would be the mercy of its silence, and the many women, cultivated, ladylike, self-reliant, commanding, thorough, untiring; and then listening to the felicitations of that group of schoolmasters over their own assumed superiority, the only appropriate argument in response seems to be that of the poet: 'To take them as I would mischievous boys, / And shake their heads together.'" The fact is that "women preponderate in schools, not because they soften the boys, but because they cost less than men." [60]

In part, male worry over the "feminization of teaching" did concern the effects of schooling on children, but it was also—and perhaps primarily—a response to the growing assertiveness of women at the end of the century. I shall return to this subject in Part V, but here I should like to anticipate that story of woman power in order to illustrate an important feature of the bureaucracies the schoolmen were creating. As we have seen, it was possible to import into the organization the subordination of women that characterized the outside society and to make that sexism work to strengthen the authority of the male managers. At the same time, bureaucracies could be regarded as inherently neutral in theory and form rather than sexist. Because they could make centralized decisions about thousands of workers, and were ostensibly committed to norms of merit and impartiality, bureaucracies rendered rapid change possible as women gained power and learned how to use it.

Power came in different forms. In the West, for example, women early gained the vote on school matters and the right to hold school offices. It is no coincidence that in 1901 the only women state superintendents of instruction were in Colorado and Idaho and that women county superintendents appeared most frequently in states on the plains and far West. Equal pay for city teachers was often the result of feminist organization. In San Francisco Kate Kennedy, a suffragist, teacher, and member of the Knights of Labor, lobbied successfully with her sister colleagues for a legislative act in 1870 that awarded women the same pay as men for equal work. Margaret Haley in Chicago and Grace Strachan in New York were strategists for massive leagues of women teachers and won justice that had been denied them when they had no power. After women received the vote in 1920, within a decade ten states passed laws providing equal pay for equal work. As in the case of the armed forces, which rapidly became desegregated after World War II, the city school bureaucracies were capable of reacting quickly to equalize the pay of men and women once women achieved the power to influence decisions. Equal pay for women no more eliminated sexism in schools than desegregation destroyed racism in the armed forces, but in both instances the response of the organizations illustrated that the bureaucratic form could lend itself to the righting of specific injustices quite as much as to the perpetuation of the inequities of the larger society. Indeed, the bureaucratic norms of reward by merit and performance—however inadequately realized in practice—in theory rendered preference by sex, or race, or religion, or class irrelevant and noxious.[61]

4. ATTENDANCE, VOLUNTARY AND COERCED

As U.S. Commissioner of Education and the leading school-man of the era, William T. Harris had reason for pride as he looked back in 1898 on the accomplishments of American educators since 1870. In those twenty-eight years, he reported, the number of pupils in public schools increased from less than 7,000,000 to 15,000,000; 71 of 100 persons between five and eighteen years were enrolled in some school as compared with 61 in 1870; and expenditures jumped from $63,000,000 per year to $199,000,000 (a rise from $1.64 per capita of total population to $2.67). The typical young American of 1898 could expect to receive five years of schooling. Of 100 students in educational institutions 95 were in elementary schools, 4 in secondary, and 1 in a post-secondary school.[62]

Five years of schooling does not sound like much today, but for the nineteenth century it represented a solid achievement. What makes the accomplishment of nearly universal attendance particularly significant is that in most cases it resulted from a broad consensus on the value of schooling rather than imposition by the force of government. As we shall see, compulsory schooling laws were only sporadically and inefficiently enforced in most jurisdictions during the nineteenth century. Albert Fishlow and others have argued that levels of literacy and school attendance were very high in the United States before the common school revival of the 1840's and 1850's—second, perhaps, only to Germany; he estimates that white adult literacy was about 90 percent in 1840, a dozen years before the first compulsory education law. Before Americans generally accepted the idea that schooling should be publicly controlled and financed they clearly believed in the education of the public. During the latter half of the nineteenth century free schooling became widely available; public education rose from 47 percent of total expenditures for schooling in 1850 to 79 percent in 1900. More than two thirds of these public funds came from local tax assessments. That Americans were willing to underwrite the education of their children with their own money is revealed in Fishlow's estimate that the opportunity costs of schooling—in terms of foregone income of students aged ten to fifteen—jumped from $24,800,000 in 1860 to $213,900,000 in 1900 (he points out that the burden of foregone labor and income fell less severely on farm than urban families since the school year in rural areas matched the seasonal need for juvenile labor, whereas in cities the demand for labor was more constant year-round).[63]

As Harris knew, attendance figures supplied by state and local school officials were approximate at best and often grossly inaccurate. Fortunately, Selwyn Troen has made a careful study, based on manuscript census returns and school reports, to determine which white children actually went to public schools in 1880 in St. Louis. During the four years from eight through eleven, schooling reached almost nine out of ten children, while only a tiny number were working. By contrast, from the age of fourteen fewer than one half attended school, and many moved directly into the work force. The earlier a child left school, the likelier it was that he entered an unskilled job: 88 percent of those who went to work at twelve were unskilled or semiskilled, whereas by age sixteen 47 percent were in those categories, and 21 percent in white-collar positions. More girls than boys stayed in school after age ten, and fewer girls had jobs (facts which suggest, says Troen, that the later years of schooling had little economic significance for girls and "served as a hiatus between the freedoms of early childhood and the responsibilities of marriage"). Attendance in school from ages thirteen through sixteen increased from 31.7 percent for the children of unskilled workers to 80 percent for the sons and daughters of professional fathers. As Troen observes, "it made little difference whether the father of a child at eight or twelve was a physician or a boatman; for most children it made all the difference a few years later." In St. Louis the drop-out age and years of attendance varied little from 1860 to 1908.[64]

It is easy to demonstrate class bias in the retention rates of different groups in St. Louis and to assert that the schools simply reflected the class structure of the city. But it is also crucial to recall that schooling played a far different role in 1880 than it did in 1970. When seen from the perspective of 1880, as Troen notes, it was a major achievement to be teaching nine out of ten white children between the ages of eight and eleven. Both citizens and educators shared a common belief that a little schooling could go a long way in equipping children for the world they faced and that it was not only permissible but desirable for youth to enter the work force in their mid-teens; in fact, about a fifth of the sons of businessmen in the sample were employed at the ages of thirteen to sixteen. There were few occupations for which extended schooling was a prerequisite in 1880, even though more and more of those occupying positions at the top of the professions and the corporate world had received some post-secondary education.[65]

In making educational facilities available, in sending their children to school mostly without effective governmental compulsion, and in underwriting the opportunity costs, most Americans demonstrated their faith in the value of formal education. Coercion was aimed at that deviant minority—that "target population," to use an ugly modern term—which did not share in the consensus. Set in the larger frame of attendance, both voluntary and coerced, the story of compulsion tells much about the "misfit" groups that were mostly located at the bottom of the social structure and how they were perceived by those at the top.

The logic of the common school ideology led directly to the conclusion that truant children should be compelled to attend school, for it was precisely such children who needed training the most. From Joseph Tuckerman in Boston in the 1830's to Jacob Riis in New York in the 1890's, reformers chastized society for neglect of the children who learned from the school of the streets "disobedience to parents, prevarication, falsehood, obscenity, profanity, lewdness, intemperance, petty thievery, larceny, burglary, robbery, and murder." If family discipline and the traditional village restraints broke down, then the school must fill the moral vacuum. "In too many cases," wrote one advocate of coercive attendance in Boston, "the parents are unfit guardians of their own children." The young people raised by such adults will become "worse members of society than their parents are; instead of filling our public schools, they will find their way into our prisons, houses of correction, and almshouses." The only remedy was "stringent legislation, thoroughly carried out by an efficient police" to force truants to go to school. The state superintendent in California wrote that

citizens should support compulsory education "to save themselves from the rapidly increasing herd of non-producers . . . to
save themselves from the wretches who prey upon society like
wild beasts." For such children, the state should establish "labor
schools, school ships, industrial and technical schools" so that
children can be taught not only how to read but also "how to
work." [66]

As common school publicists moved from persuasion to coercion their conception of schooling subtly shifted as well. In the
rhetoric of a Mann or a Barnard, public education was mostly a
kind of preventive nurture, a training in consonance with an
idealized family but supplementing it in ways that prepared
pupils for a more complex society. In the arguments of many advocates of coercive attendance, and even more so in the actions
of the police and truant officers who rounded up the street
arabs, schooling became a form of preventive detention—and
often the intermediate step on the way to more total institutionalization in a reform school or in one of the many forms of
incarceration for juveniles.

Since so many of the urban truants were poor, of immigrant
stock, and non-Protestant—in Boston in 1849, 963 of 1,066
truants had foreign-born parents—school officials were tempted
to put them in separate classes or separate institutions, despite
the common school ideology of mixing all social groups under
one roof. Even before the compulsory attendance laws of 1852 in
Boston, the school committee had created de facto segregation
by establishing "intermediate schools" catering to poor and immigrant children—mostly Irish—who did not meet the admission requirements of the grammar schools. Indeed, when blacks
in that city complained about being forced to attend all-black
schools rather than their neighborhood schools, the primary
school committee replied that they had already established
"schools for special instruction," or intermediate schools, "to
which all the white children of a certain class are obliged to go,
even though they may pass a dozen of the regular schools on
their way to them." By 1861 Philbrick argued for special industrial schools for "a class of children, more or less numerous,
which is too low down in the depths of vice, crime, and poverty,

to be reached by the benefits of a system of public education."
Stanley Schultz observes that "Philbrick was concerned less with
industrial benevolence and Christian love toward the poor than
with severing their associations with native children 'to purify
and elevate the character of the public schools.' " [67]

Many teachers and administrators did not want the unwilling
pupils which coercion would bring to their classrooms, even
though police and downtown merchants might want to get children off the streets and curb hooliganism. A Massachusetts superintendent complained in 1870 that such children disrupted
graded schools: "without any habits of study, unused to school
order with discipline, coming by compulsion and not by choice,
with no prospects of remaining longer than the law requires, and
joining classes for which they had no real fitness . . . [these
children were disqualified] for membership." [68]

When Chicago made some effort to enforce an 1889 law on
compulsory attendance, Superintendent Howland said that
3,528 of the former truants were "subject for reform schools." A
board committee on compulsory education reported that such
incorrigibles "cause sufficient disturbance to have their absence
heartily desired by the teacher and the principal." The Chicago
committee said that these children were filthy and "not fitted for
the ordinary classroom," urging that they be segregated in a
special classroom or school. The committee on compulsory education reported in 1894 that it was practically hopeless to try to
teach wayward children over seven years of age: "Careful research into the history of pauperism and criminality seems to
show that the child's bent is fixed before his seventh year. If
childhood is neglected, the child will mature lawless and uncon-
trolled and the final end will be the jail or the poorhouse."
Florence Kelley, who was chief inspector in Illinois in the administration of the child labor law of 1893, found that principals
expelled children at the age of eleven because they were "incorrigible" and found that school officials commonly flouted the intent of the law. [69]

Besides the disinclination of teachers and administrators to
teach the coerced child, there was a simple reason for the inef-
fectiveness of most compulsory education laws: in many cities
there were not nearly enough places even for those who *wanted*

to enroll. If all the children who were legally obliged to attend school had come to classrooms in Chicago in 1886, only one third would have found seats. In San Francisco, parents importuned the board to admit their children even though classrooms were grossly overcrowded; in 1881 New York had to refuse admission to 9,189 pupils for lack of room; in Philadelphia an estimated 20,000 children could not go to school for want of seats. Under such circumstances a compulsory attendance law was a farce.[70]

In 1885 Philbrick reported that only sixteen out of thirty-eight states had passed coercive laws, and these were mostly dead letters. They seem to have been sponsored largely by labor unions eager to prevent competition from child labor, by philanthropists eager to "save the child," and by politicians who saw compulsory attendance as a partisan issue (in California, for example, Republicans largely voted for it in the Senate, while Democrats largely opposed it in 1874). Forest Ensign argued that school people for the most part did not push the idea since they "did not want the poorly trained, uncultured child of the factory and workshop in their well-ordered schools." Nonetheless, the basic functions of the common school, and the increasingly accepted notion that "the children of the Commonwealth are public property" led to the conclusion that Philbrick stated in 1885: "Public instruction cannot be considered as having fulfilled its mission until it secures the rudiments of education to every child. To accomplish this object coercion is necessary." By 1900 Harris reported that thirty-one states had passed compulsory education laws, normally requiring attendance of children from eight to fourteen years of age. Although the laws were commonly ignored in some communities, and few prosecutions were made, Harris maintained that they were useful in establishing a principle accepted by the law-abiding parents. Twentieth-century educators would be faced with the full implications of preventive detention. It would not come as a surprise to find that the reform school and its curriculum would strike some educators as the best model for the reformulation of the common school for the new kinds of students entering urban classrooms.[71]

5. SOME FUNCTIONS OF SCHOOLING

As David Rothman has shown, the nineteenth century was an age of institutionalization when agencies separated the insane into asylums, the poor into almshouses, the criminal into prisons. Fear of disorder, of contamination, of the crumbling of familiar social forms such as the family, prompted reformers to create institutions which could bring order into the lives of deviant persons and, perchance, heal the society itself by the force of example.[72]

In some respects public education followed similar patterns and performed somewhat comparable functions. A certain category of people—the young—were taken away from the rest of society for a portion of their lives and separated in schools. Like inmates of the poorhouse, they were expected to learn "order, regularity, industry and temperance," and "to obey and respect" their superiors. As in some of the asylums, reformatories, and refuges, they were assorted in large groups "under a central administration" and followed an exact schedule and military routine. Schools, like other institutions, were supposed to counteract or compensate for indulgent or neglectful families.[73]

But urban schools of the nineteenth century, however routinized and rigid they may have been, were nonetheless not such total institutions as jails nor were they dead-end alleys for most of the pupils; they occupied but a short period in the lives of most children, and pupils could go home at night. They "imposed" a curriculum and an urban discipline, but they also opened up opportunities that many of the students might otherwise never have had: to read a newspaper, to compute, to know something of history and geography, to speak standard English. These new skills often created alternatives for the literate that were unavailable to the illiterate. And the structure of the school taught habits of punctuality, obedience, and precision that did help the young to adjust to the demands of the world of work. In retrospect one may claim that urban education in the nineteenth century did more to industrialize humanity than to humanize industry. Herbert Gutman has shown that the pre-industrial culture of the native-born artisan or the immigrant peasant often conflicted sharply with the demands of the factory owner, who wanted his operatives to follow a rigid daily and weekly schedule, to work steadily at segmented tasks, to follow orders strictly, and to be smoothly-meshing interchangeable parts. As we have seen, urban schools were well adapted in structure and process to transform children into modern workers. Harris wrote that in an age of "cities and the growth of great industrial combinations," it was clear that "precision, accuracy, implicit obedience to the head or directive power, are necessary for the safety of others and for the production of any positive results." The urban "school performs this so well," he remarked, "that it reminds some people unpleasantly of a machine." When educators argued that the educated worker made a better employee, it did not simply mean that he could read directions or was less likely to drink whisky or go out on strike; it also meant in effect that he was properly socialized to the new modes of production, attuned to hierarchy, affective neutrality, role-specific demands, extrinsic incentives for achievement. Some recognized that present conditions in industry were alienating, but Harris, for one, believed that the mechanization of his day was but a phase in a longer evolution that might one day largely liberate workers from the toil that had been their lot for centuries.[74]

To assert that the schools served a modernizing function for workers is not to imply that the classroom was a necessary anteroom to the factory—many pre-modern workers, after all, went directly into industry and learned the new work-discipline there—nor is it to claim that educators were attempting to create a class-biased system to teach workers their place. On the contrary, most school leaders of the nineteenth century asserted that class-consciousness was wrong and that the common school should combat group divisiveness of all kinds—class, ethnic, religious, or political.

This concern with group conflict, with threats to the existing order, pervaded their rhetoric on the purposes of public education. To be sure, many educational leaders continued to talk and write about the welfare and morality of individual children, but in the second half of the nineteenth century they worried most about the aggregate social and political functions of schooling. On all sides were threats to the fabric of society, the authority of the state: mobs and violence; corruption and radical ideas in politics; vice and immorality as village constraints broke down; immigrants who refused to become assimilated; conflict between labor and capital; and highly visible crime, poverty, and disease. In a disorderly society, schoolmen argued, the school must itself be a model of order, regularity, obedience—a prototype of a conservative republic. To such leaders, public education was the most humane form of social control and the safest method of social renewal.[75]

"If we were to define the public school as an instrument for disintegrating mobs, we would indicate one of its most important purposes," declared an educator in 1882. Mob violence exploded again and again in American cities of the nineteenth century, sparked by religious, racial, ethnic, and class conflict: the burning of the Charlestown (Massachusetts) convent and the anti-Irish riot in 1834; "Bloody Monday" in Louisville in 1855, when Know-Nothing partisans tried to bar immigrants from the polls; the Draft Riot in New York in 1863 in which mobs brutally killed blacks and burned and looted buildings; the violent railroad strike of 1877 which spread city to city from Baltimore to San Francisco, leaving in its wake scores killed, hundreds wounded, and charred, gutted trains and buildings; the Pullman strike in Chicago in 1894 that pitted federal troops against a crowd of 10,000; and many others.[76]

To educational leaders such mobs—"wild beasts, that prove their right to devour by showing their teeth," Horace Mann called them—proved the need for more efficient schooling. After the strike of 1877 the U.S. Commissioner of Education warned of "the enormities possible in our communities if the systematic vagrancy of the ignorant, vicious, and criminal classes should continue to increase," and urged that "Capital, therefore, should weigh the cost of the mob and the tramp against the cost of universal and sufficient education." The president of the NEA that year reported that he had heard a citizen say that "it was the good sense of an immense majority of working people, created, fostered, and developed by public education, that saved us from the terrors of the French Commune." In 1894, confronting industrial turmoil and Populist excitement, the NEA resolved at its annual meeting that "we deem it our highest duty to pronounce enthusiastically, and with unanimous voice, for the supremacy of law and the maintenance of social and political order." Massachusetts Governor Edward Everett warned that the militia had to be made dependable through proper schooling. His fears were not groundless: quite often militia members called out to quell riots fraternized with the mobs instead.[77]

Schoolmen continued to regard the American republic—and in particular its forms of city governance—as an *experiment* in self-government whose success depended largely on the common school. In 1842, in a Fourth of July oration, Horace Mann declared that elsewhere the experiment had always failed "through an incapacity in the people to enjoy liberty without abusing it." Politics after the Civil War seemed to many educators to confirm Mann's warnings. In 1880 a rationale for public education in Portland stressed that "the self-government of the government of the people is still on trial," and that amid the sweeping waves of immigration only the common school could train "every child in our own tongue and habits of thought, and principles of government and aims of life." One might trust "parental instinct" to educate an individual child, but the state required homogeneity; "the right of preservation of a body politic" took precedence over all other rights.[78]

Immigrants posed a sharp challenge to the school managers. Not only was it difficult to socialize them politically, but they also seemed to defy the school's goal of eliminating vice, crime, and poverty. Justifying the use of corporal punishment in schools in immigrant wards, a member of the Boston school committee declared in 1889 that "many of these children come from homes of vice and crime. In their blood are generations of iniquity. . . . They hate restraint or obedience to law. They know nothing of the feelings which are inherited by those who were born on our shores." "It is largely through immigration that the number of ignorant, vagrant and criminal youth has recently multiplied to an extent truly alarming in some of our cities," wrote the secretary of the Connecticut board of education. "Their depravity is sometimes defiant and their resistance to moral suasion is obstinate." Clearly, to wean such children from their corrupt homes and neighborhoods, to train them in industry, temperance, and obedience, would require systematic effort.[79]

Increasingly, leading schoolmen in the latter nineteenth century talked more in terms borrowed from business and social science and less in evangelical rhetoric. They argued that the structure of schools should correspond with that in large corporations. A case in point is a report submitted in 1890 to the National Council of the NEA. This statement on "School Superintendence in Cities" began by quoting Herbert Spencer's affirmation that "a differentiation of structure and a specialization of function is the law of all growth and progress." Combination, the report said, gives power, as in the case of large corporations, but the division of labor has produced "the marvelous industrial progress of the present century. . . . The specialist is the most characteristic product of modern civilization." In the evolution of schools the authors saw a corresponding principle of specialization of function. From education in the family, to combination in "the one-teacher school, the representative of the family, and modeled after it," to the development of specialized schools such as academies or colleges, and finally to large state systems, the story was one of combination coupled with differentiation.[80]

City schools, however, lagged behind the progress of other large organizations in their division of labor and expert direction. "School administration in cities is still organized essentially as it was when the cities were villages." The reason: boards of education originally performed all functions, "legislative, executive, and judicial," and refused to relinquish them. As a result, remarked William H. Maxwell, the Brooklyn superintendent, "the board of education serves several purposes and none of them well." Although most boards "have not a very lively sense of their incompetency in these directions," the remedy is obvious: commit administration "to a superintendent selected because of his known ability, not merely 'to run schools,' but to devise, organize, direct, and make successful a rational system of instruction." Maxwell described the results of lay control on the school managers: "performance without responsibility is not equal to performance with responsibility. The functions of these officers [superintendents and principals] are at best but advisory. Their best efforts may be nullified by those who hold the reins of authority." As Maxwell said, under such arrangements, even "the strongest and wisest of superintendents may well grow weary of well-doing, and instead of leading the vanguard of progress, content himself with trying to avert the dangers that continually threaten our public schools. Under such a system the strongest and wisest of superintendents may be pardoned if he degenerates into a not ignoble specimen of arrested development." [81]

As schoolmen confronted the urban social crises of the late nineteenth century, they increasingly advocated structural changes which would give themselves more power. More efficient, nonpolitical, rational bureaucracies were the answer to poverty, faulty ideologies, crime, social splintering, and class conflict. Echoes of earlier ideologies persisted; lines of actual development were as yet unclear as the century drew to a close. It was not until the midst of a successful campaign to reform the schools from the top down that a prime mover of centralization, Nicholas Murray Butler, could confidently assert, to the applause of the Merchant's Club of Chicago, that he should "as soon think of talking about the democratization of the treatment of appendicitis" as to speak of "the democratization of schools." "The fundamental confusion is this: Democracy is a principle of government; the schools belong to the administration; and a democracy is as much entitled as a monarchy to have its business well done." A common school run for the people but not by the people—but during the nineteenth century the urban villagers often frustrated the plans of the managers.[82]

PART III

The Politics of Pluralism: Nineteenth-Century Patterns

Although school managers tried to create smooth-running, rational, conflict-free bureaucracies during the nineteenth century, often with the assistance of modernizing business elites, in most cities they encountered serious opposition. At times they had to answer critics who claimed that in consolidating urban systems they were creating mindless and oppressive machines. Less often they encountered dissenters who questioned the consensus on which public education rested. In almost every city where the population was heterogeneous, contests erupted in educational politics. Although there were sometimes overtones of class assertion or resentment in such conflicts, the issues were not normally phrased in class terms but in the cross-cutting cultural categories of race, religion, ethnicity, neighborhood loyalties, and partisan politics. These concerns had great power to motivate political action, even though they may have blurred commonalities of class interest.

The biggest practical challenge to school reformers in their quest for the one best system came from those laymen who persisted in regarding themselves as part and parcel of the public schools. Both in ward committees and on central boards, laymen often retained the very powers that the schoolmen sought. Obscure or contradictory allocations of responsibility between boards and professionals produced discord between school committees and superintendents. This helped to generate different perceptions of power. Whereas some citizens saw a menacing "school ring" of bureaucrats setting up tyrannical machines, school administrators often felt that they were required to make concrete without cement, that they had responsibility without adequate authority. To many schoolmen, lay decision-making at its best tended to be inefficient meddling in the proper province of the expert; at its worst, the school system became just another source of patronage and graft to boodlers. L. H. Jones, superintendent of schools in Cleveland, complained in 1896 that "the unscrupulous politician is the greatest enemy that we now have to contend with in public education." Superintendents often found that they could examine teachers but not hire them, write a course of study but not purchase textbooks, compile reports on school architecture but not decide who would construct buildings. In many cities, wrote Jones, "the superintendent is a superintendent only in name." [1]

We have seen that there was tension in the swollen villages between the older forms of governance and the bureaucratic aims of the modernizers. School board politics was one arena in which these different interests clashed during the nineteenth century. Educational politics in cities defies easy categorization or appraisal, for perjorative labels often obscured different worldviews. To many bureaucrats the ethnic or religious or party loyalties of pluralistic urban groups were irrelevant distractions from the chief task of building a universal, efficient system. To many laymen on boards, such social differences gave urban life its meaning and politics its motive force. Whereas schoolmen often denigrated nomination of teachers by school board members as "patronage" and desired to build meritocratic hierarchies controlled by professionals, many laymen saw teaching as a good job for the girls in the ward and the power of appointment as the natural prerequisite of office for board members. (Why otherwise would men donate their time?) One man's participatory democracy was another's chaos. Although teaching Polish to pupils in immigrant wards might have seemed an unwise concession to parochial interests to a bureaucrat, it was a proud affirmation to parents from the old country. Mixed together in the political contests for control were both tangible and symbolic stakes: direct economic benefits derived from jobs and contracts, and intangible but highly important issues centering on ethnic and religious differences. Different groups sought not only cash but reaffirmations of their values and life-styles in the schools. Just as the closing of saloons on Sundays aroused a bitter controversy between native Protestant prohibitionists, who wanted to stamp out evil at its source, and German and Irish workingmen, who wanted to imbibe with their friends on their one day off, so the school became a target for cultural crusades.[2]

1. CRITICS AND DISSENTERS

To Horace Mann and most of his successors as spokesmen for public education during the nineteenth century, the supporters of the common school were the children of light and opponents the children of darkness. Since the schools were the panacea for crime, poverty, and vice, to oppose them was to ally with evil. This tradition continued in influential writings of educational historians. Witness a classic statement in 1919 of the "alignment of interests" for and against public schools during the mid-nineteenth century:

For	Against
"Citizens of the Republic"	Belonging to the old aristocratic class
Philanthropists and humanitarians	Politicians of small vision
Public men of large vision	The ignorant, narrow-minded, and penurious
The intelligent workingmen in the cities	The non-English-speaking classes
"New-England men"	

Here is Ellwood Cubberley's morality play presented as sober history. But the tradition of cloaking the public school establishment in virtue allowed schoolmen to denounce any attacks on their ideology or practices as the work of "enemies of democracy" or selfish men of small vision. One consequence has been that we lack to this day any comprehensive account of the long history of dissent against the public school establishment.[3]

But there have been dissenters of all kinds, many of them forgotten. In the present crisis of authority in American public education, there are those who say that schools lack intellectual rigor, those who detect communist influences, those who criticize the rigidity of vast urban bureaucracies, those who claim that the schools are racist and sexist, those who argue that the common school produces conformist servants of mediocrity, those who argue that education has been the opiate of the people and an excuse for neglecting basic social change. These and other charges are hardly new, but they have long been overshadowed by the consensus earnestly sought and successfully won by educational spokesmen of the last century.[4]

Even as urban schoolmen were struggling to create systems, critics attacked the structure and effects of school bureaucracies. In 1878 Professor B. A. Hinsdale of Ohio (later to become superintendent of schools in Cleveland) wrote that "for a generation our schoolmasters have gone on developing the system, the public supporting them with abundant money and influence; and now, when the work is called perfect, and we are called on to fall down and worship . . . it is seen by the discerning that the Graded School is only an appliance, that it leaves education to brain and heart where it was before, and that the new system has become inflexible and tyrannous." His special target was the mindless administrator whose trained incapacity blinded him to the results of his work, namely, archaic and rigid ritual. Absorbed in trivia, he becomes despotic toward subordinates: "there is no place where a crochety, a bumptious, or tyrannical man can do more harm than at the head of the public schools of a large city." Children are forced to learn twaddle—like "the important fact that 'napiform' means turnip-shaped"—while in practice, said Hinsdale, they "learn little in the Public Schools but the rules."[5]

Others joined in the assault on superintendents and the mechanical character of city schools. Charles Francis Adams, Jr., fresh from his attempts to reform the schools as school board member in Quincy, Massachusetts, said that typical school administrators were mere "drill sergeants" and described average city school bureaucracy as "a combination of the cotton mill and the railroad with the model State-prison." President Charles W. Eliot of Harvard denounced mass education, "which almost inevitably adopts military or mechanical methods," and deplored the inflexible routine, which degraded the "teacher's function. . . . There are many persons who say that teachers in the graded schools ought not to serve more than ten years at the outside, for the reason that they become dull, formal, and uninteresting; but, if this be true, it is certainly the fault of the system rather than of the teachers." Mary Abigail Dodge deplored the use of the factory as analogy for the school. "The thing which a school ought not to be, the thing which our system of supervision is strenuously trying to make the school into, is a factory, with the superintendents for overseers and the teachers for workmen." Instead, she argued, "teachers ought to run the schools exactly as doctors run a hospital." "The superintendent is a mere modern invention for receiving a salary, whose beneficence seldom rises above harmlessness, whose activity is usually mischievous." [6]

The impact of the rigid urban school on the child was the main concern of Joseph Mayer Rice, a pediatrician who had studied "educational science" in Germany. Rice visited schools in thirty-six cities in 1892 to prepare a series of articles for *The Forum*. What he saw profoundly depressed and angered him. The typical "atmosphere of the mechanical school is damp and chilly" whereas a classroom should be "glowing with life and warmth." Teachers followed prescribed routine, fearful of losing their jobs, forgetful of the child, although their first task was to strive "to understand him, to interest him, and to make him happy." [7]

In city after city, Rice witnessed similar episodes. In St. Louis the superintendent gave examinations to test both students and teachers and observed classes like a military inspector to see if the program was being followed. "The superintendent here reigns supreme; his rulings are arbitrary; his word is law. But in exercising his license he deprives the child of his liberty . . . the years of childhood are converted into years of slavery." The prime rule of many schools was to "save the minutes." Children were forced to sit with eyes facing forward; even when they handed material to their neighbors, they stared "straight in front of them" and groped sideways to pass or receive papers. Pupils popped up and down like automata when they recited definitions: "things appear as if the two children occupying adjoining seats were sitting upon the opposite poles of an invisible see-saw, so that the descending child necessarily raises the pupil next to him to his feet." Such recitations were just memorized "facts" from the textbooks—after all, that was what the examinations tested. Rice attended one physiology class where a ten-year-old student cried out that alcohol "dwarfs—the body,—mind,—and soul,—weakens—the—heart,—and—enfeebles—the—memory." [8]

While dissenting intellectuals criticized the one best system of urban education for its mechanical routines and its deadening effect on children, conservatives across the country fretted about the costs of new fads and frills like the high school or instruction in music or drawing. The old common school was good enough, they said; this new establishment is being run by professionals for their own advantage. In 1880, in Portland, Oregon, a crusty and conservative newspaper editor, Harvey Scott, launched an attack on the "cumbrous, complex and costly system" of the public schools. "In nearly every city there has been growing up during the last ten years an elaborate public school machinery," he wrote, "largely managed and directed by those whom it supports. Nominally it is controlled by the taxpayers of the districts, but in reality by associations of persons who live as professionals upon the public school system." What was needed, he said, was a return to "the simple yet effective system of the old common schools." Scott was sure that the citizens were "decidedly in favor of reducing the 'establishment,'—as the system has been called since it grew to its present proportions." [9]

Scott sent reporters out to gather the opinions of the businessmen of Portland about the "new-fangled, finical stuff" going on in the schools—the complex machinery, the new subjects introduced into the grades and the high school (which Scott thought quite unnecessary for the common child). Most of the businessmen interviewed thought common schools necessary, but many questioned the need for expensive "flummery." "A child who has a good English education, if he has any snap about him," said one, "will succeed better than the average graduate of the high school who knows a little of every thing." Another said flatly: "The prominent and useful men of this city are not men of high education." Some glorified the simple, cheap, old-time district school: just the three R's, under the eye and thumb of the community. And one believed that the Portland schools were "being controlled by a school ring and not by taxpayers or directors." Just inculcate the right values cheaply, said the self-made men.[10]

Scott had said that no one could expect self-criticism from the professional establishment; letters to the press from administrators like Thomas Crawford and the state superintendent of public instruction displayed a shocked and self-righteous attitude about Scott's attack. The depth of feeling against the bureaucrats was illustrated in a letter from "C" which appeared in the *Oregonian* on February 26, 1880: "We, the defenders of the common school system, are between the upper and nether millstones, the impracticables and the destructives. . . . It can only be perpetuated by relieving it of the complex character it has assumed by reason of the inflated, pedantic and self-aggrandizing character of the faculty, who from one entrenched foothold of aggression against popular rights have advanced to another, until we see the result in the superficial, overloaded and overtaxing system now prevailing." [11]

Although most critics of the school bureaucracies did not question the aim of transmitting the dominant culture through public education, other dissenters opposed the common school precisely because they treasured cultural differences which public schoolmen were attempting to destroy. This was particularly true of Catholics, many of whom bitterly resented the Protestant character of public education in nineteenth-century America. A priest in Boston said that he had heard a leading citizen there contend "that the only way to elevate the foreign population was to make Protestants of their children." In New York, Bishop John Hughes fought "to detach the children of our holy Faith from the dangerous connection and influence of the public schools." He assailed the textbooks in use that praised Luther as a great man and spoke of "the deceitful Catholics." What the schools taught the Catholic child was that "Catholics are necessarily, morally, intellectually, infallibly, a stupid race." [12]

Added to this anti-Catholic cast of the schools was a disdain for foreigners in general and the Irish in particular. Hughes quoted a textbook that declared that immigration could make America "the common sewer of Ireland," full of drunken and depraved Paddies. That Americans were preoccupied with human pollution in the republic is evident in a metaphor used in *Putnam's Monthly* to describe the function of the public school: "Our readers will agree with us that for the effectual defecation of the stream of life in a great city, there is but one rectifying agent—one infallible filter—the SCHOOL." [13]

Bishop Hughes railed at the techniques used to compel poor children—many of them Catholic—to attend schools. The Free School Society—the paternalistic forerunner of the public schools of New York City—claimed that its schools enjoyed the support of all groups, yet as Hughes said, it had persuaded the Common Council to enact decrees "depriving the parents, in time of need—even when cold and starvation have set in upon them—of public relief, unless the children were sent to those or some other schools." They sent out ladies to recruit the poor "by soothing words" and asked employers to coerce parents to send children to school. With all this, fumed Hughes, "they pretend that they have the confidence of the poor." [14]

One result of such discrimination and pressure was that Catholics increasingly dissented from the common school consensus and sought power over their own educational destiny. Leading schoolmen had trouble understanding these dissenters. In the relatively homogeneous Protestant America of the era before large Catholic immigration, Protestants had agreed to call a truce in their sectarian quarrels at the schoolhouse door and to teach in the common school an evangelical consensus they called "nonsectarian": to read the King James Bible without comment, letting it "speak for itself," as Horace Mann said. For Catholics, of course, this was hardly nonsectarian, and the influence of Protestant teachers and textbooks further undermined their religion. Boldly, many Protestant ministers, schoolmen, and politicians argued that the majority had a right to dictate religious instruction, and since the Catholics were a minority, they had to capitulate.[15]

Catholics could not accept this second-class citizenship nor this violation of their religious rights. In city after city they withdrew their children and boycotted the schools. They took their grievances to court but usually gained little satisfaction. But court cases, voluntary persuasion, and boycotts did not win justice for the Catholic cause. Increasingly, Catholics realized that only through gaining political leverage and through building their own institutions could they achieve the respect and autonomy they deserved.[16]

This quest for Catholic power aroused as much consternation then as the demand for black power today. When Catholics sought successfully to eject the Protestant Bible from the common school, Protestants thought that they were attacking the very basis of American institutions. When they demanded the removal of biased textbooks, citizens and school officials thought Catholics were trying to control the curriculum. Politicians saw a Jesuit plot in the desire of Catholics to win public support for their parochial schools, and President Grant predicted that the forces of "superstition" might precipitate a new civil war. Republicans attempted to capitalize on this Protestant backlash.[17]

The quest for Catholic power became successful, particularly in cities where Catholics gathered in large numbers. They quickly expanded their parochial school system, consolidated political power, especially in the cities, and in the twentieth century began to move more and more into the American mainstream. Aided by strong leaders in a vigorous hierarchy, proud of their religious and ethnic traditions, growing by immigration and natural increase from 1 percent of the population in 1790 to 17 percent in 1907, they helped to transform a Protestant America into a pluralistic America.[18]

Then, as now, there were anonymous dissenters to the common school:

Truant boys in Boston, pursued by police officer Oliver Spurr—most of them Irish children, probably wondering why they had to go to school when there weren't enough seats in classrooms and when signs were appearing all over town, "No Irish Need Apply."

Fishermen in Beverly, voting against a high school in 1860, refusing to pay taxes for an institution that served the children of white-collar families.

German parents in Cincinnati, refusing to send their children to a school that taught them to scorn their language and culture.

Many such dissenters withheld their taxes or their persons from the schools rather than leaving a written record of their protest.[19]

During the common school crusade a few radical spokesmen for the lower classes questioned whether education could really provide moral redemption or prosperity for the dispossessed. In New York in 1829, Thomas Skidmore asked: "Is a family, where both parents and children are suffering daily, in their animal wants; where excessive toil is required to obtain the little they enjoy; where the unkind and unfriendly passions, generated by such a wretched condition of things, reign with fell sway: is such a family in a situation to receive instruction?" No, he replied, free education under such circumstances was simply an excuse for postponing real equality: "let all remember, that those who undertake to *hold back* the people from their rights of property . . . until *education,* as they call it, can first be communicated . . . either do not understand themselves, or pursue the cause they *are* pursuing, for the purpose of diverting the people from the possession of these rights; that they may be held in bondage, even yet longer." Education, in short, Skidmore regarded as a substitute for social justice. Horace Greeley agreed: "to the child sent daily out from some rickety hovel or miserable garret to wrestle with Poverty and Misery for such knowledge as the teacher can impart, what true idea or purpose of Education is possible?" Such voices were few and faint, however, and so persuasive were the crusaders, and so hopeful were Americans that education could provide equality of opportunity—an equal chance at the main chance of wealth—that only a handful perceived the problem stated by Merle Curti in 1935: "Above all the privileged classes expected the free public school to increase wealth, secure their property, and prevent revolution, while the lower classes thought that popular education would break down class barriers, lift them into the ranks of the rich and bring about, in short, substantial equality." Curti doubted that the schools could do both tasks. "Could they leave the wealthy with all their economic power and privileges and at the same time enable the masses to enter the upper ranks without jeopardizing the position of those already on the top?" His question would gain new significance to dissenters in the 1970's.[20]

2. CONFIGURATIONS OF CONTROL

During the nineteenth century, there was great variety in structures of school governance. This helps to account for the broad spectrum of behavior of school boards and for the diverse roles of superintendents, which ranged virtually from educational dictator to file clerk.

In a number of cities, school boards emerged as the appointed subsidiary of the city council, specialized in function like departments of public works or police commissioners, when tasks became too great for mayors and councils to accomplish without division of labor. Whether from an unwillingness to delegate financial control, or from a desire for checks and balances, city councils sometimes splintered authority for different phases of school administration. In Nashville, as late as 1891, the board of public works retained control over buildings and appointment of janitors, so that "while the board of education had authority to purchase chalk, brooms, pens and soap, it could not supply furniture, stoves, or curtains." In Milwaukee, likewise, the board had no power to relieve overcrowding since the city council was in charge of new building programs. Buffalo had a baroque organizational chart: the mayor appointed janitors, the superintendent teachers; the city council bought sites for new schools, while the department of public works erected them. Fights between school boards and city councils over appropriations and over school functions were commonplace from Providence to Los Angeles.[21]

Further conflict and ambiguity stemmed from division of power among central and ward school boards, although community control had its defenders, then as now. In Buffalo taxation for new schools was not assessed city-wide but divided by districts, with the result that the rich sections (most of which had few children) paid a pittance, while the working-class residential areas with many children suffered. "Every proposed expansion of school accommodations," wrote the superintendent there in 1887, "had to wait until local objections were overcome by the pressure of imperious needs." Until 1911 each of the thirty-nine subdistrict boards in Pittsburgh had individually raised local taxes, chose teachers, built new schools, and maintained old ones—in fact, assumed all responsibility for education except buying textbooks, paying teachers, and running the high schools and the "colored schools." The subdistrict boards met in a convention every three years to elect a superintendent. Such diffusion of responsibility made everyday decisions—like where to erect a school or who should pay the bill—contentious and tangled. Long-range planning for the future was next to impossible. And in cities like Detroit, where school directors on the central committee represented individual wards, competition for funds often resulted in unequal distribution of resources.[22]

In 1885 Philbrick reported that most city school boards were large; members were typically elected from wards rather than the city as a whole and normally held office for two or three years. "Everywhere there are unscrupulous politicians," he wrote, "who do not hesitate to improve every opportunity to sacrifice the interests of the schools to the purposes of the political machine." Cities tried various ways to minimize corruption: nomination of board members by the mayor, as in New York; appointment by judges, as in Philadelphia; and selection by the city council in Chicago. In other communities citizens discussed counteracting these "political and other corrupting influences" by enfranchising women and disenfranchising illiterates. Philbrick concluded that "it must be admitted that the problem [of proper selection of school boards] remains unsolved; and without doubt this is the supreme educational problem which remains for our educational statesmen to grapple with."[23]

Political cultures in new cities in the West and South often differed from those in the older cities of the Northeast. In a number of cities relative peace reigned between school board members and superintendents. During the thirty-year superintendency of Aaron Gove, Denver had one such system. No city came closer to the ideal, said Philbrick: "the members of this board have been, from its origin, so far as I was able to ascertain by inquiry on the ground, unexceptionable in respect to character, ability, and faithful devotion to the interests of the schools." Another moderate-sized western city that won praise from educators for its school board was Kansas City, Missouri, during the tenure of James M. Greenwood. Superintendent Greenwood "gave early attention to the composition of the school board. To insure the selection of high-class citizens, and to obviate the chance of political influence, he secured a nonpartisan school board and long tenure for the members." The president of the Kansas City board testified that the members conducted their work in a businesslike manner, without speeches to the galleries, and reached all decisions by consensus. In Birmingham, Alabama, John H. Phillips served as superintendent of schools for thirty-eight years from 1883 to 1921. There a commission "made up of leading citizens" appointed a board of five members composed of "the best qualified citizens." [24]

As we have seen in examining the work of lay school board members in the "swollen village," traditional tasks for the school committeeman included visiting schools, overseeing almost all administrative details, and making most fiscal decisions. The degree to which school board members were willing to delegate some of these functions to professionals depended on many variables: their trust in the superintendent—or even their awe of him; their interest in making a personal profit or gaining political influence; their desire to represent the interests of a particular locality or group; their commitment to expertise and specialization of function; their available time and concern for the work; and their conception of their duties as representatives of the public.

The actual spheres of authority of individual superintendents differed enormously during the late nineteenth century. The definition of functions normally included supervision of teachers and preparation of the course of study, but Philbrick observed that leaders sometimes stretched the formal definition to gain more actual power. Superintendents in Boston and St. Louis, for example, both were to oversee "instruction and school management, but the superintendent of the latter city practically exercises much larger powers than the superintendent of the former. He performs the duties and exercises the powers to a large extent which are assigned in the former, and indeed in most cities, to subcommittees on individual schools or districts." Whereas William T. Harris gained de facto power to nominate teachers and transfer them and pupils in St. Louis, those tasks in Boston remained in the hands of subcommittees of the board.[25]

Aaron Gove's informal ways of influencing the Denver board of six members gave him influence comparable to that of Harris. Since the board followed the custom of having subcommittees to make decisions on administrative matters, Gove exerted his control not through formal delegation of responsibility but by being a well-informed and trusted adviser to the board and its committees. He did not limit his scope to the course of study and supervision but felt that it was his duty to participate in all "the business affairs of the corporation" of which he was "executive officer." Toward subordinates he was an absolute authority, but he was content with relatively undefined power with respect to the board—until in 1904 he crossed swords with a new consolidated board and came to believe that duties and spheres of influence of the superintendent should be clearly specified.[26]

Another commanding figure in school administration—one who appeared autocratic to most of his teachers—was William Maxwell, superintendent of the Brooklyn schools. Maxwell learned to seize power where he could. When in Brooklyn, he became friends with political boss Hugh McLaughlin, and when he needed support for some plan he "went to the Boss on Willoughby St., and if, perchance, the Boss was whittling or absorbed in deep thought, Maxwell adapted himself to circumstances. He studied the whims and foibles of the leaders and played upon their vanity to attain his ends." When he became superintendent of the unified boroughs of New York, he was expressly forbidden under the terms of the charter any "right of interference with the actual conduct of any school in the city of New York," so firm was the resistance to centralization among borough leaders, but once again he learned how to build a bureaucratic power base through influence on appointments and through exploiting the power vacuum created by an ineffectual large board of education.[27]

Men less skilled and forceful than Maxwell often ran afoul of resentful school boards. In 1869 Zalmon Richards was appointed superintendent of the Washington, D.C., schools under an ordinance that authorized him "to direct all matters pertaining to the government and course of instruction, books, studies, discipline and conduct of the public schools, and the conditions of schoolhouses and of the schools generally." Immediately an editorial in the *Washington Evening Star* warned that this "sweeping" grant of power did "away with pretty much all the duties heretofore exercised by the board of trustees," an action that "put aside the experience of so many well-informed men as are now to be found upon the school board." Within a year the trustees censured Richards for invading their prerogatives "by importing from Chicago a set of school registers," by introducing some "sound charts" he had prepared, "by precipitating a collision of authority by issuing to the teachers a mode of annual examination and promotion which has been unanimously rejected by the Board," and by sundry other faults, including "errors in spelling common words" which "excited the derision of the pupils." A subcommittee of the board wrote a report attacking Richards and contending that a proper superintendent should be suave and cooperative, and "should avoid rather than seek responsibility." It was this kind of role definition that Philbrick ridiculed when he described one kind of typical superintendent as a man whose "supreme ambition is to carry on the routine operations of the system with as little friction as possible, and with this end in view he virtually says to his board, 'I am here to obey your instructions. Tell me what to do and I will do it with alacrity and delight.' . . . All are highly gratified to be thus assured and are highly content with their amiable and industrious superintendent." [28]

As if troubles with boards were not vexing enough, superintendents sometimes faced insubordination and sabotage within the ranks of the school system, especially in cases where male principals and masters had once enjoyed autonomy. Like board members, such subordinates resented the invasion of their former privileges. Superintendent Seaver of Boston described troubles his predecessor Philbrick faced in putting a uniform course of study into operation. "Schoolmasters are usually great for passive opposition, and perhaps none were ever greater than the Boston schoolmasters of the last generation. Each was a supreme ruler in his own school district, and, relying on the support of his district committee, he could defy the interference of all other authorities, and he often did." Seaver told of a visitor who asked one of the masters of that era if he could see a class in natural science. The master said there were none, and when pressed to explain why—since science was in the course of study—replied: "We allow our Superintendent to keep it there for ornamental purposes, but we do not pretend to do anything with it in the schools." [29]

Certain political arrangements compounded the troubles of central administrators. In San Francisco, the superintendents were elected every other year—often from the ranks of principals and on the basis of party affiliation. This political turmoil undermined the informal authority of the superintendent—his formal authority was practically nil—although it did lend itself to unusually frank annual reports as a Democratic superintendent criticized the Republican principals for spending too much on repairs, or as Republican board members talked about poor discipline in schools run by Democratic principals. In Philadelphia the powerful local boards looked upon "suggestions that came from the Central Board as propositions to be opposed on principle," reported Joseph Rice. The support of this central board was of little use to James McAllister when he arrived as the first superintendent in 1883. He did not even visit some of the schools since he knew he would be unwelcome there, and had as "allies only a few of the thirty-odd local boards in the city." He was partially successful, however, in asserting control over the curriculum by writing a new course of study and giving annual examinations based upon it.[30]

Despite the adamant opposition of school managers like L. H. Jones to political bosses, there were certain structural similarities between bureaucratization in education and the consolidation of power in urban political machines. Although the inspiration and composition of the organizations were quite different, school bureaucracies and political machines both responded to the splintering of decision-making in the city: both sought to answer the question, "Who's in charge?" Astute machine bosses created complex chains of command. Daniel Moynihan points out that in Tammany the Irish built "a vast hierarchy of party positions descending from the county leader at the top down to the block captain and beyond, even to building captains. Each position had rights and responsibilities that had to be observed. The result was a massive party bureaucracy." In contrast with the flux and unpredictability and counterbalances of the visible and official government of elected offices, the machine was often stable over long periods of time—Hugh McLaughlin bossed the Brooklyn Democracy from 1862 to 1903, for example—and accountable to those who paid for influence.[31]

Although WASP reformers often portrayed the public school system and the political machine as polar opposites, each provided disciplined bureaucratic hierarchies, each sought to stabilize and centralize public decision-making, and each in different ways helped immigrants adapt to the city politically and economically. Whereas school bureaucracies sought to assimilate foreigners by teaching them English, indoctrinating them in Mugwump civics, and providing them with skills and habits needed in the urban job market, political machines helped newcomers to adjust to urban life in payment for their votes. Party machines not only offered direct relief for the poor—shelter when floods hit the river wards, Thanksgiving turkeys, hods of coal on biting February days—but also provided information and influence for families unfamiliar with the red tape and overlapping jurisdictions of city agencies.[32]

In cities where machines dominated school politics, bosses and their subordinates sometimes mediated between their constituents and the official school system. Through jobs and contracts in the schools the machine sometimes offered paths of social mobility to groups that otherwise might have been excluded. Amid the rivalries of ethnic groups, abrasive acculturation to strange urban and American ways, the machine often lubricated the points of greatest social friction. Boss Tweed's ward committees, for example, let teachers omit Protestant rituals in predominantly Catholic neighborhoods. Sensitive to the dangers of alienating voters by denigrating their religion or their folkways—for that might cost votes—machine politicians sought peace among their pluralistic supporters. If parents wanted their native tongue taught in the schools, why not? If textbooks contained scurrilous comments about immigrants, then the textbooks should be removed from the schools.[33]

But machines were a business, offering centralized power to those who wanted jobs, contracts, and services, and that often meant graft, patronage, and favoritism—the bane of the WASP school reformers. The "corruption" so frequently charged should not be dismissed as simply a code word for anti-immigrant or anti-Catholic feeling—though sometimes it was just that. Graft did siphon off funds sorely needed to build schools, provide books, and pay teachers. The opportunities for corruption in public education were enormous, as local or central boards assigned contracts for land, construction of buildings, repairs, or equipment; bought textbooks, supplies, and similar consumables; and appointed the hundreds of thousands of teachers, janitors, administrators, and other salaried officers. In the graft-ridden and yet penny-pinching schools of Philadelphia, Adele Shaw found plaster sagging over the heads of children, "the teacher constantly on the alert to warn them if it fell." There teachers had to buy supplies from their paltry salaries, and the principal had to drop a dime in the school's telephone before it would operate. Furious at the corruption in Detroit that robbed the children of the city, Mayor Hazen Pingree walked into the school board meeting on August 15, 1894, and declared "there are quite a number of the members of this board who are going to jail tonight." When committeemen refused to resign, Pingree called off their names and the police hauled them away.[34]

In another form of collective graft, textbook scandals rocked the country as huge firms collided in conflict over the vast school market. A teacher claimed that "the majority of superintendents in small cities owe their positions to 'pulls' organized by publishing houses to whose books they are friendly." Muckrakers like Upton Sinclair and Lincoln Steffens reported cases of bribery and collusion between textbook promoters, school board members, and schoolmen. Textbook salesmen were not above using alluring women as accomplices to blackmail school officials into favoring their wares.[35]

But not all swindling of the public and the children took covert forms, nor was graft the monopoly of political machines or school-related businesses. Large corporations and taxpayers "legally" bilked public schools. The Chicago schools consistently failed to receive just rentals from prestigious tenants on its school lands. In 1895, for example, the *Chicago Tribune* won a ninety-nine-year lease for its property for $30,000 while a neighboring building on half the land paid $60,000. By strange coincidence the chairman of the board of education at the time and member of the committee on school fund property was the attorney for the *Tribune*. Public utilities in that city evaded taxes on their franchises with the connivance of county and state assessors. Sanctified by law or not, such cheating of the public was hardly the monopoly of machines dominated by inner-city ethnic groups.[36]

During the latter half of the nineteenth century, superintendents were caught between their vision of an "ideal standard" of school organization and the actual configurations of school politics. Even those who had served long and devotedly were often unceremoniously fired. For most the job was a brief way-station; the average tenure of office in Los Angeles and San Francisco was two years; Omaha, Buffalo, Rochester, and Milwaukee, three; Cincinnati and Indianapolis, five. But some, like Gove and Philbrick, stayed for long terms to construct, piece by piece, bureaucratic foundations on which others would build.[37]

Would the future be different? The writings of schoolmen at the turn of the century bristled with apprehension and hope. They knew what was wrong: "the multiplication of troublesome classes and the greater influence of patronage upon political organizations and elections"; large and meddlesome boards of education; insecure and sometimes powerless status for the men who should lead; class conflict, poverty, crime, and all the other ills that the school was designed to solve. When they talked about solutions, characteristically they saw them in the form of better organization. Writing about "The Trail of the City Superintendent" Aaron Gove said in 1900 that "without question the greatest problem today is how best to administer the public-school interests of a city. . . . The history of the last two years or more leaves no doubt of the interest and even anxiety of the American community as to the direction of public schools. From our great metropolis down thru the secondary cities is found an agitation, an unrest, as to the conduct of this quasi-public corporation." In speaking of "this quasi-public corporation," he was talking about the future of the public schools of New York, Chicago, Detroit. The village school had now become urban and almost a system. A new type of expert, backed by a centralized board and an efficient staff—that might be the answer. Such a plan might weaken the influence of "troublesome classes" which had so disrupted the search for system.[38]

3. LIVES ROUTINIZED YET INSECURE: TEACHERS AND SCHOOL POLITICS

Teachers sometimes found themselves caught in the middle in contests of authority between superintendents and school boards. As a result their lives were often routinized yet insecure. Both superintendents and school boards commonly shared, so far as I can determine, the same expectations that classrooms should be run with military discipline and that teachers, like pupils, should toe the line. "I have known supervisors to go about from schoolroom to schoolroom," said one observer of city schools, "note-book and pencil in hand, sitting for a while in each room like malignant sphinxes, eying the frightened teacher, who in his terror does everything wrong, and then marking him in a doomsday book." Yet in other cases, a teacher might have to satisfy the local ward boss that she was politically orthodox. Often it was not clear who governed the schools, who hired and supervised and fired. The drive for teacher power, civil service reform, and professionalism arose in part from a widespread desire of teachers to gain more control over their destiny.[39]

It is very difficult to find out how teachers did feel about the questions of who should hire, fire, and supervise them, for they left few written records. In 1896 the *Atlantic Monthly* quoted some anonymous teachers in a series of articles designed to "get the schools out of politics." Superintendent L. H. Jones cited a few of these comments:

Nearly all the teachers in our schools get their positions by what is called "political pull."

Positions are secured and held by the lowest principles of corrupt politicians.

The public schools of this city are partisan political schools. . . . Politicians wage a war of extermination against all teachers who are not their vassals.

Jones then remarked that "it is difficult to decide which is the more startling, the innocent acceptance of the situation by teachers and superintendents, or the depth of cupidity and cold-blooded selfishness manifested by the partisan politicians, and even by members of school boards." To Jones as to many other leading schoolmen of the time, it was clear that the solution lay in civil service reform and meritocracy: school boards should appoint teachers only on recommendation of the superintendents and only on the basis of merit. Philbrick argued that "the principles of a good civil service are essentially the same as the principles of a good educational service. Hence the achievement of the civil service reform will prepare the way for this reform. The spoils system and the annual election [reappointment of teachers] are twin barbarisms, and with the abolition of the former the latter must go." Philbrick believed that "the paradise for which the teacher prays" is a job in which "he owes his position to his merit, and not to favor . . . sure that his efforts will be appreciated and recompensed." [40]

In San Francisco John Swett, principal and superintendent and pioneer of professionalism, fought for decades against the way the school board appointed teachers. The board divided hiring of new teachers equally among the twelve directors, so that if there were thirty-six to appoint, each board member would have three. The board itself gave an examination to each teacher sufficiently arbitrary that it could pass or fail individuals at will. Swett recalled that fine teachers failed to be reappointed because they forgot "the best route from 'Novgorod to Killimanjaro,' or from 'Red Dog to You Bet.'" The superintendent was never consulted or asked for recommendations. Before 1870 the board threw open all positions annually, so that the Damocles sword of non-reappointment hung over the head of even the most competent teacher. "The doors of the star-chamber were besieged until midnight," Swett wrote about the board's closed session, "by anx-

School Board Journal

Founded March 1891 by WILLIAM GEORGE BRUCE

Volume LII, Number 5   MAY, 1916   Subscription, $1.50 the Year

THE SWORD OF DAMOCLES IN THE SCHOOLROOM

"The Sword of Damocles in the Schoolroom"—A Teacher's Perspective

ious teachers, waiting to know their fate." In 1870, San Francisco reformers managed to win a new policy of hiring teachers during a "period of competency and good behavior"—hardly iron-clad tenure, but an improvement over annual election. Throughout the nineteenth century, however, San Francisco teachers won positions mainly by pull with some director. In 1880 the superintendent reported that it was "a well known fact, that the most incompetent teachers bring the most outside pressure to bear on the Directors." When the board wanted more positions to fill, it found useful the new role of "inspecting teacher," for this supervisor could recommend the dismissal of any "inefficient" teacher to the board's "Committee on Classification." Swett said that "it would be easier to make an 'informer' in Ireland, respected by the mass of the Irish people, than to make a 'head inspector' regarded in any other light than that of a spy and an executioner." [41]

In a number of the wards in Philadelphia, there was no *one* effective "department discipline" over teachers. A muckraking journalist, Adele Marie Shaw, claimed that the teacher in that city "acknowledges three distinct authorities. . . . She owes allegiance to the local board that appoints her, to the Central Board that confirms the appointment, and to the superintendent and his staff, who supervise the course of study and are supposed to regulate the standard of teaching." There were 553 superiors with overlapping jurisdictions: 504 local board members in forty-two wards, forty-two central board members, and the superintendent and his six assistants. "The salvation of the teacher is in choosing the most powerful master and in appearing, as far as possible, to serve all three." In fact the dominant master was usually the local board, she thought, since most local bosses showed "an ignorant and suspicious disregard of the superintendent" and since the central board had little real power. "The local board is the old village school board clinging to an authority whose excuse has vanished." Many of the ward committees were stepping stones for politicians and part of a large patronage apparatus. For decades it had been common for teachers to pay committeemen for positions. One new teacher who brought fifty dollars to a reform woman director was bewildered when her sponsor refused the tribute: "I was told it was customary to pay some one," she blurted out.[42]

The ward boss normally gave final approval to nominations. He had his own network of information about the schools in which janitors were often the key spies. In one school, Shaw "heard a janitor summon the principal with a peremptory 'Come here!' If there had been no visitor present, I was told, it was quite likely he would have called her by her first name." In another school, the janitor asked a substitute teacher what she could do to get votes for the "organization." When she replied "nothing," he answered: "You ain't the kind we want here." [43]

In December 1904, after some school directors were indicted for graft, a group of Philadelphia administrators and teachers mounted an attack on the patronage system, fearful that "they were taking their educational lives in their hands." Shaw observed the previous February that "there is a Siberia, both cold and hungry, for subordinates who criticize the management of the Philadelphia public schools." Fifty principals and a number of high school teachers—people of higher and more independent status than the elementary school teachers—issued a statement to the press that asserted that the system was so chaotic and conditions in classrooms so deplorable that a total reorganization was imperative. The principals' example gave courage to the Board of Managers of the Teachers' Association, which endorsed the idea of a new structure of government for the schools. "The vice of the Philadelphia system," said the president of the Teachers' Association, "is . . . that while we have grown into a great city, we have maintained a village organization." The Council of Representatives of the Teachers' Association, however, refused to submit a referendum to the membership on the reform proposals, although the Council did vote its own support for a commission to investigate the matter. Thus we know how leaders among the teachers felt, but not the views of the rank and file. In Pittsburgh the Teachers' Association of more than 600 members took an active role in reforms designed to centralize control of the schools and turn them over to experts.[44]

In the heated campaign to abolish the ward boards in New York City in 1896, teachers expressed their views openly and vociferously—and almost entirely against destroying the powers of the local committees. All of the teacher organizations fought the state legislative act that removed powers to hire and supervise teachers from the local committees and transferred these functions to a centralized board with its staff of superintendents. Teachers collected 100,000 signatures on petitions, attended mass meetings, and wrote protest letters to Mayor William Strong. Almost 4,000 teachers gathered at one meeting to hear Matthew Elgas, president of the New York Teachers' Association, denounce centralization. Elgas believed that centralization might "prove the beginning of disaster to our beloved schools," for decentralized lay authority had been the chief means of humanizing and democratizing the vast system. "It is unfair and dangerous to concentrate so much labor, power and responsibility in the person and office of the Superintendents and thereby make them a kind of educational Pooh-Bah." Far wiser was it to retain the powers of the ward trustees to hire and supervise teachers, to recommend promotions and replacements, to mediate in special decisions about religious observances or curriculum between the community and the central board, and to stimulate local interest in the common schools. Another educator praised the "representative character of the Trustees . . . which furnished an Irish Trustee to represent the Irishmen, a German Trustee to represent the Germans, and a Hebrew Trustee to represent the Hebrews." [45]

Supporters of centralization argued that teachers defended the ward system from fear of losing their jobs if they offended Tammany politicians or from worry that a more efficient system of supervision would mean more work for them. There may have been some substance to these charges—after all, teachers did owe their jobs to the trustees and had learned how to work well with them—for it is natural for incumbents to resist a sharp change in the power structure. But the teachers' testimony both in public meetings and in private letters to the mayor hardly sounded coerced or insincere. Again and again the teachers argued that the ward trustees were respectable, hard-working, honest people with a strong interest in the children of the neighborhood. "The trustees are gentlemen," said a woman who had taught in four quite different wards in the city, "and devote every spare minute and even sleeping time to the care of the schools. The present attempt to abolish the trustees is all wrong and has not been brought about by those who know our Public Schools." Speaking as the representative of the Male Assistant Teachers' Association, a principal asserted that because of the trustees' "interest *in* the children, they are necessary *to* the children." As an example, he cited his experience in the crowded tenth ward, where the schools enrolled children who were almost all "of Russian and Polish parentage, whose lives are lives of toil and privation." Practically every day, he said, "one or the other of the Trustees was . . . a visitor to the school in the interest of the children." The result was a harmonious relationship in which "Trustees were known to the parents in this community; the children knew them as their friends." The local "peculiar population had its representative on the local Board." In his present prosperous ward on Morningside Heights, the principal added, the trustees took the same active interest: "Their visits are frequent, and the very tots seem to know that *their* comfort and welfare is the object of these visits," as when trustees came one bitterly cold morning to make sure that the building was warm enough.[46]

To publicize their demand for a centralized school system, reformers had charged that education in the city was inefficient and honeycombed with corruption and partisan politics. They only thinly veiled an anti-Catholic and anti-immigrant animus that implied or asserted that things would not be well in the schools until a better class of teachers was employed. One opponent of the ward boards asserted that the new plan would "take the schools out of politics, and that is of far more importance than the alleged objection 'that it takes them out of touch with the plain people.' " The "plain people" of New York were mostly foreign and therefore incompetent to manage their affairs properly. The only way to deal with such neighborhoods was to "demand that the children of such a population be brought under American influences and instruction, even if we have to go to the farthest confines of the state to find them." During the debate in the New York legislature, a senator declared that the schools must put children of the slums "under the influence of educated, refined, intelligent men and women, so they will be elevated and lifted out of the swamp into which they were born and brought up." When one considers that over half of the teachers were probably either first or second generation immigrants, many of them Catholics from humble backgrounds, such opinions could hardly have been winning.* Class snobbery was bad enough; but when it was fortified by religious and ethnic bigotry, the reformers' claims of superiority became a call to battle.[47]

Overwhelmingly, the teachers resented the centralizers' condescension and feared what might happen to themselves if the reformers appointed their "experts" as superintendents and their "refined" ladies as inspectors. Some of the reasons for their nearly universal hostility appear in a handbill called " 'SCHOOL REFORM' " that was distributed to principals and teachers. They claimed that the inspectors might make arbitrary requirements like forcing them to wear uniforms, or that they would not understand the teachers' perspectives. Centralizers, they said, claim only to be creating "a simple and business-like administration" of the schools, but this amounts to a realignment of power, based on anti-democratic theories: "the *Fact* that stares the people in the face is the establishment of an Educational Bureaucracy." [48]

In New York, at least, where teachers had achieved a fairly stable tenure system by 1885 and thus did not face the insecurity of annual reelection, they saw few benefits and many dangers in giving up the powers of the local ward committees and substituting a centralized board with its superintendents. It is likely that in many other communities teachers feared the "educational Pooh-Bah" quite as much as the party machine and suspected that new standards of selection, retention, and supervision might render their status more precarious, not less, especially if standards were set by persons of narrow WASP sympathies.[49]

4. CULTURAL CONFLICTS: RELIGION AND ETHNICITY

Often at stake in the pluralistic politics of urban education were issues that were more cultural than economic. Many citi-

---

* In 1908 in a very thorough study of ethnicity in New York schools, the Immigration Commission discovered that 71 percent of the pupils had foreign-born fathers; 47.2 percent of teachers had foreign-born fathers, and 7.9 percent were themselves born abroad. Of the 7,029 teachers who were children of

zens who sought to influence school policies were not interested in jobs or contracts or favorable tax assessments but rather in an imposition of their values on others or in freedom to affirm their subculture in their own schools.

Certain symbolic questions dramatized and reinforced the life-style of a native-born Protestant group that once had been dominant in village America but that saw its power and influence slipping away in the cities. Temperance was one such question, as state after state passed laws requiring public schools to teach the evils of liquor (by 1901 all states had some form of "temperance" instruction). The place of religion in public education was another. Perceiving a decline of their authority and an increase in sin and disorder, Protestants waged a vigorous campaign to inculcate their morality in a society becoming increasingly pluralistic. The very people who made the WASPs nervous about the state of the nation—Catholic and Jewish immigrants in particular and urban "politicians" in general—were leading an attack on religion in the public schools. Again and again in meetings at the NEA, leaders accused Catholics of a conspiracy to defraud children of religious instruction, aided in their dirty work by "the foreign element, uninstructed in American civilization." No moral education which dispenses with the "All-Seeing Eye" could accomplish its central purpose: inculcating the life-style of the Protestant middle class. In *Our Country* the evangelical minister Josiah Strong joined the battle in 1885, claiming that lack of religion in the common school was one of the curses of the "rabble-ruled" cities.[50]

In 1888 some Protestants in Boston were outraged when the school board voted to remove an anti-Catholic textbook and to censure a teacher accused of making bigoted remarks. Accustomed to thinking of themselves as a majority and their views as the accepted consensus, they did not regard themselves as "political" but as crusaders for an obvious good: "one indisputable reason for [placing] women on the school committee," one of them wrote, "is the necessity of keeping our schools out of poli-

---

immigrants, 2,297 had Irish parents; 1,194 German parents. It seems likely that a dozen years earlier the percentage of first and second generation immigrants serving as teachers was not less than 50 percent (U.S. Immigration Commission, *Children of Immigrants,* IV, 610, 615).

tics." Ultra-Protestant groups vowed not only to remove all Catholic committeemen but also to eliminate all others who had voted with them in the textbook case. Swelled by a ten-fold increase in registered women voters, a large group of Protestant women formed a bloc-vote in response to the challenge that "no true woman will remain inactive when her religious convictions are jeopardized." Smelling victory in feminist anti-Catholicism, the city Republicans nominated only school board candidates approved by the Protestant women. They won.[51]

Like religion, bilingualism and biculturalism aroused strong feelings in public school politics. Here, nativists and immigrants clashed head-on in urban school politics. To many immigrants it was vital to assert the value of their culture by teaching their language to their children—after all, they paid taxes and deserved a say in the curriculum. Especially during the anti-foreign hysteria, induced by movements such as the Know-Nothings, the American Protective Association, and the anti-immigrant feeling of World War I, nativists demanded that the schools Americanize the children of immigrants by teaching them only in English.[52]

The politically sophisticated Germans in Cincinnati were among the first to organize to insert their language into elementary school classrooms. In 1840, German citizenry persuaded the Ohio legislature to pass a law requiring school boards to teach German whenever "seventy-five freeholders" demanded it in writing. The resulting schools were bilingual: at first children learned reading, grammar, and spelling in both English and German in the primary grades, moving on to instruction in English in arithmetic, geography, and other subjects. In 1841, "fifty prominent German citizens" persuaded the board to organize two divisions: "The elementary class, in which German and English were taught orally as well as with the use of books, and the advanced class, which was to receive instruction in English one day, and the next day in German." The election of German residents to the board advanced their cause, despite the hostility aroused by Know-Nothing agitation. In 1853, German children residing in districts where there were no special provisions for language instruction were permitted to transfer to German schools. That year the president of the board, Rufus King, observed that the Germans "may well appeal to us to preserve between them that link without which all family and social ties are lost." By 1899 there were 17,584 pupils studying German in Cincinnati, 14,248 of them in the primary grades; in the first four grades they split their school week evenly between a German teacher and an English teacher. Thus bilingual classes not only helped immigrant parents to preserve their culture but also gave positions to 186 German-speaking teachers.[53]

In St. Louis, Germans persuaded the school board to introduce their language into elementary schools in 1864. With their increasing numbers and wealth they were an effective political pressure group, for a German boycott of public schools would have seriously weakened the system. At first the board expected that only German children would enroll in these classes, but in 1871–72, Anglo-American pupils were admitted to these classes in the first three grades and the enrollment in the German classes rose 95 percent in three years to 15,769. For the most part, German was a separate subject rather than the language of instruction in the curriculum as a whole. In 1875 William T. Harris, then St. Louis superintendent, staunchly defended the teaching of the language in elementary school. By including the German minority that felt excluded, he said, the entire public system became more useful and more stable: "to eradicate caste distinctions in the community is, perhaps, the most important function of the public school system." Although Harris deplored "clannishness and the odious feeling of 'nativism,'" he saw no conflict between the Germans' desire to retain their "family ties with the old stock" and their determination that their children be "thoroughly versed in the language and customs of the country in which they are to live." "National memories and aspirations, family traditions, customs, and habits, moral and religious observances—all these form what may be called the *substance* of the character of each individual," said Harris, "and they can not be suddenly removed or changed without disastrously weakening the personality." Later leaders not so cosmopolitan or tolerant as Harris, however, abolished the teaching of German in elementary schools in 1888.[54]

That year the Missouri state superintendent of schools complained that German settlers in many districts so ruled the schools that "the schools are mainly taught in the German language." Between 1854 and 1877, responding to German leaders, eight states in the Midwest and the plains passed laws enabling local school boards or even "freeholders" representing twenty-five or fifty pupils to require instruction in foreign languages in the common school. By 1900, 231,700 children were studying German in elementary school. That year 34,232 out of a total enrollment of 40,225 in the four upper elementary grades and the high schools in Chicago were taking German, slightly under half of them of German parentage.[55]

Among the various immigrant groups seeking symbolic affirmation of their worth, Germans had high status and political clout. As they became increasingly assimilated into the dominant Anglo culture, they shifted their demands from bilingual schools—which they had achieved in Cincinnati, Baltimore, and Indianapolis—to a justification of German as an elective and separate subject for the upper elementary grades and the high schools. The change became explicit when a spokesman for the Nationalbund in 1901 declared that English should be the official language of instruction, that only foreign languages of "cultural importance or commercial value" should be taught (foremost among them German, of course), and that "no foreign language should be taught in the American public schools simply because the pupils and patrons of the schools speak the foreign languages in question. If this principle will not be recognized, we will not only have German schools but *Hungarian, Polish,* and *Italian ones as well.*" [56]

Indeed, although German or Anglophile cultural chauvinists might decry it, that is precisely what happened wherever immigrants were able to use ethnic power to their advantage. Polish, Italian, Czech, Norwegian, French, Spanish, Dutch, and other languages were introduced into public elementary schools (though usually not as the language of instruction but as a separate subject). In 1915 in Milwaukee, 30,368 children studied German in elementary schools, 3,102 Polish, and 811 Italian (the last two subjects were concentrated in a few schools in immigrant neighborhoods). In 1865 San Francisco opened its first "cosmopolitan school," which taught children in French, German, and English. The superintendent in 1875 urged that students "be required to study and recite their lessons in geography, arithmetic, etc., in the foreign language which they wish to learn," admitting that such a practice might drive away the nonimmigrant children. As late as 1917, largely because of the political demands of foreign-speaking citizens, San Francisco still taught French in four elementary schools, German in eight, Italian in six, and Spanish in two.[57]

Instruction of young pupils in foreign languages aroused much opposition, both among nativists and among ethnic groups that felt excluded. In the late 1880's there was a concerted drive in some cities and states to eliminate or curb foreign languages in elementary schools. Professing a variety of motives—economy, the need to Americanize, and others—Louisville, St. Louis, St. Paul, and other cities dropped German. The Edwards Law in Illinois (1889) and the Bennett bill in Wisconsin (1889) tried to regulate immigrant private and parochial schools by requiring that most instruction be conducted in English. As in the case of Protestant rituals in the schools, the contest over instruction in languages other than English became a symbolic battle between those who wanted to impose one standard of belief and those who welcomed pluralistic forms of education.[58]

Amid the pluralistic politics of interest groups, the cultural conflicts of Catholic and Protestant, immigrant and nativist, black and white, the position of schoolmen was an anomalous one. For the most part, they held a common set of WASP values, professed a common-core (that is, pan-Protestant) Christianity, were ethnocentric, and tended to glorify the sturdy virtues of a departed rural tradition. They took their values for granted as self-evidently true—not subject to legitimate debate. At the same time, they normally shared Horace Mann's dislike for partisan controversy in either politics or religion; the common school, after all, should rest on consensus. The battles of cultural interest groups to influence the schools simply disrupted that consensus and interfered with the task of building the one best system.

5. A STRUGGLE LONELY AND UNEQUAL: THE BURDEN OF RACE

Amid the schoolmen's quest for a one best system and the politics of pluralism the history of black urban education posed a strange anomaly. While publicists glorified the unifying influence of common learning under the common roof of the common school, black Americans were rarely part of that design. While groups like the Germans won expensive concessions like special language classes, blacks had to fight for crumbs. While schoolmen tried to erase the pauper taint from free schooling for whites, education of Negroes often seemed to be an act of charity, an occasion for self-congratulation of benevolent men. In schools that supposedly banned the lines of caste, black children became subjects of experiments in "classification" that had portents for the future.

During the nineteenth century no group in the United States had a greater faith in the equalizing power of schooling or a clearer understanding of the democratic promise of public education than did black Americans. "It is the humanizing, socializing influence of the school system, which is its most important feature," stated a group of Boston Negroes in 1846 in a petition for desegregated schools. Practically every black voluntary group, almost all black politicians, rated the improvement of educational opportunities near the top of priorities for their people. Yet across the nation many of the whites who controlled systems of public education excluded, segregated, or cheated black pupils. Negroes learned that the educational system that was to homogenize other Americans was not meant for them. As in other spheres of their lives, they learned that constantly they had to fight for rights that were supposedly guaranteed to them by the Fourteenth and Fifteenth Amendments and by democratic principles.[59]

Strategies and tactics differed from community to community, depending in part on the density of the black population, the nature of black leadership, and the degree of white prejudice. In some cities blacks argued for separate but equal schools, maintaining that such systems offered opportunities for Negroes to obtain good jobs and claiming that black children in mixed schools suffered from the insults of white children and the cruelty and bias of white teachers. In 1876 a black magazine declared that white teachers in black schools "take no real interest in their work nor in the scholars but teach and tolerate them only in order to . . . draw their money. . . . We are tired of white

The Carrie Steel School for 170 Black Children, Atlanta, Georgia, 1920

overseers." In other communities activists pressed for integrated schools, arguing that separate schools were inherently unequal. In integrated schools, Frederick Douglass said in 1872, black and white children "will learn to know each other better, and be better able to co-operate for mutual benefit." Lacking substantial political power, Negroes used some of the tactics available to oppressed minorities: court cases, boycotts, sit-ins, petitions, and lobbies.[60]

As Carter G. Woodson documented long ago, free blacks before the Civil War zealously sought education and invested much income and effort in establishing their own voluntary schools (often aided by white philanthropists and religious organizations). From first-hand knowledge and interviews of black citizens, in 1868 M. B. Goodwin wrote a history of educational opportunities for Negroes in antebellum Washington, D.C., telling of a large array of schools associated with churches, both black and white, private "seminaries" for middle-class blacks, and dozens of primary schools ranging in size from a handful of pupils to over a hundred. In a number of institutions white and black students studied side by side, although there were no public schools for Negroes. He concluded that as many free blacks attended school before the Civil War in proportion to the population as did after emancipation. That this zeal for learning galled lower-class whites became clear during a riot in 1835, when shipyard workers raged through black classrooms, demolishing furniture, breaking windows, and burning schools to the ground. In other cities, such as Boston, New York, and St. Louis, white philanthropists joined black leaders in founding private schools for Negro children.[61]

Before the Civil War, whites in northern cities often regarded public schools for blacks not as a right but as a gesture of "benevolence"—and usually a parsimonious one at that. In 1847 the New York state legislature appropriated a fund from which the trustees of incorporated villages could draw funds for separate public schools for black pupils. Although there were an estimated 11,000 Negro children in the state, the municipalities requested only $396 in 1849. These "colored schools" were independent of the regular school system, administered by the village trustees rather than by school committees; the state superintendent of common schools suspected that funds intended for black children went instead to the white public schools. In Sacramento, California, members of the city council protested that if they opened public schools to blacks, "why not open the doors of our generosity, and provide for the education of Kanakas, Chinese, and Diggers?" [62]

The major arguments that would dominate discussion of desegregation of public schools for the next century were already apparent in Boston in the 1840's. In the early nineteenth century black children were permitted to attend the Boston public schools, but few enrolled. Instead, black parents claimed that their children could gain a better education in separate schools where they would not be exposed to white prejudice, and with the aid of some wealthy whites they established their own institutions. The city gradually took over the supervision and financing of these black schools. As Stanley Schultz observes, a number of Boston Negroes changed their mind by the late 1820's and 1830's, however; they began to suspect that the only way to gain equality in education was through desegregation. The eloquent black abolitionist David Walker expressed a growing suspicion that whites were conspiring to keep black children ignorant, to keep them from the advanced knowledge that they needed for their liberation. If there were white children in the classes—in effect, as hostages—the teachers would have to teach the Negro pupils as well. At the same time that Walker called for militant action, a future black leader of a school boycott, William Nell, received honors at his school examination but failed to be invited to the mayor's dinner for the white scholars. Slipping in to the celebration as a waiter, he met a school examiner who whispered, "You ought to be here with the other boys." Nell agreed, and later attacked a power structure whose benevolence he distrusted.[63]

The drive for mixed schools split the Boston black community. A determined group of militant desegregationsists petitioned the school board and the primary school committee. When that failed, they boycotted the Smith Grammar School and set up a substitute "temporary school." Enrollment dropped from over a hundred in 1844 to fifty-three in 1849. Finally they took their cause to court. Another group of black citizens wanted to retain the segregated schools but to improve buildings and facilities and to hire a black master to replace the white teacher, who had been accused of cruelty and lack of faith in the intellectual capacity of his students.[64]

Petitions to the school committees fell mostly on deaf ears. The white committeemen said that segregated black schools in Philadelphia, New York, Providence, Nantucket, and Worcester expressed the genuine desire of the Negro communities in those cities and claimed that "outsiders"—meaning white abolitionists—had stirred up Boston black citizens who otherwise would have been content. A "petition of Sundry Colored Persons" had maintained that separate schools were inherently unequal "since all experience teaches that where a small and despised class are shut out from the common benefit of any public institutions of learning and confined to separate schools, few or none interest themselves about the schools—neglect ensues, abuses creep in, the standard of scholarship degenerates, and the teachers and the scholars are soon considered and of course become an inferior class." That was tantamount, said the white primary school committee, to believing that "colored people contaminate colored people by being together." Instead, the committee urged Negroes to "cultivate a respect for themselves, for their own race, their own blood, aye, and for their own *color*." Black might be beautiful, but black children didn't belong in school with whites, said the school committee, for there was an ineffaceable distinction "in the physical, mental, and moral natures of the two races." For both races "amalgamation is degradation." Besides, whites would "vex and insult the colored children." And since "the prejudices of color are strongest among the most ignorant," the lower-classes—notably the Irish—would be likely to leave mixed schools altogether. By thus associating prejudice with ignorance, the committee was obviously trying to avoid appearing bigoted: it was segregating the black children for their own good, using the discretionary powers of classification granted it by law.[65]

Such discretionary powers came into direct conflict with "equality before the law," thought abolitionist Charles Sumner, who used that phrase in a legal brief for the first time in the Roberts case. Using a full panoply of arguments for integration, Sumner claimed that his black client, Sarah Roberts, had every right, legal and moral, to attend the white school she passed by on her way to the black school. In a case that served as precedent for the doctrine of "separate but equal" that persisted for more than a century, Judge Lemuel Shaw decided in 1850 that the school committee had the right under its "powers of general superintendence" to classify black children as it did. After failing to win desegregation by boycott, petition, and legal action, Boston's black activists finally succeeded when a Know-Nothing state legislature passed a law in 1855 forbidding distinction "on account of the race, color, or religious opinions, of the applicant or scholar." Despite dire predictions of trouble, white and black children mingled peacefully in schools, and enrollment of Negroes increased substantially.[66]

The Civil War, the Emancipation Proclamation, and even the Fourteenth and Fifteenth Amendments failed to secure the educational rights of black children in many northern cities. It was left to state and local politics to decide "the Negro question." For a brief time during the late 1860's and early 1870's black citizens could form a powerful alliance with Radical Republicans in some cities to win educational equality; but during most of the latter half of the century they fought, mostly alone or with a few white allies, using moral suasion, lobbies, boycotts, and court action as the means of moving a reluctant majority.[67]

The legal context of the struggle was contorted and varied from state to state. In California, for example, the legislature in 1860 denied state money to any mixed school; in 1870 it passed a law stating that a board of education must set up a school for Afro-American or Indian children if parents of ten children made written application, but such a school must be separate from the white schools. This law made explicit what was often elsewhere implicit, namely that the burden of proof and effort was on blacks to obtain educational justice. In 1874 the California court affirmed that separate but equal schools for Negroes did not violate the Fourteenth Amendment. But San Francisco abandoned its segregated black schools in 1875, largely because the separate schools were costly and unpopular with the Negro community.[68]

In Illinois local officials often found ways to segregate black children even though some laws and court decisions forbade discrimination. A month after Lincoln's Emancipation Proclamation, in February 1863, the Democratic city council of Chicago passed a "Black School Law" requiring Negro children to attend a segregated school. Black parents rebelled and sent their children to white schools where teachers "refused to acknowledge their presence." When the school board voted that pupils with one eighth or less of African ancestry could attend white schools, parents used that device to open school doors. Insulted by the absurdity of determining degrees of blackness, Negro leaders "invaded the offices of the Board of Education and the Mayor" to press for repeal of the law. In 1865, Republicans passed a new city charter which abolished segregation. The state constitution of 1870 required free schools open to all and statutes in 1874 and 1889 prohibited discrimination by school officials, but Republican state superintendent Newton Bateman, who had campaigned for adequate education for black children, claimed that desegregation was "one of those matters which involve no *principle* worth striving about," surely no violation of the Fourteenth Amendment. In 1874 blacks attended separate schools in twenty-six counties, and in cities like Quincy, Cairo, Alton, and East St. Louis school boards segregated black children. The legal process of obtaining desegregation took so long, and aroused such antagonism in the local community, as Negro Scott Bibb discovered in Alton, that it was a determined and courageous black person indeed who dared to go against the prejudices of white neighbors.[69]

In Indiana black citizens had mixed feelings about desegregation. The Negro community in Indianapolis made great sacrifices to provide private schools for their children in the 1860's before the city opened public education to them. The superintendent of public schools wrote admiringly in 1866 of the large number of black people attending private schools "conducted and supported by themselves, and to a very limited extent, if at all, dependent on the charities of the public. . . . Their schools are maintained under great disadvantages—without the generous sympathy of the public generally, with very moderate funds, with buildings unsuited to school purpose, with limited or no school apparatus, with uncomfortable school furniture, with insufficient textbooks, without classification, and with teachers unskilled in the art of imparting instruction." In the name of "humanity, justice, and sound public policy," he urged, they should "receive the benefits of our common school system." The next year the city offered an old school building to blacks, who ran it as a tuition school; Negroes old and young crowded this and other schools to learn to read and write, hungry for the knowledge that had been denied them by law when they had been slaves in the South.[70]

From the beginning of the black public schools in Indianapolis, the Negro community insisted on having black teachers. In 1902, out of a total of 585 teachers employed in elementary schools, 53 were black, all assigned to the "colored schools." In 1897, a Negro member of the general assembly introduced a bill to abolish all discrimination on grounds of race, but 30 teachers from Indianapolis signed a petition opposing the measure, arguing that "if such a Bill becomes a Law, we believe that it will be detrimental to the colored people of the State; that it will deprive not only ourselves but many colored men and women of their livelihood; and that it will remove the opportunity that colored men and women now have to strive after and obtain honorable employment in our public schools." In Washington, D.C. a large number of black teachers shared the same fear, should schools be integrated in that city.[71]

That this worry about jobs was not an idle concern is indicated by the experience of New York City: for twenty-two years after mandatory segregation was discontinued in 1873, no black teachers were hired in that school system. In theory integrated schools and integrated faculties were desirable, and many black leaders in the North fought all types of segregation; but often desegregation simply meant the loss of teaching positions for blacks. Indeed, when the Immigration Commission reported on the number of Negro teachers in thirty cities in 1908, it became apparent that with one or two exceptions the only systems to hire substantial numbers of black teachers were segregated either de jure or deliberately without sanction of law. Table 1, which includes those cities in the sample with more than 1,000 black students, indicates that black teachers had a much better chance in 1908 of being employed in separate schools.[72]

Table 1. Black elementary and kindergarten teachers and black pupils in selected cities, 1908 (segregated systems are marked with an asterisk)

City	Number of Teachers	Number of Pupils
Baltimore*	285	8,014
Boston	3	1,456
Chicago	16	3,806
Cincinnati	12	2,085
Kansas City*	55	2,351
Los Angeles	0	1,059
Newark	8	1,193
New Orleans*	73	5,028
New York	43	6,542
Philadelphia*	99	7,284
Pittsburgh	0	2,792
St. Louis*	136	4,057

Source: U.S. Immigration Commission, *Children of Immigrants,* I, 8–13, 129–33.

Because the job ceiling in white institutions and the poverty of black communities severely restricted careers for the black middle class, teaching had great prestige and frequently attracted highly educated black men and women. In Washington, D.C., there were about ten applicants for each vacancy in the black school system as a whole, and positions in the high school attracted the Negro intelligentsia. In a number of cities special normal schools were established to prepare black teachers, and a substantial number of Negro graduates of leading northern universities found careers in black high schools. Both in elementary and secondary classrooms, these black teachers served as important role models for their students, visible proof that in education, at least, there could be a ladder of success for the ambitious black child.[73]

It was not only in the classroom that black educators served their communities. In a study of the functions of black schools in Cincinnati during the years from 1850 to 1887, David Calkins pointed out that the segregated school system of that city had an important impact on the political life and social and economic differentiation of the entire black community. Before the creation of the black school system, Negroes in Cincinnati had a flat occupational structure: almost all workers were unskilled laborers and servants. With the exception of ministers, most of whom worked at other jobs for survival, there were few who could claim positions of leadership. But with the employment of Negroes as teachers and administrators new career lines opened and new sources of income and prestige appeared; in the first thirty-seven years of the schools, for instance, black teachers earned over $437,000. When black Gaines High School opened in 1866, it trained teachers, offered preparation for further education, and helped to create a middle-class leadership for the city's black population. Black educators also provided a nucleus for a number of new voluntary groups and stimulated a social differentiation which helped to change the white community's stereotype of Negroes. As Calkins observes, the schools also provided a political outlet for ambitious blacks, for in the two decades before they gained full suffrage in 1870, they were empowered to elect their own school trustees. In this arena they gained skills and exercised power that became increasingly important with their enfranchisement. When the separate board for black schools was abolished in 1874, they lost this source of patronage and influence, and with the abandonment of de jure segregation in 1887, through state action, the separate "colored schools" ceased to exist officially, though they remained in fact as a "branch school system" enrolling only black children.[74]

In most cities black citizens did not enjoy the kind of political power possessed by Negroes in Cincinnati in the years before 1874. In New York, for example, the black schools were controlled chiefly by white philanthropists until 1853 when the "Colored Free Schools" were transferred to the board of education of New York. In 1857 a group of black leaders told a state investigating committee about the wretched condition of these segregated schools. They said that the board of education had appropriated one cent per Negro child and sixteen dollars per white child for sites and school buildings, even though there were 25 percent more black children attending school in proportion to their total population than white. The results were apparent in the school buildings for Afro-Americans: schools "dark and cheerless," wedged into neighborhoods that were "full of filth and vice"; one even had four feet of water in the basement. In contrast, the white schools were "splendid, almost palatial edifices, with manifold comforts, conveniences, and elegancies." It was, they said, "a costly piece of injustice which educates the white scholar in a palace . . . and the colored pupil in a hovel." The only answers, they said, were to desegregate the white schools or build new black ones.[75]

As in other cities, New York black teachers knew that they would lose their jobs if schools were mixed, and even though they were paid on the average $100 less than whites and kept down by a Catch-22 system of examiners' ratings, they had no other options. Under the ward system, blacks had little power even when they could vote, for they were so scattered across the city and their numbers were so small that they could muster little power. Indeed, in 1866 the ward committees so neglected the black schools that ten buildings were put under the central board of education (this was also the case in Pittsburgh, where otherwise ward boards reigned supreme). After the ratification of the Fourteenth Amendment in 1868, especially, New York began building new Negro schools and renovating the old ones. After a new school law opened white schools to black children in 1873, however, the attendance in the "colored schools" dwindled; in 1863 the attendance of black students in the segregated schools had been 858, but by 1880 it was only 571. Black teachers retired, went to all-black schools in Philadelphia, Brooklyn, or Washington, or were dropped. The employment question fanned a harsh debate in the black community about the board's intention to abolish the separate schools, which were becoming uneconomical by the 1880's. In 1883 a black principal and her friends campaigned to get Negro pupils to attend her school on 17th Street, giving them free lunches and transportation. But as this effort failed, and as Governor Grover Cleveland spoke out against segregation, the state decided in 1884 to close the last black schools. In a last-minute gesture, a group of black citizens appealed to the legislature successfully to retain two black schools with the understanding that they would also be open to whites. It was not until 1895, after an unsuccessful lawsuit, that a black teacher, Mrs. Susie Frazier, won an appointment to teach on a white faculty in the city.[76]

With its avowed dual system, Washington, D.C., presented still another pattern of governance of black urban education. When the Negro public schools began in 1862, a separate board of three trustees for the black system was appointed by the Secretary of the Interior because the board for the white schools shirked its dury. Although the first board had only white trustees, by 1869 two of the three were black. That year Congress passed a bill transferring its powers to the board for white schools. The black community reacted bitterly and at a mass meeting resolved that this would subject the law establishing black schools "to the chances of being again refused, or at least being negligently or indifferently executed by persons whose positions are held by tenure of local politics and the prejudices consequent thereto." Such a change, they said, would expose the black community "to political hostility in circumstances where we are powerless." President Andrew Johnson vetoed the bill. In 1873 Congress passed a bill changing the board for the black schools to a nine-man group appointed by the governor of the District; only black trustees were selected. The next year

Congress set up a common board for both sets of schools composed of nineteen members, five of whom were black, and while the size and mode of selection of the board changed, there was a "gentleman's agreement" commonly in effect that a minority of the board members would be Negro. In turn, from 1868 to 1900 the superintendent of the black schools, coordinate with the superintendent of the white schools, was a black educator. The white majority on the board retained the final power, and some said that the Negro members gained their positions by being toadies, but at least the arrangement gave blacks influence and good jobs (the last white teacher in the black schools withdrew in 1901). Apparently no other dual system of city schools had an integrated central board of education before 1940.[77]

In St. Louis black citizens lacked direct political power but won a share of influence on the schools nonetheless. The state constitution in 1865 required the city to educate Negroes; in 1866, St. Louis' white board of schools took over responsibility for a separate system of black schools. Radical Republicans on the central school board wished to build schools for Negro students, appealing to the fact that blacks were taxpayers and that the law and sentiment of the community approved schooling as "common justice to the colored people." But Democrats ridiculed the idea of "extravagant school houses for the education of Negroes" and said that if the Radicals "like to associate with niggerdom, as would seem to be the case, let them go to them, but not at the expense of the white men." In the 1866 election the Democrats won most city offices, including all the eligible school positions. Although the Radicals kept a small majority on the board of schools, they realized that public sentiment was for keeping the Negro down.[78]

Opponents of the black man had no cause to fear extravagance. The board searched for three months in vain to find anyone willing to rent rooms for a black school. For years black scholars attended classes in damp basements, dilapidated houses, and antiquated and abandoned white schools. Frustrated by such treatment, and eager for good education, black citizens were forced to build a school at their own expense in 1868. Only by constant pressure by lobbies like the Colored Educational Association, a group of teachers and ministers, did they persuade the board to provide ordinary services—and that from a superintendent and set of trustees that were, for that time and place, benevolent. Benevolence was clearly a poor substitute for justice, lobbying a shaky form of power.[79]

Like other urban groups, the black citizens of St. Louis wanted both tangible and symbolic victories. By 1875 even the Radical Republican newspaper had dismissed the idea of desegregation through a civil rights act, saying that "integration would work a great deal of mischief, and could do no good except in satisfaction of a little false pride on the part of colored children and their parents." Not surprisingly, with such white friends, the black community concentrated on equality, since they were clearly to be separate. Beginning in 1874, Negroes pressed for black teachers for their schools. In 1877 their lobby argued that white teachers had "certain false and wicked ideas" which tainted their instruction; by contrast, black teachers knew the community, understood "the wants of their pupils and how to supply them," and could raise horizons of black children "by example and intercourse." Black families voted for Negro teachers with their feet: in the first three years after the introduction of black teachers, the number of pupils rose 35 percent (1878), 20 percent (1879), and 27 percent (1880).[80]

Jobs and good buildings were essential, but black pride bridled at the board's policy of giving Negro schools numbers instead of names, as in the white schools. In 1878 the Colored Educational Association requested the board to name the schools after prominent blacks like Toussaint L'Ouverture, Alexandre Dumas, and Crispus Attucks. The board refused, suggesting instead that they be named for white "men who have distinguished themselves in the cause of the colored race." In 1890, twelve years later, the board tried again unsuccessfully with a list of white benefactors, but in two more months agreed to a list of eminent Negroes, including L'Ouverture, Dumas, Attucks, and others like Ira Aldridge, Benjamin Banneker, and Phyllis Wheatley. No doubt the black community learned much of its own history, as well as much about white men, in this battle of the names.[81]

As measured by attendance in schools and by literacy, the black faith in education in St. Louis and other northern cities persisted throughout the nineteenth century. In 1890 a larger percentage of blacks as a proportion of the St. Louis Negro population attended public school than whites—18.7 percent as opposed to 12.9 percent (although white attendance in private and parochial schools, as well as a different ratio of children to adults, may have accounted for much of the disparity). In the black seventh ward in Philadelphia in 1897, W. E. B. DuBois found that 85 percent of the Negro children aged six to thirteen attended school for at least part of the year. The illiteracy of black youth ten to twenty years old in that city was only 4 percent.[82]

Nationwide the statistics showed an enormous stride ahead, despite the lagging progress in the rural South. In 1870 only 9.9 percent of Negro children five to nineteen attended school; by 1900 the figure had jumped to over 31 percent. Of non-white men alive in 1940, those born about 1870 had on the average 2.8 years of schooling; those born about 1890 had approximately 5 years of schooling. The percentage of illiterate Negroes dropped from about 80 percent in 1870 to 44.5 percent in 1900.[83]

But where did better education lead? Were blacks only to enjoy that luxury beloved of commencement orators, the value of "education for its own sake"? A teacher in the African Free Schools of New York said in 1830 that "as the acquirement of knowledge is pleasing, delightful, and ennobling to the human mind, it is a wonder that [the black parents of the city] do not feel more interested in it for the sake of knowledge itself; but, is this abstract view of the subject sufficient to satisfy *our own minds in relation to our children* . . . ?" In 1819 a black youth gave his answer at a graduation ceremony: "Why should I strive hard, and acquire all the constituents of a man, if the prevailing genius of the land admit me not as such, or but in an inferior degree!" At the end of an education, what lay ahead? "Shall I be a mechanic? No one will employ me; white boys won't work with me. Shall I be a merchant? No one will have me in his office; white clerks won't associate with me. Drudgery and servitude, then, are my prospective portion. Can you be surprised at my discouragement?" Almost a century later the only black principal in New York, Dr. William L. Bulkley, told a reporter that "the saddest thing that faces me in my work is the small opportunity for a colored boy or girl to find proper employment." What was he to say to persuade a black youth that he should stay in school when a Negro "must face the bald fact that he must enter business as a boy and wind up as a boy"? DuBois found that 79 percent of the employed black workers in the seventh ward of Philadelphia were laborers and servants; the number of skilled workers had declined from earlier years; and of the sixty-one individuals who were listed as "in the learned professions," twenty-two were clergymen and seventeen were students. And in the years that Rayford Logan has described as a time of "Betrayal of the Negro," the employment situation in many cities got worse, not better. The St. Louis school reports told a distressing story; between 1880 and 1890 the percentage of black parents classified as unskilled rose from 62.5 percent to 75.1 percent, skilled workers declined from 255 to 171, mechanics dropped from 145 to 94, and merchants fell from 19 to 6.[84]

As the century came to a close, an episode in East Orange, New Jersey, illustrated the potential of the powers of "classification" that had been awarded to school boards and professionals by numerous court cases and by the growing trust in a pseudo-scientific technology of discrimination. In 1899 the superintendent of schools in that suburb of Newark persuaded the board to "experiment" with an "ungraded" class of "backward colored pupils." Outraged, black leaders "suspected that the 'experiment' was nothing more than a not-too-subtle entering wedge for the establishment of a completely segregated school system." In fact the practice of Jim Crow classes continued, despite angry protests and boycotts, for as a professed liberal member of the board contended, teachers and parents felt that Negroes had "different temperaments." When asked why there were no whites in the special classes, one principal replied that there were no backward whites in his school. From there it was a clear path to an "ideal state school code" written by a leading northern educator in 1914, praising the unifying force of the common school, and noting that at the same time the state might set up separate schools for "defective, delinquent, or . . . negro" children. Not surprisingly, the Alabama state superintendent asked him to come south the next year to rewrite the state's school laws.[85]

For black Americans the nineteenth-century struggle to win

educational justice had been lonely and unequal, its results impressive in themselves but problematic in their influence on the position of Negroes in the larger society. Whether they dealt with rednecks or benefactors, with tortuous jurisprudence or scientific racism, they learned that they must be wary. They wanted better education for their children and power to improve their status. Those related themes underlay debates about strategy and tactics, integration and segregation—and in the larger struggle to come in urban schools, those themes would recur.

PART IV

Centralization and the Corporate Model:
Contests for Control of Urban Schools,
1890–1940

They talked about accountability, about cutting red tape, about organizing coalitions to push educational reform, about the need to face the realities of class and power in American society. "They" were members of a movement composed mostly of business and professional elites, including university people and the new school managers. At the turn of the twentieth century, they planned a basic shift in the control of urban education which would vest political power in a small committee composed of "successful men." They wished to emulate the process of decision-making used by men on the board of directors of a modern business corporation. They planned to delegate almost total administrative power to an expert superintendent and his staff so that they could reshape the schools to fit the new economic and social conditions of an urban-industrial society. They rejected as anachronistic, inefficient, and potentially corrupt the older methods of decision-making and school politics. Effective political reform, said one of their leaders, might require "the imposition of limitations upon the common suffrage." They ridiculed "the exceedingly democratic idea that all are equal" and urged that schooling be adapted to social stratification.[1]

As we have seen, during the nineteenth century urban schoolmen and their lay allies were slowly moving toward the strategy which would shape the centralization movement during its hey-day, the years from 1890 to 1920. From the 1870's forward, reformers like Philbrick and the patrician businessman Charles Francis Adams had called for small, "non-political" boards which would delegate the actual administration of the schools to experts. But until the 1890's in most large cities the school board remained large, ward boards kept substantial powers, and the whole mode of lay management was diffuse, frequently self-contradictory, and prone to conflict. Defenders of the ward system argued that grass-roots interest in the schools and widespread participation in school politics was healthy, indeed necessary, in large cities, but centralizers saw in decentralization only corruption, parochialism, and vestiges of an outmoded village mentality. The men and women who sought centralization of control and social efficiency in urban education at the turn of the century—the people I shall call the "administrative progressives"—wished nothing less than a fundamental change in the structure and process of decision-making. Their social perspective tended to be cosmopolitan yet paternalistic, self-consciously "modern" in its deference to the expert and its quest for rational efficiency yet at times evangelical in its rhetorical tone.[2]

As Joseph Cronin and others have shown, the administrative progressives were notably successful—indeed, their success so framed the structure of urban education that the subsequent history of these schools has been in large part an unfolding of the organizational consequences of centralization. In 1893 in the twenty-eight cities having populations of 100,000 or more, there were 603 central school board members—an average of 21.5 per city; in addition, there were hundreds of ward board members in some of the largest cities. By 1913, the number of central school board members in those cities had dropped to 264, or an average of 10.2, while the ward boards had all but disappeared and most central board members were elected at large. By 1923 the numbers had continued to diminish until the median was seven members. Case studies of centralization in particular cities as well as large-scale investigations of urban school boards in general indicate that school boards after centralization were overwhelmingly composed of business and professional men.[3]

As important as the size and social-class membership of school boards was the change in the procedures of decision-making. Increasingly the model of the corporate board of directors with its expert manager became the norm. The crucial changes were the reduction or elimination of administrative subcommittees of the board and the turning over of the power of initiative and the agenda largely to the superintendent.[4]

The "administrative progressives" (1) were a movement with identifiable actors and coalitions; (2) had a common ideology and platform; and (3) gained substantive power over urban education. Their movement and program closely resemble Samuel P. Hays's interpretation of general municipal "progressive" reform. The experience of centralization in cities like New York, Philadelphia, St. Louis, and San Francisco indicates that the chief support for reform "did not come from the lower or middle classes, but from the upper class." Like reforms in public health, city government, or police and welfare work, urban educational reform followed a familiar pattern of muckrakers' exposure of suffering, corruption, or inefficiency; the formation of alliances of leading citizens and professional experts who proposed structural innovations; and a subsequent campaign for "non-political" and rational reorganization of services. Public rhetoric might portray a contest between "the people" and "the politicians," but as Hays says, the reformers wished "not simply to replace bad men with good; they proposed to change the occupational and class origins of decision-makers." [5]

During this period there was a blurring of the lines between "public" and "private" in businessmen's quest for a stable, predictable, rational social organization. While educational reformers spoke of schools as "quasi-public corporations" and emulated the business board of directors as a model of "public" control, liberal industrialists founded Americanization classes, kindergartens, and day-care centers in factories, improved working conditions and health care for their workers, and provided a variety of fringe benefits calculated to enlist the loyalty and reliability of labor. Public school managers often catered to the wishes of their "major stockholders," the business leaders, especially with regard to vocational education and citizenship training. Civic-minded elites such as the Chamber of Commerce of

Cleveland supported programs to build new schools, to improve public health, and to create playgrounds and vacation schools. "Progressive" school superintendents found such businessmen their natural allies in reform. To change the schools, however, one first needed to concentrate power at the top so that the experts could take over.[6]

1. AN INTERLOCKING DIRECTORATE AND ITS BLUEPRINT FOR REFORM

It is time to face the facts, Charles Eliot told the Harvard Teachers' Association in 1908: our society "is divided, and is going to be divided into layers whose borders blend, whose limits are easily passed by individuals, but which, nevertheless, have distinct characteristics and distinct educational needs." Freedom produces inequalities, and it is foolish to educate each child to be President of the United States. There are "four layers in civilized society which are indispensable, and so far as we can see, eternal": a thin upper one which "consists of the managing, leading, guiding class—the intellectual discoverers, the inventors, the organizers, and the managers and their chief assistants"; next, the skilled workers, whose numbers are growing with the application of technology to production; third, "the commercial class, the layer which is employed in buying, selling and distributing"; and finally the "thick fundamental layer engaged in household work, agriculture, mining, quarrying, and forest work." By discovering the talented child in the lower layers—"the natural-history 'sport' in the human race"—the school might foster mobility among the layers, but it should be reorganized to serve each class "with keen appreciation of the several ends in view"—that is, to give each layer its own appropriate form of schooling.[7]

Several key groups within Eliot's thin "upper layer" joined together in the campaign to centralize control of schools on the corporate model and to make urban education socially efficient. The most prominent spokesmen for reform were university presidents and professors of educational administration, some of the "progressive" city superintendents, leading businessmen and lawyers, and elite men and women in reform groups like the

Public Education Associations and civic · clubs. Eliot was encouraged that "a few disinterested and active men may sometimes get good legislation out of an American legislature." Three men "acting under a single leader . . . obtained from the Massachusetts legislature the act which established the Boston School Committee of five members. The name of that leader was James J. Storrow. I am happy to believe that the group were all Harvard men." In St. Louis, said Eliot, "a few citizens . . . went to the Missouri legislature and procured the abolition of their former school committee" and the enactment of a reform plan. According to Andrew S. Draper, briefly the superintendent of schools in Cleveland and later superintendent of schools for New York State, three lawyers and a businessman pushed through the Ohio legislature the bill centralizing control of education in that city.[8]

"As it becomes more and more imperative to have strong men, honest and experienced men to manage the business of great cities," Draper observed, "it also becomes, for obvious reasons, more and more difficult to secure them on the basis of an unrestricted suffrage. It is therefore meet that the best thought of the country should be turned, as it is turned, to plans for the government of cities." One cannot expect reform of urban education from the men and women who presently serve as board members or employees, he argued; "any advance . . . will have to come from outside the schools: it is more than likely to have to be made in spite of the opposition of the schools. The school boards are jealous of prerogatives; the teachers are apprehensive. . . . The leaders of the intellectual life of the city will have to evolve a plan; and the masses will have to be educated to its support."[9]

"Leaders of the intellectual life of the city"—and of its social and economic institutions as well—spearheaded the centralization movement across the nation. As men who had perfected large organizations, they had national reference groups and thought in cosmopolitan rather than merely local terms. Successful in their own careers, they assumed that what was good for their class and private institutions was good public policy as well. At the turn of the century, business and professional men increasingly valued specialized education and expertise—rejecting the earlier glorification of the self-made, undifferentiated man "who can turn his hand to anything." Increasingly they turned to universities to get standards of truth and taste, authority and expertise. These leaders were impressed with the newly developed forms of corporate structure which had revolutionized decision-making in vast business organizations. They were convinced that the way to improve urban schools was to place on school boards a few "Americans of good quality—that is honest men who have proved their capacity in private business" and to turn the schools over to the progressive expert—"a man who, knowing the shortcomings and defects in his business, is eager to try experiments in overcoming them." [10]

In 1912 two of the new "progressive experts," David Snedden (commissioner of education in Massachusetts) and Samuel Dutton (professor of administration at Teachers College, Columbia University) surveyed the movement to centralize control of schools and concluded that "no one can deny that under existing conditions the very salvation of our cities depends upon the ability of legislatures to enact such provisions as will safeguard the rights of citizens, take the government from ignorant and irresponsible politicians, and place it in the hands of honest and competent experts." Like Draper, they disdained the electorate of the great cities; like him, they wondered if it might not be possible to "safeguard the rights of citizens" by disenfranchising or at least weakening the power of the wrong sort of people by means of state action. They shared this distrust of the democratic process with a number of patrician reformers and conservative social scientists who urged reforms to take not only the schools but urban government itself out of politics. [11]

Melvin Holli has described the elite assumptions and program of such structural reformers: "the first wave of prescriptive municipal government . . . placed its faith in rule by educated, upper class Americans and, later, by municipal experts rather than the lower classes." While originally it seemed right to have patricians themselves run the city, it seemed easier and more stable and efficient to have trained experts administer urban government instead, as in the city manager plan, which was modeled largely on the structure of a business corporation. A former mayor of New York, patrician Abram Hewitt, argued in 1901 that "ignorance should be excluded from control . . . city business should be carried on by trained experts selected upon some other principle than popular suffrage." Columbia Professor Frank Goodenow, who was active in school reform, argued that urban decline in New York began in 1857 when "the middle classes . . . were displaced by an ignorant proletariat, mostly foreign born." Goodenow and other theorists thought that southern methods of disfranchising blacks might be adapted to the urban North once people realized that "universal suffrage inevitably must result in inefficient and corrupt government." In 1891 an NEA committee on state school systems endorsed the idea of limiting "the elective franchise by excluding the grossly ignorant and vicious classes," thereby making a compulsory common school the doorway to citizenship. In 1909 Ellwood Cubberley expressed a point of view common among WASP educators when he declared that the "new immigrants" from southeastern Europe were "illiterate, docile, often lacking in initiative, and almost wholly without the Anglo-Saxon conceptions of righteousness, liberty, law, order, public decency, and government." James Bryce explained, however, why the structural reformers did not succeed in open disfranchisement of the newcomers: "Nobody pretends that such persons are fit for civic duty, or will be dangerous if kept for a time in pupilage, but neither party will incur the odium of proposing to exclude them." [12]

Although patrician reformers and elite theorists won some victories in their campaigns to sanitize and professionalize city government generally, the failure of economy-minded structural reformers to provide better services to the masses of the urban residents often made their triumphs short-lived. In education, however, the process of "keeping the schools out of politics" through charter reform, boards of "successful" men, and expert direction proved to be more durable than in most other sectors of city politics—in part, probably, because many of the school reformers were committed to substantive social reforms within the schools as well as reform of school governance. Economy was sometimes a major motive in educational reform, but quite often the schools on the corporate model cost considerably more than the ones they replaced.[13]

One great advantage of the network of urban school centralizers was its access to—and frequently control of—the mass media and the magazines read by opinion leaders. In the battle to destroy the ward school boards in New York, for example, the reformers enjoyed nearly total control of news and editorials in the major newspapers of that city as well as an inside track to such periodicals as *Harper's Weekly, The Outlook,* and *The Critic.* Thereby they could define the nature of the problem in such a way that their remedies seemed self-evident and opposition to reform selfish and misguided. Grass roots politics of education in the ward system could be defined as corruption or parochialism. Practically unchecked power to classify students and to differentiate the curriculum could be defined as the legitimate province of the professional expert. A shift of the method of selection of school boards to favor the upper-middle and upper classes could be explained as a means of getting "better" public officials. The slogan "get the schools out of politics" could disguise effective disfranchisement of dissenters. The quoted opinions of "experts" could be used to squelch opposition. Most of the educational muckrakers—like Rice, Adele Marie Shaw, and other writers for popular magazines—agreed that the source of the evils they described was corruption and lack of expertise in running the schools, thereby accepting the centralizers' definition of the problem.[14]

University presidents and professors of educational administration helped to create a useful consensus of "experts" on the reorganization of urban schools. Presidents Charles W. Eliot of Harvard, Nicholas Murray Butler of Columbia, William Rainey Harper of Chicago, and Andrew Sloan Draper of the University of Illinois achieved national prominence in the movement, speaking before reform associations, writing in national periodicals, and masterminding political strategy in a number of cities. When he was a professor at Columbia, Butler and elite allies commanded a "school war" (his term) in 1896 which destroyed the ward school boards in New York. Harper was chairman of an educational commission in Chicago whose report in 1899 was a compendium of centralist reforms. His roster of advisers for the report listed some of the most eminent university presidents of the day: in addition to Eliot, Butler, and Draper, it included David Starr Jordan of Stanford, Daniel Gilman of Johns Hopkins, and J. G. Shurman of Cornell. It was common for presidents to become city superintendents and vice versa: Andrew Draper left the Cleveland superintendency to become head of the University of Illinois; E. Benjamin Andrews managed the Chicago schools after serving as president of Brown University; Josiah Pickard went to the University of Iowa as president after serving as Chicago superintendent; Daniel Coit Gilman was a prominent candidate for the New York superintendency (Butler declared that had Gilman served "for two or three years," he would have reorganized "the New York school system and put it on its feet"). Harper, Gilman, and Harvard's Abbott Lawrence Lowell were school board members in Chicago, Baltimore, and Boston, respectively. Eliot, Butler, and Jordan all served as presidents of the NEA, while Draper and Gilman were presidents of departments of the NEA. Eliot, said the Brooklyn superintendent, "has done more to accelerate educational progress in this country . . . than all the professors of pedagogy taken together." [15]

Essentially, these university presidents regarded the ideal role of large city superintendent as parallel to their own careers. In explaining to Mayor Gaynor of New York why school board members should not be paid, Butler made an analogy to his own board of trustees at Columbia, arguing that the paid professional—the president or superintendent—should be in command with only general oversight by the governing board. Schoolman William Mowry said urban school boards should treat superintendents the way the Harvard Corporation dealt with President Eliot. The city superintendent was to be a captain of education, a commander whose scope was limited only by the reach of his statesmanship. "The types of men that the educational methods of America have developed appear to me to be entirely different from what we produce at home," wrote the British investigator Alfred Mosely in the report of his education commission in 1903. Butler, he thought, not only was a scholar but also had "the initiative and organizing capacity that are required in a railroad president or chairman." Eliot, likewise, ran a great university but also stepped "out into the area of public affairs" and was "one of the moving spirits of the Civic Federation," an organization which sought accommodation between big business and big labor. Entrepreneur Harper of Chicago managed the University of Chicago after he "actually himself raised the money to bring it into existence." Such educators felt at home with the men of great wealth and power and worked easily with them to bring about changes in the structure of urban schools which might permit wide powers for the new managers of urban education.[16]

University presidents also appreciated the challenge of the city superintendency and the opportunity for universities to prepare the new managers. In introducing William Maxwell to a University of Chicago convocation, President Harper declared: "I am convinced that next in difficulty and in importance to the work of the president of the United States stands that of the superintendent of schools of our great cities." Butler told the Merchants' Club of Chicago that the superintendency is a "learned profession" and that "nobody is too big to be superintendent of schools of the City of Chicago." In a eulogy of the "new profession" of the school superintendency in 1898, President Charles F. Thwing of Western Reserve University wrote that "the present drift in American education is away from democratic toward monarchical control." The king needed a university training.[17]

The actual job of helping to create a "learned profession" out of the superintendency fell to another key group in the interlocking directorate of centralizers, the professors of educational administration. Although they lacked the power and access to the intimate circle of the business elite enjoyed by university presidents, most of them admired businessmen and were in turn often accepted by corporate leaders as useful allies. By the turn of the century, specialized university training was becoming the hallmark of the "expert" so touted by progressive reformers. A key problem facing the professors of education was to find a base of knowledge on which to build this expertise. When Cubberley started his career at Stanford in 1898, for example, he wondered how to define the field. This was no trivial matter; President Jordan told him that he must either make the education department intellectually respectable in three years or see it abolished. Cubberley faced staggering obstacles. As he examined the literature of education, he discovered how scanty it was: a few works in the slowly emerging field of psychology; a handful of books by experienced educators recounting professional folklore; a few writings of European educational theorists, supplemented here and there by the works of an American like W. T. Harris—hardly the basis for scientific expertise. Thus Cubberley had to discover what it was he should be teaching, had to convince his colleagues that it was worth academic credit, and had to recruit students who thought the training was worth their tuition. He succeeded, as did other professors at centers like Teachers College, Columbia, and the University of Chicago.[18]

The new professors of educational administration gave the stamp of university approval to elitist assumptions about who constituted good school board members and to the corporate model of school organization. They tried to develop "scientific" ways of measuring inputs and outputs in school systems as a tool of management, and to elaborate ways in which the school might rationalize its structure and curriculum to fit new industrial and social conditions.[19]

University professors and presidents had an advantage denied to many schoolmen in the field: they were not vulnerable to pressures from school boards and thus could speak their minds while still keeping their jobs. Superintendent Seaver of Boston, for example, served on NEA committees which decried the system of administering schools by subcommittees of the board, but at home he had to cope with the tangle of overlapping jurisdictions they created (in fact, even his authority to ring the no-school bell on snowy days was in doubt). The New York school board forbade even the eminent William Maxwell of New York on one occasion to attend the meetings of the NEA. The newsman Truman DeWeese observed in 1900 that "the relations of schoolmen to school boards have tended to discourage fearless discussion on their part of the manifest flaws and abuses of the system." As a result of this reticence or resistance of school officials, lay reform groups in a number of cities found it useful to employ university professors to give advice—usually knowing in advance what the advice would be, for by the second decade of the twentieth century the wisdom of professors of educational administration had become canonical. As school boards became reformed, they increasingly demanded university-trained experts, thereby expanding the market for courses in educational administration.[20]

By 1913 the new set of experts had become quite cohesive and well linked with influential lay centralizers. When a member of the Chamber of Commerce and of the school board in Portland, Richard Montague, wrote a dozen professional educators that year asking their advice about people to conduct a survey of the city's schools, he received the following nominations (the asterisk marks those cases in which the person nominated was also one of the letter writers; the numeral indicates the number of times the person was suggested):

*Ellwood P. Cubberley of Stanford 8
*Edward C. Elliott of Wisconsin 8
*Paul H. Hanus of Harvard 7
*George D. Strayer of Teachers College 7
*Charles H. Judd of Chicago 4
*Edward Thorndike of Teachers College 3
 James H. Van Sickle, Supt. of Springfield, Mass. 3
*E. C. Moore of Yale 3

Thirteen others were mentioned in the letters, including Leonard Ayres of the Russell Sage Foundation and David Snedden, Commissioner of education in Massachusetts. The leading university experts, like their presidents, became nationally known, peripatetic speakers and consultants. They spoke not only with each other, as in the small in-groups of the Cleveland conference composed of men like Judd, Cubberley, Elliott, Hanus, and Strayer, but also to patricians concerned with educational reform.[21]

As case studies of centralization in individual cities illustrate, the most politically potent segment of the movement was leading business and professional men. Often their wives and daughters took an active part in the movement through organizations like the Association of Collegiate Alumnae, the Public Education Associations of New York, Philadelphia, and other cities, and the women's auxiliaries of civic clubs. In 1898 delegates from local educational societies met to form the Conference of Eastern

School Politics in Philadelphia, 1907, as seen by Cartoonists

Public Education Associations, a coalition which met in different cities each year to share reform strategies and "to learn from trained experts in the educational world the results of efforts along special lines that lead to a broader development of school life." In its early years the Public Education Association (PEA) of New York relied heavily on Nicholas Murray Butler for advice, its president saying in 1896 that "a meeting of the Association without Dr. Butler was like the play 'Hamlet' with Hamlet left out." [22]

In turn, Butler and his elite allies found the PEA useful in the "school war" against the ward boards, for the society women proved to be effective lobbyists in Albany, having tea with the governor's wife and buttonholing legislators. The society ladies also prodded their husbands' sense of duty. Mrs. Cornelius Stevenson chided the leisured gentlemen of Philadelphia at a joint meeting of that city's Public Education Association and the department of education of its Civic Club: "they actually take a decided pride in their contempt of public service; and in this country—which is supposed to be governed by the will of the majority—the children of educated and well-effected parents are brought up to look with horror and disgust upon the idea of taking an active part in city affairs." The members of the New York PEA wanted to make the school board a fit place for a gentleman and the public schools—which their own children often did not attend—fit places for resocializing the children from the "peculiar environment" of the neighborhoods "below 14th Street." If the New York school system "had not adapted itself to, or conquered, that environment," said the Visiting Committee of the PEA, "it was clearly no system at all." Herbert Welch told the Philadelphia elite that their model should be Samuel Chapman Armstrong, "the great teacher of the negro and the Indian," who was as "great a practical genius in the education of plebeian races as Arnold in the education of an aristocracy." [23]

The elite reformers often combined paternalistic sentiment—which harked back to the days of charity schools—with hard-headed modern notions about school organization. As members of a national business elite they exchanged ideas about strategy and structure; St. Louis reformers, for example, borrowed a plan developed by a New York commission, while businessmen from Boston and St. Louis advised merchants in Chicago about how to reorganize their school system. Chambers of Commerce as well as reform associations and municipal research bureaus funded by the rich spread news of urban reforms to a national constituency. [24]

One important phase of reform was the restructuring of urban school politics to promote more representation by elites on school boards—that is, to give more power to *their* people. A small "non-partisan" board elected at large was well calculated, they thought, to accomplish this purpose. As neighborhoods became increasingly segregated by income—and often by race and ethnicity as well—election by wards reduced the percentage of positions on the board available to urban elites. But if members were elected at large under a "non-partisan" system which was independent of place of residence or party endorsement, leading businessmen and professionals could use the media and their reform associations for publicity to give name-familiarity and hence an edge at the ballot box. In cities where they trusted the mayor, some reformers preferred appointment rather than election. And in fact, the proportion of elite board members rose sharply after charters that destroyed the ward system in cities like Philadelphia, Pittsburgh, and St. Louis. In the next section we shall examine the change in Philadelphia and St. Louis. In

Pittsburgh, as the method of selection of board members shifted from election to appointment, the fifteen members selected in 1911 "included ten businessmen with city-wide interests, one doctor associated with the upper class, and three women previously active in upper-class public welfare."[25]

Experts in education customarily agreed that "successful citizens" made the best school board members and that the ward system produced corruption and inefficiency. "Wards came to be known as the 'fighting third,' 'the red-light fourth,' 'the socialistic ninth,' or the 'high-brow fifth,' " wrote Cubberley, "and the characteristics of these wards are frequently evident in the composition of the board of education." In 1892 the U.S. Commissioner of Education, William T. Harris, stated what was to become the conventional wisdom in writings on school administration. There are three common types of school board members, he said: "First, the businessmen chosen from the class of merchants, bankers, and manufacturers, or professional men who have no personal ends to serve and no special cause to plead. . . . Second, there are the men representing the element of reform or change . . . honest and well-meaning, but . . . prone to . . . an unbalanced judgment. . . . A third class of men . . . is the self-seeking or selfish man." The first, of course, were the superintendent's natural allies; the second he must "educate into broader views" (and he might even adopt some of their suggestions "after freeing them from all features of danger to the established order").[26]

This notion that successful men were disinterested found nearly universal expression in the early textbooks on school management. A board composed of such people, argued the administrative progressive, would run the business efficiently, respect the expertise of the superintendent, and consider the needs of the city as a whole rather than those of wards or interest groups. Any necessary diversification of the school program could safely be left in the hands of the superintendents "who will really represent the interests of the children."[27]

Rare indeed was the schoolman who would argue that businessmen did not necessarily represent the good of the polity at large. The most influential doubter and dissenter was Professor George Counts, who wrote that the supposed disinterestedness of the elite "is a pious fraud. The member of a dominant group, because he is peculiarly tempted to identify the interests of society with the interests of his class, is particularly inclined to regard himself as a spokesman for society at large." [28]

Statistics on school board membership in cities after the centralization movement indicated that business and professional men did indeed predominate on urban boards. Scott Nearing found in 1916 that more than three fifths of the members of city committees were merchants, manufacturers, bankers, brokers, real estate men, and doctors and lawyers. Subsequent studies by George Struble and George Counts confirmed that wage-earners and women were grossly underrepresented. [29]

Simply getting "successful" men on school boards was only part of the solution. In a number of cities—especially those that elected small boards from the population at large and not by wards—it is likely that elites had all along enjoyed disproportionate membership on school committees. Such seems to have been the case in Denver and Portland, for example; and even in Boston and New York, those centers of centralist reform, the central boards of education had usually included many leaders in business and the professions. But even with "disinterested"—that is, "successful"—board members, archaic patterns of decision-making frustrated the effectiveness of even the most efficient businessmen. Under the older traditions of lay management inherited from the village school, school board members handled myriad administrative details. [30]

Boston was a case in point. In 1874 reformers complained that members of the school committee thought too much about their own districts, decided minutiae of administration in subcommittees, and indulged in "too much speech-making." A quarter of a century later Boston reformers were still making the same charges. Supervisors of special subjects like drawing or music were accountable not to the superintendent but to subcommittees of the Boston board. S. A. Wetmore, who served on the pre-reform Boston committee from 1894 to 1897, said that "the superintendent and his supervisors are mere figureheads." "The feeling that I should be called upon to formulate a course of study for a primary class, or a Latin school, or a manual-training school, became oppressive," he wrote, "when I realized that I was not what is called 'equipped' for such service; nor did I hanker for the opportunity to designate what text-books should be used in the schools; a task which, in fact, amounts to nothing more than choosing between text-book publishing houses." Factions in the board—religious, political, ethnic, commercial, even academic—had full play, especially in the battle over textbooks. "If we can't have Frye's *Geography*," asserted a member of the board after a memorable textbook struggle, "they shan't have Metcalf's *Grammar*." James Storrow, prime mover behind the 1905 bill to reduce the board to five members, complained that the old committee of twenty-four members had conducted its business— most of it properly the duty of the superintendent—in twenty-nine closed-door subcommittees, while using the public meetings strictly for unnecessary debate: "The desks of the members were grouped in horseshoe form around a rostrum, where sat the presiding officer. Proceedings were very formal; points of order were constantly raised; formal debates were held; many epithets were hurled back and forth; and type-written speeches were often delivered, intended more for the galleries and the newspapers than the members of the Board." [31]

In Philadelphia, Scott Nearing studied how one respectable board operated under the old system of subcommittees. The superintendent was ineffectual, while the real work of the board was delegated to ten subcommittees which dealt with such matters as textbooks and supplies, the election of teachers, and buildings. Of 1,386 resolutions approved by the board, all but 63 emanated from the subcommittees (whose recommendations were usually accepted without discussion). "The great corporations of the country are governed by small boards of directors," observed Nearing. "It is a recognized fact that business can be effectively transacted in no other way." [32]

To many of the reformers it was clear that the way to run a school system was the way to run a railroad—or a bank, or U.S. Steel, or Sears Roebuck, or the National Cash Register Company. Eagerly the centralizers seized on the corporate model of control as the appropriate means of decision-making in urban education. "This is a time when prodigious efforts are being exerted to concentrate interests managed by many under a system whereby they can be controlled by one corporate authority," said

Harvey H. Hubbert, an elite member of the Philadelphia board of education. Not only commerce and industry but also "religious and moral movements are being combined in vast organizations, under one executive head." It was only natural to apply this principle of corporate consolidation to education, he argued.[33]

Indeed, it was an age of consolidation. The capitalization of corporations valued at a million dollars or more jumped from $170 million in 1897 to $5 billion in 1900 to more than $20 billion in 1904. Many of the men who supported the centralization of schools had helped to shape that corporate model and to build the trusts. The same corporate model of expert, centralized administration would serve other organizations equally well: universities, churches, the city manager form of government, welfare services, public schools, philanthropy, and other organizations affected with the public interest. Gone was the commitment of most business leaders to Herbert Spencer's doctrine of minimal government and the tradition of laissez-faire, within which Toulmin Smith could define "centralization" as "that system of government under which the smallest number of minds, and those knowing the least, and having the fewest opportunities of knowing it . . . and having the smallest interest in its well-working, have the management over it, or control over it." The New York lawyer Stephen Olin argued that ward control of education was "primitive," a relic of the days when each neighborhood had its own watchman and volunteer fireman. "Mulberry Bend may not control its own police, nor Murray Hill assess its own taxes, nor Hell's Kitchen select its own health inspectors." No, the day had come to "organize on a modern and rational plan our great and costly system of public schools." [34]

To many schoolmen the corporate model of school governance was not only "modern and rational" but the answer to many of their biggest problems. They wished to gain high status for the superintendent—and here he was compared with that prestigious figure, the business executive. They were tired of "politics" which endangered their tenure and sabotaged their attempts to improve the system—and here was a board that promised to be "above politics." They wanted to make of school administration a science—and here was a ready-to-use body of literature on business efficiency to adapt to the schools. The administrative progressives were quick to develop the implications of the corporate model and to anticipate possible objections to it on democratic grounds. Whereas in the past they often used loose factory analogies for the public schools, they were now quite precise in drawing a strict parallel between the governance of business corporations and the governance of schools.[35]

Educational administrators drew elaborate comparisons between the roles of business leaders and superintendents. In the Denver school survey in 1916 Professor Franklin Bobbitt of the University of Chicago summarized "the principles of good management" in two columns, one for a manufacturing company employing 1,200 and the other for a school system of the same size. In his detailed comparison, citizens became stockholders, the superintendent of schools the manager who divides up the functions of the organization and chooses staff, while "the superintendent and his corps . . . do the work according to the plans and specifications approved by the board." At the end Bobbitt concluded that "when it is asserted that educational management must in its general outlines be different from good business management, it can be shown from such a parallel study that there is absolutely no validity to the contention. All kinds of organizations, whether commercial, civic, industrial, governmental, educational, or other, are all equally and irrevocably subject to the same general laws of good management." In his survey of the San Francisco schools, the U.S. Commissioner of Education Philander Claxton reproduced Bobbitt's chart verbatim. In 1917 educator William Theisen argued that educational administrators should emulate the patterns of centralized organization of eight business firms he examined in detail.[36]

The movement to institute the corporate model of school politics spread rapidly. In many ways the key element in the new model was the power of the superintendent to influence major decisions of the school board. In 1901 a Massachusetts schoolman surveyed practices in 233 towns and cities in his state. He found that superintendents were gaining duties formerly handled by the school board, though the prerogatives of the school managers were by no means firmly established. With but few exceptions superintendents had the power to design a course of study, call and conduct teacher meetings, promote pupils, and inspect and direct the work of teachers. In ninety-two of the systems they had full control over the selection of textbooks, in ninety-five over the nomination of teachers. But the appointment and dismissal of teachers was still firmly in the board's hands, although superintendents were gaining greater advisory powers and in about sixty towns had joint responsibility. A study of the duties of school superintendents in 1923 indicated that the managers were continuing to win power to initiate board actions on such crucial decisions as hiring staff, determining new educational policies, firing staff, and determining the scope of the curriculum and selecting textbooks.[37]

The ideal board was gentlemanly and businesslike—qualities most likely to be found in gentlemen of business. Meetings of the board were to be brief, free of "oratory," and shaped by an agenda in which the superintendent had a primary initiative. One of the biggest differences between the behavior of the old large boards and the new small ones, the reformers reported, was that members no longer spoke to the galleries or worked for particular constituents. A businessman who served for fourteen years as chairman of the Kansas City, Missouri, board of education prided himself on never making a speech in all that time. "The work of the board," wrote the Boston superintendent after the committee was reduced to five in 1905, "is conducted in a conversational tone; speeches made for political effect that were common in the larger board no longer are delivered. The deliberations of the board are not essentially different from those of a board of directors." Superintendent Ben Blewitt of St. Louis told the Chicago city council that under the school charter that conferred most powers of initiation on him, the school board often completed its work in about twenty minutes. Repeatedly the theorists who urged the corporate model of school administration presented conflicts of value, debate, and representation of the interests of special groups as "inefficient" and unnecessary in a properly functioning system of governance.[38]

What, then, was the need for a board of education at all if the professional experts were to initiate most policies and to have a free hand in administering the schools? As professor of government at Harvard and a frustrated member of an unreconstructed Boston school board, Abbott Lawrence Lowell admired expertise but felt that even professionals might lose "the sense of perspective." Universities and hospitals find it useful "to bring to bear on questions of general policy the good sense of outsiders or laymen." So, too, urban schools. And since "gusts of discontent . . . ruffle all democracies from time to time," Lowell wrote, it also helps to have a board "to act as a buffer between the professional force and the public—a body that sanctions the acts of the experts and assumes the responsibility for them." The efficiency expert Leonard Ayres agreed that a board might "keep the professional schoolman from exceeding the educational speed limit" and said that the status of its members in the community could legitimize the actions of the superintendent.[39]

Wallace Sayre has observed that an educational bureaucracy—like other large organizations—"works persistently towards stabilizing its relationship to each of the other elements in its field of forces in ways that will maximize its own autonomous role." As we have seen, during the nineteenth century the politics of urban schools—and especially the ward system—disrupted professional autonomy. During the years from 1890 to 1920, however, the administrative progressives and their lay allies developed an ideology that served to protect the schools from such an external "field of forces." They helped to establish what Sayre would later call a "body of doctrine, a set of serviceable myths" which asserted that education was "a unique governmental function," that only educators were "proper guardians of the educational function," that citizens should "not be influenced in their responses to educational questions by their structured associations or organizations . . . (save perhaps in parents' groups) or as members of a political party," and that "political parties and politicians are institutions not to be trusted." Thus the common school, a prime agency for the perpetuation of democracy, was led by persons who made it a matter of principle to distrust one of the central institutions of democratic government, the political party.[40]

In urging the corporate form of external school governance and internal control by expert bureaucrats, the centralizers were, of course, simply exchanging one form of "political" decision-making for another. They were arguing for a relatively closed system of politics in which power and initiative flowed from the top down and administrative law or system took the place of decisions by elected officials. They wished to destroy the give-and-take bargaining of the ward system, the active lay influence through subcommittees of the board, the contests over cultural and tangible values that had characterized the pluralistic politics of many large cities. Instead, they wished to centralize control and differentiate functions over a large geographical area in a "modern and rational" bureaucracy buffered from popular vagaries. As Samuel Hays writes, such consolidation and systematization of decision-making "was closely related to professionalization. . . . The scope of interest of the professional concerned with such matters as education, health, welfare, and public works was increasingly universal rather than parochial, increasingly cosmopolitan rather than local. . . . [The professionals] found corporate systems of decision-making to their liking, and they approved them not only because of their scope of coverage, but because of their coercive potential." [41]

In the generation following 1920 it was only a lonely maverick here and there in the educational establishment who dissented in theory from Sayre's "serviceable myths" or the benefits of the corporate model, although the realities of educational politics often departed from the norms. So familiar—and seemingly so inevitable—would centralized city bureaucracies become that many Americans would later forget the bitter contests of power and the conflict of values that had attended their origins.

2. CONFLICTS OF POWER AND VALUES: CASE STUDIES OF CENTRALIZATION

Although there was a good deal of agreement on the principles of school reform among members of the interlocking directorate, the tactics and consequences of centralization differed city by city. For that reason, in this section I shall analyze the process of centralization in four cities at different points of time: the abolition of ward boards in New York in 1896, the centralist reforms of 1905 in Philadelphia, charter revision in St. Louis in 1897, and the introduction of the corporate model of school governance in San Francisco in the 1920's. Running through these episodes is a common theme with some local variations. In each case, the proponents of reform were members of highly educated civic elites who believed that structural reforms were necessary to create efficient, rational, and "non-political" school bureaucracies. The opponents of centralization tended to be those who had a political or occupational stake in the system or who viewed the reformers as snobbish intruders. In New York and San Francisco, in particular, the centralizers managed to alienate a large proportion of the teachers by their publicity and tactics. In all of the cities, some lower-class or middle-class ethnic groups such as the Irish spoke out against the "aristocratic" premises of the reformers.[42]

Specific political strategies and tactics depended much on the local political context. In New York, Philadelphia, and St. Louis, the reformers went to respective state governments for enabling legislation, whereas in San Francisco they had to appeal to the voters of the city to amend the charter. Thus in each case but San Francisco, there was a complex interplay of state and city politics. Although the New York bill was ostensibly nonpartisan, its advocates widely proclaimed it as a victory over Tammany Hall. In Philadelphia, the temporary alliance of patrician reformers with a Republican boss, William Vare, helped to secure the passage of their measure through the Republican Pennsylvania legislature. St. Louis reformers relied on a Democratic Missouri government to secure their charter revision for a city where the political machine belonged to the Republicans. In San Francisco, opponents of centralization tended to see it as an anti-Catholic and anti-Democratic measure. Although the tactics and consequences of the reforms varied from city to city, in each case the central ideology and central strategy were similar, marking these episodes as part of a nationwide urban "progressive" campaign, part of an organizational revolution which had earlier transformed other sectors of American life and which now was reshaping urban education.[43]

The abolition of the powers of the ward boards of education in 1896 was only one battle in a long campaign to centralize control of the New York schools. This struggle began with reform plans in the 1880's and finally culminated in a seven-man board for greater New York in 1917. But the contest in 1896 was in some respects the most critical, for it destroyed the decentralized power which had sustained a grass roots lay influence in the schools.[44]

David Hammack has made a careful study of the alignment of social groups advocating and opposing centralization during this "school war" of 1896. The coalition that supported the bill to abolish the ward boards was composed, he writes, of "three over-lapping elites: aggressive modernizers from business and the professions, advocates of efficient, non-partisan municipal government, and moral reformers determined to uphold Protestant virtues in polyglot New York City." Individuals from these groups had been active in previous campaigns for educational reform in the Good Government Clubs, the Public Education Association, and the Educational Commission appointed by Mayor Gilroy in 1893 to make a blueprint for modernizing the schools. In 1896, Nicholas Murray Butler and Steven Olin organized a "Committee of 100" to arouse support in the city and in the legislature for the centralization bill. While Butler and his fellow political strategists did the day-by-day work of steering the bill through the legislature, the membership of the Committee of 100 gave financial support, publicity, and the weight of its collective prestige to the campaign.[45]

The Committee of 100 (actually 104 members) contained a remarkable cross-section of the city's leaders in corporate business, the professions, and "society." Ninety-two were listed in the 1896 *Social Register*. Graduates of leading colleges and universities, they commonly belonged to elite social and philanthropic organizations. Forty-nine were lawyers, mostly in corporate practice. In addition, eighteen bankers and a handful of merchants and manufacturers joined the committee. Highly successful men in other professions—doctors, professors and university administrators, editors, and "professional spokesmen for genteel culture" like Clarence Steadman—rounded out the committee. Accustomed to broad and long-range planning in their own organizations, and conscious that careful public investments paid off in public stability and predictability, they took an active interest in services such as police, roads, docks, mass transit—and education.[46]

The members of the Committee of 100 made a fetish of being "non-partisan" in local politics. Fifty-eight belonged to the City Club, which had "made municipal 'non-partisanship' a principle to rank with the gold standard and civil service reform." Generally they despaired of controlling the party machinery of either the city Democrats or Republicans, for they represented a class numerically small though economically dominant. Instead, they sought to capitalize on their legal and organizational skill, anti-Tammany propaganda in the press, and the ideology of disinterested expertise and efficiency which they were trying to popularize.[47]

Butler adapted his techniques of persuasion to the audience, using snob power when he sent society ladies from the Public Education Association to call on Governor Morton's wife in Albany, or attacking incumbent Superintendent John Jasper of New York as an untrained "common man." In the newspapers, however, he insisted that the centralization movement was an uprising of the people against the Tammany machine. When an opponent of centralization called its advocates "aristocrats and theorists, without any intimate knowledge of our public school system," one of Butler's group angrily replied that such a fomenter of "class distinction" was "an enemy of public peace, and either a fool or demagogue." The argument that one needs to know the system at first hand was silly, he said: "when the principles of pedagogy found useful in the 10th Ward can be distinguished from those indicated in the 20th, when the unfolding of the pupil's mind in the 3rd Ward presents different problems from that of the 6th, then, and not until then, let us continue Educational Subdivisions along Ward lines." [48]

In private, however, many reformers were willing, indeed eager, to make distinctions along lines of class, political party, and religion. In 1896, when Mayor Strong was facing a decision whether to sign the bill abolishing the ward boards, supporters of the measure urged him to approve the bill in order to weaken Tammany Democrats and the Catholic Church. One advocate of abolishing ward boards argued that it was not wise "in a city like this so impregnated with foreign influence, languages and ideas that the school should be controlled locally; for in many localities, the influences that would control would be unquestionably un-American. In some districts there are vast throngs of foreigners where one scarcely hears a word of English spoken, where the mode of living is repugnant to every American." He told Mayor Strong that the local trustee system might work well in uptown wards, but on the East Side, people "are incapable of judging the efficiency" of the schools. In the slums "daily life . . . is largely based upon the experience that a great many desirable things come through political influence, that this is the natural way of the world, and that it is useless to kick against it." Thus the immigrant poor were obviously unfit to manage their own educational affairs, according to the centralizers. As we have seen, many reformers thought little better of teachers and administrators; clearly subordinate educators needed experts to tell them what to do.[49]

In order to persuade the public of the need for reform, Butler and his allies claimed that the schools were miserable. The photographer-muckraker Jacob Riis wrote Mayor Strong that "a management which leaves 48,000 children . . . to roam the street, deprived of school accommodation, sends truants to jail, and makes a laughing stock of the compulsory education law, is not fit to exist. . . . In common with all right-minded, public spirited citizens I pray that you will sign the bill." In the legislative debate on the bill a senator cited Dr. Joseph M. Rice's indictment of the New York schools to prove that the results of instruction "were far below the standard attained in other cities; that the methods employed in the class-room were nothing short of 'dehumanizing'; that the whole system was not only antiquated but actually pernicious." Although he provided ammunition to the centralizers, Rice actually opposed granting one superintendent power over the whole school system of the city, believing instead that New York should be divided into twenty decentralized districts.[50]

The persons who defended the ward trustees and opposed the centralization bill were neither so eminent nor so well organized and financed as the reformers. In typical caricature, Butler described the critics of his bill as "a small clique of individuals who derive either prestige, power or patronage, from the existing system." No such simple categorization of them as agents or dupes of Tammany will suffice, however. Hammack has isolated four main groups as vocal opponents of centralization: "business and community leaders from Harlem and the Bronx; Republican as well as Democratic party officials; some spokesmen for various Protestant, Catholic, and Jewish committees; and nearly everyone engaged in the operation of public schools, from teachers to School Commissioners." While the reformers had concentrated their rhetoric upon what Riis called "the battle against the slum," it was, as Hammack states, "the middle class areas which most vigorously opposed centralization." Defenders of the ward system resented the efforts of the elite "400" to run their schools. Their social perspective and scope of business was local, often linked with specific religious or ethnic communities, but they did not fear the pluralism of the larger society. In their willingness to accept the social diversity of the city and to give each group its political voice, they were in a sense more cosmopolitan than the educated, nationally oriented elite, which wanted to make all children alike through efficient schooling. For many of the opponents of centralization, political parties were a means not only of achieving modest personal advance and influence but also of resolving or accommodating differences of value and power in a heterogeneous city. Hammack points out that the decentralized system of school governance, like political parties, "increased citizen participation in city government and thus helped to tie various groups together. No one called for a system of separate schools for the various religious and national groups. What they did demand was recognition of the integrity of each group's cultural heritage, and proportional representation of each group in the schools." [51]

Many laymen as well as teachers resented the reformers' charges that the quality of education in the city was poor. A journalist wrote the mayor that she had come to New York expecting that the schools were miserable since Dr. Rice had portrayed them in such grim terms, and since the teachers had not risen *"en masse* to resent his open insult. . . . when they did not I thought that just possibly his statements were true." But when she visited a variety of schools, she "found exactly the reverse. . . . Not only intelligent and well-bred teachers who were doing their duty and doing it well, but [also] happy and well-trained children." Local control of schools guaranteed that educators would be responsive to the wishes of the community, said others, whereas the centralizers were mostly aristocrats who sent their children to private schools and based their criticisms of public schools on snobbery or misinformation. The school bill, said one opponent, "was born in aristocracy, sired by amateurs and damned by 'butterflies.' . . . In approving the bill, the theories of the fashionable idler are endorsed. In disapproving it, the intelligence, experience and conscience of the faithful teacher is dignified." [52]

The centralizers won the school war of 1896 when Mayor Strong signed the bill abolishing the ward boards in April of that year. By September, however, Butler was gloomy, for the central board of education had frustrated his designs. The "men of education and of standing" on the board were outnumbered by the "political place hunters and looters" and by a third group of ignorant men who "would die at the stake sooner than harbor a new idea or favor any policy emanating from the enlightened portion of the community." In league with these sinister and ignorant school board members was John Jasper, superintendent of schools in New York since 1879, "one of the shrewdest and most far-sighted politicians in the city." To Butler, Jasper was the personification of the untrained superintendent who "has no conception of what modern theory and practice of education mean"—in short, the type of leader that the university-educated new managers were to replace. "New York wants common schools for common people," declared an opponent of Butler on the board. "The superintendent ought to be a common man. Mr. Jasper is good enough for me." The elite who had pushed the centralization bill through the legislature lobbied to have Daniel Coit Gilman, president of Johns Hopkins University, chosen as superintendent. But at the last moment, Gilman withdrew his name and Jasper was reelected by the board. Jasper then persuaded the board to employ fifteen assistant superintendents and ten supervisors who were largely his old cronies—including all of the former assistant superintendents and two of the principals who had most strongly opposed the new bill. [53]

Clearly the battle for reform—for centralization of control in a corporate board with delegation of power to experts—was not over for Butler and his allies. An important step toward centralization came, however, when William Maxwell became superintendent of schools in the five consolidated boroughs of New York in 1898. Adroitly, Maxwell exploited the weakness of an unwieldy and ineffectual board of forty-six members and arrogated many of the powers to himself de facto. When a new charter reduced the size of the board to seven in 1917, most important decisions were already being made within the massive bureaucracy Maxwell had built. This was the crucial outcome of the contest of power and values in 1896: by destroying the network of local political control of schools through ward committees, the "school war" had created a vacuum of power and influence which the managers were ready and able to fill.[54]

As we have seen, the Philadelphia school system of 1904 seemed to the muckraker Adele Shaw a classic case of corruption, selfishness, impoverished schools, intimidated teachers, and cheated children. Things would change, she wrote, only when Philadelphians abandoned "the old village prejudice and the tenacity of association that prefers to see in office a bad neighbor rather than a good man from a remoter street." But the full story was not so simple, of course, though the evils Adele Shaw and the other muckrakers exposed were genuine enough. The "old village prejudice and the tenacity of association" that helped to preserve the local boards represented not simply an archaic style of decision-making but an alternate view of urban life, one that was anathema to the modernizing elite which had sought since 1881 to change the politics of education in Philadelphia.[55]

It took the patrician reformers a generation to bring about the reform of 1905. In the early 1880's the Public Education Association allied itself with a group of upper-class reformers called the Committee of 100. Sam Bass Warner has observed that these reformers were mostly wealthy lawyers and businessmen who "turned participation in government into a philanthropic activity. These . . . [men] carefully defined themselves as amateurs, helping out for a brief time, as if the municipal corporation were ordinarily someone else's affair." In 1885 the Public Education Association tried to destroy the ward boards, resolving that "all merely local and artificial divisions should be abolished both in the management of the schools and in the appointment of the members of the Board of Public Education, so that the interest of the whole community may always be kept in view." [56]

Local leadership and constituencies, however, were hardly "artificial" or undesirable to the majority of the members of the ward boards. When the Public Education Association and its allied Municipal League presented bills to the legislature in Harrisburg in 1891 and in 1895, they met strong opposition from the representatives of the local boards. In 1891 the reorganization bill sailed through the Senate with the support of the state and city machine leaders, who "were working to break the independent strength of the ward organizations." But the bill was killed in committee in the House, partly because of the pressures placed on Philadelphia legislators by the ward officials. In 1895 the major leaders within the Republican party organization supported the reform bill, but once again the friends of the ward boards triumphed. [57]

A major spokesman for the opponents of centralization was the feisty William Taggart, who broadcast his scorn for the reformers at the hearings in Harrisburg and in his newspaper, *Taggart's Times*. People are perfectly content with the schools, and all this fuss, he said, "does not represent the general demand or sentiment in this city." Instead, he claimed, "This bawling and whining about the 'degradation' and 'inefficiency' of our schools" comes mostly "from the old maids in the Civic Club, from a handful of educational cranks, from the University clique which is anxious to boss the whole school system, and from the newspapers which are anxious to please powerful advertisers." In part Taggart saw the reformers as people on the make—and in pointing out the "University clique" as a group with something to gain from increased power, he was more accurate than those who claimed that the "experts" were totally disinterested. Taggart also resented the reformers' snobbery: "The real object is an effort of the so-called social status people, who have no faith in the system of boilermakers, carpenters, painters—in short the bone and sinew, as well as the good common sense element to be found among our mechanics as well as businessmen in all our wards—to take a hand in the management of our public schools." Many of these centralizers, said another editor, were not educated in the public schools and did not even live in the city.[58]

As William Issel has shown in his analysis of school centralization in Philadelphia, the reformers were indeed mostly "social status people." From 75 to 100 percent of members of organizations active in in movement were listed in either the Philadelphia Blue Book or the Social Register. Furthermore, they looked to other elites elsewhere and to the universities for guidance. In 1904 Charles W. Eliot presented a plan for structural change to the Public Education Association, and on various occasions Nicholas Murray Butler, G. Stanley Hall, and William H. Maxwell also came to the city to advise on its educational reorganization. Martin Brumbaugh, a professor of education at the University of Pennsylvania, was on the commission that wrote the Reorganization Act of 1905 and later became the first city superintendent under Philadelphia's new charter. Wiser than their New York counterparts, the Philadelphia reformers tended to portray teachers and principals as the unhappy victims rather than the allies of unscrupulous politicians.[59]

Conviction of school directors for graft in 1903, coupled with forceful exposure of corruption in the city and in the schools in national magazines and local newspapers, helped to revive the reform movement. Centralizers transformed the stagnant Municipal League into a Committee of 70 dedicated to "rescue Philadelphia from political degradation." This time some administrators and teachers in the schools joined the battle, fearful that "they were taking their educational lives in their hands." One sign that participation in the movement was indeed tricky is the fact that Superintendent Edward Brooks did not even mention in his annual report for 1903 the scandals that shook the schools during that year. The city political machine supported the school reformers, probably from a mixture of motives: to control the local ward politicians, to respond to the public demand for "honesty and efficiency," and to improve the system by opening new high schools. Likewise the state leaders favored a bill proposed by the school reorganization commission, and the measure passed the legislature with but one dissenting vote.[60]

The new law abolished practically all the powers of the ward boards and reduced the central board by half to twenty-one members, appointed by judges and chosen from the city at large rather than by ward. The reforms were a partial victory for the conception of public education advanced for over a generation by patrician reformers and educational experts. It was, said the jubilant reformers, "Philadelphia's revolution of 1905." But like all revolutions, it would bring new problems of its own when the bureaucratized and massive school system later failed to respond to the changing needs and character of the Philadelphia population during the twentieth century.[61]

Like Philadelphia and New York, St. Louis went through a familiar cycle of exposure of corruption and inefficiency by muckrakers, a call for a better "class of men" in office by elite civic groups, and a successful appeal to the state legislature to change the structure of control of the city's schools. In preparing the bill of 1897 that reorganized the school system, the St. Louis reformers borrowed liberally from the recommendations of Mayor Gilroy's commission in New York City, from the experience of Cleveland, where a small elite group centralized the system of control, and from the recommendations of the NEA Committee of 15 on the governance of city schools. In turn, St. Louis' pattern of administration became a model for other cities.[62]

An abortive attempt at reform in 1887 taught the centralizers that it was not sufficient simply to devise ways of getting good men into office; it was also essential to create a structure that would prevent bad men from doing harm. Reformers had backed a law in 1887 which reduced the school board from twenty-eight, elected by wards, to twenty-one, with seven elected at large and fourteen by wards. The revised board of 1887 included seventeen of a slate of twenty-one nominees of a reformer's "citizen's ticket." In comparison with a board for 1886, it represented, Elinor Gersman found, a marked increase in social prominence as measured by education, occupation, listing in *Gould's Blue Book* or honorific biographies, and residence in fashionable neighborhoods. But by 1896, the Republican city machine had regained control of the school board and used it for graft and patronage.[63]

Confronted with such corruption, the elite reformers realized that they had not only to devise better election procedures, but also to restrict board functions. The elite members of the St. Louis civic federation found willing allies in the Democratic Missouri legislature, since both were eager to curb the power and spoils of the city Republican machine. In 1897 the legislature passed a new charter which prescribed strict standards of eligibility and conduct for school board members: each of the twelve board members had to swear an oath of political nonpartisanship and to declare that "he will not be influenced, during his term of office, by any consideration except that of merit and fitness, in the appointment of officers and the engagement of employees"; he was forbidden to hold any other concurrent office; and he was prohibited from voting on any contracts in which he had a financial interest. The chief purpose of the charter, said Edward C. Eliot, a key reformer, was to take "the schools . . . out of politics" and to persuade "men of standing and position in the community to accept this duty as a public trust." [64]

As Elinor Gersman has shown, "men of standing and position" did in fact become school board members under the new charter. Whereas professionals and big businessmen constituted only 14.3 percent of the 1896 board, in 1897 they made up 83.3 percent of the board. In 1903, Edward Eliot reported that members of the board continued to enjoy high status: "three lawyers of high standing; three businessmen at the head of their respective occupations; two civil engineers, one of whom has a national reputation; a physician; the manager of the leading German newspaper in St. Louis . . . ; a retired railroad capitalist . . . ; and last, but not least, Dr. C. M. Woodward, Director of Manual Training School, and Dean of the School of Engineering and Architecture of Washington University." In 1906, Eliot reassured the Chicago Merchants' Club that the right people were still in control of the St. Louis schools.[65]

In retrospect, the St. Louis reforms were important not so much for making school board membership attractive to "men of standing" as for greatly expanding the power of the superintendent. Indeed, critics of the new charter accused the new superintendent under the new plan, Louis Soldan, of having conspired with the Civic Federation members to create an autocratic regime: "Soldan is supreme. He is a pedagogic Pope, absolutely infallible, unamenable to anyone or anything." In fact, the superintendent did have enormous power of initiative in virtually all matters concerning the schools: the appointment of staff, the selection of textbooks, plans and contracts for buildings, the determination of the curriculum, and normal decisions about everyday running of the schools. "What is left for the school board to do?" asked Edward Eliot. "The answer is: Only those things which lie within the qualifications of men of general intelligence and business ability, not experts in education or construction." In Eliot's view, running schools was a task for experts, while policy questions were few and far between. The superintendent distributed a printed agenda in advance, and the board disposed of it expeditiously. Now and then a board might reject a recommendation of a superintendent, but it was not the business of a member to initiate anything.[66]

During the 1890's, some of the national spokesmen for centralization had suggested actually *eliminating* the school board entirely, the acme of power to the professional. The St. Louis reformers settled for the next best thing: hedging the board and liberating the school manager. They justified this transfer of power not only as a means of eliminating political corruption, but also as an opportunity for expertise and charismatic leadership. Like progressives elsewhere, the St. Louis reformers blended "science" with evangelism, organizational savvy with Horatio Alger mythology. If you give a superintendent full and complete responsibility, Edward Eliot told schoolmen at the NEA in 1905, "under such a system great men could be developed. A railroad president of the highest rank who has attained a leading position while still quite young in years, said to me a short time ago that no one knows what a man can do until he is given the opportunity. It was the principle on which his success had been attained." Similar exhortations permeated the early literature on school administration: the leader was not only the trained expert, but the free-ranging creator, the crusader who inspired his organizational followers. Was the superintendent a man on a white horse or a man on one end of a telephone? If the qualities of charisma and scientific expertise today seem antithetical, or at least jarring when linked together, it is perhaps because it is apparent today how men become shaped by the organizations they inhabit and because it seems increasingly difficult for a single person to transform a bureaucracy. But in the early twentieth century the faith of patricians in the charismatic and scientific captain of education mirrored their worship of the captains of industry and finance who were transforming the corporate economy.[67]

A charismatic man, Alfred Roncovieri faced a hostile audience when he talked to the Commonwealth Club of California on November 14, 1917. The elected superintendent of schools of San Francisco since 1906, Roncovieri realized that not only his position but his whole conception of school politics in a pluralistic city were under attack in this gathering of elite business and professional men and their wives. U.S. Commissioner of Education P. P. Claxton had just completed a survey of the city schools—largely at the invitation of influential laymen—and had concluded that the city should adopt the closed system of the corporate model of school governance. To Roncovieri that represented a repudiation of "our splendid progressive San Francisco system of direct government by the people." It was the right of the people, he said, "to choose their superintendent of schools, the one public official who, through their children, comes nearest to their homes and firesides." In answer to those who claimed that an elected superintendent would necessarily clash with the members of the school board, he replied: "After all, from the clash of ideas among public officials the people get light. It will not do to have too much harmony among public officials." He had been elected, and reelected, he said, because he knew what the parents wanted—had he not listened to them, and addressed them in French and Italian in their colonies? What citizens wanted, and what the teachers gave them, was "honest school work," upholding "the standards of manners, of morals and of real work," not "fads" and "pedagogical experiments" or "showy effects." Differences of opinion there must be in a cosmopolitan city, but the proper way to resolve these was by the give and take of rule by the people, not by edict from the top down.[68]

Until the long tenure of Superintendent Roncovieri—which would stretch from 1906 to 1923—the normal condition of San Francisco school politics had been conflict and instability. In the fifty-three years prior to 1906 there had been twenty-one super-intendents (three appointed and eighteen elected). Urban reformers had tried unsuccessfully in 1883, 1887, and 1895 to change the charter under which the city ran its schools. They finally succeeded in ratifying a new charter in 1898 which attempted to locate full responsibility in the mayor for politics and appointments of staff and to separate "politics and administration." In theory, the new charter allowed voters to determine basic policies at the polls by voting for a strong mayor, while the actual administration of the city's affairs would be in the hands of paid experts. Accordingly, the schools were to be run by a bipartisan board of four directors, appointed by the mayor and each paid $3000 per year, together with an elected superintendent of schools who was an ex officio member of the board.[69]

Although he thought the new regime infinitely preferable to the old corrupt one, Ellwood P. Cubberley wrote in 1901 that the San Francisco plan was unacceptable: "the system is double-headed and certain to result in conflicts. The directors can hardly earn their salaries unless they assume duties which of right belong to the superintendent." An elected superintendent must be a local politician, while the job demanded the best trained person available anywhere in the nation. The board of education should be composed of unpaid businessmen who simply performed minimal "legislative work." The present plan was merely "a stage in the evolution of the city's educational system" toward the corporate model which lay ahead. What was needed now, said Cubberley, was "an awakening of the better elements of the city's population. . . . If a few such clubs as the Merchants, the Unitarian, the California, the Century, and the Association of Collegiate Alumnae were to begin a serious study of the problems, . . . it would in time work à revolution in the management of the public schools." [70]

Cubberley was prophetic, but the revolution took longer than he anticipated. In the spring of 1913 some members of the Association of Collegiate Alumnae, bothered by complaints "that grammar school graduates do not fit into business and commercial houses," decided to organize a "School Survey Class" to study the schools. They invited school officials, education professors like Cubberley, and others to speak, and hired as official investigator Agnes de Lima, who would later win recognition as a publicist for child-centered education. Mrs. Jesse H. Steinhart was the prime mover in the study and in later efforts to reform the governance of the schools. The Association then published a report in 1914 comparing school conditions in San Francisco with those "in other progressive communities" and found the local system sadly wanting.[71]

Within six months of this survey the San Francisco Chamber of Commerce and the San Francisco Public School Society began negotiating with U.S. Commissioner of Education Philander P. Claxton to conduct a thorough examination of the city's schools. The board of education was less than enthusiastic: it insisted on a veto power over any investigator suggested by the U.S. Bureau of Education and refused to pay anything for the report. The manager of the Chamber of Commerce raised the necessary funds through private subscription. The survey commission began its work in 1916. Claxton's chief policy recommendation—to replace the "dual organization" of paid board members and an elected superintendent with the corporate model of control—echoed Cubberley's contention of 1901 that "the system is double-headed and certain to result in conflicts." Indeed, Roncovieri contended that the Claxton study was "trite and general" and that most of it "could have been written without . . . ever visiting San Francisco." Significantly, when Claxton wanted local citizens to verify data in the report, he submitted it not only to school officials but also to the president of the Chamber of Commerce and to Mrs. Steinhart.[72]

School governance was the crux of the argument that followed Claxton's report. To the system of "dual control" of paid board and elected superintendent Claxton attributed "such evils as may exist in the public-school system of San Francisco." Without a "proper official subordination" the teachers and administrators "are constantly in uncertainty as to whether they should regard the superintendent and his deputies or the board of education and its committees as their immediate official superiors." This ambiguity produced "unrest" in both schools and community. Roncovieri and his allies disagreed, claiming that Claxton's surveyors had formed their opinions not from observation of the schools but from conversations and correspondence with a "select few" outside the schools: "certain persons intent on discrediting our schools, and of placing responsibility for what is wrong and what is alleged to be wrong, on certain features of school government which only they desire to change, are using this unjust criticism to prejudice the minds of our citizens." [73]

The members of the local elite who brought in Claxton had reason to believe that he would propose the corporate model of school control, for that had become the conventional wisdom of professional leaders, while Roncovieri and San Francisco educators were out of step. Claxton produced little evidence to justify his charges of "evils" and "unrest," but he devoted eight pages of his report to quotations from experts on "Principles of School Organization and Management." Five of these pages detailed the elaborate analogy between schools and manufacturing corporations written by Franklin Bobbitt of the University of Chicago, concluding that "the principles of good management in the school world are identical with the principles of good management in the business world." Not surprisingly, this ideal appealed to the businessmen and leading professional men in the Commonwealth Club, who applauded a speaker who declared: "The citizens are the stockholders; the board of education are the directors; the superintendent is the technical expert and general manager." [74]

Roncovieri disagreed with the corporate model. A musician rather than a trained educator, a union member active in the Union Labor Party, he saw school politics as a matter of accommodation, controlled conflict, rather than a closed system. It is true that there have been disagreements between the board and the elected superintendent, he said: "Such disagreements were actually foreseen, if not actually desired, by the makers of the charter. . . . With a board which cannot remove the superintendent and a superintendent who cannot remove the board, it is obvious that the outcome of all differences is a full and free discussion and a final settling vote, and the people come into their own and learn the whole truth." He maintained that this was "the American way—and it is a good way!—the only way in which the people come into their knowledge of what is going on, which is clearly their right and due." Such shared responsibility and independence was not a liability but a virtue, Roncovieri argued, for it offered a balancing of power and multiple means of redress of problems.[75]

A pluralistic system of school control matched the pluralistic nature of the city's population, Roncovieri believed. Persons who taught during his years of office were often uncertain about just who *was* superintendent. "Some were quite positive that Roncovieri was 'just another board member,'" wrote Lee S. Dolson in his history of the San Francisco schools, "and that one of the actual members of the Board, who had been supervising their work, was the 'real superintendent.'" Either board members or the superintendent might mediate the cultural conflicts that were bound to arise. A writer in the Catholic *Monitor* described how the system handled a request of a birth-control advocate to teach "sex hygiene" in the schools: "The school board handed her case to Mr. Roncovieri, who, like a gentleman, looked into her methods, and assembled several mothers' clubs to discuss the question. . . . The conclusion arrived at by the teachers, the superintendent, and the mothers' clubs, was that sex hygiene was no subject for children or a classroom, but must be reserved for the parents and the home." [76]

As an elected official, superintendent Roncovieri felt responsible to the entire citizenry, not simply to a business-dominated school board. He was sensitive to the wishes of labor unions, ethnic groups, and religious organizations. He rejected the idea that the purpose of the schools was simply to produce products desired by employers: "We are too prone to judge our children by adult standards. That is particularly true of business men, and it is not fair." In addition, the school should not "be held wholly responsible. The home and the church are just as great factors in the development of the boy's mentality and character." If foreign-born parents wanted their children to study their home language in the public school, that was legitimate.[77]

In 1918 and 1920 proponents of the corporate model of school governance mounted campaigns to persuade the electorate to change the charter by means of Amendment 37, a measure designed to abolish the elective superintendency and to institute an unpaid board of seven lay members appointed by the mayor. The issue provoked sharp class, ethnic, and religious conflict. In favor of Amendment 37 were many of the groups and individuals who had criticized the schools and had helped to invite Claxton: the Chamber of Commerce, the Association of Collegiate Alumnae, and the Commonwealth Club, now joined by other associations such as the San Francisco Center of the California Civic League, the San Francisco Real Estate Board, the City Federation of Women's Clubs, and other high-status organizations. A number of anti-Catholic individuals, convinced that Catholics were running the system, added fuel to the fire.[78]

Ranged against the corporate model of Amendment 37 were a variety of citizens: members of the Teachers' Association, spokesmen of some labor unions, Catholics, Irish, and apparently large numbers of "common men" who resented the drive for power by the elite organizations. In contrast with the cosmopolitan perspective and experience of the elites, they tended to have a local or parochial point of view. In a letter to the *Bulletin,* Matthew Sullivan accused the advocates of trying "to dictate to the common people of San Francisco how they should manage their schools." The members of the Public Education Association, he wrote, are listed in the *Blue Book,* but where among the sponsors do you find laboring men or school people? Angered by charges that the employees of the district were political hacks and by the charter provision that board members could not be chosen from teachers, the San Francisco Teachers' Association protested "the libelous statements published in extravagant and numerous advertisements in the daily papers, paid for by secret influences interested in the passage of Amendment 37." The newspaper of the building trades claimed that the proponents of the measure "believe the people are not intelligent enough to control directly their public schools. They urge that the 'direct control' . . . be given to a 'superman' who, they claim, knows better the educational needs of the people than the people themselves. . . ." It declared that "an unsalaried school board . . . means disfranchisement of the 'common people,' because the great mass of the common people are poor people, and consequently none of them could afford to become members of the school board." The whole affair, said a correspondent in the *Monitor,* "was conceived, born, and nursed in the Chamber of Commerce conspiracy; it is the child of Claxton, and the baby that Mrs. Jesse Steinhart is now showing about in her big limousine is not her own, but another's darling." As soon as men from the Chamber of Commerce enter the board, they will hire "an Eastern, imported, high-salaried 'superintendent' " who will force teachers to "wear the Chamber of Commerce collar." An Irish newspaper contended that the amendment was "engineered by the hucksters, bigots, profiteers, uplifters, sex hygienists and birth controllers who pose as the intellectuals of San Francisco." [79]

When the amendment came to a vote in 1918 and in 1920, Irish districts voted against the measure by a large majority. The amendment failed to pass in 1918—possibly because of the extravagant publicity of the proponents—but on the second time around it passed by a narrow margin. In addition to a resurgence of anti-Catholicism—apparently part of a nationwide campaign—two factors seem to have tipped the balance of votes in the 1920 election: the firing of a school principal, which advocates of Proposal 37 portrayed as a sign of corruption in the system; and the support by certain labor groups that apparently hoped to have some influence over vocational training in the schools. In any case, by November 1920, Cubberley's prediction about a "revolution" in school governance finally came true. [80]

The groups which had actively promoted Amendment 37 now had access to power. Of the seven directors Mayor James Rolph appointed, three were members of the California Civic League; three were leaders of the Jewish community, which had provided much of the impetus behind the reform; and a majority were members of the business elite. After selecting an outside expert as superintendent—Joseph Gwinn, Columbia-trained, who became president of the National Education Association the day he took up the San Francisco superintendency—the board and its manager were ready to translate their theories into practice. For symbolic as well as practical reasons they chose to move headquarters out of city hall into a new administrative building. Soon Gwinn and his cooperative board had set up a new table of organization, collected the multiple facts on which "scientific" education depended, built specialized schools and curricula, shifted the schools to a 6-3-3 plan which included junior high schools, tested and sorted children by IQ scores, and introduced the techniques of business management and modern instruction that were being developed in the university schools of education. Reform from the top down had opened the way for the administrative progressives to transform education in the city of San Francisco.[81]

3. POLITICAL STRUCTURE AND POLITICAL BEHAVIOR

As we have seen, the administrative progressives in urban education put great faith in structural reforms. They believed that centralization and the corporate model not only would put successful men on school boards but would also insure a rational and expert process of decision-making. They normally portrayed their struggle for structural reforms as a contest of unselfish and enlightened citizens against the forces of corruption, inefficiency, and ignorance. Often the rhetoric justifying the structural changes betrayed inconsistency or ambivalence. They praised the democratic purposes of public schooling but sought to remove the control of schools as far as possible from the people. They believed that education should be "scientific," yet their ethnocentrism blurred the line between fact and value when they looked at culturally different groups. Skeptical of social reformers or panaceas in other domains, and conservative in their public philosophy, they nonetheless maintained a utopian trust in progress through structural reforms in education.[82]

"Accountability" was a word they sometimes used to describe their goal; "bureaucracy" was a negative label they pinned on features of the system they wished to change. They deplored the way in which school systems were perforated with lay influences they regarded as extraneous. They wanted to seal the city schools off from "political" forces by remodeling them on the business corporation in which supposedly influence entered at the top and percolated down rather than slipping in through holes in the sides of the organization. Once the system was thus shielded, they thought, it would be possible to pin down responsibility within the organization and to give professionals autonomy within their individual spheres.[83]

When the administrative progressives used the word "bureaucracy," they seemed to mean roughly what Thomas Carlyle connoted when he coined the term in his phrase "the Continental nuisance called 'Bureaucracy.'" "Bureaucrats" were people tied up in their own red tape, eager to avoid responsibility, preoccupied with preserving their own position or power, or so constricted by rules that they could not exercise their professional judgment. The educational results of such traits, they thought, were the lock-step routines of nineteenth-century urban schools. One educator said in 1894 that "in all cities, and most of all in large ones, the tendency toward machinery and bureaucracy is very strong in all kinds of work. It is hard for the individual to exert his force." In a survey of the New York schools in 1911, another reformer said that "the board of Superintendents has become bureaucratic, and hence non-progressive." [84]

What the structural reformers wanted to do, then, was to replace a rather mechanical form of public bureaucracy, which was permeated with "illegitimate" lay influence, with a streamlined "professional" bureaucracy in which lay control was carefully filtered through a corporate school board.

With their great trust in these structural changes, the administrative progressives were often blind to the ways in which older forms of political behavior—both external to the system and internal, among the employees—could creep back into the remodeled structures. Often they also were not aware that astute school managers, like Superintendent Edwin J. Cooley of Chicago, could change the decision-making process without structural changes. Sometimes the approved changes in structure, as in Chicago in 1917, could turn school governance into a nightmare if political conditions were wrong. In their scheme there was little possibility of accommodation between "party bosses" and the benign reform of centralization of control of schools, yet such marriages occurred—for example, in Boston Mayor James Michael Curley found a small and centralized board of education a great convenience when he built his machine. And finally, many of the reformers underestimated the potential for conflict between a superintendent with nearly autocratic powers and his school board, on the one hand, and his staff, on the other. Some of these complex interactions between political structure and political behavior illustrate a problem perennial in educational reform, namely the lure of the structural panacea and the bane of unintended consequences in behavior.[85]

In Chicago the administrative progressives took more than two decades—until 1917—to enact their notions of centralization, and then the reforms boomeranged. Not that the Chicagoans lacked proper advice and assistance. In the 1890's groups like the Civic Federation, the Municipal Voters League, and the Public School Committee (formed in response to Rice's exposé of the Chicago schools) looked to other cities' plans and experience in structural reform. In 1899 the mayor's Educational Commission under the chairmanship of President William Rainey Harper of the University of Chicago proposed the standard centralist changes—small board, strong superintendent, and the rest—and quoted as authorities the familiar roster of Philbrick, Eliot, Draper, Maxwell, Harris, Butler, and forty-four other consultants. In 1906 three elite reformers came to Chicago to tell the Merchants' Club how and what to reform—Edward C. Eliot, key member of the new St. Louis board; James Storrow, a patrician who had been a prime mover in the Boston reforms the year before; and the peripatetic Nicholas Murray Butler. In 1916 a subcommittee of the city council heard advice from experts Charles Judd of the University of Chicago, Leonard Ayres of the Russell Sage Foundation, and superintendents Ben Blewitt of St. Louis, Charles Chadsey of Detroit, Frank Spaulding of Minneapolis. The remarkable uniformity of opinion from all these men indicated that within the directorate groupthink prevailed.[86]

In the state legislature at Springfield elite leaders in the civic organizations and their professional allies lobbied for bills to enact the Harper recommendations in 1899, 1901, 1903, and 1905. Not until 1917 would a centralized bill pass (it reduced the board from twenty-one to eleven members and legally defined increased powers for the superintendent). The scrappy head of the Chicago Teachers' Federation, Margaret Haley, led the assault on the Harper bill in the legislature. She and many of her followers distrusted Harper, who as a member of the school board in 1898 had voted against pay raises and who was, they feared, trying to create a monopoly of teacher training for his department of education at the University of Chicago. Critics of Harper said that he sought "an educational trust" comparable to the Standard Oil of his benefactor, John D. Rockefeller. The women teachers also resented the suggestion in the Harper report that many of the teachers were incompetent and that male teachers should be attracted by paying them higher salaries. But most of all they distrusted giving "one-man power" to a superintendent. Teachers were also understandably upset that Harper suggested paying the superintendent $10,000 at a time when the top teachers' salary was $800.[87]

Failing new legislation, the structural reformers in Chicago sought to change the system by hiring a new superintendent. Butler expressed the belief of many reformers when he told the Chicago merchants that "the greatest force in this world is the force of personal example; and the best school systems that we have had in America have had some great, strong, vigorous human personality to look up to." The reformers' first experiment in charisma was E. Benjamin Andrews, president of Brown University, who replaced Albert Lane as superintendent in 1898 (Harper, then on the board of education, thought Lane lacked formal education; Andrews, who had been president at Denison University when Harper was a professor there, Harper acknowledged as his "intellectual father"). But Andrews failed the test. Teachers came to know him as autocratic "Bulletin Ben," who sent them countless directives, including one telling them not to criticize their superiors. The school board was annoyed when Andrews insisted on "sitting in the front row at its meetings and speaking without being spoken to." Andrews got his walking papers in 1900.[88]

The next superintendent, Edwin Cooley, succeeded in carrying out many of the purposes of the administrative progressives even though he continued to operate under the old structures of governance. When Cooley accepted the position as superintendent in Chicago, he declared, "I will go in as an educator, and not as a politician." That was a politic thing to say. When Cooley's admirers praised him they spoke of his "unusual tact and administrative diplomacy." Diplomat or politician, Cooley knew how to gain and use power to obtain the *results* sought by structural reform without the formal reorganization. In 1902 a newspaper reporter wrote that Cooley "had no rainbow theories about school boards. He knew that a board of twenty-one members, appointed by a mayor largely to accommodate certain geographical, racial, and political considerations, could have no great veneration for educational theories, nor could it be expected to regard the superintendent as an infallible autocrat in school affairs." Cooley knew that most of the important decisions took place in the subcommittee sessions rather than in the full board meetings, which tended to ratify subcommittee decisions and make a show of policy discussion about other matters. Accordingly, Cooley went first to the subcommittees to present a proposal—if they disagreed, he might raise the same issue again in that committee or another—and with this groundwork he won "every proposition" submitted to the board. He gained greater control over the appointment and retention of teachers by making wry use of a resolution passed by the board itself, directing him to "report all political efforts to influence his recommendations." When Cooley announced at an open meeting that eight board members had tried to influence his nominations of teachers, he could hardly be faulted for following orders.[89]

In 1917 the legislature finally passed a bill cutting the board from twenty-one to eleven, providing for appointment of the board by the mayor, defining duties of board and superintendent, giving the superintendent a four-year term, and granting tenure to teachers (which was the main reason the teachers supported the measure). Then came not the "non-political" and rational efficiency sought by the reformers but first anarchy and then boss rule and corruption. William Thompson, who later gained national notoriety for threatening to punch King George of England in the snoot, was in city hall when the task of appointing the eleven new school board members fell to the mayor in June 1917. Although the common council failed to approve his nominations, his board took over and appointed a new business manager and attorney. A year later a court reinstated the old board of twenty-one as the legal governing body, and until October 1919, when the council approved Thompson's new eleven nominees of that year, there was not a legally unquestioned board of education. In the spring of 1919 the board of twenty-one members appointed Charles Chadsey as superintendent, but

Thompson's board locked him out of his office and appointed Peter Mortenson as its superintendent. Although a court found six members of the Thompson board guilty of conspiracy in denying Chadsey his legal position, and implicated Mortenson in their actions, Mortenson was reappointed. With his own board and their man as boss of the schools, Thompson's machine then proceeded to rake graft from the sale of school sites, equipment, and jobs. The custodial engineers, who were key figures in the network of boodle, raised a slush fund of $90,000 for a board member after an increase in their salaries in 1920. In 1921 the board spent $8,714,065 on "incidentals," including "phonographs costing the board $187 each, dear at $40," and unwanted equipment by the carload while teachers had to buy necessary materials out of their own pockets. After a grand jury investigation made such corruption public in 1922, Mayor Thompson lost the election to William Dever, who promised to take the schools out of politics and appointed starchy William McAndrew as superintendent. But four years later, Thompson won again in a campaign which made McAndrew's alleged pro-British sympathies and autocratic traits a prime issue; he then fired McAndrew and resumed his quest for patronage and rake-offs. To please his ethnic constituencies Thompson urged schools to teach children about Irish, German, Polish, and other ethnic heroes, and his board hired relatively large numbers of black citizens as teachers and nonprofessional employees.[90]

Although structural reformers argued that the centralized corporate model could free the schools from the clutches of bosses like Thompson, in practice there was no reason why machines could not take over centralized school systems. Some bosses prided themselves on a hands-off policy, of course, and the insulated character of the corporate model made it possible to designate the schools as off limits if one so chose. Boss William Vare of Philadelphia declared himself "an ardent champion" of the school code "which divorced the schools entirely from politics," boasting that the city "is a great center of education and its school laws are as good as those of any municipality in America." He even urged the nomination and helped secure the election of Martin Brumbaugh as governor of Pennsylvania, he wrote, because of his "splendid success as the Superintendent of Schools of Philadelphia." Similarly, Boss George Cox of Cincinnati "boasted that he had taken the schools and the police departments out of politics." But in Boston, in 1931, in a time when jobs for the faithful were scarce and profits from patronage alluring, Mayor James Michael Curley found it easy to capture the five-person "reformer" board in that city, as did corrupt politicians in Los Angeles in the Depression. Indeed a centralized board and an internal pyramid of power could make it easier for an unscrupulous machine to dominate the schools if the staff acquiesced in stretching the civil service regulations and in awarding contracts to the right people.[91]

Not only organized machines but most city politics relied heavily on ethnic and religious loyalties to win votes. Although to the structural reformers such considerations were anathema—partly because the WASP could be so easily outvoted in the big cities—ethnic factors quickly reentered the arena of school politics when control became centralized and as the corporate model became fashionable. No political structure could negate such deep forces in urban society. In pluralistic cities like New York and San Francisco with boards appointed by mayors, political parties found it essential to balance school board nominations on ethnic and religious grounds. In Boston the largest ethnic group, the Irish-Catholics, won more than 80 percent of the school board positions since 1931, Joseph Cronin reports, for there the elected small board gave their political organization powerful leverage.[92]

Within urban systems different ethnic groups often moved up the hierarchies in succession, strengthening their hold through informal networks of information and influence. These informal lines of communication often coexisted with a firmly held belief in the system of authority and in the merit classifications of the bureaucracy. Thus Peter Schrag found in the 1960's that in Boston all members of the board of superintendents—the top administrative staff at 15 Beacon Street—were Catholics, all over fifty, all but one graduates of Boston College, and all but one Irish—but they praised Boston's "impersonal, objective standards of appointing and promoting teachers, its examinations and point scales, its rigid rules and practices governing advancement within the system." As Schrag observed, the informal network of friends with its fast grapevine often worked better than "the system that some civil service reformer dreamed about a half century ago." [93]

Structural reformers claimed that giving the superintendent a larger and more clearly defined sphere of authority could create a more stable and conflict-free position, according to the norms of the corporate model, but in many cities, both school boards and subordinates resented what they saw as the autocracy of the new captains of education. In Chicago, for example, McAndrew faced unending insurgency and sabotage from angry teachers. Six teachers in Cleveland sought an injunction against Superintendent Frederick when he blacklisted them for organizing a union in 1914. "You are out of harmony with the public, your real employer," the judge told the superintendent. "In your loyal service to your nominal master, the board, you have drifted away from your real master. . . . The system is sick, very sick. Two things only will cure it: light and air, agitation and ventilation." [94]

Superintendent James H. Van Sickle aroused hostility from teachers in Baltimore when he came to the city under a reform charter of 1898. He served an elite new board of education in what he called a "progressive movement." Among his first tasks was firing sixty teachers and eliminating many principals appointed by the previous board. "Mutiny" soon developed in the teaching force, wrote George Strayer, especially in reaction to a new promotional examination run by the superintendent and two appointees. Teachers had to pass this barrier—including "an impersonal test of the correct and effective use and interpretation of English"—before they could advance in salary. Then as now it was easier to talk about merit than to assess it, and teachers organized to fight the superintendent (although some of the "more progressive element," said Strayer, supported Van Sickle). The two largest organizations, the 1000-woman Elementary Teachers' Association and the Public School Teachers Association, headed by a man, both tried to persuade the board to give up the merit scheme. In the spring of 1911 they helped to elect a Democratic mayor, who promptly assembled the school commissioners and told them that more than a thousand of the teachers "have lost confidence in the fairness and good faith of

Mr. Van Sickle, and are in a state bordering on revolt." The new school board fired the superintendent and appointed two of the teacher leaders, both of whom had been charged with "insubordination," to important administrative posts.[95]

Many school board members as well as teachers resisted giving superintendents autonomy to run the schools as they saw fit. The editor of the *American School Board Journal,* William Bruce, bitterly attacked a report by a committee of the NEA chaired by Andrew Draper. Draper's plan would basically have made the school board into a rubber stamp. He charged that committeemen "override and degrade a superintendent, when they have the power to do so, until he becomes their mere factotum." Through cartoons and editorials and letters solicited from subscribers, Bruce attacked Draper and his colleagues as despots. One cartoon portrays "The Modern Feast of Herod" and shows Draper serving up the head of the people in a bowl, declaiming, "a superintendent alone must rule. Henceforth behead all school boards." An article in the same journal in 1916 called "Why Superintendents Lose Their Jobs" described the insecurities of high office and said that *nothing, absolutely nothing, is of more vital consuming interest to the average superintendent of schools than the tremendously important question of whether he will be retained in his present position for the coming year. He knows from statistics, observation and experience that he is in the most hazardous occupation known to insurance executives. . . . No gambling house would be sufficiently reckless to bet on the chances of re-election for school superintendents three years or even two years ahead."* Significantly, the author was an *anonymous* "veteran fighter in the field of American education." [96]

In 1918, elected superintendent Roncovieri told the San Francisco Commonwealth Club that it was futile to suppose that the corporate model would necessarily promote "harmonious relations" between school board and superintendent. "The human equation is ever present, and in so far as San Francisco is concerned no such upheavals have occurred as happened in Berkeley when Superintendent Bunker tried to recall the Board of Education and failed, and in Denver recently when Superintendent Cole succeeded in recalling the members of the Board of Education that were opposed to him." Progressive Superintendent

J. H. Francis was not reelected in Los Angeles when elite factions fought other elite factions in the city in 1914. "Even men like Superintendent Van Sickle, formerly of Baltimore, resigned," said Roncovieri, "rather than submit to being bossed by those who stood over him as members of the Board of Education." One cannot legislate a structure that will ordain harmony, he argued.[97]

Structural reform could offer, then, no sure relief from insecurity of office for the leaders, insubordination by employees, corruption and machine domination, ethnic influence and informal networks of power within the system, or any of the other forms of political behavior that the corporate model was designed to minimize. Structure did count, however, though not always in the manner intended. With centralization and the corporate model in the large cities came the growth of vast and layered bureaucracies of specialized offices, differentiation of patterns of schooling to the specifications of a new "science" of education, Byzantine organization charts, tens of thousands of incumbents protected by tenure, and many people within the city bewildered about how to influence the behemoth that had promised accountability.[98]

PART V

Inside the System: The Character of Urban Schools, 1890–1940

One August day early in the century, Helen Todd climbed the long stairs of a converted warehouse on Lake Street in Chicago. When she reached the attic, the smell of turpentine and the blast of heat from the cement furnace nauseated her. Inside were fourteen girls aged fourteen or fifteen sitting on stools and lacquering canes. After inspecting the room, she sat down to talk with some of them: "How can you stand it here, children?" she asked. "Why don't you little girls go to school? 'School!' cried one who had given her name as Tillie Isakowsky, aged fourteen years and three months, shaking her head until her red bows trembled. 'School is de fiercest t'ing youse kin come up against. Factories ain't no cinch, but schools is worst.' " All over the city in her rounds as factory inspector, Helen Todd heard similar stories. She asked 500 children this question in 1909: "If your father had a good job and you didn't have to work, which would you rather do—go to school or work in a factory?" Of these 500, 412 said they preferred the factory. Bewildered, Todd jotted down their reasons:

"Because it's easier to work in a factory than 'tis to learn in school."

"They ain't always pickin' on you because you don't know things in a factory."

"The children don't holler at ye and call ye a Christ-killer in a factory."

"They're good to you at home when you earn money."

"What ye learn in school ain't no good. Ye git paid just as much in the factory if ye never was there."

In the basement of a building in the stockyards, Inspector Todd stumbled over a thirteen-year-old boy who had huddled there, hoping she would not discover him. He wept bitterly when told he would have to go to school, blurting between his sobs that "they hits ye if yer don't learn, and they hits ye if ye whisper, and they hits ye if ye have string in yer pocket, and they hits ye if yer seat squeaks, and they hits ye if ye don't stan' up in time, and they hits ye if yer late, and they hits ye if ye ferget the page." Again and again she heard the same story: 269 children said they preferred factory to school because no one hit them there. They were more "push-outs" than "drop-outs." [1]

At the turn of the century Chicago was the center of a movement to humanize schooling and to train teachers to understand the natural learning processes of children. The charismatic progressive Francis Parker taught hundreds of teachers at the Cook County Normal School in the years from 1896 to 1899, showing them his techniques for employing the child's curiosity as the easy and pleasant path of instruction. John Dewey was developing his progressive philosophy and practice of teaching at his famous Laboratory School at the University of Chicago. "What the best and wisest parent wants for his own child," he told an audience in Chicago in 1899, "that must the community want for all of its children. Any other ideal for our schools is narrow and unlovely; acted upon, it destroys our democracy." One of Dewey's strongest advocates, Ella Flagg Young became superintendent of the Chicago schools in 1909. Barely five feet tall, a woman of great courage, intelligence, and compassion, she taught teachers about Dewey's "new education" when she served as instructor at the Normal School from 1905 to 1909. Like her friend Jane Addams, she was most concerned about reaching the children of the slums, largely second generation immigrants (67 percent of Chicago pupils in 1909 were children of foreign-born parents).[2]

Obviously there was a gap between what leaders intended and what children perceived.

The view from the top and the view from the bottom sometimes was different in New York, too. Although imposing and stern in appearance, with his frock-coat and walrus moustache, Superintendent William Maxwell felt deeply about the suffering of the poor. He knew that thousands of children came hungry to school each day and that stomach pains gnawed at them as they tried to study; he thought providing cheap lunches in schools the "most pressing of all school reforms." He proudly told of a principal on the lower east side who was so loved and respected that as she picked her way through the crowds and the pushcarts on the street, children smiled at her, older boys tipped their caps, and bearded men greeted her. He helped to install baths in schools so that children who had no water in their flats could get clean. He marveled at the ability of teachers who instructed pupils who could speak no English; in one school alone there were twenty-nine different languages or dialects. He stayed in the city during the steaming summer months partly to encourage those teaching in the vacation schools, where hundreds of thousands of children went voluntarily to learn crafts and nature study. Maxwell told with delight about a little girl, Leah, who invited her teacher home to eat at a table set just like the one in the picture in a magazine her teacher had lent to her.[3]

But for all this dedication, the response from "crowded, ignorant, prejudiced, and highly excitable people" was often distrust. In 1907, Maxwell said teachers in an East Side school faced a riot in which "frenzied mothers and fathers by the thousands besieged the school." The reason: parents thought that "the children's throats were being cut." The school had 150 children whose adenoids were enlarged—a condition assumed to contribute to mental retardation. When eighty parents refused to take their children to clinics to have the adenoids removed, the principal decided to bring in a surgeon to operate on the children in the school. For days thereafter, whenever a health board doctor appeared in the ghetto, "it was a signal for a mob to storm the gates of the schoolhouse." To these Jewish parents the school was capable of genocide.[4]

Different perceptions of urban schools were equally meaningful to different people—to school managers, educational scientists, black parents, first and second generation immigrants, teachers, and the heterogeneous millions of children and youth called students.

For the administrators at the top of city school systems, together with their mentors in universities and lay allies, the years from 1890 to 1940 represented largely a success story whose plot was apparent early in the twentieth century, though details sometimes were in doubt. As Cubberley taught in his popular history of public education, the public school was part of a larger social evolution whose beneficence was not to be doubted by the faithful. Challenges like Americanization of immigrants abounded, to be sure, but the strategies to respond to them were to be found in "science," in administrative efficiency, and professional specialization. For leading schoolmen it was mostly an age of confidence inspired by a dream of social efficiency.[5]

The administrative progressives believed that they knew what was wrong with the old one best system which Philbrick and his peers had labored to create: it was too "bookish," rigid, and undiversified, ill-adapted to the great variety of students flooding the upper grades of elementary schools and the secondary schools and poorly serving the needs of the economy for specialized manpower. The modernized one best system should "meet the needs of the children," but these needs and social demands could be assessed scientifically and the system reshaped accordingly. Intelligence testing and other forms of measurement provided the technology for classifying children. Nature-nurture controversies might pepper the scientific periodicals and magazines of the intelligentsia, but schoolmen found IQ tests invaluable means of channeling children; by the very act of channeling pupils, they helped to make the IQ prophecies self-fulfilling. Likewise, the differentiation of secondary education into tracks and the rise of vocational schooling represented a profound shift in the conception of the functions of universal education.[6]

In one respect, however, the administrative progressives continued and indeed accentuated one of the earlier purposes of public schooling: the Americanization of the foreign-born and their children. In the two decades bracketing World War I, especially, concern for homogenizing American beliefs and behavior reached a fever pitch. Just as it was the educator who decided which differences among children were significant in the tracking of children into a differentiated system, so it was leading schoolmen and powerful native-American interest groups that determined the proper pattern of socialization to American norms. With but few dissenters, policy-makers in these years saw pluralism as a peril.[7]

Although for purposes of official policy pupils were members of a "unitary community" of persons who differed in ways measurable individually by the tester and significant to the psychologically trained counselor or administrator, they were also members of different ethnic and religious and class groups. Just as welfare workers were trained to think in psychological ways and to regard their "cases" as individual problems, so teachers and administrators often came under the spell of the individualistic orientation of the psychologists who dominated educational thought. Educators often failed to see that many problems children faced in school were sociological and economic in character and were, in C. Wright Mills's terms, "public issues" rather than "personal troubles." Early in the century, as now, the culture of the school poorly fit the culture of certain subgroups in the population. That Italian-American children, for example, scored an average of eighty-five on IQ tests and dropped out of school in droves indicated not a plethora of individual problems but a mismatch of institutional demands and group norms and behavior. To explore this phenomenon it is useful to look at two groups—Italians and Jews—who differed markedly in their response to schooling.[8]

It makes little sense to malign the intentions of schoolmen in their campaign to differentiate the structure of schools, to classify students, to socialize in uniform ways. With but few exceptions their motives were good, their belief in the objectivity of their "scientific" procedures manifest, their achievements in the face of massive challenges impressive. But some unforeseen consequences of administrative progressivism become most clear when one looks at the educational experience of those citizens at the bottom of the social structure, in particular those who became victims without "crimes," black Americans.[9]

The changes in schooling affected teachers as much as students. As persons in the middle of the growing school bureaucracies, teachers were often restive. When they became better educated and learned a rhetoric of professionalism, they more and more objected to being functionaries. As they seized power here and there in their unions and professional associations, they demanded greater security, autonomy, and pay. Women, especially, gained new assurance and won equal pay and greater influence. But the tensions of being "professionals" at low levels within hierarchical organizations persisted, largely unresolved.[10]

1. SUCCESS STORY: THE ADMINISTRATIVE PROGRESSIVES

Looking back in 1930 on the previous quarter century in city school administration, George D. Strayer of Teachers College, Columbia, saw twenty-five years of steady progress. The keys to this success were "the application of the scientific method" and "the professional training of school executives," he believed. At the beginning of the century "a relatively powerful and able group" of administrators had been dubious about the benefits of educational science, he said, but by 1930 almost all influential schoolmen had become converts. The results were everywhere apparent: "better organization of the administrative and supervisory" employees into line and staff categories; the differentiation of the "traditional elementary school and senior high school" into institutions like junior high schools, vocational schools, and junior colleges that "provide unique opportunities for boys and girls who vary greatly in their ability to acquire skill and knowledge"; grouping of pupils by scientific tests; the expansion of high schools with multiple tracks until they enrolled 50 percent of students of high school age; extensive revision of the curriculum; the keeping of detailed records on students, from IQ's to physical history and vocational and recreational interests; and rapid upgrading of the standards of training for all professional personnel. The principle underlying such progress was "recognition of individual differences" and the consequent attempt "to adjust our schools to the needs and capacities of those who are registered in them." [11]

Statistics revealed the magnitude of the transformation and

A New York Elementary Classroom, 1942

suggested the character of the challenges schoolmen faced as education became increasingly universal through the high school years. The costs of city schools in 1910 were twice as high as in 1900, three times higher than 1890. From 1890 to 1918 there was, on the average, more than one new high school built for every day of the year. Attendance in high schools increased during that period from 202,963 to 1,645,171, an increase of 711 percent while the total population increased only 68 percent. The curve of secondary school enrollment and graduation continued to soar: in 1920, 61.6 percent of those fourteen to seventeen were enrolled, and high school graduates represented 16.8 percent of youths seventeen years old; in 1930, the figures were 73.1 percent and 29 percent; in 1940, 79.4 percent and 50.8 percent. As these statistics suggest, during the first two decades of the twentieth century compulsory schooling laws were increasingly effective. From 1900 to 1920 educators became less am-

183

A New York High School Classroom, 1938

bivalent about coercion than they had often been during the nineteenth century. Gradually school accommodations began to catch up with demand, the size of classes diminished, and the gospel of social efficiency helped create a commitment to universal education as an achievable goal. State aid increasingly was tied to average daily attendance, and thus stimulated the pursuit of truants. School leaders joined muckraking journalists, foes of child labor, and elite reformers in political campaigns to translate their concerns into compulsory schooling and child labor laws. In part as a consequence of the new laws, school systems developed new officials whose sole purpose was to insure universal attendance (usually to age fourteen). Members of these new bureaucracies—school census takers, truant officers, statisticians, and school social workers—became experts in "child accounting." [12]

As city systems grew in size and bureaucratic complexity, the number of specialized administrative offices and administrators expanded dramatically. In 1889 the U.S. Commissioner of Education first included data on officers "whose time is devoted wholly or principally to supervision." The category was new enough to cause confusion—and indeed statistics on the number of administrators and their nonteaching staffs are still hard to determine. That year 484 cities reported an average of only 4 supervisors per city. But from 1890 to 1920 the number of "supervisory officers" jumped from 9 to 144 in Baltimore, 7 to 159 in Boston, 31 to 329 in Detroit, 58 to 155 in St. Louis, 235 to 1,310 in New York, 10 to 159 in Cleveland, and 66 to 268 in Philadelphia. Robert and Helen Lynd pointed out that in 1890 in Middletown the superintendent was the only person in the system who did not teach, but by the 1920's there was between the teacher and superintendent "a whole galaxy of principals, assistant principals, supervisors of special subjects, directors of vocational education and home economics, deans, attendance officers, and clerks, who do no teaching but are concerned in one way or another with keeping the system going." Problems were met "not by changes in its foundation but by adding fresh stories to its superstructure." [13]

Schoolmen created special programs for retarded, deaf, blind, delinquent, gifted, anemic, and other groups of children, and specialized tracks and schools for vocational and other special training. With such differentiation came dozens of new job categories, programs of professional preparation, and many new bureaus and officials. Specialists of all sorts formed their own professional associations: superintendents, secondary school principals, elementary school principals, counselors, curriculum directors, vocational education teachers, high school teachers of art, music, English, social studies, and many others. Together with the rapidly expanding college and university departments and schools of education, professional associations helped to persuade state legislatures to pass laws requiring certificates for the various specializations. Replacing the earlier licenses based on examinations, the new certificates were based on completion of professional training and legitimized specialists by *level*—kindergarten, elementary school, junior high school, high school, and so on—and by *function*—principal, guidance counselor, school librarian, supervisor, or teacher of vocational subjects, and so forth. In 1900 only two states had specialized credentials; by 1930 almost all states had elaborate certification laws. In the

decade following 1912, fifty-six cities created research departments that kept track of the new credentials and bureaus, tested
the "intelligence" and achievement of pupils, helped to channel
students, and amassed statistics for "child accounting" and business management.[14]

In the half century following 1890, then, there was a vast
influx into urban schools of youth who previously might have
gone to work or roamed the streets, pushed into the classroom
by child labor laws and compulsory attendance or attracted by
new curricula, activities, and facilities. At the same time, the
structure of urban schools became enormously complex and differentiated for diverse groups in the population.

Differentiated education was not a new phenomenon in city
schools, of course. We have seen that schoolmen sometimes
treated groups like the Irish poor or black children in a manner
different from the mainstream of children in the common
school. But the goal of uniform education had been an attractive
one in the nineteenth century both for practical and ideological
reasons. Many of the innovations designed to offer differentiated schooling in the nineteenth century stemmed not so much
from career educators as from wealthy philanthropists, merchants, and industrialists. Influential lay people, for example,
founded private kindergartens for poor children in cities as far
apart as Boston and San Francisco; in a number of cities they
privately funded the first public trade schools and commercial
high schools, as well as "industrial schools" for the children of
the poor; they supported the first program of vocational guidance; they created "parental schools" and other institutions for
truants and pre-delinquents; and they sometimes subsidized municipal research bureaus, which were the forerunners of research departments of city school systems. Through these programs the elites sought to reach children bypassed by the public
schools or to provide skills or services absent in the one best system. Thus kindergartens or industrial schools had taken children off the slum streets; commercial or trade schools had
taught skills which industrialists or merchants wanted; vocational
counselors in settlement houses had helped boys and girls find
jobs. Piece by piece such new agencies were added to the public
school structure.[15]

School Board Journal

Founded March 1891 by WILLIAM GEORGE BRUCE

Volume XLVII, Number 6

DECEMBER, 1913

Subscription, One Dollar per Year

APROPOS OF RECENT SCHOOL SURVEYS

Survey Experts: Double, double toil and trouble;
Fire, burn; and, cauldron, bubble.

A Critical View of School Surveys

But the administrative progressives were not content with piecemeal reform, however much they might agree with the specific changes pioneered by lay elites. After all, the corporate model of school governance was predicated on the idea that experts should design and run the system. Education professors like Strayer, Judd, and Cubberley were training superintendents at Columbia, Chicago, and Stanford. The new "school executives" were taking control of big cities and the professional associations. Together they were developing new strategies for public schooling as well as differentiated structures. A group of such educational leaders formed the "Cleveland Conference," which agreed at a meeting in 1918 that the time was ripe for "a radical reorganization" of schooling and concluded that changes would "go on in the haphazard fashion which has characterized our school history unless some group gets together and undertakes in a cooperative way to coordinate reforms." [16]

The administrative progressives were convinced that "traditional education"—the old one best system—was profoundly anachronistic and flawed. In their journals, they attacked the old uniform curriculum, the undifferentiated structure, the recitation methods, and the skimpy training of teachers typical in nineteenth-century city schools as rigid, unscientific, wasteful, and inhumane. They were evangelists for new educational goals of science and social efficiency. They still wanted a one best system, but it was to be a more complex, differentiated organization adapted to new social and economic conditions.[17]

Social efficiency demanded a new relationship between school and society. The administrative progressives believed that the schools should better prepare students for the tasks they would face in life. To them the old idea that a common school grounding in the three R's would suffice for any career and that public education could train any boy to be President of the United States was clearly absurd. Cubberley wrote that urban schools should "give up the exceedingly democratic idea that all are equal, and that our society is devoid of classes," and should adapt the school to the existing social structure. "Increasing specialization . . . has divided the people into dozens of more or less clearly defined classes," he wrote, "and the increasing centralization of trade and industry has concentrated business in the hands of a relatively small number. . . . No longer can a man save up a thousand dollars and start in business for himself with much chance of success. The employee tends to remain an employee; the wage earner tends to remain a wage earner." It was clear that "success is higher up the ladder now than it was a generation ago, while the crowd about the bottom increases every year." Simple realism decreed that the public schools should prepare some students directly for subordinate roles in the economy while it screened out those fit for further training in higher education. As we shall see, the "science" of psychological measurement would enable schoolmen to retain their traditional faith in *individual* opportunity while in fact the intelligence tests often were unintentionally biased against certain groups.[18]

The vocational education movement clearly expressed the type of reform Cubberley had in mind. During the nineteenth century some educators regarded industrial education as appropriate for low status people, and they experimented with different versions of skill training in reform schools and in institutions for black and Indian youth.[19] But specific vocational preparation spread to other segments of the population, especially when private donors founded commercial and trade high schools in large cities. In city after city businessmen decided that the regular school curriculum did not provide skills they needed in industry or commerce. They gave large sums to establish special schools; in New York, for example, J. P. Morgan endowed the New York Trades Schools with $500,000. By the early twentieth century most such commercial and technical schools founded by philanthropists had been absorbed into the public system, and businessmen in the National Association of Manufacturers and Chambers of Commerce were calling for greatly expanded vocational instruction in urban schools. By 1910 the movement had won broad support, with endorsements from the NEA and the American Federation of Labor (which had long been suspicious of the trade schools as sources of scab labor, but which apparently joined the movement in the hope of sharing in its control and improving the earnings of skilled labor). By 1918 the advocates of vocational training helped to secure federal funds through the Smith-Hughes Act.[20]

As Norton Grubb and Marvin Lazerson argue, the vocational

education movement was significant not so much for the numbers of students who actually enrolled in industrial curricula or courses—normally under 10 percent—but because it represented an increasing conviction "that the primary goal of schooling was to prepare youth for the job market" and that the way to do this was through vocational guidance and testing, junior high schools, and differentiated curricula. Most arguments over the character of vocational education concerned who should control it—the existing school boards, or new governing groups—and whether industrial schools were "simply a mechanism of social class stratification offering second-class education." By and large educators successfully fought separate boards of control, and instead they included vocational schools, tracks, or courses within the comprehensive system. The question of stratification proved more complex, as the vocational program often became a dead-end side track for lower-class youth.[21]

William H. Dooley, principal of Technical High School in Fall River, Massachusetts, described in 1916 how industrial education could serve the student he described as the "ne'er-do-well" (educators have been prolific in names for the "laggard," "slow learner," "retarded," "reluctant," "hand-minded," "disadvantaged," child who does not fit the system). Dooley maintained that schooling should be mostly adapted to the 85 percent of pupils who would become workers in industry and commerce and who were in danger of becoming cogs in the machine. Untrained, such people might become technologically unemployed, a condition that "breeds discontent that threatens the existence of our government." The old patterns of learning to work on a farm or through apprenticeship no longer worked for city children, nor did the older forms of moral socialization operate effectively. Now a child might wake up in the morning to find his parents off to the mill, go to school dirty and hungry, and "spend the day and evening on the streets, with the result that the dormant vicious tendencies are allowed to develop instead of being stifled by proper parental influence." Schools that teach an abstract curriculum and promote students on the basis of a literary test fail the "motor-minded" child. An efficient school, on the other hand, will measure and account for every child, providing different opportunities depending on his or her needs.

"Unskilled and socially inefficient" children of new immigrants constituted a particularly troublesome subset of the "ne'er-do-well" class. It would be unwise to forbid such children to work in factories between the ages of fourteen and sixteen, thought Dooley, for "they have descended from ancestors who mature early in life and have intensely practical ideas, and therefore should develop useful industrial habits during the early part of adolescence." It is only misguided "groups of social workers in this country attempting to tear down our institutions" who would force "unjust legislation on the community, such as compulsory full-time education for children up to sixteen years of age or over." No, what these children need is the industrial discipline of a job supplemented by a vocational part-time school. However harsh Dooley's attitude may appear today, his concern for the millworker's child was genuine and his proposal for a continuation school was at least an advance over a ten-hour day of unbroken drudgery.[22]

Not all administrative progressives agreed with Dooley's particular specifications for the proletarian child or with Cubberley's open avowal of class-based education, of course. But the underlying principle of differentiating schooling to meet the needs of different classes of pupils—as determined by the educational expert in the light of the presumed career of the student—almost all would have accepted. This was the heart of the doctrine of social efficiency. It was partly for this reason that the educational sociologist David Snedden so admired the experiments possible in reform schools, for there the experts had a preselected population over whom they had virtually total social control.[23]

The school survey became a favorite technique to spread the program of the administrative progressives. Hollis Caswell reported that there were sixty-seven surveys of city school systems by outside experts published during the period from 1910 to 1919 and 114 in the years from 1920 to 1927. During the first years of the survey movement it was common for laymen in elite organizations like a Chamber of Commerce to bring in experts to point out faults in the schools and to propose the corporate model of reform. This gave administrative progressives an opportunity to castigate "traditional education" and the village model of school governance, but it was a bit hard on incumbent board members and school employees.[24]

Two such surveys were one conducted under the direction of Harvard's Paul Hanus in New York City in 1911–12 and the study of Portland, Oregon, written by a task force under Cubberley and published in 1913. The Hanus staff claimed that the uniform curriculum in New York represented the "idealism" of an earlier time and was quite out of place under modern economic conditions. The surveyors claimed that mental independence became a form of insubordination and that the hierarchy had created "bureaucratic control all along the line," from the superintendent on down, rather than professional "cooperation under leadership." Principals and supervisors were mere inspectors, certifying compliance with the rules; most teaching, not surprisingly, was mechanical.[25] In Portland Cubberley's team found similar conditions. They concluded that "the most fundamental principle observed in the conduct of the Portland school system is the maintenance unchanged of a rigidly prescribed, mechanical system, poorly adapted to the needs of either the children or the community." Since both principals and teachers had no chance to make decisions, the result was "a uniformity that is almost appalling." The curriculum was "vivisected with mechanical accuracy into fifty-four dead pieces." Because authority was so diffused in the board's subcommittees, the superintendent was reduced to a drill sergant.[26]

The script was a familiar one, and insulted superintendents like New York's Maxwell and Portland's Rigler could justly claim that the "experts" had made up their minds before coming, that they had misinterpreted what they saw, and that they had neglected many achievements of recent vintage. Because of some of the early attacks on traditional educators by administrative progressives, surveys earned a bad reputation in some quarters, especially among those superintendents, like Rigler, who were deposed. But as the movement matured, it became increasingly a device for "progressive" superintendents to enlist the aid of outsiders to make changes they wanted anyway. By the late 1920's most of the superintendents not only survived the surveys but applauded them. When Leonard Koos sent inquiries to twenty-five superintendents whose cities had been surveyed, fourteen of the eighteen who replied said that they favored the studies.[27]

Supporting the survey movement was a network of university professors, administrative progressives in the city school systems, the U.S. Bureau of Education, lay reformers in civic organizations, and foundations. Rockefeller's General Education Board set up its own division of school surveys, which did studies of Gary, Indiana, and several states. The Russell Sage Foundation supported numerous surveys, including one comparing "efficiency" of education in the forty-eight states. The Cleveland Foundation backed a large-scale study of schools in that city. In 1917 a writer in the annual report of the U.S. Commissioner of Education commented that in doing surveys "private philanthropy has taken the initiative, as so often, in doing work for which the Government was not yet ready," but added that the Bureau of Education was by then ready to perform that service. For a brief period the Bureau and state education departments conducted the most surveys, but by the early 1920's the customary agency was a special bureau for survey research located in a college of education.[28]

Raymond Moley reported that more than three-quarters of the recommendations of the Cleveland education survey were rapidly put into effect. Caswell found that many innovations favored by the administrative progressives were incorporated in city systems after surveys, often as a direct result of the study. Table 2 indicates some of these changes as reported by superintendents in fifty cities, and together they constitute an index of the program and priorities of the administrative progressives. The administrative progressives saw success in such statistics and good reason to believe that their influence on the structure and processes of American urban education was growing. Few were the voices raised in public dissent against their general program. And the administrative progressives found articulate allies across a wide political spectrum.[29]

In the *New Republic,* the liberal intellectual Randolph Bourne applauded Cubberley's Portland survey, saying that "it stirs enthusiasm because it shows the progress that has been made in clarifying the current problems and the ideals which must be realized if the public school is to prepare the child of to-day for intelligent participation in the society of which he will form a

Table 2. Changes in school systems of fifty cities after surveys

Change	Following Survey (%)	Direct Result of Survey (%)
Clearer definition of duties of board and superintendent	46	57
Abolition or reduction of standing committees of board	34	53
Hiring of personnel only on recommendation of superintendent	34	53
Addition of specialized administrative staff	54	44
Adoption of improved system of pupil records	62	42
Adoption of improved financial accounting	56	36
Increase in per-pupil expenditure	64	28
Improvement in qualifications for teachers	62	45
Increase in teachers' salaries	74	35
Adoption of ability grouping	52	38
Reduction in percent of overaged pupils	66	36
Reduction in percent of failure	64	31
More frequent use of standardized tests	60	40
Revision of curriculum	68	47
Curriculum differentiated for slow and fast pupils	50	32
Courses added to curriculum	48	38

Source: Caswell, *City School Surveys,* 60–72.

part." Traditional education in Portland, he wrote, "seems more like the ritual of some primitive tribe than the deliberate educational activity of an enlightened American community," yet precisely that is "the type that still prevails in the majority of our cities." [30]

Scott Nearing, a professor of economics who would soon be fired for his liberal views, was as impressed as Bourne with the program of the administrative progressives. In his book *The New Education* he described the changes in the Cincinnati schools wrought by Superintendent Dyer and his staff. Dyer, he said, tried the radical experiment of trusting his principals and teachers to adapt the curriculum to the children. "Up here on the hill, in a wealthy suburban district," Dyer told his staff, "is a grammar school. Its organization, administration and course of study must necessarily differ from that other school, located in the heart of the factory district." It was up to the principals to adapt the school to the people.

What this might mean became clear in the Oyler School, on the wrong side of the railroad tracks and surrounded by factories and little houses. There the principal appealed to the factory owners to support a manual training program. Later with the help of Dyer he set up pre-vocational programs in which "subnormal" elementary pupils could spend a whole day a week, while others spent a smaller proportion of their time in shop work and domestic science. The boys turned out marketable products in workrooms patterned on real factories. A manufacturer told Nearing that he supported the schools gladly because they made good citizens and because he believed "that the material prosperity of a people is directly related to the mental and manual equipment of its people." At the Oyler School the principal worked through the mothers' club to change patterns of child-raising and to upgrade the appearance of the neighborhood. Discipline problems vanished, more children went to high school, the school became a center of "community"—it was Nearing's model of the "new education." [31]

Then as now, personal concern and energy could sometimes transform a school and thereby change the lives of children. For writers like Nearing and Bourne, who lived by words, rhetoric like "meeting the needs of children" and "cooperation" distinguished the new education from the old and predisposed them to praise what they called "progressivism." They saw a challenge to the schools in the new floods of children entering classrooms, a crisis of urban community, a traditional education that had outgrown its inspiration and calcified its routines.

But "progressivism" in education was a label that was loosely applied to diverse reformers, philosophies, and practices. I have argued in Part IV that one wing of reformers, whom I have called "administrative progressives," constituted a political-educational movement with an elitist philosophy and constituency. They tried to transfer control of urban education to a centralized board and expert superintendent under a corporate model of governance. Within the system they focused upon differentiating the structure and fulfilling the goals of social efficiency and social control. Thus they were primarily concerned with organizational behavior and the linkage of school and external control, with aggregate goals rather than individual development of students.

These administrative progressives had little in common in aim either with the small libertarian wing of educational progressivism or with the small group of social reconstructionists who dreamed in the 1930's of using the schools to construct a new social order. In some ways the forerunners of A. S. Neill and the free school advocates of today, the libertarians sought to make the school conform to the trajectory of the individual child's growth. They drew on Freud and avant-garde artists and intellectuals to criticize the repressiveness of the traditional school structure and curriculum and to urge the individual self-expression of the child instead. The social reconstructionists—whose ideas were stated most forcefully by George Counts in *Dare the School Build a New Social Order?* (1932)—argued that schools should undermine the capitalistic system by instilling left-liberal ideology in schoolchildren. Although their writings are fascinating to read, the libertarians and radicals had little practical impact on urban schools.[32]

The administrative progressives found little admirable in either of these versions of educational progressivism. They did, however, often pay attention to innovations advocated by philosophers, psychologists, and curriculum theorists in schools of education, who translated John Dewey's ideas into classroom procedures. These "pedagogical progressives" spoke about the "project method," the "activity curriculum," and other ways to "meet individual needs" of children by subverting the hegemony of established school subjects. The curricular reformers who advanced such ideas normally took the hierarchical structure of differentiated schooling as a given and concentrated on inspiring the teacher to change her philosophy, her curriculum, and her methods in the classroom. In the hortatory, individualistic style of these pedagogical progressives there was little threat to the established power of the school managers; indeed, as David Swift has said, by promoting more subtle techniques of teaching students and less overt control of teachers, the "new education" probably made both more tractable. And the broadened views of what should be learned in school made schoolmen less accountable for Philbrick's old goal of inculcating "positive knowledge." [33]

It was difficult, indeed, to express the spirit of John Dewey's version of cooperative, democratic schooling within a hierarchical bureaucracy, and for the reason Dewey stated in 1902: "it is easy to fall into the habit of regarding the mechanics of school organization and administration as something comparatively external and indifferent to educational purposes and ideals." We forget, he said, that it is such matters as the classifying of pupils, the way decisions are made, the manner in which the machinery of instruction bears upon the child "that really control the whole system." It was no accident that when Dewey and his daughter Evelyn described teachers who exemplified his ideals of democratic, active education in *Schools of Tomorrow,* they concentrated on small and private schools rather than large and public systems. A gifted teacher in a one-room country school house might alone turn her class into Dewey's model of social learning, but changing a large city system was more difficult, for Dewey's ideas of democratic education demanded substantial autonomy on the part of teachers and children—an autonomy which, as we shall see, teachers commonly lacked. Predictably, the call for a "new education" in urban school systems often brought more, not less, red tape and administration, more forms to fill out and committees to attend, more supervisors, new tests for children to take, new jargon for old ideas. The full expression of Dewey's ideal of democratic education required fundamental change in the hierarchical structure of schools—and that was hardly the wish of those administrative progressives and their allies who controlled urban education. As Robert and Helen Lynd concluded in their report on abortive "progressivism" in Middletown, "in the struggle between quantitative administrative efficiency and qualitative educational goals . . . the big guns are all on the side of the heavily concentrated controls behind the former." [34]

2. SCIENCE

When Alfred Kazin returned to the Brownsville neighborhood in Brooklyn where he grew up, the sight of the school reminded him "of those Friday morning 'tests' that were the terror of my childhood." Self-effacing parents yearned to hear of "every fresh victory in our savage competition for 'high averages,' for prizes, for a few condescending words of official praise. . . ." On the teacher's desk sat the "white, cool, thinly ruled record book" in which all defects of character were entered, all percentages averaged, all merits duly noted, "columns and columns in which to note everything about us, implacably and forever." [35]

At about the same time, in 1922, John Dewey reflected on the meaning of the constant testing, categorizing, and competition he saw around him. "Our mechanical, industrialized civilization is concerned with averages, with percents. The mental habit which reflects this social scene subordinates education and social arrangements based on averaged gross inferiorities and superiorities." The school system was becoming a vast filtering system, he feared, unaware of its own biases: "we welcome a procedure which under the title of science sinks the individual in a numerical class; judges him with reference to capacity to fit into a limited number of vocations ranked according to present business standards; assigns him to a predestined niche and thereby does whatever education can do to perpetuate the present order." [36]

From different perspectives, Kazin recalling his childhood and Dewey speaking as social philosopher, each was responding to a function of schooling that was gaining greater importance: educators were increasingly serving as the gatekeepers to opportunity. In this task schoolmen turned more and more to "scientific" measures of ability and achievement. What they sought was a technology which would enable them to differentiate children, for selection was prerequisite to specialized treatment. Through such a technology the needs of the student, the needs of the educational system, and the needs of the larger society could be more precisely calibrated and the connecting parts more smoothly meshed.[37]

One of the first questions to occupy the minds of educational scientists was the high rate of "retardation" (or students who were over-age or repeated the same grades) and "elimination" (or children who left school). In an age that worshipped efficiency, over-aged students and school leavers were signs of malfunction that required analysis and correction. Besides the waste of money and effort, forcing children to repeat grades was inhumane. "They are thoroughly trained in failure" by such a procedure, wrote Leonard Ayres: "under our present system there are large numbers of children who are destined to live lives of failure. We know them in the schools as the children who are always a little behind physically, a little behind intellectually, and a little behind in the power to do. Such a child is the one who is always 'It' in the competitive games of childhood." [38]

Beginning in 1904, Superintendent Maxwell of New York printed tables indicating that over a third of the children in the elementary schools of the city were over the normal age for their school grade. "How vividly do we recall the attention which Dr. Maxwell's figures attracted," wrote an educational statistician. The news spread fast by word of mouth, was published in magazines and newspapers, and quoted at conventions. "One superintendent could whisper to another, 'Have you heard of the awful conditions in New York? Forty percent of the children are too old for their grades!' With Pharisaical satisfaction yet gravely as befitted the sad occasion, the other would reply, 'Yes, the school conditions in New York are very bad; but then you know what you must expect when politics run the schools.' " After shaking their heads over Tammany, superintendents would then go home confidently to "collect the information as to the ages and grades of the pupils under their care. Whereupon, like as not, in one community after another a solemn hush ensued." In most cities failure in school was a way of life for vast numbers of children.[39]

In 1908, Edward T. Thorndike had aroused the alarm of citizens and the ire of superintendents with his study "The Elimination of Pupils from School," which concluded that almost half the pupils entering school did not reach the eighth grade. The next year Leonard Ayres's book *Laggards in Our Schools* used sober statistics to analyze this dramatic problem. With a generous definition of "normal age"—two-year spans, starting with six-to-eight-year-olds for the first grade—Ayres showed a remarkable decrease in the number of children in each elementary grade from one to eight. Chicago, for example, had 43,560 pupils in first grade, only 12,939 in the eighth. Even with allowances for the absolute increase in population of younger children and cumulative child mortality among the older, the rate of elimination and retardation of children was staggering. Ayres estimated that about 33 percent of all pupils were "laggards": promotion rates varied in cities he studied from 71 percent in Kansas City to 84 percent in Chicago. "The general tendency of American cities is to carry all of their children through the fifth grade, to take one-half of them to the eighth grade and one in ten through high school," Ayres concluded.[40]

Ayres found no clear explanation for the different rates of failure in the different schools. Illness, irregular attendance, late entrance, inadequate compulsory laws or lax enforcement all contributed their part. Some immigrant groups had higher rates of "retardation" than "Americans," but some foreign groups had lower. Pointing out that nationwide there were "more illiterates proportionally among native whites of native parents" than among the children of immigrants, Ayres took basically a wait-and-see attitude toward the question "Is the immigrant a blessing or a curse?" He noted that there was little correlation between the retention of pupils and the number of foreign-born citizens in a city.[41]

While ethnic differences in retardation and retention were cloudy, he found clear sex differences: 13 percent more boys repeated grades than girls, and 17 percent more girls completed elementary school. *"These facts mean,"* said Ayres, *"that our schools as at present constituted are far better fitted to the needs of the girls than they are to those of the boys."* [42]

As a statistician, Ayres believed that one prerequisite to reform was "a better knowlege of the facts." It was scandalous, he thought, that "in hardly a city in the country can the school authorities tell how many pupils begin school each year, or how fast they advance, or what proportion finish or why they fall out, or where or why they lose time." In addition to better "child accounting" Ayres advocated stronger compulsory education laws and enforcement, more thorough medical inspection, flexible grading, and "courses of study which will more nearly fit the abilities of the average child." While here and there he dropped a hint that the reason for failure lay within the child, Ayres mostly blamed educational systems which taught children to fail.[43]

The revelations of Ayres, Thorndike, and others came at a critical point for urban schoolmen, for costs were mushrooming and criticisms of public schools were heard on every hand, especially from business groups. To retain children for two years in the same grade occupied scarce classroom space and cost additional teacher salaries. The drop-out figures startled even well-informed schoolmen. In 1908 Andrew Draper, then Commissioner of Education for New York state, confessed that he had "assumed that practically all of the children who do not go to the high schools do finish the elementary schools." All over the country commentators called the elimination of pupils a sign of inefficiency. "Those of a more gifted imagination have seen in . . . [these statistics] evidence of a conspicuous failure of our schools to accomplish the purpose for which they are designed," wrote Ayres, "while those more cautious by nature have not hesitated to make it a reproach upon certain cities that their upper grades contained relatively fewer pupils than those of other localities." It had been common in the nineteenth century for schoolmen to regard a relatively low rate of promotion to high school as a symptom of high standards, and hence good schools, but that changed with the unfavorable publicity. The fact of high rates of over-aged or "retarded" pupils was not a new phenomenon—indeed in six cities Ayres studied retardation was lower in

1906–07 than in 1895–96 (31.6 versus 39.9 percent)—but by 1908 it became a problem because of new public awareness and criticism and new conceptions of schooling.[44]

"Retardation" was manmade, of course, an educational artifact. The classification of pupils was not divinely inspired or imbedded in the order of nature; much less were the curriculum and standards of promotion unalterable. Even before Ayres's study many educators had criticized the existing system for sorting and advancing pupils as rigid and inhumane. It was, they thought, a procrustean bed in which the wits of the slow student were unduly stretched and the interest of the quick pupils amputated. Children entered a grade, were exposed to its uniform curriculum, had their performance assessed, and either passed to the next grade or stayed behind. A crude sort of winnowing took place, a kind of survival of the fittest in which the academic proletariat was *lumpen* at the bottom and the talented rose. Many school people believed that they must devise new and better ways of adapting the school to different kinds of children and of sorting heterogeneous children more intelligently into a differentiated school structure.[45]

A New York district superintendent, Julia Richman, described in 1899 both the pedagogical problem and her response to it. She pointed out that the armies of "hold-overs" commonly repeated the class they had taken previously, mixed together with a miscellaneous assortment of bright and average children. Normally they did not catch up even then: "they remain unambitious and apathetic, and in schools where the ability of the pupil to answer a fire of questions is the gauge of the teacher's success, they constitute the most unwelcome element in every class." Richman's solution was to divide the children on the basis of teachers' recommendations and examinations on the standard curriculum into "the brightest material," "medium material," and "the poorest material." She told the teachers in each sorted class to adapt the pace of instruction to the capacity of the pupils. Accordingly, no children simply repeated material they had already studied at the standard rate. She found that this step toward tailoring instruction to the child resulted in more sympathetic and effective teaching and a much higher rate of promotion. "I see my bright children no longer handicapped in their onward march," she concluded; "I see my slow ones eagerly reaching out to grasp the patient, helping hand. I see them all believing in themselves, and at last growing thru self-help and self-development." In 1903 she turned her attention to the 1,719 children in her district who would not complete fourth grade by the time they reached fourteen and were eligible to apply for job permits. These were often children who had just arrived in the country, or who had been turned away from overcrowded schools, or "whose minds were spoiled" by poor teaching. She realized that many of these students had "developed a street shrewdness which makes it absurd to give . . . training designed for the baby mind." The best teachers should be assigned to special classes for these students and alerted, said Richman, to detect the reasons for retardation and to find appropriate remedies.[46]

Despite the efforts of educators like Richman, the situation in New York had not much improved by 1922, when superintendent William L. Ettinger called on his staff to face the facts. That June, 83,000 out of 716,000 pupils were not promoted. About 46 percent of all students were retarded, 20 percent for one term and the rest for two or more. There was enormous variability in ages of pupils in a given grade and in the percentage of over-age students in a given school. Such figures, he argued, proved the failure of the "classification on the basis of unstandardized, informational tests" which formed the rationale for semiannual promotion. There was light on the horizon, however, for "the rapid advance in the technique of measuring mental ability and accomplishments means that we stand on the threshold of a new era in which we will increasingly group our pupils on the basis of both intelligence and accomplishment quotients and of necessity, provide differentiated curricula, varied modes of instruction, and flexible promotion to meet the crying needs of our children." [47]

The problem Ettinger described was genuine enough, and given the almost evangelical faith in science of many educators, it was natural that they would turn for a solution to the newly developed technology of group intelligence tests. It would be far better, thought the administrative progressives, to be able to identify the able, the normal, and the slow from the start, to provide them with appropriate instruction, and by secondary school to sort them out according to their likely careers.

In World War I came an important breakthrough in this process of differentiation. Like urban schools, the army then faced a mass of humanity which it was expected to train and then to place in different slots in a complex organization. A group of leading psychologists gathered to develop group intelligence tests which could classify recruits. Prior to that time there had been some preliminary work on group IQ tests, based partly on the work of Alfred Binet, but here at the beginning of the war was an opportunity for a mass experiment. In a little over a month the psychologists wrote and field-tested the examinations. The resulting Alpha and Beta tests were given to 1,726,966 army men.[48]

At first the testers expected that they could identify only those at the two ends of the intelligence spectrum—the unfit and the leaders—but as they investigated the validity of the test, they found that there was a high correlation between the test score and an officer's rating of the efficiency of a soldier in his position. As Joel Spring points out, the chief validation of the test was an officer's assessment of "practical soldierly value." Hence the tests became increasingly used to fit individuals into specific jobs. In short, the tests had *consequences:* in part on the basis of a short group examination created by a few psychologists in about a month, testee number 964,221 might go to the trenches in France while number 1,072,538 might go to offices in Washington.[49]

But results of the tests had other consequences as well. They seemed to prove that the social order was close to a meritocracy since the fittest seemed mostly on top. They helped to fix on the mass institutions of education, civil service, and business narrow standards of what constituted ability. All this was no malevolent plot. In the war the psychologists were men trying to make democracy work efficiently in what they believed was a great cause. They saw themselves as scientists and on occasion changed their minds when evidence proved them wrong in their assertions and assumptions. They even had their moments of utopian dreaming of a smoothly running, conflict-free society where talent rose and ruled benignly. But the effects of their technology of objective discrimination need to be assessed as well as their intentions.[50]

In 1923 one of the original creators of the army tests, Carl Brigham, wrote *A Study of American Intelligence,* which analyzed ethnic and racial differences in "intelligence" as judged by data from the tests. He found what he thought was conclusive proof that "representatives of the Alpine and Mediterranean races are intellectually inferior to the representatives of the Nordic race." At the bottom of all white groups were black Americans. The mixing of genes from Europeans of poor stock was bad enough, he said, but "we must face a possibility of racial admixture that is infinitely worse . . . for we are incorporating the negro into our racial stock." Low scores of southeastern Europeans on the army tests confirmed WASP belief in the immigrants' inferiority and gave powerful arguments to those Congressmen who voted to discriminate against them in the immigration restriction laws of the 1920's. The tests appeared to give scientific validation to garden-variety social prejudice.[51]

It was, of course, relatively easy to disprove Brigham's shaky "science," and to his credit he disavowed his own interpretation in 1930. Studies which grouped scores by states, for example, showed that the predominantly "Nordic" white soldiers from the South "made the lowest scores of any registered by white soldiers in America"—and Negro soldiers from certain northern states scored well above whites from certain southern states. Another critique of Brigham's assumptions matched army Alpha scores by states with the Ayres index of efficiency of schooling in these states and found a coefficient of correlation of .58. Clearly something more than genes was at work.[52]

For the most part, the scores in the army Alpha tests correlated well with the prestige and pay of occupations in the occupational world. Accordingly, the army test experience prompted school testing experts to urge the use of IQ scores in vocational guidance and in the assignment of students to lanes leading to different careers.[53]

It was this long-range selection function of the schools that most interested Professor W. B. Pillsbury of the University of Michigan. He recognized the defects in existing tests and admitted that psychologists "have only the vaguest notion of what intelligence is." Nonetheless, he argued, men differed enormously in their mental ability. "If we have a body politic in which only fifteen percent of the citizens can be expected to make any important contributions, and possibly not more than half are able to understand clearly the real problems of the state," he asked rhetorically, "have we the machinery for selecting the men who are best fitted for the higher grades of work, or are we allowing our best to waste time with unimportant affairs while lesser intelligences are struggling vainly with the great problems?" Supposedly the function of the schools was to create intelligence rather than to discover it, but given the great importance of heredity, he thought, schools mainly winnowed out the "incompetents" and rewarded the "competent," but they did this inefficiently. Better testing would allow them to perform their sifting scientifically.[54]

Such meritocratic proposals, however, were of less interest to urban school officials than were the practical tasks of classifying the millions of heterogeneous pupils gathered in classrooms by compulsory education. And to those children, the debates over the validity of IQ measures meant less than the way the tests were used in their everyday lives. To illustrate: one could say that threading a needle in three seconds is a test of intelligence and then deal with children on the basis of their performance. Whether the test had any validity as a test of "innate mental ability" or not, it would surely have consequences for the pupil—and those consequences could feed back to the child in such a way as to fulfill the prophecy made by the test.

Prior to the army tests, mental examinations were often popularly associated with disordered minds—feeble, sick, in some way peculiar (Binet had first designed his individual examination to discover feeble-minded children). But during the war, magazines and newspapers carried favorable accounts of the army testing program and helped to convince parents that there was nothing abnormal about their children being tested.[55]

In 1921 the president of the National Association of Directors of Educational Research observed that educators quickly seized on the new group intelligence tests as a means of sorting children for instruction: "Teachers, administrators, and supervisors . . . have received the adaptations of the group intelligence examination to school uses with open arms and all too often with uncritical acceptance of what has been made available." Tests became a fiscal bonanza for their makers. When the army tests were first opened for "commercial distribution the publishers accepted the offer as an adventure, printing a lot of 10,000." But when a group of psychologists revised the army scales for school use, under a grant from the General Education Board, 400,000 copies of the resulting "National Intelligence Test" were sold the first six months on the market. A year later Lewis Terman reported that there were a dozen group tests available for all levels of the educational system and estimated that not less than two million children were tested in 1920–21; shortly, he said, "we may expect the number to exceed five millions." [56]

Indeed, as Paul Chapman has observed, the IQ testing movement swept the nation as an educational crusade, often starting from university centers like Columbia and Stanford. Articles and books glowed with testimonials of principals and teachers about the value of the tests. "The importance of this new psychological tool for the improvement of school administration has been recognized everywhere," wrote Terman, "with a promptness which is hardly less than amazing." Terman felt it necessary to warn against false hopes: "the over-enthusiastic will gradually learn that not even the universal use of intelligence tests will bring us to an educational millennium." [57]

School people did admit that sometimes parents were unhappy about the way their children were classified. One director of testing thought that the task of dealing with parents was best delegated to teachers because "many parents are more willing to comply when the decision appears to have been made by the teacher" rather than "handled by an impersonal system operated in some central administrative office." In point of fact, however, it was often the central research bureau that gave the tests and segregated the children, and "for the sake of uniformity" the director thought that teachers should have a document outlining official policy and giving canned answers to objections from parents. [58]

Sometimes teachers were skeptical, too. In Los Angeles "the task of converting these 'sinners' " fell to a principal who sought to convince them that tests were not "composed in the darkroom of a rat-infested laboratory by some 'exchange professor' who could not speak English." One of the main selling points to teachers was that the impressive and seemingly objective numbers used in IQ and standardized tests made it easier to convince irate parents that their child's mark in a class or the grade placement was fair.[59]

The early advocates of using IQ tests in school administration urged that they be employed to segregate students by ability, to aid in vocational guidance, to detect unusually able or retarded students, and to diagnose learning problems. In 1925 the U.S. Bureau of Education told how 215 cities used intelligence tests (35 of these cities had populations of 100,000 or more). The *group* IQ tests were most heavily used in the elementary grades, and there primarily for administrative purposes: 64 percent of the cities used these IQ tests to classify students into homogeneous groups (62 percent used them to supplement the teachers' estimates of ability); 46 percent used them to diagnose the causes of pupils' failures as opposed to 19 percent to diagnose causes of success; tests were more often used to compare the efficiency of teachers or of school systems than to guide changes in curriculum or methods. In junior high schools and high schools group tests continued to be used to organize classes by ability, but they also became important in guiding students in the choice of courses and careers. Cities employed *individual* intelligence tests largely to diagnose serious learning problems and to sort out subnormal children. In 1926 a U.S. Bureau of Education survey discovered that 37 out of 40 cities with populations of 100,000 or more reported that they used ability grouping in some or all elementary grades and a slightly smaller percent used ability grouping in junior and senior high schools. As Terman had predicted, the intelligence testing movement was transforming administrative practice in urban schools. In 1932, three fourths of 150 large cities reported using intelligence tests in assignment of pupils.[60]

What this meant in practice we can examine in case studies of individual school systems. One of the first cities to use IQ tests in massive reorganizations of the schools was Detroit. Detroit had been a leader in standardized testing in such subjects as mathematics. The large staff of the Psychological Clinic of the Detroit schools—eleven psychological examiners—developed and tested a new intelligence examination for six-year-olds in the spring and summer of 1920. In September of that year they gave it to 11,000 children entering first grade. On the basis of scores on that test they divided the pupils into three groups: X, the top 20 percent; Y, the middle 60 percent; and Z, the bottom 20 percent. The Y group then pursued the regular curriculum while the X group had an enriched course of study and the Z group a simplified one. Since tests supposedly measured "fundamental differences in native ability," the Detroit testers were confident that the intelligence test was an invaluable "instrument of *classification;* it establishes the intelligence-group to which the pupil will almost surely be found to belong and in which there is every reason to believe, other things being equal, that he will do his best work." [61]

Terman thought that an experiment in classification by tests in Oakland, California, was "the best hope for a satisfactory solution of the problem of individual differences" in educational administration. His student Virgil Dickson was director of research in that city and carried out a massive program to differentiate students through testing. In a study of why children failed to be promoted, Dickson concluded that "mental tests given to nearly 30,000 children in Oakland prove conclusively that the proportion of failures due chiefly to mental inferiority is nearer 90 percent than 50 percent." The obvious solution, he said, was to track students, and "it was the invariable testimony of teachers in charge of special limited classes, where pupils of similar mental ability have been grouped together, that these pupils behave better, work better, and accomplish more than they did under the former classification with the regular grade pupils." Dickson's rule was to "find the mental ability of the pupil and place him where he belongs," which meant in practice to direct him into one of five tracks from "accelerated" to "atypical." The standards for placement were based on the student population of the whole city, so that one school in a poor part of the city had more than 50 percent of students in "limited" (or slow) classes and only a rare child for an accelerated class, while another in a rich neighborhood had more than half in fast classes and only 3 percent in a limited class.[62]

Since "pupils of inferior intelligence" were "the ones who drop out" of the junior high school grades, special tracks were devised for them which would give them "instruction aimed definitely toward civic and social relationships required of useful members of society" and hold them in school by offering them vocational training in subjects like sheet metal work, agricultural work, sewing, and cooking. Removing these pupils "from the regular classes relieves both the teacher and the class of a great weight." Dickson said that this "policy of segregation" should continue in senior high school since secondary education faced the responsibility "of 'educating' a large number of pupils who are of high school age but are admittedly unable to cope with the requirements of the standard high school curriculum." Such a "system is more democratic than former systems," he concluded, "because it offers to every child a freer opportunity to use his full capacity." [63]

Dickson quoted some reactions of administrators and teachers to the new system. The assistant superintendent in Oakland praised the new system of mental testing as "the most important factor in effective educational administration that has been introduced in recent years" and "a prime agent for educational efficiency and economy." A principal thought it a great advantage to "segregate the slow, misfit children." A teacher commented in language reminiscent of a religious revival that "tests have thrown floods of light on problems that have hitherto baffled me. I have felt my way in darkness as to what should be done in many cases. Now I proceed with more light." The new plan even created some humorous moments, Dickson said, as when a substitute teacher unaware of the changes took over fast and slow English sections. "It was a school joke until the end of the second day, when she reported, 'There must be some mistake, because all of the "stupids" seemed to be in one class.' " [64]

Some smaller cities joined the testing movement with fervor equal to that of Oakland. Superintendent C. R. Tupper of Miami, Arizona, a copper-mining city of 10,000 inhabitants, was bothered by the high rate of retardation of pupils and hired a tester from Stanford to give group intelligence tests to all children in the second through eighth grades. When the results were assembled in charts in colored inks, Tupper discovered that "there was practically no retardation"—that is, children were actually performing at their mental level (or in other words, the fault lay not in the teachers but in the genes of the children). Half of the pupils were of Mexican background; for the most part these were the pupils who tested low, did poorly in school, and dropped out early. The obvious solution was to create a special vocational curriculum for Mexicans in their segregated classrooms.[65]

Energetically, Tupper undertook "a 'selling campaign' . . . subsequent to regrouping, in order to make the program 'stick.' " He held teachers' meetings in which he quoted "the opinions of leading educators . . . in order to acquaint them with the trend of expert opinion." He emphasized that teachers' judgments tended to be subjective and told them "that it is a part of every teacher's professional duty to become familiar with the nature, purpose, and use of tests." He fed articles to the newspaper which showed that the new method of grouping resulted in "a very considerable saving, both financial and human." He spoke to the Rotary Club with illustrations on multicolored charts. He maintained that the plan of grouping children by "homogeneous mental development" and giving them a "diversified course of study adapted to class groups" was the only way to cope with "the shifting nature of the school enrollment and . . . the wide diversity in ability, mental development, character, social position, and previous training of the cosmopolitan enrollment in the Miami schools." He did not say how the Mexican population reacted to the new way to meet "individual differences." Professor Terman was pleased with Tupper's "initiative and courage." [66]

In another small city, another superintendent was putting mental tests to work to differentiate his school system, using much the same pattern that Tupper followed: hiring an examiner, making the charts, setting up tracks, revising the curriculum. He found some interesting correlations between ethnicity and ability. The children of immigrants constituted 63 percent of the pupils in the slow track, 36 percent in the normal group, and 26 percent in the fast. Some parents objected to the classifications, but did not protest to the officials; that's just what you would expect, said the administrator, from parents who "do not come to the schools and learn what is being done *for their chil-*

dren." Teachers were generally pleased with the plan, he said, although they should be rotated out of the slow classes "for a year or two in order to relieve any strain that might result from continued work with defective children." [67]

"Defective children" was the theme of much research into the relation between ethnicity and intelligence done after the supposed revelations of the army tests. In a study of schoolchildren of Italian, Portuguese, and Mexican extraction in San Jose, California, and neighboring communities, Kimball Young clearly showed where the hereditarian view of "inferior races" could lead in education. Young proposed to determine whether the poor showing of these "Latin" pupils in schools was "due: (a) to their alleged language handicap, or (b) to the lack of native mental endowment." Since he believed that IQ tests did by and large validly indicate "native mental endowment" and that general intelligence was transmitted by heredity "and hence exist[s] *relatively* independent of the effects of environment," his task was simple. He only had to demonstrate that the "Latins" were far behind grade level proportionately, and that their IQ scores were low. Having shown this to his satisfaction, and having convinced himself that the disparities were not accounted for by differences in languages, he then turned to the implications for the schools.[68]

Here he encountered a problem: the traditional rhetoric had stressed a common school, with common learnings; the new rhetoric of the testers talked of *individual* differences as the key to differentiation; but Young had apparently discovered inerasable *ethnic* disparities. He fudged: "the problem for the school administrator is not fundamentally one of race but of the educability of all the pupils with whom he deals. Of course, if the bulk of the mentally retarded in any given school system, such as San Jose, turn out to be of Latin stock, then in one sense the question does involve racial differences." Whether residence here will raise intelligence or not, immigration will bring "retarded material which the public schools have to handle," and educators have no choice but "to care for the on-coming generations from these inferior stocks" already here. A new set of policies must grow from studies of intelligence and consideration of "what the children of the present will be doing in later life in industry or agriculture or business." [69]

Young then outlined what such a new policy for San Jose might look like. All children would take group intelligence tests and be assigned to classes according to ability. A new research director should be appointed to supervise the work. The first need in curriculum revision was to prepare "children for their proper economic life activities in accordance with their abilities," also giving them "the intellectual and moral heritage of the past . . . so far as they can assimilate it." The public must abandon "the ideal that education wipes out all differences . . . and the older notion of Plato . . . that education is for selection." It was clear that the Latins would mostly be made of iron, the gold composed of more favored stocks. Young suggested that educators investigate how colonial groups "of like racial extraction" were being trained "in the Philippines, Hawaii and Porto Rico." [70]

On a note of uplift Young urged schoolmen in San Jose to use the school as a means of building a sense of community and of rehabilitating "those social values upon which our political structure rests." There, he said, people can come to "learn anew the human values of neighborhood co-operation and common purpose." [71]

A man who could write that "the original American settlers in the Santa Clara valley were almost entirely of North European ancestry"—surely a surprise to the Mexican Californios—could not be expected to realize that the "Latins" had their own deep loyalties of family and community. Furthermore, as Leonard Covello and other writers have shown—and as we shall examine later—there was often a profound dissonance between the values and mores of the Italian or Mexican family or youthful peer group and the behavior rewarded in school. Indeed, the Italian girl who did *not* leave school to help the family was often regarded as selfish; the Italian boy who tried hard to please the woman teacher was often ridiculed by his friends; for both, the school might lead nowhere desirable. The routine competition according to impersonal norms in school, the kind of quick, abstract verbalism often rewarded there, the kind of knowledge and skills sampled on intelligence and achievement tests—these often seemed part of an alien and unattractive world to the kinds of immigrants' children who did poorly on intelligence tests.[72]

Of course not all educators and surely not all citizens fell in line with the intelligence testing movement in the schools. Especially in the 1930's, school people began to attack homogeneous grouping as an undemocratic practice. They also urged, and used, measures other than IQ scores to sort children. A professor of educational psychology at the University of Minnesota warned that credulous educators accept "mental tests as a mysterious instrument with which they are able within thirty minutes to judge a high school pupil's value to society." "It is not possible, I think," wrote Walter Lippmann, "to imagine a more contemptible proceeding than to confront a child with a set of puzzles, and after an hour's monkeying with them, proclaim to the child, or to his parents, that here is a C− individual." Such a process would be not only contemptible but inane, Lippmann thought, for "all that can be claimed for the tests is that they can be used to classify into a homogeneous group the children whose capacities for school work are at a particular moment fairly similar." There was nothing wrong with using the tests to fit the child into the school, he thought, but the broader social implications of the movement alarmed him. "If, for example, the impression takes root that these tests really measure intelligence, that they constitute a sort of last judgment on the child's capacity, that they reveal scientifically his predestined ability, then it would be a thousand times better if all the intelligence testers and all their questionnaires were sunk without warning in the Sargasso sea." [73]

It was precisely the broad potential uses of tests that deeply antagonized the members of the Chicago Federation of Labor. In 1924 the Federation issued a slashing report on testing that attacked in particular the use of tests in vocational guidance. Ever since the psychologists had discovered correlations between IQ scores and occupations in the army tests, experts like Terman had repeatedly suggested that data on "intelligence" be used not only for classifying students into homogeneous groups but also for channeling them into curricula, for occupations could be ranked by the intelligence needed, from professional and business on down to unskilled labor. The members of the Federation reacted bitterly to the application of this channeling by IQ: "the alleged 'mental levels,' representing natural ability, it will be seen, correspond in a most startling way to the social levels of the groups named. It is as though the relative social positions of each group are determined by an irresistable natural law." The Chicago school research department added figures showing that the scores of children pursuing the different curricula did match the levels required in the occupations to which the schooling led, with two-year vocational students on the bottom. "The selection of courses," said the Federation statement, "is naturally determined very largely by the social and economic status of the pupil." Poor children can only afford to go to secondary school for two years, while well-off parents can send their children to college. "Here again the so-called 'mental level' ascertained by the 'intelligence tests' corresponds in an astounding exactness with the social and economic status of the family," said the unions. "Has a new natural law been discovered which binds each individual to a place in society and against which struggle is hopeless?" In the testers' claims the Federation saw nothing new, but rather "the ancient doctrine of caste." It said that "developments in other cities show the classification of pupils into so-called 'superior' and 'inferior' groups, the former of which are encouraged by official 'counselors' to go on into the high school while the latter are advised by these 'vocational counselors' to end their school life at the age of fifteen years when the average child graduates from 'junior high.' " Labor saw this as a "brand of inferiority . . . placed upon all productive workers through the medium of propaganda emanating from the public school." [74]

As rhetoric escalated on both sides in the 1920's, scholars developed a more sophisticated understanding of "intelligence," but schools went on making discriminations between pupils through testing. Sometimes these discriminations were subtle and designed to diagnose and prescribe for individual children with severe learning problems. Some lower-class children did well on the IQ tests and were encouraged to continue their schooling into college; the tests may well have promoted social mobility for such high performers. There were, indeed, complex problems of classifying students for a differentiated school structure, and quite probably subjective judgments by teachers would have been at least as questionable as the supposedly objective intelligence tests. But perhaps the most significant result of the testing movement was that the notion of great and measurable differences in intellectual capacity became part of the conventional wisdom not only of school people but of the public—a development so pervasive in its influence that it is exceedingly difficult to perceive today how people conceived of differences in cognitive performance before scientists taught us to think of this as a function of "intelligence." Even if the scientists' ideas about "intelligence" were entirely capricious—which they surely were not—the testing movement in the schools would have had enormous effects because of the way in which scores influenced the behavior of professionals and the self-concept of the children who lived in classrooms.[75]

The problem with the discriminations schoolmen made was not that they paid attention to differences, but that their technology of testing was limited in scope. They so often confused individual variation with gross social inequalities associated with poverty, oppression on the basis of color, or other features of the multiple subcultures of a highly plural society. "Is the place of the so-called lower classes in the social and industrial scale the result of their inferior native endowment," asked Terman, "or is their apparent inferiority merely a result of their inferior home and school training?" This was a view from the top down, the very way of phrasing the question implying a standard that the *tester* could determine. In Michigan a psychologist noted that Italians who worked in grim conditions in mines scored unusually low on IQ tests. "The employers of labor in these locations recognize the low mentality of their employees, and one of them stated frankly that men of higher intelligence would not remain in the location because of the character of the work." Why did their children score low on tests? Different people had different answers. The easiest answer to social injustice was to blame the victim.[76]

3. VICTIMS WITHOUT "CRIMES": BLACK AMERICANS

"If every child who fails of promotion were coated in black," wrote Oakland research director Virgil Dickson about "mental tests and the inferior child," "we would have at least one out of every four thus labeled before the first grade had been finished." By the sixth grade "more than one half of our children would thus have earned a coat of black, many of them several coats." To have been *born* black was normally to have been labeled a failure—an inferiority all too often justified by a bogus science— as millions of Negro children learned in school systems which were consciously or unwittingly racist. Black Americans arrived in northern cities in large numbers at a time when centralization had undermined ward school politics, when educators were increasingly empowered to make classifications of pupils according to *their* notion of what was best for the client, when the results of biased tests were commonly accepted as proof of native ability, when those in control of schooling generally agreed that the function of schools was to sort and train students to fit into the existing order, and when much writing in education and social science tended to portray black citizens as a "social problem," linked in research and library classification schemes with delinquency, prostitution, and disease—when they were considered at all. Sociologists often saw blacks as cripples. Thus it was no accident that a leading northern educational statesman would write, as we have earlier seen, that segregated schools might be wise for "defective, delinquent, or . . . negro" children. Indeed, while northern white educators wrote copiously about immigrants, the administrative progressives were, for the most part, strangely silent about black children. The inferior status of blacks was a fact of life to which the schools in their "realism" must adjust.[77]

When a number of black educators bitterly attacked such acquiescence to racism, they were joined by a few white allies who refused to believe that the promise of American education did not extend to Negroes. Indeed, such leaders believed that the victimization of blacks presented an agenda for reform, not of education alone but of the entire society. The normal rhetoric of "democratic education" sounded weird when set against the social reality the black child knew. "As long as Negroes are the victims of lynching, police brutality, disfranchisement, residential covenants, higher rents, segregation, unsanitary living conditions, meager recreational opportunities, and other forms of discrimination," wrote one educator, "the social-civic aim of education is defeated." Doxey Wilkerson, one of Gunnar Myrdal's staff members, argued that the task of "differentiating" education for black children was to discover what Negroes should *know* and *do* about such injustices as job discrimination, economic exploitation, denial of civil liberties, high rates of disease and death, stereotypes of inferiority, and inadequate opportunities for education.[78]

Such a militant use of schooling won few converts in the years from 1890 to 1940, however. Three studies by educators on the "adjustment" of schools to the black community reveal more common ways of translating the success story of the administrative progressives into an appropriate form of Negro education. In 1921, Berlinda Davison studied the schooling of blacks in the San Francisco Bay region. She found that all but a handful of the 393 Negro men in her sample were working at unskilled jobs as laborers, janitors, porters, and the like, but 18 percent of these had attended high school and 9 percent went to college. Among those who had attended college were eleven common laborers and twenty-three others in blue-collar occupations. The number of years of education had little correlation with the type of work the black men pursued, and skilled workers were rarely able to follow their trades because of discrimination in unions. After giving such proof that years of schooling did not pay off for the fathers, she went on to urge that all children be given intelligence tests to see if they were qualified for "(1) professional classes, (2) semi-professional classes, (3) ordinary skilled workers, (4) semi-skilled workers, (5) unskilled workers." After talking of the poverty and multiple problems children faced simply to survive, she accounted for the high number of over-aged children by their "low mentality," quoting Dickson's doctrine that "there is one cause of retardation that is preponderant and that cause is low mental level." In the teachers' comments explaining the failure of the black children, again and again the phrase "low mental level" cropped up, nudging "laziness" and "indifference" as favorite labels.[79]

In 1928 a Cincinnati principal, Mary Holloway, studied how to relate her junior high school to a black community characterized by "low economic status . . . crowded living conditions, false standards of conduct, and general lack of intelligence." One important task, she thought, was proper guidance about sex, since over half the girls first learned the facts of life from friends, meaning that "but a small minority have a sane, healthy attitude toward the subject because of a lack of scientific knowledge and terminology on the part of the informants." In other ways, too, the school should guide the morals and mores of the girls, acting *in loco parentis*. But "realism" was the order of the day in fitting children into the economy. She advocated Terman's plan of using IQ tests to give proper vocational guidance and felt that students should give up the idea of becoming nurses since the local training schools discriminated against blacks. The best job available to most black girls was domestic service, but even here whites were taking over the field. "While racial prejudice is given by the negro girl as the cause for this discrimination, they themselves are often at fault. The great gap existing between their home environment and the one in which they seek to find employment, is possibly the greatest handicap in qualifying for efficient domestic service." Hence the school should remedy that cultural deprivation and fit the girls to work for rich folk.[80]

In 1920, Philip A. Boyer tried to apply "the principles of efficiency underlying scientific management in industry" to a Philadelphia elementary school that enrolled almost 80 percent black children. He felt it unnecessary to adapt the school to the Caucasian children since they were "representative of average middle-class whites. Special treatment . . . has therefore been regarded as unnecessary." Blacks, however, were different: the "excess of females in the negro population" and the large proportion of unmarried men present "difficult social and moral problems"; housing was unsanitary, and crowding and lodgers created moral dangers; 58.3 percent of Negro women worked, thereby disrupting home life; "studies of the psychology of the negro point to a somewhat lower than average mentality, less subject to the inhibitions of the higher mental powers"; and the "social life of the negro is too much outside the home." It was hard to get the children to come to school because of the "indifference of parents," an opinion "often acknowledged by them without the least concern." But truant officers persisted, serving 174 notices of prosecution on parents and actually indicting fifty-five. These black parents were partially responsible for the 42 percent of children who were over-age, since they were likely to "permit or encourage irregular attendance at school." Nonetheless, a school social worker, Boyer said, "has done much to improve home conditions in order that a satisfactory basis for successful school work can be established." He then went on to recommend that the school classify pupils more carefully by ability and institute opportunity classes and ungraded work, stressing pre-vocational skills and proper attitudes. Most important "the work of the school should be punctuated throughout with such *moral* attributes as regularity, punctuality, responsibility, neatness, accuracy, tenacity of purpose, truthfulness, honesty and purity of thought and action." The end result would be a community school " 'Vitalized' and 'Magnified' " which would "become the great democratic socializing agency." [81]

Although Boyer and some of his fellow educators were sincerely concerned abou the "Negro problem," their response was not to try to use the school to expose and correct the racism of American society but rather to "adjust" the black child to the white middle-class norms educators accepted unquestioningly. At the same time, their trust in the statistics on "retardation" and in intelligence tests made them locate the cause of school failure in the child or in his family and neighborhood. The classification of Negro children often reflected these same assumptions. In Cleveland, for example, 25 percent of the children assigned to "special classes" for defective children in 1923 were black, even though in theory mental retardation was equally common among whites. Likewise, 50 percent of all work permits issued to Negro girls in that city were marked "retarded," signifying that the students had not "passed the seventh grade by reason of mental retardation." By contrast, only 4 percent of all native-born white children received "retarded" work permits. In the Kinsman School twenty-four black children were absent in 1930 because they had no shoes, twelve for lack of clothing. Coming mostly from terrible schools in the South, they struggled against great odds to keep up with their age-mates. Black children were refused entrance to commercial and academic schools because of low scores on IQ tests even when their grades were superior; one administrator told a Negro mother that a high score was necessary "to keep the lower elements out." [82]

Educators puzzled about what sort of vocational training to give to black students. In the theory accepted by many of the administrative progressives, the school system sorted out students by ability and probable careers and educated them accordingly. This presupposed an economic order that would be open to talented recruits from the lower ranks of society; indeed, the notion of a school-filtered meritocracy was becoming the twentieth-century version of the earlier self-made man ideology. But for blacks such a system mostly did not work, since racism in the unions of skilled workers and in white-collar occupations tended to exclude Negroes. The job ceiling kept blacks mostly in unskilled, hard, dirty, dead-end occupations that no one else wanted.

Were schoolmen simply to accept the low job ceiling as a given and to prepare Negroes to be good janitors and housekeepers? If so, how much and what kind of schooling did a janitor really need? Or was it the duty of schoolmen to open up new career opportunities for black graduates, to perforate the job ceiling to let talented individuals slip through? Or did such piecemeal progress simply postpone the major reconstruction of society that would create genuine equality for blacks and other dispossessed groups? During the years from 1890 to 1940 some schoolmen adopted each of these alternative ways of coping with the relation of schooling to employment for black students, but most appear to have accepted the racism of unions and employers as a fact they could do little about.

A number of observers in the early twentieth century believed that the occupational level of blacks in northern cities had declined rather than advanced in the previous half century. Many former slaves and free blacks were skilled craftsmen who were barred from their trades by unions or by industrial developments that made the crafts obsolete. In a number of cities immigrants cornered a large share of occupations formerly available to Negroes, such as catering, barbering, and the more skilled forms of domestic service. A black principal in New York, William Bulkley, observed that "if a boy . . . wants to learn a trade he must commit a crime," for only in a reformatory could a black child acquire a manual skill since in business he "runs sheer up against a stone wall." Bulkley and some allies among Negroes and white liberals formed an organization to create new job opportunities for blacks in the city (this group became the forerunner of the National Urban League).[83]

But the task of overcoming prejudice was enormous. In 1915, a social investigator reported that in New York "there was a general belief among school principals, social workers, and colored clergymen that the restriction of industrial opportunities because of their race was sapping the ambition of the colored boys and girls, and that they were not making the effort put out by their parents and grandparents to secure an education." Again and again principals told her of their failure to place highly qualified black graduates in positions as clerks, machinists' apprentices, dressmakers and in other trades.[84]

As Negro enrollment in high schools soared in the 1920's and 1930's, and as the practice of vocational guidance became more firmly institutionalized in urban schools, a number of studies examined the connection between schooling and vocation for blacks. Literacy among blacks increased from 42.9 percent in 1890 to 90 percent in 1940; Negro high school enrollment jumped from 19,242 in 1917–18 to 254,580 in 1939–40 (an increase from 1.6 percent of total black enrollment to 10.5 percent). In a study of about 20,000 black high school graduates and nongraduates, a U.S. Office of Education expert on Negro education, Ambrose Caliver, found that the more schooling a black person achieved, the more dissatisfied he was with his job. The reasons for this are not far to seek: study after study showed that black students aspired to professional or other white-collar occupations that were closed to all but that small number who could make a living serving the needs of the black community or who could find one of the relatively few jobs available in the civil service.[85]

In Minneapolis, for example, there were no black counselors for Negro children, and white counselors had little knowledge of the "job outlook for Negroes." The career choices of Negro schoolboys in that city differed sharply from the actual patterns of employment of black men: 58.6 percent of the male students chose professional jobs, whereas only 4.4 percent of men were so employed in 1935; 70.1 percent of Negro employees worked in unskilled jobs, whereas only 2.5 percent of boys selected unskilled positions. Parents shared similarly high aspirations for their children's careers.[86]

Given the great disparity between aspirations and actual career opportunities, the attitudes of guidance officers and principals toward the curriculum choices and careers of black students became an especially crucial influence. In the mid-1930's Virginia Daniels made a survey of 159 secondary schools in all parts of the nation enrolling black students to determine "Attitudes Affecting the Occupational Affiliation of Negroes." Her data revealed few differences between the opinions of northern and southern schoolmen on the key issues (most respondents from the southern schools were black). For that reason the figures for North and South will be combined here, and her two top categories of agreement, "generally" and "frequently," will be merged in the list below.

Percentage of Agreement with Statements

1. "There are very few Negro employers in the community; hence, Negro youths must look to white employers for work and accept such limitations as are thereby imposed."   96.2
2. "Union membership is denied to Negroes; they are thus prevented from entering occupations which are controlled by trade unions."   69.8
3. "Employers refuse to accept Negroes for the more socially desirable jobs, regardless of qualifications of ability and character."   92.4
4. "Promotion is denied to Negroes because of the insistence that inspectors, sub-foremen, and foremen—men vested with minor authority—must be white."   88.7
5. "It is believed that members of the Negro race are ill-adapted for work with machines."   50.3

6. "It is believed that all Negroes are persons of a low
   order of ability."   57.2
7. "It is believed that Negroes are inefficient or irresponsible or both."   65.4
8. "Various groups exert pressure on employers to retain white workers or to displace Negroes with
   whites."   54.1
9. "Employers hire no Negroes because they fear there
   will be racial friction if white and Negro workers are
   employed in the same plant."   42.2
10. "The spirit of the community is to keep Negroes at
    the bottom of the economic scale where wages are the
    lowest and jobs are the most hazardous."   59.0

It was only on the last question that there was a decided difference of opinion between northern and southern respondents,
39 and 79.2 percent respectively.[87]

Daniels reported that schoolmen largely agreed that Negro
students aspired to positions well above those designated for
them by racist communities, despite their recognition that they
might have to accept the common conception of "Negro jobs."
The most talented students especially chafed under the limitations. "Respondents in five cities had comments to make concerning this attitude of acceptance of 'Negro jobs,' " she wrote.
"From East Orange, New Jersey, comes the statement that Negroes seldom accept it while in school but 'after school.' The
guidance officers of Philadelphia, Pa., feel that it is accepted by
all Negroes 'except those who have initiative,' while those of
Milwaukee, Wis., feel that Negroes 'indirectly accept because
they feel their lot is hopeless.' "[88]

Both in their reaction to the questions about prejudice in hiring and in their individual comments, schoolmen made it clear
that they recognized that equality of opportunity was a lie for
black Americans. They saw the human cost and the pain. Should
schools prepare Negro students for careers not yet open to
them? If they did not, how could blacks ever extend their scope
of employment? Was it the task of schoolmen to fight racism in
the community? About 73 percent of northern respondents said
that they agreed that counselors should "attempt positively to

dispel racial prejudice so as to provide a wider range of occupational opportunities" for blacks, yet only one third thought it advisable for Negroes "to organize their power as consumers to force occupational openings from white-owned businesses which now depend on Negro buyers." And almost one third of counselors in the North thought that blacks should "be counseled merely to enter those lines of work in which there is reasonable expectancy of obtaining employment." [89]

Here and there a few school people aggressively sought to place Negroes in "non-Negro" jobs. Lloyd M. Cofer, a counselor in Detroit, fought "to break down the occupational barriers" against blacks in skilled trades by putting pressure on the United Auto Workers: "we told them that opening the doors of skilled trades to Negroes would do more good than all the speeches they could make or organizers they could hire if they were really sincere about recruiting blacks into the union." A group of teachers in Philadelphia made the rounds among manufacturers, union leaders, and public and private employment agencies to drum up opportunities for unemployed blacks and to expand the range of jobs Negroes could fill. In New York, a black schoolwoman, Elise Johnson McDougald, successfully fought both with a bigoted principal of the Manhattan Trade School and with employers to admit and hire more black girls in the millinery and dressmaking trades. The black activist Doxey A. Wilkerson attacked those who "proclaim vociferously that the proper role of vocational guidance—as in the case of all education—is to adjust the individual as best it can to prevailing mores of the occupational world, and not to seek its reconstruction." [90]

One measure of the willingness of school systems to counteract racism in the job market was the hiring of black teachers and other employees. Most systems failed this test badly. There was no shortage of trained black teachers—teaching was one of the favorite career choices of black high school girls, and there were many training programs for black teachers in both North and South. Precise data on the number of black teachers in northern cities is impossible to find, since most school reports did not list teachers by race, but in 1940 Doxey Wilkerson gathered good estimates from teachers and civic leaders in various black communities. He found that in eighteen of twenty cities with more than

7,000 black inhabitants there were some Negro teachers. In twenty-eight cities in his sample with fewer than 7,000, however, only four employed black teachers. Table 3 shows his figures for

Table 3. Number of black teachers and school administrators in cities with a large black population

City	Negro Population 1930	Blacks on Instructional and Administrative Staff
New York	327,706	Over 800
Chicago	233,903	About 300
Detroit	120,066	About 80
Cleveland	71,899	78
Pittsburgh	54,938	3
Cincinnati	47,818	148
Los Angeles	38,894	About 54
Newark	38,880	11
Columbus	32,774	About 75
Springfield, Ill.	20,000	None
Boston	20,574	?
Dayton	17,077	80

Source: Wilkerson, "Negro in American Education," I, 72.

a dozen cities with a large black population. The figures offer an interesting study in contrasts. The N.A.A.C.P. praised the New York system for hiring black teachers without prejudice on grounds of merit. As Mary Herrick has shown, the black community in Chicago enjoyed a fair degree of political power through its support of the Thompson machine (though it did not receive its proportionate share of the more prestigious or lucrative positions at the disposition of the machine). Of the remaining cities, Cincinnati, Columbus, and Dayton stand out as relatively prominent employers of black teachers and also as systems which hired a number of black administrators quite disproportionate to those hired in the other cities. What these cities together with Philadelphia, Gary, and Indianapolis had in common, in contrast with the many cities with no black professionals, or only a handful, was that there was generally a high degree of conscious segregation of black pupils in separate schools—and normally black teachers were only allowed to teach in these institutions.[91]

Philadelphia is a case in point. In 1907, Superintendent Martin Brumbaugh wrote that separate buildings for black children with Negro teachers had accomplished two purposes: "First, it has given to the colored child better opportunity to move at its own rate of progress through the materials of the curriculum, which rate of progress is in some respects different from the rate of progress of other children. Second, it has enabled the Board of Education to give employment to a group of deserving members of the colored race." Thus the desire of this administrative progressive to segregate black children because of their alleged mental differences coincided with job opportunities for Negro teachers. In 1940, Clara Hardin found the same basic plan in operation. "To a Negro born and reared in New York City, where no records are kept by color of students," she wrote, "and where Negro teachers may teach classes of white children in the public schools, the system of allowing the all-Negro schools to continue in Philadelphia may appear to be a form of 'Jim Crowism.' The Philadelphia Negro leaders are usually reticent on the subject, especially with outsiders." But she argued that "one can scarcely blame those who are employed in the school for keeping silent and wishing to maintain the *status quo.* They know that a majority of the 360 Negro women and 92 men who were employed as teachers in Philadelphia, in 1940, would be replaced by white teachers, if mixed schools became the rule." Their main strategy was to have black teachers appointed to the desegregated high schools.[92]

One reason many cities had few black teachers was that superintendents buckled before white protest. A leading administrative progressive, Frank Spaulding, described his way of assigning black teachers when he was superintendent in Cleveland: "I had been surprised to find that my staff included about sixty colored teachers. In none of my previous superintendencies was there a single colored teacher." The old hands in Cleveland told him that the policy was to take "advantage of the fact that among the city's numerous nationalities . . . there were some sections in which no objection was made to the color of teachers." When the black novelist Charles Chesnutt protested this policy, Spaulding told him that he would not debate "abstract principle" with him, and that it was simply his job "to see that the schools operate as efficiently as possible. Efficiency demands harmony and cooperation." When whites rejected black teachers, that destroyed "harmony and cooperation." That settled the matter.[93]

Judging from the prejudices of many white teachers in Cleveland at that time, black parents had their own cause for protest. About 1930 a word association test was given to 200 teachers who taught in predominantly black schools in the city. The word "Negro" was mentioned, and the teachers put down the first thought that came to mind. Here are the responses: slavery—43; antipathy—39; color—18; sympathy—4; music—4; and so on through a list of mainly negative nouns and adjectives.[94]

Indeed, many blacks were profoundly ambivalent about having Negro children taught in mixed schools by white teachers. As the volumes of *The Crisis* and the voluminous files of the N.A.A.C.P. attest, blacks vigorously fought dozens of attempts by whites to segregate them in cities and towns all over the nation, for they knew from bitter experience that separate schools in the South had been almost invariably unequal. Lacking direct political power—for there were only a tiny number of cities where there were blacks on school boards or where they had influence proportional to their numbers—they turned to the courts to defend the tenuous equity that integration promised. But again and again blacks expressed in autobiographies and poems, in truancy and protest, their sense of rejection in schools dominated by a white power structure over which they had little influence.

No one had more skillfully punctured the arguments of white segregationists in the North than W. E. B. DuBois. In an article in 1929, DuBois rejected the argument that black children were inferior and therefore needed special treatment: "their poverty is part of a universal problem; their retardation is due to wretched Southern school systems; their dullness comes from poor food and poor homes and there is absolutely no proof that it is Negroid." He pointed out that separate schools would inexorably become *"less well-housed, less well-supported, less well-equipped and less well-supervised than the average public school."* Segregation was a denial of democracy and could produce only unending hatred and conflict: the black man educated apart "is going to believe that the world of white folk is armed against the world of black folk, and that one of these days they are going to fight it out to the bitter end." [95]

But by 1935, after he had left his position with the N.A.A.C.P., DuBois had concluded that "race prejudice in the United States today is such that most Negroes cannot receive proper education in white institutions." Although in some communities, blacks and whites could prosper in schools together, he believed, "there are many public school systems in the North where Negroes are admitted and tolerated, but they are not educated; they are crucified." For decades DuBois and other Negroes like Carter Woodson had been discovering and teaching the black heritage, and he was convinced that the "main problem of Negro education will not be segregation but self-knowledge and self-respect." This search for power and self-definition might lead to a separation that was not imposed but sought.[96]

By 1940, Doxey Wilkerson believed that black education "in the North is characterized by tendencies toward structural separateness. This fact is seen in the fairly general exclusion of Negroes from policy-making and administrative functions in the public school system, the small number of Negro teachers, the definite trend toward the segregation of white and Negro pupils and teachers in separate schools, and in the more or less informal exclusion of white and Negro pupils and students from selected activities in schools and in institutions of higher education." He found, moreover, that "the degree of such separateness tends to be most pronounced in areas where the Negro population is relatively most heavily concentrated, and where the general social status of the Negro is lower than in the North as a whole." Whether sought or imposed, this structural separateness was to become massive as ghettos expanded in central cities after 1940; the poverty and racism that produced the nation within a nation became a bitter heritage for the future.[97]

4. AMERICANIZATION: MATCH AND MISMATCH

"The problem of the city is the problem of a revolution—a revolution brought about by an industrial evolution with an immigrant invasion." This was a common view of educators early in this century. It was not the small number of black children but the diverse multitudes of first and second generation immigrant children that posed the most visible challenge to school people as they went to work in northern cities at the turn of the century. In December 1908 investigators for the U.S. Senate Immigration Commission tallied the ethnic origins of students in thirty-seven cities across the nation, including most of the largest cities and those with the largest concentrations of immigrants. They counted more than sixty nationalities and discovered that 58 percent of all students had fathers who were born abroad. Of the large cities, New York led with 72 percent, followed by Chicago (67), Boston (64), Cleveland (60), and San Francisco (58). Jews accounted for 18 percent of these pupils, Germans for 12, and Italians for 6. By contrast only 3 percent of the sample was black.[98]

As the major port of entry for immigrants, New York struggled to provide seats for the tens of thousands of newcomers streaming into the city. From 1899 to 1914 there was a 60 percent increase in school enrollment. In September 1897, 500 children clamored to gain admission to P.S. 75 but were turned away; the building, built for 1,500 pupils, already contained 2,000. On a single day after the arrival of a steamer as many as 125 new children would apply to P.S. 110. In 1905 the *New York Times* estimated that from 60,000 to 75,000 children were denied admission to school for lack of space, while the previous year almost 90,000 children attended school only part-time. Inside the classrooms it was not uncommon to find sixty to eighty students. Educators joked that teachers should have prior experience in a sardine factory before being hired to work in the New York schools.[99]

In 1903 a reporter, Adele Marie Shaw, visited twenty-five New York schools to see how the system was coping with its task of converting "a daily arriving city-full of Russians, Turks, Austro-Hungarians, Sicilians, Greeks, Arabs, into good Americans." "I chose New York City . . . ," she wrote, "because New York's problem is so difficult that once solved it would shed a calcium light upon the problems of other places." She witnessed an outward homogenization of ethnic newcomers. In a classroom near the Brooklyn Bridge built for twenty pupils she saw sixty-five children of many nationalities. When she first visited, two Cubans had just arrived in the class; they eagerly imitated the other children. "I saw the small class a few days later," she said, "and the two were already melted into the rank and file and were losing the distinctly foreign look." Like the other children, they soon "begin to be ashamed of their beautiful Spanish name, and will revise its spelling in deference to their friends' linguistic limitations. Esther Oberrhein in the entering class changes to Esther O'Brien in the next grade. Down in Marion Street a dark-eyed son of Naples who came last spring as Guiseppi Vagnotti appeared in September as Mike Jones." The photographer accompanying her was startled to find that the ethnic "types" had vanished in "the extraordinary homogeneousness of upper-grade children."

Shaw was astonished at the patience and skill of some of the lower grade teachers, who could entrance children and help them to forget the overcrowded, dreary rooms with their flickering gas jets and stifling air. In one such class, she wrote, "I became so absorbed I overstayed my hour. It was here that Garcia, Mendelssohn, and Joshua sat in the same row and made well-proportioned pictures with yellow crayon, and a nasturtium for model." Other teachers expressed a "tone of continual exasperation" that "would blight the forthputting powers of a Macaulay." "Who told you to speak out?" "You—are—not—still." "Don't stand in my class with pencil, pen, or book in hand." "You dirty little Russian Jew, what are you doing?" Shaw said to one teacher, " 'These seem like nice boys.' 'I haven't found them so,' answered the teacher sourly, and a sudden animation and general straightening lapsed into stodginess." But so difficult were the tasks the teachers faced with their huge polyglot classes that one should "admire and not carp at the woman who keeps her temper, treats them like human beings, and teaches them to speak English," wrote Shaw.[100]

"If it hopes to Americanize a school population chiefly of foreign parentage," Adele Shaw concluded, the school system "must use abnormal means. . . . To educate the children of our adoption we must at the same time educate their families, and in a measure the public school must be to them family as well as school." If children come to school dirty, the teacher must teach them how to keep clean. If children cannot learn because they are hungry, the school must provide cheap lunches and teach proper nutrition. If students come to class with physical defects, then the system must provide free medical inspection. If the child learns to be delinquent on the streets, then the schools should provide playgrounds and vacation schools. If youth or their parents have no place to study or find recreation in the evenings, then the school should become a community center after class hours. If grown boys and girls arrive without a knowledge of English, then special "steamer classes" should be created for them. By and large, the newcomers flocked to take advantage of the voluntary services as soon as they were provided early in this century.[101]

Indeed, not only in New York but elsewhere educators were largely optimistic in facing the unprecedented task of assimilating the millions of immigrants. Some believed that the "new immigrants" were genetically inferior and hence beyond the power of environment. Some believed that schooling could not overcome the terrible effects of poverty. A few thought that the schools should not attempt to uproot children from their parents' cultures and argued that America could become a confederation of disparate, close-knit, organic ethnic communities. But the great majority of administrators and teachers were probably ethnocentric, proud of American middle-class standards, and confident that schooling could change the many into one people, *e pluribus unum*. While they spoke little about the segregation of black people, they deplored the congregating of white ethnic groups in their own colonies and believed the schools should integrate the immigrant into American society.[102]

Educators' rhetoric of Americanization was often messianic, a mixture of fear outweighed by hope, of a desire for social control accompanied by a quest for equality of opportunity for the newcomers under terms dictated by the successful Yankee. The principal of DeWitt Clinton High School in New York, for example, wrote in 1902 that "education will solve every problem of our national life, even that of assimilating our foreign element. . . . Ignorance is the mother of anarchy, poverty and crime. The nation has a right to demand intelligence and virtue of every citizen, and to obtain these by force if necessary." He went on to claim that a "pupil's very association with intellectual and honorable men and women [in school] tends to inspire toward higher standards of living." Another educator argued that the clustering of immigrants in their ghettos arrested their development as citizens and stymied their social mobility. "In a commonwealth such as the United States social inequalities are largely the result of difference in up-bringing, and to this extent the problem of assimilation is one of *education* in the broadest sense of the word. In all progressive communities the school is recognized as the chief instrument of socialization and civilization." "If the standard of living in the tenements is to be raised from that of the poorest classes in Italy and Russia to the American standard," said William Maxwell, "it will be done through the teaching of home making in the public school." [103]

The social origins of those who set and carried out policies in public education helps to explain the confidence of school people in "the American standard." As we have seen, especially after centralization and the abolition of ward boards, the members of school committees tended to come disproportionately from the upper reaches of the occupational and social structure—people who had been successful within the system and had no reason to question its soundness or authority. A study of 850 superintendents in the early 1930's revealed that 98 percent of them were native-born, 90 percent Anglo-Saxon, and 85 percent of rural or small town origins; and most of them had enjoyed at least modest mobility into positions of white-collar authority. Raised in relatively homogeneous surroundings, in the village heartland of traditional American values, such men acquired a conservative ethnocentrism by birthright.[104]

A much larger percentage of urban teachers were offspring of immigrants than the superintendents in that sample—in 1908 the Immigration Commission found that 43 percent were second generation immigrants—but almost six-sevenths of those came from the British Isles, Germany, and Canada (non-French). There is a good deal of evidence that most of these second generation teachers were quite as ardent about Americanization as the native-born, and as converts, perhaps even more fervent. One Cleveland teacher, herself a newcomer, spoke thus at an NEA convention: "I am an immigrant, a stranger in a strange land. . . . Please notice me, take hold of me, lead me. . . . Try to protect me from my own inexperiences. Take me in as a member of your great and glorious family. *I want to belong.*" A

Adult Naturalization Class in a Public School

sociologist in Cleveland—where half of the children came from
homes where English was not spoken—observed that many
teachers took a "provincial self-satisfaction . . . in their Americanism," a comment echoed by many other witnesses. Especially
during the apex of 100 percent Americanism during World War
I and the Red scare in its aftermath, it was dangerous to be a
teacher whose conformity and patriotism were in doubt; in 1917
in Cleveland Superintendent Spaulding recommended firing any
teacher "whose sympathies are proved to be with our country's
enemies" (it was not necessary, he said, to express disloyalty in
words, since teachers influenced pupils merely by the "convictions and fundamental desires of the . . . heart").[105]

"Americanization" was a highly complex process. In part it en-
compassed the general pattern of socialization we have already
examined in nineteenth-century schools, namely the kind of
"modernization" of behavior and beliefs which has been world-

wide during the past century. In order to achieve at even modest levels in an urban-industrial society citizens needed to acquire certain kinds of common competence: to manipulate language and numbers, to follow clock time, to fill out forms and thread bureaucratic processes, to learn styles of thinking and affective expression congruent with the demands of a complicated, interdependent society. As individuals entered impersonal organizations, they learned that often they were rewarded or punished insofar as they measured up to specialized standards of performance. Thus for some immigrant children the urban public schools—with their stress on language and mathematics, their norms of punctuality and standardized performance—helped to bridge the rural folk cultures of their parents and the expectations of those who held power in American society.[106]

But because of the rainbow-like overlay of ethnic differences, Americanization was more than modernization. Like an immigrant from Poland, a native American from the farm also had to learn to cope with the complexities of life in crowded cities, but the Pole, as ardent Americanizers saw it, not only had to learn new skills but also had to shed an old culture. It was reasonable for educators to presume that insofar as the immigrant wanted to participate in the public life of the American city he needed to learn English or arithmetic or to gain familiarity with American economic and political institutions, just as he or she needed to learn to drive on the right-hand side of the road. But in their demands for total assimilation, for Anglo-conformity, many educators went further: nothing less would satisfy them than assaulting all forms of cultural difference, than creating a sense of shame at being "foreign."

Nowhere did the definition of "American" behavior and traits emerge more sharply than in the textbooks aimed at foreigners. Just as the Italian immigrant learned, often for the first time, what it meant to be defined as "Italian," so "Americans" became self-conscious about what the proper end-product of American training should be when they prescribed for the newcomers. Textbooks for immigrants stressed cleanliness to the point of obsession, implying that the readers had never known soap, a toothbrush, or a hairbrush. The California Immigration Commission primer for immigrant women declared: "Dirty windows are bad"; "A dirty sink is bad"; "A dirty garbage can is bad." It went on to tell mothers to send their children to school, clean and on time: "Do not let your child be tardy. If you do, when he grows up he will be late at his work. Thus he will lose his job, and always be poor and miserable." Many of the readers prescribed diet, health precautions, and even proper clothes and recreation. Sara O'Brien's *English for Foreigners* expressed the classic Mugwump ideal of politics: "Without law and order, property and even life would be unsafe. . . . These men who make and carry out the laws of the city are city officials, and are chosen by the people. The people should choose only honest and unselfish men for these offices." She closed her discussion of the American flag with a phrase to copy: "America is another word for opportunity." [107]

There is no reason to suppose that the Americanizers were being hypocritical in talking of opportunity or in preaching Anglo-conformity and middle-class standards. They were mostly true believers and perhaps were accurate in believing that in an opportunity structure dominated by WASPs the immigrant youth would find success easier with an Anglicized name, "correct" speech, a scrubbed face, and well-starched collar. Prejudice closed many doors, even in supposedly meritocratic organizations. Educators, after all, did not create ethnocentrism or bigotry in American society. In many accounts of childhood by second generation immigrants it was the other children who first introduced them to terms like "Dago," "Sheeny," "Jap," or "Polack." It was often other pupils who made fun of the Mexican child's tortilla, the Chinese boy's pigtail, or the Jewish boy's praying shawl. Probably this kind of ridicule or group pressure at school or at work, coupled with the influence of the mass media, had quite as much to do with the outward assimilation of members of immigrant groups as did conscious instruction in school. But accommodation to American ways was often only partial and limited to the public part of people's lives. In the primary groups of family, friends, and neighborhoods, the offspring of immigrants often returned to ethnic enclaves.[108]

Many educators felt ambivalent or guilty about splitting children away from their parents. After all, the family was supposedly an institution that needed to be strengthened, not undermined. One Americanizer warned that "we have no right to educate a child away from its parents, and failure to recognize this truth has caused a serious breach between the old and the new in the family and has led to serious results in the social life of these foreign communities." Many observers commented that the positions of parents and children were becoming reversed, as fathers and mothers depended for guidance on the young, who knew English and could interpret the workings of American society. This led, they felt, to increased disrespect for parents, to delinquency, and to alienation among the second generation. From her long experience as teacher, principal, and superintendent on New York's lower east side, Julia Richman realized that the more successfully the school Americanized the child "the more it is weaned away from the standards and traditions of its home. The parents remain foreign; the children become American. There is thus created an almost unbridgeable gulf between the two." The answer, said Richman and most educators, was not to stop assimilating the child but to Americanize the parents as well: "If we have given the child other, and let us hope better, standards, then let us build a bridge between the Americanized child and its foreign parent, so that the parent can cross the bridge to join the child on the American side." [109]

In parents' meetings and other communications between the school and immigrant parents there was to be no doubt about who was in charge. Immigrants must learn how to fit into the one best system. "They must be made to understand what it is we are trying to do for the children," wrote Richman. "They must be made to realize that in forsaking the land of their birth, they were also forsaking the customs and the traditions of that land; and they must be made to realize an obligation, in adopting a new country, to adopt the language and customs of that country." A sociologist observed that the reason "why there are not more parents' associations is to be found in the discouraging and managerial attitude of many school principals." They feared, he said, the loss of their prerogatives and resented parents who butted into school business. One principal's idea of how to maintain "sympathetic contact" between the home and the school was to send home notes attached to deficient homework saying that "this work is below the average of the class" and to notify parents

Italian Father and Son at Table

when the child was tardy or truant. Such treatment often made both children and parents feel that they were on probation. A Chicago child complained that "school ain't no good. When you works a whole month at school, the teacher she gives you a card to take home, that says how you ain't any good. And yer folks hollers on yer an' hits yer." In a number of cities adult educators tried to reach parents by requiring pupils to take notes home instructing parents that they should come to Americanization classes to learn English.[110]

Increasingly, educators began to realize that self-respecting immigrant parents would be insulted by such negative and one-sided contact. In 1913 the U.S. Commissioner of Education observed that "for the enrichment of our national life as well as for the happiness and welfare of individuals we must respect their ideals and preserve and strengthen all of the best of their Old World life they bring with them. We must not attempt to destroy and remake—we can only transform. Racial and national virtues must not be thoughtlessly exchanged for American vices." Some school people sought a real partnership between teachers and immigrant parents, a blending of cultures in the schools rather than an injection of Americanism.[111]

From his own experience as an immigrant from Aviliano to New York, Leonard Covello knew how painful forced assimilation could be to children and parents alike. He recalled the evening when he first brought home his report card for his father to sign. "What is this?" asked his father, "Leonardo Covello! What happened to the *i* in Coviello? . . . From Leonardo to Leonard I can follow, . . . a perfectly natural process. In America anything can happen and does happen. But you don't change a family name." The son explained that his teacher found Covello easier to say, and he wanted it that way too. When his mother joined her husband in protest, Leonard made the reply that was all too familiar to immigrant parents: "Mama, you don't understand." "Will you stop saying that!" she replied. "I don't understand. I don't understand. What is there to understand? Now that you have become Americanized you understand everything and I understand nothing." Covello and his friends did their best to keep their mothers away from school, for they were ashamed of their shawls and Italian speech. Hearing nothing of Italy or Italians in school, except for Columbus, he "soon got the idea that 'Italian' meant something inferior."

As he grew older and became a teacher, however, Covello's views changed. In 1920 he began teaching Italian to rough east-side boys at DeWitt Clinton High School and became a kind of father-confessor to them. "To put it bluntly," the principal told him, "it will be your job to look after these boys." Covello spent many hours talking in Italian to parents, seeking to bridge the sharp gap that separated them from the school and their children. As a teacher he did his best to give his students pride in their Italian heritage. He fought the "intelligence-test insanity" that downgraded Italian pupils because they lacked vocabulary and didn't flourish under the pressure of the test-giver with his stop watch and whistle.[112]

When Covello became principal of the new Benjamin Franklin High School in East Harlem, he had a chance to put into practice his ideal of a community school. He lived within walking distance of the school in the crowded slum in which only 9 percent of the residents were native-born whites of native-born parents. His school contained twenty-five different ethnic groups, of which the largest were Italian, Puerto Rican, and black (in that order). In 1935 Covello and his colleagues organized a Community Advisory Council designed to bring the people of the neighborhood into the school and to extend the school into the community. Students gave plays in Spanish and Italian, parents' associations held meetings in several languages, and the curriculum extolled cultural pluralism and assaulted negative ethnic stereotypes. During Wednesday "open house" while Covello talked with parents in his office, he could hear in the distance the classes in which adults were learning English, a parent-teacher meeting in the library, "while from the auditorium might come the shrill sounds of an argument that meant the Community Advisory Council was in session." Such a time, he wrote, "came closest to fulfilling my dream of the school as an integral part of the community."[113]

As in Covello's case, other educators came to believe that the nation should welcome ethnic diversity within its larger unity and that it was un-American to be bigoted. A Mexican boy, Ernesto Galarza, recalled that his elementary school in Sacramento "was not so much a melting pot as a griddle where [the principal] Miss Hopley and her helpers warmed knowledge into us and roasted racial hatreds out of us." In a neighborhood filled with Mexican, Polish, Japanese, Korean, Italian, and other immigrants, Miss Hopley kept telling the students why they were in school: "for those who were alien, to become good Americans; for those who were so born, to accept the rest of us. Off the school grounds we traded the same insults we heard from our elders. On the playground we were sure to be marched up to the principal's office for calling someone a wop, a chink, a dago, or a greaser." Teachers tried to pronounce the children's names correctly and encouraged them to share their cultures with others in the class. "No one was ever scolded or punished for speaking in his native tongue on the playground. . . . It was easy for me to feel that becoming a proud American . . . did not mean feeling ashamed of being a Mexican." Not that Miss Hopley was a luke-warm patriot: she once stopped the entire assembly of children in the middle of singing the national anthem because two men were walking by within earshot with their hats on (it later turned out that the two men were the superintendent of schools and a distinguished visitor).[114]

Even under the best of conditions Americanization of the children tended to produce strain between parents and children in the home.[115] A Jewish girl, Mary Antin, recalled that her father had written to the family in Polotzk that free education in the United States was "his chief hope for us children, the essence of American opportunity," yet with assimilation to America came a "laxity of domestic organization, . . . [a] sad process of disintegration of home life" that was "the cross that the first and second generations must bear." Rumanian peasants resented the fact that their children refused to speak their language in the family. Polish parents became upset because public school teachers scarcely mentioned the old country, and if they did, only to heighten American superiority. Angry because her son was disobedient, an Italian mother asked a countryman if American schools taught children to be bad. A sensitive observer of Americanization wrote that a "fear of losing the children haunts the older generation. It is not merely the natural desire of parent to retain influence over child. . . . It is a vague uneasiness that a delicate network of precious traditions is being ruthlessly torn asunder, that a whole world of ideals is crashing into ruins; and amidst this desolation the fathers and mothers picture themselves wandering about lonely in vain search of their lost children." [116]

Although they feared losing their children through Americanization, the great mass of immigrant parents also saw schooling as a doorway to new opportunities. John Daniels, a sociologist who traveled all over the nation studying biculturalism, wrote in 1920 that "if you ask ten immigrants who have been in America long enough to rear families what American institution is most effective in making the immigrant part and parcel of American life, nine will reply 'the public school.' " The immigrant watches his children "go into the kindergarten as little Poles or Italians or

Finns," wrote Daniels, "babbling in the tongues of their parents, and at the end of half a dozen years or more he sees them emerge, looking, talking, thinking, and behaving generally like full-fledged 'Americans.' " Timothy Smith has shown how fervently the immigrant press in this country praised education, both public and private. Indeed, many of the ethnic parochial schools claimed that they Americanized children even more effectively than the public schools, in part because they built on rather than destroyed family, religious, and ethnic traditions. In the Hebrew Institute in New York children eagerly memorized the Declaration of Independence printed in parallel columns of English and Hebrew.[117]

Statistics of attendance and literacy document this immigrant faith in schooling. Leonard Ayres reported in 1909 that nationwide there were forty-four illiterate native white children of native parents compared with only nine per 1000 among the white children of immigrants. Likewise, 72 percent of second generation children and 69 percent of foreign-born children aged five to fourteen were in school in comparison with 65 percent of children of native parentage. Much of the national discrepancy, of course, resulted from minimal schooling of southern whites, but in most northern cities the attendance of immigrants' children equalled or excelled that of the native born. No brigades of attendance officers could have coerced such masses of children into school if their parents had strongly opposed public education.[118]

It is essential, however, to examine differences in attitudes toward education and in achievement levels between ethnic groups, for "immigrants" varied enormously among themselves. Talking of *the immigrant* masks these disparities. In early 1909 investigators for the U.S. Senate's Immigration Commission did an intensive study of the rate of progress of different ethnic groups in twelve cities in the East and Midwest (not including New York, which will be discussed separately below). Defining a "retarded" pupil as "one who is 2 or more years older than the normal age for his grade" (using six years as the normal age for first graders), the Commission found the following percentages of retardation: [119]

Native-born	30.3
Foreign-born, total	40.4
English-speaking	27.3
Non-English-speaking	43.4
German	32.8
Russian Jew	41.8
South Italian	63.6
Polish	58.1
Swedish	15.5

Retardation rates were generally lower for those children of all nationalities whose parents spoke English, whose fathers had become citizens, and whose fathers had lived for long periods in the United States—all indicating the importance of familiarity with and commitment to the environment. Not surprisingly, age at arrival in the country greatly influenced retardation: 91.8 percent of all foreign-born pupils who immigrated at age ten or over were retarded, compared with 43.5 for those who entered under six. There were, however, some critical differences between groups in the importance of exposure to American soci-´ ety. Among children of immigrants whose fathers had lived for twenty years or more in the United States, the children of Russian Jews had a retardation rate of only 29.7 percent as compared with a rate of 55.4 percent for South Italians. Studies of retardation conducted in Minneapolis and St. Paul in 1919 and in New York in 1931 produced quite similar rates of retardation among some of the same groups investigated by the Immigration Commission in 1909, indicating that the ethnic differences in school performance persisted over time.[120]

The Immigration Commission also found important disparities among ethnic groups in their rates of school attendance, although these were less striking than rates of retardation. Table 4 indicates varying rates of attendance among different ethnic groups in certain cities during the period from the opening of school to December 31, 1908. With the exception of Russian Jews, low attendance rates closely matched high rates of retardation.[121]

Studies of high school attendance and drop-out rates by eth-

Table 4. Percent of children attending primary grades, 1908

Ethnic Group	Attendance Rate			
	90% +	75–90%	50–75%	50% or less
Native-born	72.6	15.2	7.3	4.9
Foreign-born, total	74.4	13.0	7.4	5.2
English-speaking	72.8	14.4	7.6	5.1
Non-English-speaking	74.8	12.7	7.3	5.2
German	82.4	9.2	5.1	3.3
Russian Jew	70.9	16.4	7.3	5.5
South Italian	68.4	14.1	11.1	6.3
Polish	69.4	14.3	9.6	6.6
Swedish	82.2	10.0	3.7	4.1

Source: U.S. Immigration Commission, *Children of Immigrants,* I, 103, 108.

nicity yielded results which closely paralleled rates of retardation, truancy, and IQ among immigrant groups. In 1911 Joseph Van Denburg reported that secondary students in New York whose fathers were born in the United States, Russia, England, and Germany contributed disproportionately large numbers to the high school population, while children of Irish and Italian fathers were poorly represented. Studies during the 1920's also showed substantially higher high school retention rates for the same groups than for children of Irish, Italian, and Polish parents.[122]

When one examines the occupational diffusion of immigrant groups, one discovers that by and large those groups who stayed longest in school moved disproportionately into the higher status occupations. Drawing on decennial census reports, which provide at least a gross indication of occupational mobility, E. P. Hutchinson compiled figures about the occupations of male first and second generation immigrants in 1910, 1920, and 1950 (see Table 5). With some exceptions, he found that the children of immigrants tended to approximate the typical distribution of all white workers more than did first generation immigrants. They also tended to cluster more in the high-status jobs. Indeed, by 1950 the second generation of white immigrants not only ranked higher in occupational prestige than the first generation but they

Table 5. Relative concentration of male foreign-born white workers and native white workers of foreign or mixed parentage, by major occupation group, 1950, 1920, and 1910

Major Occupation	Foreign-Born White			Native White, Foreign or Mixed Parentage		
	1950	1920	1910	1950	1920	1910
Proportion of category as a percent of total white male work force	9.9	22.4	24.7	21.8	21.0	19.8
Proportion of all white male workers as index	100	100	100	100	100	100
Professional, technical, and kindred workers	76	64	63	110	108	103
Farmers and farm managers	45	49	52	68	76	71
Managers, officials, and proprietors, except farm	131	114	107	111	105	111
Clerical and kindred workers	56	44	44	119	148	158
Sales workers	71	72	73	107	122	129
Craftsmen, foremen, and kindred workers	114	118	120	103	112	117
Operatives and kindred workers	102	142	154	105	109	116
Service workers, including private household	189	162	149	106	104	117
Farm laborers and foremen	75	37	34	54	77	81
Laborers, except farm and mine	132	167	182	95	81	81

Source: Adapted from Hutchinson, *Immigrants and Their Children*, 202, 216.
Note: Gainful workers 10 years of age and over in 1910 and 1920; experienced civilian labor force 14 years of age and over in 1950.

had more than their proportionate share of white-collar jobs in the entire labor force. It could be argued, then, that through his children the immigrant shared in the American dream of success.[123]

But in occupations as in schooling, it is highly misleading to talk about "the immigrant." Here specific ethnic groups showed marked disparities. Using Hutchinson's index figure of 100 as a normal distribution, one finds the relative concentrations of white male second generation workers of certain groups in selected occupations were: Mexican—22 professional, 500 farm

Saluting the Flag in the Mott Street Industrial School, New York, c. 1889–90

worker; Russian (as approximation for Jewish)—193 professional, 65 operative; Italian—79 professional, 141 operative; French Canadian—75 professional, 164 operative. In general the groups that had highest rates of school attendance and retention—such as immigrants from the British Isles, Scandinavia, Germany, and East European Jews—had significantly higher occupational status in the second generation. By contrast, the children of groups that collectively experienced difficulty in school were heavily concentrated in the blue-collar occupations in 1950.[124]

By comparing statistics on schooling and occupations of ethnic groups I do not intend to imply any simple causation. The transaction between social class and schooling is two-way and highly complex. Dozens of studies have demonstrated that the social class of parents explains much of the variance of children in school performance. At the same time, scholars have pointed out that amount of schooling plays a role in social mobility, the pre-

Americanization Class in Milwaukee, with Golda Meir as the Statue of Liberty

cise degree being almost impossible to assess but clearly substantial—for the children of immigrants as for old Americans. One reason for the importance of extended schooling, of course, is that employers and occupational associations have steadily increased the educational requirements for entry into many prestigious occupations.[125]

If one thus assumes that for most groups success or failure in school had consequences not only inside the system of education but to a degree outside as well, it becomes all the more important to ask why certain immigrants prospered academically while others did not. One approach to this question is to examine the impact of prejudice both in the larger society and within the classroom. This is surely important, but it leaves much unexplained. At the very time when anti-Semitism was burgeoning—when observers reported teachers calling children a "dirty little Russian Jew" or "little kike," Jewish pupils were achieving in school at high levels. Chinese and Japanese pupils met gross discrimination and cruelty—in 1906 they were segregated in special schools in San Francisco and were assaulted by roving gangs of toughs—yet they also generally did well in school.[126]

Another approach might argue that a desire to assimilate rapidly American norms, to disavow the parents' culture, characterized those who adjusted rapidly to their teachers' expectations and hence succeeded in school. But here one must explain the relative success of the Germans, who often insisted on bilingual public schools, or of the Jews and Japanese, who preserved their languages and cultures through their own networks of private schools meeting after school or on weekends. Merely coming from a home where the parents spoke a language other than English or struggled to preserve their folkways did not by itself explain poor performance of the second generation in school.[127]

Among immigrants, as among the general population, poverty correlated highly with academic failure, yet not only individuals but whole groups transcended initial poverty to succeed in school. In 1900 the Tenth Ward on New York's lower east side had more than 700 persons per acre squeezed into dismal tenements, the most densely crowded area in the United States, yet in its schools a disproportionately large percentage of Jewish children attended regularly and proceeded to high school. Joseph Van Denburg reported that the median monthly rent paid by parents of high school students in New York—of whom a large number were Russian Jews—was $15, a sum barely adequate to purchase two to four rooms in a jammed tenement.[128]

Surely prejudice, clinging to old cultures, and poverty had much to do with a lack of fit between ethnic groups and the schools. Still, it seems likely that there is more to the conflict than what meets the eye and ear, that beneath superficial differences between ethnic groups lay a kind of deep structure of family and community values, roles, and behavior that may have coincided or clashed with the expectations and demands of urban public education. Such deep structures may reflect differences of class, religion, urban or rural residence, national traditions, methods of child-raising, and other powerful influences. They involve both cognitive structures and value patterns. A contrast of the experiences of South Italians and Jews in New York City may illuminate this transaction between subcultures and the urban school system.

Two cautions. First, any attempt to categorize the experience of a group obviously tends to blur differences between individuals and subsets of the group. There were many thousands of Jews who performed poorly in school (most of the schools on the lower east side had special classes for such pupils); among these alienated students were rebels who threw inkwells at teachers, who cursed principals who washed their mouths out with non-kosher soap, who reveled in the life of the street. Likewise, a large percentage of South Italian pupils proceeded at a normal rate through school, some using education as a stepping stone to distinguished careers. Talking of collective experience is useful chiefly to explain gross statistical differences, such as general rates of retardation or retention.[129]

Second, in examining the fit or conflict between an ethnic group and the schools one needs to remember that the relationship is two-way, that the educational system may be largely responsible for the *mis-fit*. Contrasting two groups, one relatively successful in school and one relatively unsuccessful, does not entail praising the one and blaming the other. Schools have sometimes helped to destroy family and community cultures that met human needs and values more fully than did the culture they sought to instill (one thinks in this connection, for example, of the disastrous federal educational policies for American Indians).

Before immigrating, most New York Jews had already adapted to industry and the city. Thus it is useful to look briefly at their experiences in Europe, which shaped their adaptation to schooling in the United States. In the mid-nineteenth century the Jews of Eastern European cities turned increasingly from petty commerce and crafts to semi-mechanized production of textiles, toys, cigars, and other goods in household sweatshops and small workshops controlled by merchant capitalists. Buying Singer sewing machines, whole families made the manufacture of clothing "the great Jewish metier." Rigid quotas normally barred all but a handful of Jews from advanced education, and even when the Russian government did relent and try to attract them into state schools, leaders resisted assimilation: "As long as we are not granted civic rights," said one, "education will only be a misfortune for us." [130] But oppression helped to strengthen the respect of Jews for their religion and for the intellectuals who interpreted the sacred books. "Talmudic scholarship, an unrelenting task-master and an end in itself, earned the highest social esteem," Moses Rischin has observed. Families proudly supported the learned men who spent their days in reading the Torah and disputing its meaning. Not only the family but the whole community reinforced intellectual ambitions among the young.[131]

Irving Howe wrote that "it was a distinctive trait of the Jewish immigration that it brought to these shores not the ignorant and hopeless, but the most vital and articulate agents of a fully-developed culture." To many Jewish immigrants the opportunity to attend free schools was one of the wonders of New York, for freed of the educational quotas and barriers to opportunity they faced within the Pale of settlement, they believed that the future was theirs for the taking. "All for the children" was a familiar saying as the parents justified their sacrifices in the present. A characteristic feature of modernization, this future orientation meshed well with the demands of the public schools.[132]

Superintendent Maxwell sought to create a system of free education in New York leading from gutter to graduate degree, and many Jewish families saw the schools as the ladder to the professions. Moses Rischin estimates that "by the turn of the century youngsters of East European origin had become a majority at the city's free institutions of higher learning." In October 1917, 10,000 parents and children rioted in Jewish neighborhoods in New York to protest the introduction of the "Gary plan" into the city's schools, for they believed that it would condemn youth to blue-collar occupations and prevent upward mobility. Children wandered from school to school in mobs in the Williamsburg and Brownsville sections of Brooklyn, breaking windows, tangling with the police, and trying to disrupt classrooms. At a mass meeting "one mother cried out from the platform against the Gary system, shouting: 'We want our kinder to learn mit der book, der paper und der pensil [*sic*] und not mit der sewing and der shop.' " Jews demanded power to the parents: " 'Dey are unserer kinder, not theirs.' " [133]

For the most part, New York educators praised the educational zeal of the Jewish population. Superintendent Maxwell admired the "national genius for education" of the Jews, while another observer commented that "Jewish children are the delight of their teachers for their cleverness . . . obedience and general good conduct, and the vacation schools, night schools, social settlements, libraries, bathing places, parks and playgrounds of the East Side are fairly besieged with Jewish children eager to take advantage" of these opportunities. A less enthusiastic teacher agreed that Jewish children were "mentally alert, colorful . . . the backbone of my class, but they can be an insufferable nuisance because of their constant desire to distinguish themselves." [134]

In his brilliant autobiography *Walker in the City* Alfred Kazin gives a view from the other side of the desk, a sensitive Jewish boy's impressions of school in Brownsville. "All teachers were to be respected like gods, and God Himself was the greatest of all school superintendents." Teachers "were the delegates of all visible and invisible power on earth—of the mothers who waited on the stoops every day after three for us to bring home tales of our daily triumphs; of the glacially remote Anglo-Saxon principal, whose very name was King." Kazin recalled that constantly he was told that "the road to a professional future would be shown us only as we pleased" the teachers by showing "an ecstatic submissiveness in all things." And academic performance was only part of the test: one also had to acquire *character*—the quality possessed by teachers, by Principal King, and above all, by President Theodore Roosevelt, who looked down disapprovingly from his portrait in the auditorium. The alternative to success was "going bad" and Sing Sing. "Anything less than absolute perfection in school always suggested to my mind that I might fall out of the daily race, be kept back in the working class forever, or—dared I think of it?—fall into the criminal class itself." Surely the contest, however successful the child appeared in the eyes of condescending teachers or self-abnegating parents, bore its price for the second generation. And the poignant letters to the editor of the *Jewish Daily Forward* showed that parents often felt rejected by their successful children.[135]

But for the South Italian child the contest often took different forms. Whereas the typical Jewish immigrant from Eastern Europe was urban in background and middle class in outlook, if not in income, in the old country, the average South Italian immigrant was a peasant, a *contadino*. Leonard Covello has estimated that 78 percent of Italian newcomers in New York had been peasants, unaccustomed to cities and new to an industrial discipline. "Their folkways and mores in the realms of religion, social life, economic organization, and education abounded in vestiges of a civilization of by-gone eras," wrote Covello; "ancient customs and practices were survivals, 'not merely as symbolical residues of the past but retained the force of primeval verities.' " Even in their practice of Roman Catholicism South Italians found their behavior at odds here with custom in Irish-dominated churches.[136]

The *contadino* believed strongly in education but meant by it something far different from the bookish schooling that attracted Jews. Education was centered in the family, the bastion of warmth and security from which the peasant looked out on the world, often with suspicion. Over the generations on the farm the father and mother had taught children the economic skills they needed to survive, the attitudes and behavior they needed to wend their way in the social world of the village, the world-view that explained the unfamiliar. Extended schooling was unnecessary, a luxury for the upper classes. When big enough to help in the fields or the kitchen, the child merged into the adult work force; there was no such thing as "adolescence" in peasant families. An Italian immigrant recalled that "in America [his countrymen] sought to find freedom from various deviltries of the Italian government. Among these were the attempts (not always successful) to introduce compulsory education which the peasant in southern Italy considered more of a burden than a blessing." [137]

In America as well, South Italian parents often resisted coerced school attendance. School taught modern ways of thinking that held old folkways up to ridicule and undermined the family's authority. Italian children in New York had high rates of truancy, often with the parents' connivance. It was absurd for a healthy son to be cramped in a classroom when he could be out working, helping to support the family; and what good would all that learning do a daughter—better she help her mother until she found a husband. A. P. Giannini, an Italian banker in San Francisco, said he would lend a worker $25 "with no better security than the callouses on the borrower's hands." Hard work, loyalty to the family—*that* mattered. "Mother believed you would go mad if you read too many books, and Father was of the opinion that too much school makes children lazy and opens the mind for unhealthy dreams," recalled one second generation Italian. Not only a lack of a tradition of books and intellectualism but also a belief in fate made the postponed careers, the future orientation implicit in schooling, foreign. When the richest man on the street could read neither Italian nor English, when chance played such a role in life that one needed to live in the present, what was the point of all that schooling? [138]

For educators, to whom success in life started with success in the classroom and who relished the "ecstatic submissiveness" of pupils, the Italians often seemed incorrigible. "The southern Italians," wrote district superintendent Julia Richman, "as a class, lack education themselves, and are indifferent to the advantages of education for their children." A teacher complained that "Italian children were usually more crude in manner, speech, and dress than non-Italian children. . . . These children, especially the boys, were a source of constant irritation to teachers." Others agreed that the Italians were hard to discipline, irresponsible, and again and again expressed the stereotype that they were good chiefly at manual and artistic tasks. Some teachers responded warmly, especially to the Italian girls, but often the classroom was a battlefield.[139]

Archie Bromsen, a sociologist who attended school in an Italian neighborhood, has left a vivid account of the conflict between South Italian boys and their teachers. At school "the boy is subjected to criticism, not for his misdemeanors, but because he acts as he has been taught to act." There the child learns "that he is not an American, but an Italian child of the slums; it is in the school that the one institution which is an integral part of his nature and devotion—his home—is constantly subjected to objections." Naturally, he rebels both against the teacher and the lessons. As she attacks his dialect, he persists in his linguistic delinquency; as she tries to get him to take baths, he takes pride in the ring on his neck; as she cautions him on diet, he buys a lunch of hot dogs, candy, and cigarettes; and finally, "as a boy in the graduating term, he masturbates in the classroom during an admonitory lecture on the evils of self-abuse." And teachers fight back against the dirt, the smuttiness, the defiance: "what a bunch of little animals they are, one and all! If one could only get transferred! They are so dirty!"

The conflict often left the Italian boy suspended between two worlds. His father, eager to assert traditional authority, began to appear ignorantly despotic. A gang of adolescents often became a refuge half-way between the family and the school. Real life belied the bland civics of the textbook, which was purged of "all the crudities and unpleasantnesses of reality." The policeman at the corner was really not the "gentleman hero of the peace" but a guzzling, "big, fat Irish bastard." "The school has drilled him for his part in a democratic paradise," wrote Bromsen, "but instead, he finds himself assigned to no enviable position in a blue-eyed aristocracy." For what has he endured school? "He has been educated for the Presidency, and he becomes a truck driver." [140] High truancy and drop-out rates, an average IQ score of eighty-five, negative teacher stereotypes—these were the symptoms of this conflict for the South Italian child.

The fact that many immigrants did well in school seemed to place the burden of failure—indeed, often of shame—on those who did not. To be sure, school people did make adjustments in the system to fit immigrants' children in certain ways: steamer classes for older children who did not speak English, a new stress on hygiene and civics, new opportunities for after-school recreation and continuation schooling, for example. But by and large they believed that the child had to fit the system, and that when whole ethnic groups were misfits, they should shape up. Helen Todd, who looked at school from the point of view of the Polish and Italian child-workers she saw daily, asked in 1913: "Would it not be possible to adapt this child of foreign peasants less to education, and adapt education more to the child? To reach into the home and console and protect and cooperate with him better than we do? Nothing that a factory sets them to do is so hard, so terrifying, as learning. . . . We do not make our education fit their psychology, their traditions, their environment or inheritance." Could schools adapt to the learning styles, the deep structures of family and community values, of those children who met failure? Her question remained as pertinent sixty years later.[141]

5. "LADY LABOR SLUGGERS" AND THE
PROFESSIONAL PROLETARIAT

In September 1899 Marian Dogherty left her Cambridge home early to ride through the tree-shaded, quiet streets to her new job as teacher in the Hancock school in Boston's North End. The principal, Mr. Dutton, took her to her classroom with its fifty-six desks bolted to the floor and extra, movable ones in the rear, its "high platform where the teacher sat." The platform, she thought, "was her throne and helped to fix her above the rest of the world in the minds of the children. If they desired to converse with her, they had to step *up;* when they returned to their own quarters, they must step *down*." As the Jewish and Italian girls marched in, faces shining from soap and dresses stiff with starch, they were models of deportment on that first day of school. "Even the janitor seemed to them a celestial being, for when he shuffled in and banged the furniture about, an awe rested on their innocent faces, because he was a part of that great system that held them in its benign but awful hand." The hierarchical order seemed fixed and immutable; a student, chastised for her temper, later wrote a theme for Miss Dogherty: "I must not slam the door when I am mad, nor answer back the teacher. Teachers are sometimes aggravating, but we must put up with them because the city pays them to be like that."

But one day "I became aware that a teacher was subservient to a higher authority," Marian Dogherty observed. One day in came Mr. Dutton to take his seat on the platform next to her and to hear the recitations. "Our principal was a stickler for the proprieties, and the proper way to read in the public school in the year 1899 was to say, 'Page 35, Chapter 4,' and holding the book in the right hand, with the toes pointing at an angle of forty-five degrees, the head held straight and high, the eyes looking directly ahead, the pupil would lift up his voice and struggle in loud, unnatural tones." Miss Dogherty had properly trained the toes and arms, but she thought reciting chapter and page "a cold douche on the interest of a story." The principal was not amused by the children's prodigious ignorance of the proprieties. As he left, disconcerted, the children chorused: "Good afternoon, Mr. Dogherty." "As for me," recalled the teacher, "only centuries of the civilization process kept me safe. Had I followed my primitive instincts—but it is no matter!" For the rest of the day, stretching to twilight, she coached the children on how to address the august principal, impersonating his mannerisms with an earnestness born of her own respect for the "benign but awful" power of the system.[142]

The same docility among teachers frustrated Angelo Patri when he became a principal in New York and sought to humanize the rigid school he inherited. "Free at last, my own master," he exulted as he entered the fortress-like building. "I am limited only by my own vision." But he, like the teachers there, found himself trapped by the force of sociological custom. As he passed a classroom, he saw a teacher smiling at a pupil. "I was glad and walked towards the teacher. Instantly the smile disappeared, her body grew tense, the little boy sat down and all the other little boys sat up stiff and straight and put their hands behind them." Patri grew despondent. "I've tried to have the teachers and children feel that I'm their friend," he told the former principal, but instead "they are afraid of me!" "Afraid of you? Of course they are and they ought to be," replied his predecessor. "You'll find them well trained. . . . Take my advice if you want any peace of mind and keep them under your thumb." Patri urged the teachers to praise children who came to school clean. Miss North took that as an order, and bought blouses for the students so that the class could get an A from the authorities. There sat the children, each with a light-colored shift, each with a "primer carefully covered in brown paper with a red edged name-paster precisely fixed in the centre of the front cover." Miss North and her pupils were well trained.[143]

That was the way it was supposed to be, said Aaron Gove, the veteran superintendent of the Denver schools, as he addressed the NEA audience in 1904. The teacher was hired to perform a duty assigned by the superintendent. "It is comparable to the turning out of work by an industrial establishment, the performance of a task assigned by the chief of police of a city, or communicated to a soldier while on duty." A superintendent and his line officers necessarily had despotic authority, "but that despotism can be wielded with a gloved hand." Gove deplored the notion that teachers should take part in the decision-making process in schools: "An apparently growing feeling seems to exist—in truth it does exist, especially in one of the large cities of the country—that the public-school system should be a democratic institution, and that the body of teachers constitute the democratic government." [144]

He was talking about Chicago. Margaret Haley, a paid organizer for the Teachers' Federation there, preceded him on the NEA platform and had just urged that "teachers have the courage of their convictions" and take democracy seriously in their own lives. "Democracy is not on trial," she told the NEA, "but America is." Teachers need to organize for their part in the great battle taking place in the larger society and in the schools. "Two ideals are struggling for supremacy in American life today: one the industrial ideal, dominating thru the supremacy of commercialism, which subordinates the worker to the product and the machine; the other, the ideal of democracy, the ideal of the educators, which places humanity above all machines, and demands that all activity shall be the expression of life." Across the nation teachers are underpaid, insecure in tenure, overworked in jammed classrooms, and denied a voice in policy because of "the increased tendency toward 'factoryizing education,' making the teacher an automaton, a mere factory hand, whose duty it is to carry out mechanically and unquestioningly the ideas and orders of those clothed with the authority of position, and who may or may not know the needs of the children or how to minister to them." She quoted John Dewey: "If there is a single public-school system in the United States where there is official and constitutional provision made for submitting questions of methods of discipline and teaching . . . to the discussion of those actually engaged in the work of teaching, that fact has escaped my notice." How can the child learn to be a free and responsible citizen if the teacher is bound? How can an autocratic school teach the process of democracy? Only if teachers joined with workers "in their struggle to secure the rights of humanity thru a more just and equitable distribution of the products of their labor" could teachers become free to "save the schools for democracy and to save democracy in the schools." [145]

Margaret Haley saw women classroom teachers as a white-collar proletariat. A study of teacher salaries, tenure, and pensions in city schools published by the NEA in 1905 documented her contention. Recall that urban schools at that time were generally meccas for teachers by comparison with town and rural schools. In 467 cities the average salary of 68,730 women elementary teachers was $650. In all but 4 out of 48 cities studied, unskilled municipal laborers on street and sewer work earned more in a year than beginning teachers, while the minimum wage paid molders was almost double that for teachers. In 1911 an intensive examination of teachers' salaries and the cost of living in Cincinnati, Hamilton (Ohio), Denver, Atlanta, and New Haven revealed that their financial situation had generally declined since 1905 because of the rise in prices (from 1896 to 1911 the cost of fifteen food staples increased 50 percent). In the five cities unmarried women elementary teachers saved only from $30 to $90 a year on the average. In Denver two thirds of the unmarried women elementary teachers under twenty-five reported that they had no real or personal property. In 1911 elementary teachers still earned less than many types of unskilled female employees as well as male unskilled employees, despite the fact that their average years of schooling had increased to approximately thirteen years. Their typical work day was about eight hours. Only 2.5 percent of women teachers were married; of twenty-six men teachers up to age thirty-five who reported, only nine were married. In many places there were rules against employing married women teachers, and even those free to wed, like men teachers, often found marriage financially impossible. Teachers testified that worry over making ends meet and providing for the future added immeasurably to their nervous burden. Hear their voices: "The strain is so great and the salary allows no sum for recuperation. There is no line of work which so drains vitality." "If I could get something else that would pay better, I would give up teaching in spite of the fact that I love the work, but after teaching ten years most of us are unfit for anything else. We give the best years of our lives to the work and how few live to enjoy the pension!" "I am so worn out from teaching sixty pupils that most of my money goes for medicine and trips for my health." [146]

The school was often, as Willard Waller said, "a despotism in a state of perilous equilibrium." Teachers needed to keep tight rein on their pupils, but they also felt powerless to influence policies dictated by their superiors. Drawing on her experience as a school board member in Chicago, Jane Addams said that teachers were so restricted "that they had no space in which to move about freely and the more adventurous of them fairly panted for light and air." An English educator, Sara Burstall, generally admired American education, but she observed that so little initiative is granted to teachers that they feel little more "than a cog in a machine. All this must have the effect of driving the best men out of the profession." "No more un-American or dangerous solution of the difficulties involved in maintaining a high degree of efficiency in the teaching corps of a large school system can be attempted than that which is effected by what is termed 'close supervision,'" wrote Ella Flagg Young in 1901 soon after she had resigned from her position as assistant superintendent in the Chicago public schools to protest against autocratic Superintendent McAndrew. It was this petty degradation, she said, that drove many self-respecting men and women from the classroom. [147]

In her career as organizer of the Chicago Teachers' Federation (CTF), Margaret Haley brought teachers for a time into the mainstream of progressivism in the city in alliance with the labor movement and with liberal and radical reformers. As Robert Reid has documented in his perceptive study of Haley, she and the CTF fought for higher salaries, pensions, and tenure; opposed administrative centralization of power and worked to establish teachers' councils; affiliated the CTF with the Chicago Labor Federation and worked on union issues with Samuel Gompers and other leaders; mobilized teachers in support of women's suffrage, local and state elections, and progressive measures such as child labor legislation; and pressed suits against

utility companies, the *Chicago Tribune,* and other business corporations to force them to contribute their legal share of school
taxes.[148] Eloquent, witty, warm, with piercing blue eyes, Haley
was an activist so effective that her foes called her and her
friends "lady labor sluggers." In 1915 Carl Sandburg wrote that
"for fifteen years this one little woman has flung her clenched
fists into the faces of contractors, school land lease holders, tax
dodgers and their politicians, fixers, go-betweens and stool
pigeons. . . . Over the years the Tribune, the News and the
ramified gang of manipulators who hate Margaret Haley have
not been able to smutch her once in the eyes of decent men and
women of this town who do their own thinking." [149]

Haley's CTF was the earliest teachers' organization to win and
exercise real power. By and large, the earlier voluntary associations of educators had been a mixture of social club and self-
improvement society, often differentiated by sex and status (for
example, in Chicago the male principals had their George Howland Club and the handful of women principals attended the
Ella Flagg Young Club). College presidents and state and city superintendents dominated the NEA, an organization whose influence depended on whether the captains of education wanted to
follow their own advice, and that of peers, when they returned
home from the yearly meeting. In the year when the CTF was
born, 1897, the membership of the NEA was a paltry 1,857;
from 1857 to 1900 the membership exceeded 2,000 only during
nine years. By contrast, between March and December 1897,
2,567 dues-paying women teachers joined the CTF, over half of
the Chicago teachers. The CTF addressed real grievances of
teachers in a politically astute manner.[150]

At the first meeting of the CTF the teachers adopted as its
purpose "to raise the standard of the teaching profession by
securing for teachers conditions essential to the best professional
service, and to this end, to obtain for them all the rights and
benefits to which they are entitled." From the start they interpreted this mandate in a hard-headed and broad fashion.
Realizing that unity of aim and resistance to administrative co-
optation were essential, they limited membership to elementary
teachers (which meant, in effect, to women). Their first goals
were a sound pension system and higher salaries. From 1877 to

1897 the salary for beginning elementary teachers had remained at $500, while the maximum was $825. By contrast, the high school teachers and administrators (mostly male) had received raises varying from 14 to 100 percent. With a petition in hand from about 90 percent of the women grade school teachers, the CTF extracted from the school board in 1898 a promise to increase salaries at the top of the scale for teachers who had taught eight or more years. In 1899, however, the board infuriated the CTF by reneging on the raises, arguing poverty.[151]

By 1900 the CTF had employed two former teachers as full-time organizers paid at the regular teacher's salary, Margaret Haley and her equally vigorous friend Catherine Goggin. They and an attorney probed to find new school funds for salaries. Several of the largest corporations, they discovered, were paying no taxes at all to the city, and a number of public utility companies such as the gas, electricity, telephone, and transit corporations, were paying no tax on franchises valued at about $200,000,000. Goggin and Haley detailed the facts to the tax authorities; no action ensued. Only through persistent court suits did the CTF force the State Board of Equalization to do its legal duty. After the utility corporations had pressured the federal courts to lower the tax assessment from $2,300,000 to $600,000, the Chicago school board received $249,544.77 and used it for everything but paying the higher salaries it had legally appropriated but not paid in 1898–99. Again the CTF resorted to the courts and forced the board to give teachers the salaries. In the process of this battle, the CTF learned many things: that board promises meant little; that corporations had their own version of law and order; and that the CTF needed powerful political allies.[152]

In 1902 the CTF sought such allies when it voted to affiliate with the Chicago Federation of Labor. "The only people you can depend on to act permanently with you," said Margaret Haley, "are those whose interests are identical with yours. We expect by affiliation with labor to arouse the workers and the whole people . . . to the dangers . . . confronting the public schools from the same interests and tendencies that are undermining the foundations of our democratic republic." Ella Flagg Young had doubts about the wisdom of this labor link, but she fully understood the motives of the CTF activists. She recalled that the women teachers used to come into the Committee on School Management, which she attended as a district superintendent, to ask the board to raise their pay. "I can see that committee now," she later wrote, "as they sat there and listened calmly, with their immovable, expressionless faces. When all had spoken, the chairman askt [*sic*] whether there were any more to speak. There were no more; hence they were dismist [*sic*]: and then the smile that went around that table!" The teachers talked, the "result was—nothing!" And after such encounters with a group of smirking businessmen, said Young, is it surprising that they should have decided that they needed voting power, that "they were compelled to go in with those who had felt the oppression and the grind of the power of riches"? [153]

Under Haley's aggressive leadership the CTF worked for a variety of reform measures in addition to the meat and potatoes issues of higher salaries, pensions, and tenure for teachers. In so doing it constituted in Chicago an important element of the working-class liberalism which J. Joseph Huthmacher has identified as crucial to urban "progressivism." Like factory workers, CTF members knew at first hand the arbitrariness of superiors and the difficulties of making ends meet on tiny wages; with them the impulse to fight the entrenched power of corporations came more from the problems of daily experience than from some ill-defined "status anxiety." Unlike the "administrative progressives" in education, who identified with corporate wealth and sought elite allies, they worked with labor unions to secure their goals. Unable to vote, members of the CTF appealed to their brothers, fathers, other male relatives, and neighbors; they spoke at ward meetings; they collected signatures on petitions; and Margaret Haley, in particular, reported vividly on the actions of boards and councils, mayors and governors, courts and business courtiers. The CTF spearheaded campaigns for municipal ownership of street railways and for child-labor legislation. With its labor allies the teachers' union managed to prevent passage of several bills to put into effect the centralization of school governance advocated by the Harper Commission in 1899 (Haley called Harper's plan one-man rule comparable to Rockefeller's role in Standard Oil). The CTF helped to elect Judge

Edward Dunne as mayor, while he in turn appointed liberal board of education members who approved many of the union's policies, such as the establishment of teachers councils to shape educational policy and the abolition of a secret rating system of teachers by administrators (part of a merit pay scheme). For a time this activism paid off, but the organization discovered that it had created fierce enemies in its legal and political forays, especially its attacks on corporate tax dodgers.[154]

The most successful foe of the CTF was Jacob Loeb, a businessman who became president of the board of education in 1916. In 1915 as board member Loeb proposed a regulation forbidding teachers to be members of trade unions. Not only the CTF but Samuel Gompers and local labor leaders regarded the Loeb rule as an assault on unionism. Four officials of Chicago and Illinois labor federations wrote a letter to the governor which claimed that the corporate elite on the board were attacking the labor movement and trying to use the schools to "create for them a body of trained, efficient, and somewhat servile workers" at the lowest cost in taxes. Gompers had fought a successful battle against a similar anti-union ruling in Cleveland the year before—indeed the superintendent there had been fined and jailed for blacklisting union teachers—and came to Chicago to join Haley in her fight. A judge wrote an injunction against the first Loeb ruling, but the next year under Loeb's chairmanship the board refused to rehire sixty-eight teachers. The cause for firing them was clear, since most were prominent in the CTF and had received good to superior ratings on their teaching. The Supreme Court of Illinois upheld the ouster, maintaining that the board had "the absolute right to decline to employ or re-employ any applicant for any reasons or for no reason at all. . . . It is no infringement upon the constitutional rights of any one for the board to decline to employ [him] as a teacher in the schools and it is immaterial whether the reason for the refusal to employ him is because the applicant is married or unmarried, is of fair complexion or dark, is or is not a member of a trade union or whether no reason is given for such refusal." "This is the happiest day of my life," exulted Loeb; "there will be no more labor unions in the public schools." [155]

The unsuccessful confrontation with Loeb proved to be a

turning point in the history of the CTF. Concerned about reinstating the fired teachers, Haley compromised with Loeb, and the CTF withdrew from the American Federation of Teachers and the Chicago Federation of Labor. In 1918 Haley also withdrew from the NEA, in which, as we shall see, she had been a prime mover for greater teacher power. Discouraged by the increasing influence and prestige of the business and bureaucratic forces she had been fighting for two decades, she concentrated on, preserving gains already won by cultivating alliances with local politicians.[156]

In the flush of her early victories over the tax-dodging corporations, however, Margaret Haley had dreamed of linking together the professional proletariat of woman teachers into a national organization. A reporter visited her in Chicago in 1905 when she was president of the National Federation of Teachers (NTF), a loose alliance of local teacher federations, many of them inspired by her CTF. All day the telephone rang, the in-box filled with letters from teachers in Tennessee, Iowa, North Dakota, asking Haley's advice about how to raise their pay, how to prevent teachers from being fired capriciously, how to go to court to secure their rights, how to get legislatures to pass laws favorable to teachers. One day, when teachers better understood the need for affiliation with labor and for political action, surmised the reporter, Haley would create "a great union of working women" that might have the power of the blacklist, the combined force of the labor movement, and real political power.[157]

Created in 1899 in Los Angeles, the NTF reorganized in 1901 with membership open only to classroom teachers. Its immediate goal was to put "into the hands of the grade and classroom teachers a weapon keen enough to cut the N.E.A. loose from the traditions that have bound it to the ideas and ideals of the eastern university people, which the teachers describe as standing for conservatism almost amounting to stagnation." For a time members of the NTF met concurrently with the NEA and sought its endorsement of the resolutions they passed, since the NEA could lend, thought Haley, "weight and dignity to our movement." [158]

In the NEA the position of classroom teachers, and especially women, had been an anomalous one throughout the nineteenth century. In 1910 Ella Flagg Young became the first woman president of the NEA, but when she had attended her first meeting of the association in 1867, she found that women were only "permitted to sit in the gallery and listen to discussions carried on by the men." Until 1866 the NEA followed the practice common in other teachers' associations of excluding women teachers from membership, even though they might attend meetings and write essays to be read aloud by male members. Although a few women were elected as officers of minor sections of the NEA, like the kindergarten or child study departments, very few ever spoke at major meetings or held powerful offices. In 1909, for example, there were no women trustees or members of the executive committee, and only one of the eleven vice-presidents was a woman; of the speakers at the general sessions, only one of fourteen speakers was a woman—this despite an overwhelming predominance of women members. Men also dominated the state teachers' associations. The editor of the *Western Journal of Education* lamented in 1909 that in the California organization "the women seem to lack the championship of a leader and are content to meekly pay their dollars and form the audience for the speakers, while the men show their educational efficiency by doing the thinking part in the lobbies of halls and hotels." That same year, however, Ella Flagg Young predicted that women would one day take their rightful leadership: "Women are destined to rule the schools of every city. I look for a large majority of the big cities to follow the lead of Chicago in choosing a woman for superintendent. In the near future we shall have more women than men in executive charge of the vast educational system. It is woman's natural field and she is no longer satisfied to do the greatest part of the work and yet be denied the leadership." [159]

Women like Haley and Young were hardly willing to let the men do their thinking. Fresh from victories against corporate tax dodgers in Chicago, Haley and her allies took on the "educational trust" that largely controlled the affairs of the NEA. In Boston in 1903 Haley started her campaign to turn the NEA into "the medium for expressing the most urgent needs in education," especially "better conditions for the teachers." That year Charles W. Eliot was president; he explained to suffragists that there were no women speakers because Mechanic's Hall had an all-male policy. Not daunted, the CTF hired its own hall and invited Young and other speakers, who attacked the NEA for its undemocratic organization and pressed for tenure, pensions, and higher salaries for teachers.[160]

On the NEA floor Nicholas Murray Butler proposed that the NEA president appoint the nominating committee rather than vesting power of nomination in persons chosen by the state associations. Barred from the rostrum, Haley rose from the audience to oppose Butler's porposal as a plan to create "a self-perpetuating machine" which would "keep out the women, who form nine-tenths of the membership of the National Education Association." It represented the same centralization of power she had been fighting in Chicago. She won in the vote that followed, and managed to persuade the assembly to work for higher teacher salaries. The program committee next year gave her a place on the program.[161]

As a member of the old guard, Butler bitterly resented Haley and her allies. Once the NEA had been a meeting ground of the educational aristocracy, he wrote in his autobiography, "not only men of great ability, but men of exceptional character and personality." In the twentieth century, however, it "fell into the hands of a very inferior class of teachers and school officials whose main object appeared to be personal . . . advancement." Haley saw the NEA governing clique as part of a "powerful, persistent, silent and largely successful conspiracy to make a despotism of our entire public school system," and she decided to try to oust the old guard by electing a sympathetic woman.[162]

In 1910 Haley combined forces with leaders of New York's militant Interborough Association of Women Teachers to plan strategy for the election of Ella Flagg Young. The nominating committee recommended a man, but for the first time in history a woman stood up to give a minority recommendation. The hundreds of women wearing Ella Flagg Young buttons had done their politicking well; in the vote that followed, Young received 617 of 993 votes of the active members. The press called the outcome a "triumph without parallel in the history of women's organizations." During Young's administration and that of the next four presidents—all endorsed by Haley—the NEA paid increasing attention to classroom teachers, endorsing higher salaries, equal pay for equal work, women's suffrage, and advisory teachers' councils. In 1913 the NEA approved a new organization advocated by Haley, the Department of Classroom Teachers, a group that stemmed from the League of Teachers Associations (composed largely of urban women elementary teachers).[163]

Haley's success in Chicago had encouraged other women teachers to organize. The largest other group was New York's Interborough Association of Woman Teachers (IAWT). A Manhattan seventh-grade teacher, Kate Hogan, began the organization in 1906 to press for equal pay for women teachers. That year an astute and energetic district superintendent named Grace Strachan took over as head of its executive committee. By 1910 14,000 members had joined. Despite school board attempts to prevent teachers from engaging in "politics," and moves to gag and punish leaders, the IAWT won important allies among labor unions, the mass media, women's associations, civic and religious leaders, and most important, politicians in the city and in the state legislature. By persistent work in Albany and arousal of public opinion at home, these voteless women secured in 1911 a law requiring that they should be paid the same as men doing the same work. In other cities teachers made similar demands. Whereas in 1904–05 in a sample of sixty-four cities with populations over 100,000 only 18.7 percent of women received the same pay as men for the same jobs, by 1924–25 79.7 percent had won equality.[164]

For a brief time, and in certain cities, skilled and fearless women were able to channel the resentment and quest for power of elementary teachers into effective organizations. Clear-cut grievances such as unequal pay or failure to pay promised higher salaries; a strong sense of group-consciousness; politically astute leaders who could analyze power relationships incisively and plan strategy accordingly—these were preconditions for organized militance.

Partly because of the counter-thrusts of the "lady labor sluggers," the blunt autocracy of Aaron Gove went out of style during the twentieth century. Increasingly administrators talked of cooperation, of democratic administration, of professionalism, of science, and not of the army, the police, or the factory opera-tive. The new "professionalism" made the old administrative bluntness obsolete in the 1920's and 1930's, and it helped to sat-isfy the status-hunger of underpaid educational workers. More and more administrators were told that they should "socialize" teachers the way teachers were to "socialize" children in the classroom: have them form committees on this and that, give them symbolic recognition (every other year a woman was presi-dent of the NEA from 1918 on), blur the actual lines of power. While some administrators really believed in "democratic ad-ministration," and genuinely tried to restructure authority in school bureaucracies, quite as often they manipulated teachers to arrive at conclusions the management had predetermined. Forms administrators used to rate teachers clearly indicated the premium placed on conformity, groupthink, cooperation (read *obedience*); the forms never inquired (to my knowledge) if teachers had a sense of humor—that was too subversive a quality for the professional bureaucrat. Worried about teacher unrest, the managers learned to coopt teachers rather than dictate to them, but when teachers persisted in independent behavior, prompt sanctions usually followed.[165]

Especially for the women, who constituted the great majority of teachers, the social pressures against militant organization were many. There was a high rate of teacher-turnover nationally (one fifth in 1919, for example). In the society as a whole women were trained to be submissive to men, and the schools permit-ted few to rise into high administrative positions (one paternal-istic male educator wrote a 280-page book telling them how to spend their recreational time!). Communities often regarded teachers as public property. City teachers remained subordinate members of elaborate bureaucracies, and new layers of adminis-trators often meant more bosses. Marian Dogherty wrote in the 1940's about Boston that "I became increasingly aware of . . . subservience to an ever growing number of authorities with each succeeding year, until there is danger today of becoming aware of little else." In the face of such obstacles, urban teacher unions would not gain substantial strength until the 1960's, when new conditions and new leaders would profoundly upset the calculus of power in urban schools.[166]

Epilogue: The One Best System under Fire, 1940-1973

If the educational reformers of Cubberley's generation had known in 1910 the statistics of American education a half century later, they would probably have exulted, confident that their aims would become fulfilled. In 1960 over 46,000,000 students were in school, constituting about 99.5 percent of the children aged seven to thirteen years, 90.3 percent of youth aged fourteen to seventeen, and 38.4 percent of those aged eighteen and nineteen. In 1966, 93.4 percent of all public school teachers had bachelor's degrees or higher. Pupil-teacher ratios were drastically reduced from 1910, federal and state aid was expanding school funds at a rapid rate, and splendid new school buildings were appearing all across the country as capital investment zoomed upward in the 1950's and 1960's. The reformers of 1910 would probably have welcomed the specialized structure and increased functions of the schools, the varied curriculum, the expanded number and role of educational experts as confirmations of their plans and dreams for American schooling. Yet if they had been able to look more closely, they might have discovered that in the late 1960's American public education was undergoing an unprecedented crisis, especially in the cities. Their one best system, so laboriously constructed, was under fire.[1]

Indeed, "crisis" became one of the common words in the

school lexicon during the years from 1940 to 1970, although it denoted different problems in the three decades. In the 1940's observers worried most about the critical shortage of funds and wondered how the cities could ever hire enough teachers and build enough schools to educate the multitude of children born during the war. Their strategy for reform fell well within the conventional wisdom of public education, however: more of the same, an upgrading and expansion of the familiar, would solve the basic problem.

In the 1950's the cold war intensified debate and action in a different sort of crisis: was American schooling too soft, too inefficient, too unselective to sustain the nation in its conflict with Russia? Sputnik dramatized concerns that began to emerge in the late 1940's. A fixation on internal subversion and external threat helped to turn attention away from developments that had far greater importance for the future of urban education, the demographic and economic changes taking place in the metropolis.

By the 1960's, however, schooling had become one of the prime weapons in the war on poverty and a central concern not only of policy-makers but also of the dispossessed, especially the people of color struggling for a greater share of power in cities. When muckrakers and sober scientists made it increasingly clear that the educational establishment was not fulfilling newly raised expectations, anger and disillusionment erupted, optimism gave way to doubt or despair, and many Americans came to question both the ideology and the institutions of public education. A new crisis was at hand, promising to be more serious and long-lasting than the previous ones.[2]

It is, of course, difficult to see the events of one's own time in perspective. Often people in the past have failed to perceive trends or events that later historians identified as central or pivotal. Recognizing that observations and conclusions need be tentative, I hazard the conjecture that historians a hundred years hence may consider the ferment of the 1960's and 1970's to be a major turning point in the history of American education, comparable in impact to the common school crusade of the mid-nineteenth century or the program of the administrative progressives in the early twentieth century.[3]

The "crises" of the 1940's and 1950's I see as controversies and

"Be Sure to Give Mine Special Attention"—from *Herblock's*
Special For Today (Simon & Schuster, 1958)

programs carried out largely within the familiar ideology and structure of the common school, even echoing previous episodes (the race between accommodations and mushrooming population, after all, characterized the earlier periods of greatest immigration and urban growth; arguments about "hard" and "soft" curriculum and methods and over the use of schools as sorting and selecting agencies in a meritocratic society were common well before the cold war).[4]

By the end of the 1960's, however, established assumptions and practices were questioned. Many people questioned whether equality of input in schooling was enough to promote equality of opportunity (some doubted that schooling had much to do with equality at all). Outcast groups eager for power argued that "keeping the school out of politics" was a smokescreen for elite, white rule. Critics of the establishment claimed that the professionals had neither the expertise nor the empathy to design schooling appropriate for all groups. Although scholarly books prior to 1965 had scarcely mentioned teachers, courts, ethnic groups, or students as elements in the power equation in school governance, by the 1970's teacher unionization, collective bargaining, judicial decrees, student rights, and community control upset the politics of education. People on both ends of the ideological spectrum began to propose basic alternative structures of schooling—vouchers, performance contracting, radical decentralization, free schools, alternative schools within the public system—and even the abolition of compulsory schooling or the deliberate deschooling of society.[5]

And while critics argued, urban teachers and students often went to work amid violence, strikes, drugs, armed guards in the corridors, and bureaucratic breakdown.[6]

During the Depression and the 1940's a number of educators called attention to the grossly unequal distribution of educational opportunities in the United States. "If formal educational attainments condition entrance to some economic and social spheres, and if great opportunities for educational advance are open to some groups while the educational facilities for others remain meager," warned Newton Edwards in 1939, "it is obvious that education becomes an instrument of social stratification and of regional and racial inequality." Far from being "the bulwark of democracy," he argued, public schools "may in fact become an instrument for creating those very inequalities they were designed to prevent." [7]

Researchers documented that educational attainment and credentials were becoming increasingly important in employment and found shocking differentials in educational finance. In 1940 an investigator asked employers in eighteen industries what was the minimum education they required of the persons they hired. He found that entrance into white-collar occupations depended heavily upon the degree of schooling. While employers required only minimal schooling for workers in unskilled, semiskilled, service, and skilled jobs, they demanded high school graduation for a majority of persons hired as managers and as clerical and sales workers; a majority of those hired as professionals or semiprofessionals needed a college degree. Yet in 1940 2,000,000 children aged six to fifteen were not in any school, and by mid-decade probably half of the most talented students dropped out of school before they had "the kind and amount of schooling which would be justified by both their ability and the demands of our way of life." In 1939–40 about 19,500 children attended schools costing $6,000 per classroom, while twice that many attended classrooms where the unit cost was less than $100: the upper 10 percent of schools spent $4,115 to the lowest 10 percent's $500. Worse off than city schools were those in the countryside. Clustered below the national average of $1,600 per classroom unit were the predominately rural states, bottoming out in Mississippi with its $400. Normally the poorest states and communities were making the greatest proportional sacrifice. Most exploited were the black schools of the states which maintained segregated systems. There the median expense for white classrooms was $1,166, for Negro $477. [8]

Significantly, a pamphlet financed by the NEA and the American Council on Education which publicized these inequities was entitled *Unfinished Business in American Education*. The job facing the public and educators was to *complete* the school system according to the traditional ideology and practice of the common school. A similar theme ran through the book by *New York Times* reporter Benjamin Fine published in 1947, *Our Children Are Cheated*. In his view, the *crisis* was fiscal and moral, a failure to live up to the traditional ideology, to reestablish the upward curve of educational progress broken by the Depression and the war. For six months Fine traveled all over the United States, talking with educators and legislators, visiting classes in big cities and mountain hollows. His conclusion: the public school system was near breakdown. Teachers were deserting the profession because of low pay and miserable morale; classes were overcrowded and double sessions were multiplying; parents were losing confidence in the public schools and sending their children to private schools instead; because of moratoria on building during the Depression and the war many communities had ancient, disintegrating, school facilities (in New York alone there were 200 schoolhouses over fifty years old).[9]

The most serious problem was the shortage of teachers, already serious before the population bulge of about 13,000,000 wartime babies hit the elementary grades. Partly to fill the gaps left by the 350,000 teachers who left the classroom, more than 125,000 people were teaching on emergency certificates, further diluting already minimal standards for competence (less than half of the teachers in 1947 had completed a college education). Although the nation would require hundreds of thousands of new teachers, enrollments in teacher training programs were well below capacity. "It's just impossible to get the teachers we need," the San Francisco superintendent told Fine. "We'll take anyone who wants to teach." When 450 school superintendents were asked if teacher morale was worse than before the war, 54 percent replied yes. Angered at their low salaries and poor working conditions, tens of thousands of teachers were striking or joining the American Federation of Teachers. A newly militant Latin teacher in Buffalo declared after joining a walkout on a blustery day in February 1947: "I've always been opposed to strikes. . . . I don't think it's right to keep the children out of school. But it looks as though the city wants it this way. Aren't teachers supposed to be human beings? How long do you think we can be stepped on?"[10]

Joining teachers in the drive for adequate financing for public schools were a variety of other interest groups. Each expressed traditional arguments. The National Association of Manufacturers and the Chamber of Commerce both argued that better education results in higher income. The American Federation of Labor complained that low teacher salaries, arbitrary administration, and political maneuverings were undermining the democratic purposes of the schools. The Congress of Industrial Organizations passed a resolution calling for an extension of opportunities in areas "where educational facilities are absent or meager" and endorsing federal aid for free schooling for adults.[11]

By the 1950's the united efforts of such groups and their political allies began to result in greatly improved conditions. Capital outlays for education jumped from $53,856,000 in 1943–44 to $1,477,322,000 in 1951–52. In 1953 the New York board of education closed a school built in the 1840's at the same time that it charted a $500,000,000 program of capital expansion for 312 new schools and additions. Total expenditures for all public schools increased from $2,906,886,000 to $10,955,047,000 in the decade after 1945, far outpacing the growth in the population of students. The disparities of educational expenditures between states, and between communities in states, and even within socioeconomic neighborhoods of the same districts, however, remained shockingly high, belying the goal of equality of opportunity revived by the reformers at the close of World War II.[12]

One reason for the overshadowing of the claims of the poor and the victimized minorities in the cities was preoccupation with the cold war during the late 1940's and 1950's. During one year of World War II the United States spent more for military purposes than it had expended on public education during the entire history of the nation. In 1955, a "peacetime" year, the federal government spent over $40 billion, almost four times the total expenditures for public education. But the cold war influenced the schools in many ways other than financial: under the influence of McCarthyism, many liberal and radical teachers were fired or silenced; pressures for ideological conformity became intense for students as well; little children in elementary schools learned passive fear as an official way of life as they huddled under their desks in mock atomic attacks; and competition with Soviet expertise became a leitmotiv of educational policy (recall that increased federal aid to education entered in the National *Defense* Education Act of 1958). Opinion-makers in education focused public attention on the need for cultivating talent as a weapon in the contest with communism. In the past, the schools had often glorified patriotism in its military forms and had put the schools at the service of the war effort, but not until the cold war did the needs of a military-industrial complex assume lasting and great prominence in educational policy. In the anxious fifties, many liberals—both pedagogical and political—were on the defensive.[13]

There were, of course, liberal policy-makers who saw no conflict between the meritocratic view of equality of opportunity and the new requirements of the military-industrial complex. Such persons also often combined a search for social justice with eager anti-communism. The educational statesman James Bryant Conant, for example, helped to call public attention to the desperate poverty of urban blacks in these words: "Communism feeds upon discontented, frustrated, unemployed people. . . . With what kind of zeal and dedication can we expect them to withstand the relentless pressures of communism?" The black youth in the ghettos who were "out of school and out of work" were "social dynamite," he argued in *Slums and Suburbs* (1961). "Leaving aside human tragedies," he added, "I submit that a continuation of this situation is a menace to the social and political health of the large cities." The urban riots of the mid-1960's helped to confirm his analysis.[14]

As Conant indicated, enormous demographic and economic changes were taking place in American cities in the three decades following 1940. These developments riveted the attention of educational reformers during the 1960's. "If, for a long period of years," Newton Edwards warned in 1939, "we draw each succeeding generation in disproportionately large numbers from those areas in which economic conditions are poorest and the cultural-intellectual level the lowest, if the population reserves of the nation are to be recruited from a definitely underprivileged class, and if we fail to make good the deficit by conscious educative endeavor, the effect on our culture and on our representative political institutions may be appalling." Indeed, the millions of people who migrated to the central cities from rural areas from 1940 to 1970 did come predominately from the most poverty-stricken and educationally parched areas of the

The View from the Schoolhouse Window: New York, 1935

republic—blacks from the rural South, where they had lived for generations in the shadow of the plantation; Puerto Ricans who emigrated from abject hovels on the island; Appalachian whites from isolated settlements that often had changed little since the eighteenth century; Mexicans from factories in the field in California. Victims of neglect or oppression, blacks in Mississippi moved to Chicago or New York, Chicano field workers in the San Joaquin Valley settled in barrios in Los Angeles, Native Americans left their reservations to attempt to put roots down in Oakland. Millions more migrated from slum to slum in the cities; during the period from 1955 to 1960, about half of the Negro migrants to northern cities came from other metropolitan areas.[15]

With federal subsidies through F.H.A. housing loans and freeways, middle-class whites fled the cities in vast numbers in the postwar years. In all central cities, there was a net loss of whites of 1.2 percent between 1960 and 1970, while some of the largest cities lost considerably more (New York, 9.3 percent; Chicago, 18.6; Cleveland, 26.5; St. Louis, 31.6; and Philadelphia, 12.9). Taking their place during that decade, in large part, were blacks: for all central cities there was an increase of Negro population of 32.6 percent, while there was an increase of over 50 percent in Boston, Newark, Milwaukee, New York, and Los Angeles. Blacks formed a majority of the total population in 1970 in three large cities—Atlanta, Newark, and Washington, D.C.—but in 1966–67 nonwhite pupils formed a majority in the public schools of ten major cities.[16]

In part as a result of urban migration patterns, central cities in the 1960's contained a disproportionate number of the old, the poor, and the unemployed. In 1969 one tenth of urban whites lived at or below the poverty line, one fourth of urban blacks. Among parents of schoolchildren the incidence of poverty rose more sharply than in the general population. "In 1950 it was estimated that one child out of every ten attending public schools in the nation's fourteen largest cities could be considered socioeconomically disadvantaged," report Raymond Hummel and John Nagle. "By 1960 this proportion had increased to one in three, and it is believed that by the early 1970's it had risen to approximately one out of every two." [17]

During the early twentieth century, industries in central cities absorbed a large proportion of the lower-class immigrants streaming into the metropolis. During World War II and in the 1950's and 1960's, however, many industries built plants in the suburbs. In 1947 60.8 percent of industrial workers in the nation's twelve largest metropolitan areas worked in central cities; by 1970 the figure had dropped to less than 40 percent. At the same time, overall employment in manufacturing dropped sharply in relation to white-collar clerical and service occupations; blue-collar workers outnumbered white-collar employees by one million in 1950, but by 1970 there were 47,700,000 white-collar workers and only 27,400,000 blue-collar workers. Many of the areas of projected growth in employment—commerce, construction, and clerical occupations, for example—were precisely those in which people of color had historically faced severe discrimination. Moreover, many of the white-collar jobs required higher standards in basic skills of reading, writing, and computation than did the older entry jobs in industry, posing a sharper challenge to the school system than it faced when the general educational attainment of the population was lower and occupational demands for academic competence were less rigorous.[18]

As we have seen, in the past black parents and students in cities often had high aspirations for the progress of the race through education, even in times when the job ceiling created, in effect, an occupational caste system. The *Brown* desegregation decision of the United States Supreme Court in 1954 gave hope to American Negroes across the nation that at last their quest for educational justice had the sanction of law. In the *Brown* case the Court affirmed belief in the central "importance of education to our democratic society" as "the very foundation of good citizenship." Indeed, it was because the school was so crucial that segregation on the basis of race denied black children "the equal protection of the laws guaranteed by the Fourteenth Amendment." "Today," said the Court, schooling "is a principal instrument in awakening the child to cultural values, in preparing him for later professional training, and in helping him to adjust normally to his environment. In these days, it is doubtful that any child may reasonably be expected to succeed in life if he is denied the opportunity of an education." Segregation, of course, denied the professed ideology of the common school, which in theory sought to mix all kinds of children under the unifying roof of the public school. Hence the Supreme Court was not so much stating a new principle as correcting an old abuse.[19]

The slow, painful, and still incomplete drive to enforce the new law of the land in the nation's schools made education a staging ground in the quest for racial justice. After *Brown*, supposedly with the rule of law on their side, blacks sought to enroll their children in all-white schools, only to find that troops had to be called out to protect little girls from white mobs. "It was incredible to a Negro woman who had been a servant in a white house for twenty years," wrote Louis Lomax, "that her employers would cringe and hide while white trash threw bricks at her grandson on his way to school." Daisy Bates told black parents in Little Rock that the students should stick it out.

"We've got to decide if [desegregation]'s going to be this generation or never." [20]

Some border cities with dual systems—like Washington, D.C., St. Louis, and Baltimore—desegregated fairly soon. But in most northern cities the legal situation was more cloudy, for there the segregation in the schools resulted mostly from residential patterns rather than from legal policy—de facto rather than de jure—although to the child in an all-black school the lawyers' technicalities probably made little difference. Ghetto residents, the poor, people of color generally, knew at first hand what scholarly studies revealed in cities like Detroit and Chicago: their schools were shortchanged, as statistics on run-down buildings, uncertified teachers, crowded classrooms, and inadequate equipment and books attested. The demand for desegregation in northern cities was for most blacks a quest for equality and quality in schooling more than some vague aspiration for mixing of ethnic groups; the white power structure could be trusted to teach Negro children adequately only if there were white children there as well, for practical experience had taught blacks that segregated schools had almost always been unequal.[21]

But the search for better education through desegregation proved disappointing. In New York, for example, the school board had issued in December of 1954 a ringing declaration that schooling "in a racially homogeneous setting is socially unrealistic and blocks the attainment of the goals of democratic education, whether this segregation occurs by law or by fact." A decade later, after numerous commissions and studies but little action, the number of schools with 90 percent or more Negro and/or Puerto Rican pupils had jumped more than 200 percent. After all the promises, the Harlem Parents' Committee declared in 1965, "standards and achievement in the segregated schools are still woefully inadequate, and there are more such schools every year." In the North, urban school boards and school leaders often rejected or sabotaged black demands for mixed schools, even in smaller cities where desegregation was relatively simple to implement. Ironically—in view of northern stereotypes—it was often southern cities which finally mixed the races in school most completely (under court pressures against dual systems, to be sure). In a number of cities, where ghettos were enormous—as in Chicago—and where almost all the pupils were black—as in Washington, D.C.—mixing of balanced populations of white and black was next to impossible within district boundaries. In any case, the campaign for desegregation in cities showed disappointing results nationwide when the Civil Rights Commission reported its findings in 1967: in all but a handful of large cities, the percentage of Negro students in schools with enrollments from 90 to 100 percent Negro increased markedly after *Brown.* At the end of the 1960's legal pressures were mounting to bus children across district lines, but powerful public reaction encouraged parents and politicians to resist court decrees.[22]

Another response to black demands for better schooling was the movement for "compensatory education." Responding to pressure from black militants and their white allies, many schoolmen informed black communities that the real problem was that their children were "culturally deprived." Pioneered by grants from foundations in the late 1950's and early 1960's, and fueled by large federal sums under Title I of the Elementary and Secondary Education Act in 1965, compensatory education was designed to improve the academic achievement of children who did not perform well in school, especially the poor and people of color. Just as the *Brown* decision and desegregation were attempts to institutionalize the professed ideology of a democratic *common* school, so the compensatory education movement was an effort to make the one best system work for "the culturally deprived." [23]

Psychologists and educators argued that the reason poor children often failed in school was that they lacked certain experiences in the home and community that enabled others to succeed—in short, that they had a "cultural deficit." In 1964 an assistant superintendent in Boston explained what such deprivation meant: "Many of these children have low aspirational levels. . . . By virtue of their limited background [they] fail to meet the expected outcomes as defined in Curriculum Guides. . . . It is our hope to raise the achievement of these pupils closer to their potentials which have for too long been submerged by parental lack of values." The chairman of the Boston school board put the matter more succinctly: "We do not have inferior schools; we have been getting an inferior type of student." The problem lay in the child, not in the educational or social system.[24]

Much of the effort of the early researchers and practitioners in compensatory education was well intentioned, some of it successful. A great deal of compensatory education in the 1960's resembled earlier attempts to teach and socialize the European immigrant child. What most professionals took for granted was the normal science of education (which was based largely on the psychological assessment of *individuals*) and the one best system (which was the existing structure and basic curriculum of the urban school). The researcher might never know that the same child who mumbled monosyllables in the classroom could also play imaginatively with words when rapping with friends on the street corner. The high school teacher saw a child who struggled with mathematics in the high school; she did not know that he might be the statistician for the numbers racket on his block. The mismatch in the culture of the school and the culture of the community, apparent to the ethnologist, might show itself only as "deprivation" in the classroom. But black psychologist Kenneth Clark saw the cultural deficit model as a cruel alibi, a new version of an old myth: "Just as those who proposed the earlier racial inferiority theories were invariably members of the dominant racial groups who presumed themselves and their groups to be superior, those who at present propose the cultural deprivation theory, are, in fact, members of the privileged group who inevitably associate their privileged status with their own innate intellect and its related educational success." [25]

For the most part, the effort and funds poured into compensatory education did not result in the goal of increased academic achievement (although later, more sophisticated efforts, as in some Head Start programs and in the Upward Bound program, did show gains). To be sure, the actual funds that reached ghetto schools were often small, prompting the comment that pouring in funds at the top of school bureaucracies was like feeding a horse in order to feed the sparrows. Often large sums went to pay new middle-class bureaucrats to administer the new programs. As ghetto parents learned about the low achievement scores and continued failures of their children, they increasingly lost faith in the expertise of the professionals. What they had feared was simply a personal misfortune—that their child could not read—was revealed to be a public problem of epidemic proportions. A joke made the rounds among blacks in New York: "What do you think of education in Harlem?" asked one parent. "I think it would be a good idea," replied the other. Those of a more bitter cast of mind began to talk of deliberate educational genocide.[26]

By the mid-1960's there was a new mood among the dispossessed. As Langston Hughes said, when a dream is too long deferred, it may explode. The hopes and expectations of the poor and people of color had been raised by the civil rights movement and by the "war on poverty." The *Brown* decision had promised that the common school might finally include all children—but whites resisted. The professionals had said that with more money and attention they could improve schooling for the educationally outcast—but reading scores continued to decline. Hope shifted to disillusionment and anger, and bitter rhetoric and violence escalated.[27]

One reason for the depth of concern was the mushrooming literature of criticism. Earlier periods of reform had their muckrakers, like Joseph Rice of the 1890's, but the volume and impact of the new exposés were unprecedented. Best sellers like *Up the Down Staircase* and *Death at an Early Age* ranged in tone from satire to flagellating anger, while dozens of lesser-known books and articles laid bare the faults of unresponsive bureaucracies, the despair or suffering of those at the bottom of the social and educational system, the violence in city schools, the awesome scope of educational failure. In this literature tales of success were few and reforms often abortive.[28]

In addition to these vivid and popular accounts, the 1960's produced many sober and detailed studies like the Coleman Report and *Racial Isolation in the Public Schools*. Cities and states released figures on the achievement levels of different districts, schools, and student populations—data which heretofore had been largely a secret of the bureaucracies. Such studies revealed that despite efforts at compensatory education the children of the poor and depressed minority groups tended to fall further behind in academic achievement in each year of schooling.[29]

Such evidence and popular literature appeared at a point in time when parents and policy-makers alike were newly aware that schooling had become crucial as a gateway to desirable employment. Increasingly the United States has become a credentials society—a development Ivar Berg has dubbed "the great training robbery"—and employers have shown little disposition to relent in their demand for educational requirements for employees. Hence schooling has gained consequences undreamed of during the nineteenth century; today educational failure condemns most drop-outs to low-level jobs or unemployment.[30]

This new public awareness of the failings and the significance of education has created a strong tension between the traditional ideal and the perceived actuality of urban education, especially among the "culturally different." In contrast with the democratic theory of public education, the ghetto parent saw that his child's school was segregated, that he had little voice in determining school policies, and that his child would graduate woefully ill-prepared to compete in a complex technological society.

As a result, many members of outcast groups demanded community control by their own people in place of the traditional corporate model of governance which sought to rise above "interest groups"; they substituted self-determination as a goal instead of assimilation; they rejected "equality" if that meant Anglo-conformity, sameness, and familiar failure in the "one best system." To many blacks the schools were not "above politics" but part of the struggle for black power. While he would have fought that kind of community control, arch-segregationist Senator Theodore Bilbo would at least have understood the principle. "All this talk about taking the schools out of politics is a huge joke to intelligent people," he said. "It means nothing except to take the schools out of your politics and put them in my politics." Many members of the so-called mainstream culture argued that the pluralism of the society should be reflected in the schools and that all students and parents should have a greater degree of choice among alternative forms of schooling.[31]

While groups outside the structure of the school system were demanding new influence and proposing new forms of education, realignments of power were taking place within the urban schools. An astute observer of the politics of education, Stephen

Bailey, observed in 1969 that "reading standard books, mono-graphs, and articles about school boards is a little like studying modern geography with a pre-World-War-II textbook, and a pre-World-War-I atlas. The continents are there; the mountains and lakes and rivers are there; but nothing else is the same." Teachers, students, ethnic communities gained quite new mean-ing in the 1960's as power groups.[32]

The greatest inside challenge to the existing distribution of power came from newly militant teachers, and specifically from the American Federation of Teachers. Although it would have seemed as unlikely in 1960 as a future President Nixon visiting Peking, by the end of the decade there was serious talk of merg-ing the NEA and the AFT into one massive and powerful orga-nization. As we have seen, urban teachers have from time to time become militant, but the results were often only sporadic and local. When they coalesced into power blocs they were often responding to specific grievances such as unequal or grotesquely inadequate pay, they had a strong sense of group identity and mutual protection, and they found skillful leaders who raised ex-pectations and provided political strategy. Similar circumstances gave rise to teacher militancy during the 1960's. In the 1950's, urban teacher salaries lagged behind those in the suburbs and fell far short of those in occupations with similar training, vio-lence in the schools and pressures from outside increased, and teachers continued to "have little or no say in the formulation of school policy." While teacher shortages and stronger tenure poli-cies gave greater security to the rank and file union member, de-termined and capable leaders like Albert Shanker emerged in the AFT.[33]

The turning point in teacher power came with two successful strikes waged by the United Federation of Teachers in New York City, which helped to add 53,000 members to the AFT (one half of them in New York). "By winning our two strikes, in 1960 and 1962 in New York City," said former AFT President Charles Cogen, "we set a pattern of teacher militancy for de-cades to come." In between these strikes the UFT won a collec-tive bargaining election in New York City in contest with an NEA coalition. In 1962 the NEA adopted a resolution on "pro-fessional negotiations" which set it on a course of competition

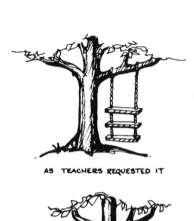

AS TEACHERS REQUESTED IT

AS PRINCIPALS ORDERED IT

AS CENTRAL OFFICE DESIGNED IT

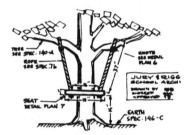

AS BOARD OF EDUCATION APPROVED IT

AS MAINTENANCE INSTALLED IT

WHAT THE STUDENTS WANTED

(C) THE TEACHER PAPER

with urban unions. While the NEA's "professional negotiations" differed in important respects from "collective bargaining," stressing the use of state educational agencies rather than labor precedent to settle disputes, the lines between the two sometimes became hard to distinguish, just as the NEA's "professional sanctions" came to bear a strange resemblance in some cases to strikes. During the 1960's the pace of militance rapidly increased in both organizations. From 1946 to 1965 NEA-affiliated groups conducted twenty-two "work-stoppages" enlisting 16,450 teachers; almost double that number of teachers in NEA groups stopped work in 1966 alone. In September 1967, about 100,000 teachers went out in union strikes in a number of cities, including Detroit and New York.[34]

Although the AFT was much smaller in membership than the NEA—about 135,000 to 1,000,000 in 1969—the union won power in many big cities by winning elections to represent the teachers in salary negotiations. The distinction between union and professional association became less and less sharp as the decade of the 1960's progressed. In an NEA poll of teachers in 1965 nine tenths favored group action in bargaining with employers; by 1968 two thirds of teachers in another NEA poll believed that strikes were acceptable. At mid-decade an NEA official observed that public school teachers worked in "a state of ferment bordering on rebellion." This changed the rules of the game for administrators as well. As Alan Rosenthal said, the key questions for superintendents became "*how* they will negotiate and on *what kinds* of matters," not *whether* they should negotiate. Agreeing on the principle of common action, in Los Angeles the union merged with the NEA affiliate to conduct a strike in 1970. In June of 1972 the New York State Teachers' Association joined forces with the UFT to form the New York State United Teachers, a massive organization numbering almost 300,000. The architect of the merger, UFT President Albert Shanker, envisaged that one day there might be a nationwide union of teachers: "The wave of the future in education is the A & P, not the corner grocery," he was quoted as saying.[35]

This drive for teacher power plunged leaders like Shanker into battle with other groups eager for change. Pressing for ever larger scope for negotiations, the UFT bitterly fought the movement in the mid-1960's to vest greater control of schools in de-centralized boards of education; indeed, the long and bitter strike of 1968 in New York—which polarized black and white to an unprecedented degree there—focused on the powers of local boards with respect to teachers. Because of their common op-position to community control, the union and the supervisors—former adversaries—joined forces. The UFT managed to per-suade the New York legislature to grant only minimal influence to the thirty-one local boards in its decentralization law of 1969, and then cooperated with other interest groups—notably Catho-lics—to elect local board members who would help to neutralize the black and Puerto Rican demands for larger power over edu-cation (in 1970, of 279 members of these boards, only 16.8 per-cent were black, 10.8 percent Puerto Rican; in twelve districts in which over 85 percent of the students were black or Puerto Rican, only half had boards in which a majority of the members were of those ethnic groups). Although the UFT and leaders like Shanker had been active in the campaign for civil rights and against racism, many ghetto residents perceived the quest for teacher power as an assault on their own legitimate aspirations and prerogatives.[36]

The AFT fought not only certain kinds of community control but also other proposals for change, such as performance con-tracting to outside business groups and vouchers, which might threaten job security. In addition, through collective bargaining teacher unions sought greater power over educational policies as well as higher salaries. In 1969 Alan Rosenthal reported that 185 teacher leaders in five large cities believed that teachers had minimal influence over personnel policy, curriculum, and school organization. Leaders like Shanker believed that American edu-cation could not be reformed until teachers could determine the form and content of schooling. Citizens had the right to decide "what the ends of society will be," he said. "Once they determine that, once they decide they want their kids to be able to read and count and do a lot of other things, then I think it is up to the ex-perts [the teachers] to decide how you structure or organize ma-terials in such a way it will effectively accomplish those pur-poses."[37]

From the late 1950's, when teachers had little influence, to

1970 a powerful new alignment of forces took place in urban schools, one comparable in potential impact to the centralization of control in small boards and powerful superintendents at the turn of the century. Whether teachers would indeed gain the kind of autonomy Shanker dreamed of was uncertain. Legislative demands for "accountability," as in California's Stull Bill, and taxpayer revolts against increasing teacher salaries indicated that the obstacles to full power for the organized teachers were many. But at the very least, teachers were the group with the greatest power to veto or sabotage proposals for reform. No realistic estimate of strategies for change in American education could afford to ignore teachers or fail to enlist their support. No meaningful improvement of life in classrooms could take place without the skill, empathy, strength, and commitment of teachers.[38]

In educational reform the decade of the 1960's has produced optimistic promises, raised expectations, bold experiments, some successes—and despair, failure, distrust, and neglect (both benign and otherwise). New strategies have popped up with astonishing speed: integration, compensation, community control, performance contracting, vouchers, alternative schools, deschooling—and the list goes on. Some of these innovations the reader will recognize as old wine in new bottles; others are comparatively novel. In short, the reform scene today is a kaleidoscopic confusion of contending interests, of different assessments of need, of rhetorical panaceas and jarring hopelessness.

A number of critics of American schools have argued that citizens have traditionally expected schools to accomplish broadscale social change quite beyond their scope or power, that our faith in education has become a surrogate for other kinds of needed social justice, such as income redistribution, greater industrial democracy, adequate housing, and equitable medical services for all. There is, I believe, much truth in this observation, but even in a more just and egalitarian society, some kind of schooling would continue to be essential so long as that society remained complex, technological, and interdependent. And for the dispossessed to have any kind of chance in the present social system, they would need far more competence than they are now gaining in such basic skills as reading and mathematics and greater knowledge of how the socioeconomic system works. To say that schooling does not explain as much of social mobility as some people have naively assumed in the past is not to say that it has no consequences; insofar as employers make decisions about whom to hire on the basis of skills or educational attainment, then the poorly schooled are mostly relegated to unemployment or to the worst jobs.

Intellectuals talk about deschooling and abolishing compulsory education, but there is little evidence that parents want compulsion to cease or that those committed to the present system—such as school employees—would be likely to fold up their tents and slink away. Indeed, the September 1973 Gallup poll on education reported once again, as in four of the previous five years, that citizens are most worried about "lack of discipline"; 76 percent of the national sample answered "extremely important" to the question "How important are schools to one's future success. . . ?" (19 percent replied "fairly important"). Even in the inner city, where conditions in the schools are often worst, polls suggest that residents are basically committed to public education. When urban parents were asked in 1968 what they thought of their children's schooling, 93 percent in Columbus and in Cincinnati, Ohio, said they thought their youngest child's teacher was doing an average or better than average job. They gave similar ratings to principals, and three fourths of those who acknowledged that the schools were facing unique and difficult problems said they thought the schools were coping reasonably well with them.[39]

Despite the efflorescence of proposals for alternatives to public schooling, it seems likely that effective improvement of the education of the urban poor will occur within the public schools if, indeed, it is to come about at all. With the waning of the reform impulses of the 1960's and the retreat of many part-time warriors on poverty, it has become apparent that the basic task of teaching the children of cities will still depend, as it has in the past, on those with full-time and long-term commitment, especially the teachers. Effective reform today will require reassessment of some cherished convictions about the possibility of finding a one best system, about the value of insulating the school from community influence, about the irrelevance of ethnic differences. To succeed in improving the schooling of the dispossessed, educators are increasingly realizing that they need to share power over educational decision-making with representatives of urban communities they serve, that they need to find ways to teach that match the learning styles of the many ethnic groups, that they need to develop many alternatives within the system and to correct the many dysfunctions of the vast bureaucracies created by the administrative progressives. Old reforms need to be reformed anew, for today many lack confidence in the familiar patterns of power and authority that developed at the turn of the century. Substantial segments of this society no longer believe in centralism as an effective response to human needs, no longer trust an enlightened paternalism of elites and experts, no longer accept the inevitability or justice of the distribution of power and wealth along existing class and racial lines. To create urban schools which really teach students, which reflect the pluralism of the society, which serve the quest for social justice—this is a task which will take persistent imagination, wisdom, and will.

NOTES

BIBLIOGRAPHY

INDEX

Notes

The bibliography gives full citations for works listed in abbreviated form in the notes.

PROLOGUE

1. For some recent—and sometimes conflicting—interpretations of educational historiography, see Cremin, *Cubberley;* Greer, *Great School Legend;* Church, "History of Education as a Field of Study"; Sloan, "Historiography"; Beach, "History of Education"; Tyack, "New Perspectives."

2. Scholars in sociology and political science have shown an increasing interest in schools. For introductions to the literature and research possibilities, see Brim, *Sociology and the Field of Education;* Bidwell, "The School as a Formal Organization"; Kirst, ed., *State, School, and Politics.*

3. On the value of comparative study of education, see Cremin, *Cubberley,* 50–51. See also Woodward, ed., *Comparative Approach to American History.*

4. Wiebe, *Search for Order;* Wiebe, "Social Functions of Public Education"; Wirth, "Urbanism"; Handlin, "Modern City"; Warner, "If All the World Were Philadelphia."

5. Gans, *Urban Villagers;* Merton, *Social Theory,* 387–420; Vidich and Bensman, *Small Town.*

6. Kimball and McClellan, *Education and the New America;* Berg, *Education and Jobs.*

7. Shepard, ed., *Thoreau's Journals,* 176–77.

8. N. Harris, review of Katz's *Irony of Early School Reform;* Greer, *Great School Legend;* Karier, Violas, and Spring, *Roots of Crisis;* Kozol, *Free Schools.*

PART I. The One Best System in Microscosm: Community and Consolidation in Rural Education

1. Eggleston, *Hoosier School-Master,* 1; this letter (not dated), together with a variety of records of a rural school in Ashland, is deposited in the O. C. Ap-

plegate Papers, Library of the University of Oregon; I am much indebted to the late Martin Schmitt for calling them to my attention. Manuscripts quoted here were included in an article on Ashland published in the University of Oregon Library Journal *Call Number* (Spring 1966), 13–23.

2. A number of the critical books and articles by professional educators will be cited below, as well as personal reminiscence about one-room schools.

3. Barber, *Schoolhouse at Prairie View*, 1.

4. Burton, *District School*, 107; Shatraw, "School Days," 68–71; Smith, "Protestant Schooling"; Tyack, "Kingdom of God and the Common School"; C. Johnson, *Country School, passim*.

5. MS report of Ashland School, 1865, O. C. Applegate Papers; Peil, "Oregon School Days," 200; Nelson, "Red Schoolhouse," 305.

6. C. Johnson, *Country School*, 4, 56–57; Nelson, "Red Schoolhouse," 306; Hazard, *Pioneer Teachers*.

7. C. Johnson, *Old Time Schools*, 102; Dick, *Sod-House Frontier*, ch. vi; John Miller to Oliver Applegate, June 21, Aug. 15, 1863, O. C. Applegate Papers.

8. Dallas et al., comps., *Lamplighters*, 28, 129.

9. Kirkpatrick, *Rural School*, 39–40.

10. Peil, "Oregon School Days," 206.

11. Elsbree, *American Teacher;* Beale, *Freedom of Teaching*.

12. John Miller to Oliver Applegate, Feb. 16, 1867, O. C. Applegate Papers. It should be noted that there were many rural schools where neither the teachers nor the communities they served had any real power over education. Examples of such colonial, powerless institutions are schools on Indian reservations, or rural black schools in the South, or schools attended by migratory workers' children. Such dispossessed groups rarely had any voice even in that bastion of participatory democracy, the rural school district.

13. Garland, *Son of the Middle Border*, 112; Masters, *Across Spoon River*, 39; C. Johnson, *Old Time Schools*, 159; letter of C. T. Lloyd to author, May 11, 1966. For a general study of textbooks, see Elson, *American Textbooks*, esp. chs. vii–ix.

14. Henry Cummins to Oliver Applegate, Feb. 17, 1863, O. C. Applegate Papers; John Miller to Oliver Applegate, Apr. 15, 1863, O. C. Applegate Papers; Oregon Superintendent of Public Instruction, *Report for 1874*, 58–59.

15. Cubberley, *Rural Life and Education*, 105–106.

16. Kirkpatrick, *Rural School*, 140–41; Keppel, "Myth of Agrarianism in Rural Educational Reform."

17. Cubberley, *Rural Life and Education*, 55–56, 70–71, chs. ii–iv; Committee of Graduate School of Education, Nebraska, *Rural Teacher of Nebraska*, 27–28.

18. O. M. Smith, "Rural Social Center," 110; Cubberley, *Rural Life and Education*, 106–107; Eggleston and Bruere, *Work of the Rural School*, 20–21; Carney, *Country Life and Country School*, ch. ii.

19. Cubberley, *Rural Life and Education*, 113; for the role of one evangelist in awakening country people, see A. Shaw's account of Superintendent O. J. Kern's work in Illinois, "Common Sense Country Schools."

20. Committee of Twelve, "Report," I, 820–21.

21. Oregon school regulations, as quoted in Raymer, "Superintendency in Oregon," 154–55, 138; letter from Robert Ginter to ed., *Portland Telegram*, Oct. 23, 1922.

22. Cubberley, *Rural Life and Education*, 306–307, 183.

23. Alford, "School District Reorganization," 355–57; Joint Committee on

Rural Schools, *Rural School Survey of New York State*, I, 257, 200ff.; Woodring, "One-Room School," 152.

24. West, *Plainville*, 80–81; Selznick, *Leadership in Administration*, 5–22; Gump and Barker, *Big School, Small School*, ch. xii; Burnett, "Ceremony, Rites, and Economy in the Student System of an American High School."

25. Alford, "School District Reorganization," 362; E. B. White, "Letter from the East," 36.

26. Lieberman, *Future of Public Education*, 34–36; Levin, ed., *Community Control of Schools*.

27. Alford, "School District Reorganization," 353; Vidich and Bensman, *Small Town*, xviii.

PART II. From Village School to Urban System:
Bureaucratization in the Nineteenth Century

1. Katz, *Class, Bureaucracy, and Schools*, chs. i–iii; Tyack, "Bureaucracy and the Common School"; Dalby and Werthman, eds., *Bureaucracy in Historical Perspective*.

2. Higham, *From Boundlessness to Consolidation*, 26–27.

3. W. T. Harris and Doty, *Theory of Education in the U.S.*, 12–13; Katz, *Class, Bureaucracy, and Schools*; Gutman, "Work, Culture, and Society," 555; for the bureaucratization of welfare services, see Lubove, *Professional Altruist*.

4. U.S. Bureau of the Census, *Historical Statistics*, 14, 139, 427; Schultz, *Culture Factory*, 286; Jackson and Schultz, eds., *Cities*, 99.

5. Still, *Milwaukee*, 230–53; Wirth, "Urbanism."

6. Richardson, "To Control the City," 272, 273–89.

7. Lane, *Policing the City*.

8. Grund, *Aristocracy in America*, 162; Dwight, *Travels*, IV, 449–52, 466–68; Tyack, *Ticknor*, 13–18, ch. vi.

9. Schultz, *Culture Factory*, 134–38; Katz, *Class, Bureaucracy, and Schools*, 59–62; *Reports of the Annual Visiting Committees of the Public Schools of the City of Boston, 1845*, as reproduced in Caldwell and Courtis, *Then and Now in Education*, 165, 185–86, 226–27. For the sake of conciseness and uniformity, I will hereafter cite city school reports in this abbreviated form: *Boston School Report for 1845*.

10. School reformer, as quoted in Schultz, *Culture Factory*, 148, 146–47; Ticknor, "Free Schools."

11. *Seventh Annual Report of the Board of Education* (Boston); Schultz, *Culture Factory*, 138–53.

12. *Boston School Report for 1845*, 203, 168, 173.

13. Ibid., 194–98; on the immunity of the masters, see *Boston School Report for 1903*, 20.

14. Nash, *Philadelphia Public Schools*, 18, 20–21, 25, 28–33; Philbrick, *City School Systems*, 16.

15. Herrick, *Chicago Schools*, 37, 26, 36.

16. Ibid., 28–29, 37–38.

17. Ibid., 38, 39–50.

18. Marble, "City School Administration," 166, 165; W. A. Mowry, *Recollections*, 9; Lazerson, *Urban School*, ch. i; Wohl, "The 'Country Boy' Myth."

19. Philbrick, *City School Systems*, 58–59, 8, 57, 8, 10–11; Draper, "School Administration," 27.

20. Philbrick, *City School Systems*, 47.

21. Kaestle, "Urban School System: New York," 342, 366–67.

22. Bishop, as quoted in Schultz, *Culture Factory*, 151, 103–104; Winship, "What the Superintendent Is Not."

23. Philbrick, *City School Systems*, 115–16; Kaestle, "Urban School System: New York," ch. v; Katz, *Class, Bureaucracy, and Schools*, 70–71.

24. Schultz, *Culture Factory*, 141–53; Kaestle, "Urban School System: New York," 366–67.

25. Gear, "Rise of Superintendency," ch. ix; Wesley, *NEA;* Schmid, "Organizational Structure of NEA"; Kaestle, "Urban School System: New York," chs. iv–v.

26. Wade, *Urban Frontier*, 314, 317; *St. Louis School Report for 1857*, 324–29, 354–69.

27. *St. Louis School Report for 1871*, 31–32.

28. Philbrick, *City School Systems*.

29. Barnard, "Gradation of Public Schools," 456, 457–58.

30. Philbrick, "Report of the Superintendent (1856)," 263; Bunker, *Reorganization*, 19–24; Schultz, *Culture Factory*, 125–31.

31. Shearer, *Grading of Schools*, 21; Bunker, *Reorganization*, 35; Goodlad and Anderson, *Nongraded Elementary School*, 44–49.

32. Philbrick, *City School Systems*, 67, 59; Cremin, "Curriculum-Making."

33. Herrick, *Chicago Schools*, 42–43.

34. W. T. Harris, "Elementary Education," 32–34.

35. Philbrick, *City School Systems*, 65; Finkelstein, "Governing the Young."

36. *Portland School Report for 1874*, 4; *Portland School Report for 1877*, 16.

37. *Portland School Report for 1874*, 8–9; Powers and Corning, "Education in Portland," 45, 327.

38. *Portland School Report for 1878*, 16–18; *Portland School Report for 1882*, 37–39; Dillon, "Portland Public Schools," 26–27.

39. White, as quoted in Button, "Supervision in the Public Schools," 33; Philbrick, *City School Systems*, 47.

40. W. T. Harris and Doty, *Theory of Education in the U.S.*, 14; on the hidden curriculum, see Fantini and Weinstein, *The Disadvantaged;* Dreeben, *On What Is Learned in School*.

41. *Portland School Report for 1876*, 8–9; Powers and Corning, "Education in Portland," 51; *Portland School Report for 1881*, 29; *Portland School Report for 1882*, 27–28; Winship, "What the Superintendent Is Not."

42. MacRae, *Americans at Home*, 601–603.

43. Baltimore School Board Committee, as quoted in Finkelstein, "Governing the Young," 373–75, 378.

44. "July, 1868, Two Representative Schools," as quoted in Finkelstein, "Governing the Young," 381–84.

45. Ibid.; Greer, *Great School Legend*, 36–37.

46. Finkelstein, "Governing the Young," 134–35; I shall return to the use of educational science in Part V below.

47. Rice, *Public School System*, 98.

48. Krug, *High School*, I, 3–6; Herrick, *Chicago Schools*, 41.

49. U.S. Bureau of the Census, *Historical Statistics*, 207; Krug, *High School*, 13–14; Herrick, *Chicago Schools*, 82.

50. Katz, *Irony of Early School Reform*, 39; Troen, "Popular Education," 31; Krug, *High School*, 12–13; Philbrick, *City School Systems*, 23, 26–27.

51. Committee of Ten, *Report*, 41; Philbrick, *City School Systems*, 31; Krug, *High School*, 11–12.

52. Payne, *School Supervision*, 42–43, 13–14, 17; Barnard, "Gradation of Public Schools," 461, 459; W. T. Harris, "Elementary Education," 6–8; Elsbree, *American Teacher*, ch. xxiii; Krug, *High School*, 3–6; Herrick, *Chicago Schools*, 41.

53. "School Mistress"; Gove, "Limitations of the Superintendents' Authority," 154; Elsbree, *American Teacher*, 201, 203.

54. Button, "Supervision in the Public Schools," 32; Warfield, "How to Test the Quality of a Teacher's Work"; Anderson, "Qualification and Supply of Teachers," 423–30; *Portland School Report for 1881*, 31–37.

55. Coffman, *Social Composition of the Teaching Population*, 82, 28. In *The Political Life of American Teachers* Harmon Zeigler reports that "maintaining discipline is much more of a problem for male teachers than for female teachers; indeed, one suspects that the crisis in authority is related to the recruitment of male teachers" (24).

56. Elsbree, *American Teacher*, 554; Philbrick, *City School Systems*, 127; *Report of the Committee on Salaries*, 52.

57. Elsbree, *American Teacher*, 431–35, 278; *Report of the Committee on Salaries*, 23, 54, 74.

58. U.S. Commissioner of Education, *Report for 1873*, cxxxii–cxxxiv; *Report for 1887*, 225; *Report for 1892*, II, 669–71. (For the sake of conciseness and uniformity, I shall cite in this abbreviated form the annual reports of the Commissioner of Education which were published in Washington, D.C., by the Government Printing Office. These reports covered educational matters for the *school* year, e.g., 1898–99; in all cases, I shall refer to the latter year in citations.) Philbrick, *City School Systems*, 127–30; Strachan, *Equal Pay*.

59. Hamilton [Dodge], *Common School System*, 96, 99, 123, 302–303.

60. Ibid., 309, 310–11, 315.

61. U.S. Commissioner of Education, *Report for 1901*, II, 2407; DeFord, *They Were San Franciscans*, 136–45; Dolson, "San Francisco Public Schools," 245–46; Reid, "Professionalization of Public School Teachers"; Strachan, *Equal Pay;* Elsbree, *American Teacher*, 451.

62. W. T. Harris, "Elementary Education," 3–4, 54. The panic of 1873 did not much influence the rising curve of enrollments and expenditures; Tyack, "Education and Social Unrest, 1873–1878."

63. Fishlow, "Levels of Nineteenth Century Investment in Education," 418–19, 423, 427, 435.

64. Troen, "Popular Education," 27–31.

65. Ibid., 31–37; W. Miller, ed., *Men in Business*.

66. *San Francisco School Report for 1873*, as quoted in Dolson, "San Francisco Public Schools," 173, 120–23, 345–53; Schultz, *Culture Factory*, chs. x–xi; *San Francisco School Report for 1854*, 31–32; San Francisco Schools Circular no. 52, 1884.

67. *Report to the Primary School Committee, June 15, 1846, on the Petition of Sundry Colored Persons*, 5; Schultz, *Culture Factory*, 278–79, 299; Katz, *School Reform*, 135.

68. Massachusetts superintendent, as quoted in Ensign, *Compulsory School Attendance*, 63.

69. Abbott and Breckinridge, *Truancy and Non-Attendance in Chicago,* 60–62; Herrick, *Chicago Schools,* 60–62, 64, 66; Dolson, "San Francisco Public Schools," 177–80; Perrin, *Compulsory Education,* ch. iii.

70. Herrick, *Chicago Schools,* 58; Philbrick, *City School Systems,* 154–55.

71. Ensign, *Compulsory School Attendance,* 173; Philbrick, *City School Systems,* 185–87; Berkowitz, "Educational Rights of Children"; W. T. Harris, "Elementary Education," 21–24; Drost, *Snedden,* 67, 72–74, 77.

72. Rothman, *Discovery of the Asylum,* 64–66, 285.

73. Ibid., 188, 235.

74. W. T. Harris, "Elementary Education," 4–6, 11, 16; Gutman, "Work, Culture, and Society"; Curti, *Social Ideas of American Educators,* 318–21; Herriott and Hodgkins, *The Environment of Schooling,* 26–27, 84–88.

75. W. T. Harris and Doty, *Theory of Education in the U.S.,* 12; Eaton, *Relation of Education to Labor,* 117, 121; M. P. Mann and Peabody, *Moral Culture,* 107–108.

76. Educator, as quoted in Lazerson, *Urban School,* 30; Wade, "Violence in the Cities."

77. H. Mann, *Life and Works,* IV, 345; U.S. Commissioner of Education, *Report for 1877,* viii; National Education Association, *Addresses and Proceedings for 1877,* 6; Everett, *Orations and Speeches,* II, 318; Curti, *Social Ideas of American Educators,* 215.

78. H. Mann, *Life and Works,* IV, 354–55, 364–65; *Portland School Report for 1880,* 34–35 (Portland) *Oregonian,* Feb. 25, 1880.

79. Boston school committee member, as quoted in Lazerson, *Urban School,* 33; Northrup, *Report,* 35; Ensign, *Compulsory School Attendance,* 204.

80. Committee on City School Systems, "School Superintendence in Cities," 309.

81. Ibid., 310–12.

82. Chicago Merchants' Club, *Public Schools and Their Administration,* 40.

PART III. The Politics of Pluralism: Nineteenth-Century Patterns

1. Jones, "Politician and Public School," 810, 812; Gilland, *Powers and Duties of the City-School Superintendent,* ch. vi; Reller, *City Superintendent of Schools,* ch. viii; Cronin, *Control of Urban Schools,* chs. iii–v; Yeager, "School Boards," 974.

2. For discussions of how similar issues influenced the police in New York and Boston, see Richardson, *New York Police,* and Lane, *Policing the City.* For other studies of the force of cultural issues in politics, see Gusfield, *Symbolic Crusade,* and Kleppner, *Cross of Culture.*

3. Cubberley, *Public Education in the United States,* 164–65; see also Cremin, *Cubberley.*

4. For samplings of current dissent, see Gross and Gross, eds., *Radical School Reform;* and Carnoy, ed., *Schooling in a Corporate Society.*

5. Hinsdale, *Our Common Schools,* 32, 28–29, 30–31.

6. Adams, "Scientific Common School Education"; C. W. Eliot, "Undesirable and Desirable Uniformity," 82, 86; Hamilton [Dodge], *Common School System,* 91.

7. Rice, *Public School System,* 23.

8. Ibid., 95, 31–33, 60.

9. (Portland) *Oregonian,* Feb. 9, Feb. 23, 1880.

10. Ibid., Feb. 21, 1880.

11. Ibid., Feb. 26, Mar. 1, 1880.

12. Boston priest, as quoted in Schultz, *Culture Factory,* 306; Hughes, as quoted in Kaestle, "Urban School System: New York," 311, 314, 315; Tyack, "Onward Christian Soldiers."

13. Hughes, and *Putnam's Monthly,* both as quoted in Kaestle, "Urban School System: New York," 315–16, 294.

14. Hughes, as quoted in Katz, *Class, Bureaucracy, and Schools,* 13; Lannie, *Public Money and Parochial Education.*

15. Billington, *Protestant Crusade,* ch. xiv; Tyack, "Kingdom of God and the Common School."

16. Tyack, "Catholic Power, Black Power, and the Schools."

17. Billington, *Protestant Crusade,* ch. vi; Dorchester, *Romanism,* 85, 115ff.; Higham, *Strangers in the Land,* 28–29.

18. I have developed some parallels and differences with black power in my article "Catholic Power, Black Power, and the Schools."

19. Schultz, *Culture Factory,* 298–300, 291; Katz, *Irony of Early School Reform,* 19–50, 272–79; Shotwell, *Schools of Cincinnati,* 289–97.

20. Skidmore, *Rights of Man to Property,* 369; Greeley, *Hints toward Reforms,* 219; Curti, *Social Ideas of American Educators,* 199.

21. Cronin, *Control of Urban Schools,* ch. iii; Reller, *City Superintendency of Schools,* 150, 156; Gear, "Rise of Superintendency," 17–19.

22. Buffalo superintendent, as quoted in Reller, *City Superintendency of Schools,* 151, 152, 156.

23. Philbrick, *City School Systems,* 15–16.

24. Ibid., 15; Reller, *City Superintendency of Schools,* 162–63 (the description of Greenwood is in Reller's words); Dabney so described the Birmingham board situation in *Universal Education in the South,* II, 402–404.

25. Philbrick, *City School Systems,* 54; W. T. Harris, "City School Supervision."

26. Gear, "Rise of Superintendency," 160–62.

27. Abelow, *Maxwell,* 28; Palmer, *New York Public Schools,* 274; Berrol, "Immigrants at School," chs. i, iii.

28. Reller, *City Superintendency of Schools,* 164–67; Philbrick, *City School Systems,* 59.

29. *Boston School Report for 1903,* 20–21.

30. Rice, *Public School System,* 149–50; Dolson, "San Francisco Public Schools," chs. iii–v; Nash, *Philadelphia Public Schools,* ch. ii.

31. Glazer and Moynihan, *Beyond the Melting Pot,* 226.

32. Vare, *My Forty Years in Politics,* 118–19; Dorsett, *Pendergast Machine,* 41; McKitrick, "Corruption," 505–508; Merton, *Social Theory,* 71–82.

33. Mandelbaum, *Boss Tweed's New York,* 69; Cornwell, "Bosses, Machines, and Ethnic Groups," 28–34.

34. A. Shaw, "Public Schools of Boss-Ridden City," 4464; Holli, *Reform in Detroit,* 27–28; Salmon, *Patronage.*

35. "Confessions of Public School Teachers"; "Confessions of Three School Superintendents"; Steffens, *Autobiography,* 451; (Portland) *Oregonian,* Sept. 23, 24, Oct. 28, 1894.

36. Herrick, *Chicago Schools,* 77–79, 101; Reid, "Professionalization of Public School Teachers," ch. iii.

37. Reller, *City Superintendency of Schools,* ch. vii.

38. Ibid., 173; Gove, "Trail of the City Superintendent," 219; Gove, "Duties

of City Superintendents"; Gove, "Limitations of the Superintendents' Authority"; Gove, "Contributions to the History of American Teaching"; Johnson, "Captain of Education."

39. Gilbert, *School and Its Life*, 85, 83; Gilbert, "Freedom of the Teacher," 165–67.

40. Jones, "Politician and Public School," 814–15, 813; Philbrick, *City School Systems*, 116.

41. Swett, *Public School System of California*, 78; *San Francisco School Report for 1880*, 423; *San Francisco School Report for 1892*, 130–31, 132.

42. A. Shaw, "Public Schools of Boss-Ridden City," 4461–62.

43. Ibid., 4462–63.

44. Nash, *Philadelphia Public Schools*, 58–61; Shaw, "Public Schools of Boss-Ridden City," 4460; Issel, "Modernization in Philadelphia School Reform," 379; Issel, "Teachers and Educational Reform," 220–23.

45.. Hammack, "Centralization of New York City's Public School System," ch. iii. In Mayor Strong's papers at the New York Public Library, Box 6147 contains letters to Strong advocating or opposing the bill to eliminate the powers of the ward boards; Box 6063 contains public speeches and publicity. In the following notes, I will cite the author of the letter or speech, the date, and the box number. Matthew J. Elgas, "Arguments against 'The Compromise School Bill,' " April 18, 1896, Box 6063; letter of Jacob W. Mach to Mayor Strong, April 16, 1896, Box 6147.

46. Letter of E. Slight to Mayor Strong, April 10, 1896, Box 6147; "School Trustees and the Children," statement of W. T. Nicholson to Mayor Strong, no date, Box 6063.

47. Letter of W. Phinley to Mayor Strong, April 17, 1896, Box 6063; unsigned and undated statement, p. 4, Box 6063 (Hammack ["Centralization of New York City's Public School System," 124] says that this was probably written by Board of Education President MacKay).

48. Handbill, " 'SCHOOL REFORM,' " Box 6063.

49. Philbrick, *City School Systems*, 117; Haley, "Why Teachers Should Organize."

50. Mayo, "Object Lessons," 7, 9; Jay, "Public and Parochial Schools," 172; E. E. White, "Religion in the School," 297; Strong, *Our Country*, 55; Tyack, "Onward Christian Soldiers"; Gusfield, *Symbolic Crusade*, 13–24, ch. vii.

51. Merk, "Boston's Historic Public School Crisis," 182–83.

52. Fishman, *Language Loyalty*, 233–36; Kleppner, *Cross of Culture*, 168.

53. Shotwell, *Schools of Cincinnati*, 291–93, 301; *Cincinnati School Report for 1900*, 64.

54. *St. Louis School Report for 1875*, 114–15, 111–13; *St. Louis School Report for 1866*, 37; *St. Louis School Report for 1878*, 67.

55. *Chicago School Report for 1900*, 235, 239; Fishman, *Language Loyalty*, 234–35.

56. Fishman, *Language Loyalty*, 236; emphasis added.

57. *San Francisco School Report for 1875*, 56–57; Andersson and Boyer, *Bilingual Schooling*, I, 17; *Proceedings of the Board of School Directors, Milwaukee*, May 14, 1915, 434; Dolson, "San Francisco Public Schools," 108; Claxton et al., *San Francisco Survey*, 560–61.

58. Pierce, *History of Chicago, 1871–1893*, III, 367–38, 385; Fishman, *Language Loyalty*, 236; Kleppner, *Cross of Culture*, 158–68.

59. *Boston Primary School Report for 1847,* 10; Fishel, "The North and the Negro," chs. iv, v, vii; Weinberg, *Race and Place.*

60. *Christian Recorder,* as quoted in Silcox, "Pursuit of Black Education," 16; Foner, ed., *Frederick Douglass,* IV, 288–90.

61. Woodson, *Education of the Negro;* Litwack, *North of Slavery,* 113–52; Heller, "Negro Education in Indiana"; Goodwin, "Schools for the Colored Population, District of Columbia," 222, 201.

62. Sacramento City Council, as quoted in H. H. Bell, "Negroes in California, 1849–1859," 152; *New York Superintendent's Report for 1849,* 12–13.

63. Schultz, *Culture Factory,* 171–74; Mabee, "A Negro Boycott," 341.

64. Mabee, "A Negro Boycott," 347, 352; Schultz, *Culture Factory,* 196–97.

65. *Boston Primary School Report for 1847,* I, 23, 13, 7, 14, 5; Schultz, *Culture Factory,* 197–98.

66. Darling, "Prior to Little Rock," 129, 142; Mabee, "A Negro Boycott," 355–61.

67. Fishel, "The North and the Negro"; A. O. White, "Jim Crow Education."

68. Stephenson, *Race Distinctions,* 177; Dolson, "San Francisco Public Schools," 115–20; *San Francisco School Report for 1875,* 58, 133.

69. Homel, "Black Education," 11–12, 7; Stephenson, *Race Distinctions,* 179–80; Meier and Rudwick, "Early Boycotts of Segregated Schools: Alton."

70. Thornbrough, "The Negro in Indiana," 318, 321–22, 323.

71. Ibid., 333–34, 337–38; Green, *Secret City,* 102, 110, 134–36; Hose, "Schoolhouse," 259–70.

72. Dixon, "Education of the Negro in New York," 62; U.S. Immigration Commission, *Children of Immigrants,* I, 8–13, 129–33.

73. Meier and Rudwick, "Early Boycotts of Segregated Schools: East Orange"; Parks, *Learning Tree,* ch. viii; Green, *Secret City,* 131; Terrell, "High School for Negroes in Washington."

74. Calkins, "Black Education: Cincinnati, 1850–87," 5–11.

75. Aptheker, ed., *History of the Negro People,* 399–401; Thurston, "Ethiopia Unshackled: Education of Negro Children in New York," 219–20.

76. Thurston, "Ethiopia Unshackled: Education of Negro Children in New York," 220–22; Dixon, "Education of the Negro in New York," 63–65, 67–68.

77. Goodwin, "Schools for the Colored Population, District of Columbia," 261; Dabney, *Schools for Negroes, District of Columbia,* 199–205, 216; Green, *Secret City,* 135.

78. Gersman, "Separate but Equal: St. Louis," 6; G. L. Mann, "Education for Negroes in Saint Louis," ch. iv; Troen, "Education and the Negro: St. Louis," 2–6.

79. Gersman, "Separate but Equal: St. Louis," 6; Troen, "Education and the Negro: St. Louis," 2–6.

80. Troen, "Education and the Negro: St. Louis," 12–14.

81. Ibid., 11; Gersman, "Separate but Equal: St. Louis," 18–19.

82. Gersman, "Separate but Equal: St. Louis," 28; DuBois, *Philadelphia Negro,* 89–90.

83. U.S. Bureau of the Census, *Historical Statistics,* 213–14.

84. Andrews, *New York African Free-Schools,* 120, 132; Baker, *Following the Color Line,* 39; DuBois, *Philadelphia Negro,* 100, 126; Gersman, "Separate but Equal: St. Louis," 16.

85. Meier and Rudwick, "Early Boycotts of Segregated Schools: East

Orange," 24, 26; Cubberley, *State and County Educational Reorganization,* 4; J. B. Sears and Henderson, *Cubberley.*

PART IV. Centralization and the Corporate Model: Contests for Control of Urban Schools, 1890–1940

1. Draper, "Plans of Organization," 1.
2. Draper, *Crucial Test,* 4–5; Chamberlain, "City School Superintendent," 401.
3. Cronin, *Control of Urban Schools,* chs. iv–v; Morehart, *Legal Status,* 11; Morrison, *Legal Status,* ch. ii; Rollins, *School Administration,* 24–31, for useful statistical charts; Cubberley, *Public School Administration,* ch. viii; D. Mowry, "Milwaukee School System," 141–51; Moehlman, *Public Education in Detroit,* 173–80.
4. Douglass, *Status of the City Superintendent;* Theisen, *City Superintendent.*
5. Hays, "Politics of Reform," 159, 163; Cremin, *Transformation of the School;* Callahan, *Education and the Cult of Efficiency;* Kimball and McClellan, *Education and the New America;* Wiebe, "Social Functions of Public Education"; Filene, "Obituary for 'the Progressive Movement.' "
6. Spring, *Education and the Corporate State;* Randall, "Progressivism"; Korman, *Industrialization.*
7. C. W. Eliot, "Educational Reform," 217, 219, 220.
8. C. W. Eliot, "School Board Reform," 3; Draper, "Plans of Organization," 304–305; C. W. Eliot, "Educational Reform," 222.
9. Draper, "Plans of Organization," 299–300; Draper, "Common Schools in the Larger Cities."
10. C. W. Eliot, "Educational Reform," 218; Handlin, *Dewey's Challenge to Education;* C. W. Eliot, "School Board Reform," 3.
11. Dutton and Snedden, *Administration of Public Education,* 122–23.
12. Holli, *Reform in Detroit,* 162; Hewitt, Goodenow, National Education Association Committee, and Bryce, as quoted in ibid., 178–79, 172–75; Cubberley, *Changing Conceptions of Education,* 15.
13. Holli, *Reform in Detroit,* 178–81; D. F. White, "Education in the Turn-of-the-Century School."
14. Hammack, "Centralization of New York City's Public School System," 30–31.
15. Butler, "Editorial," 201; Wesley, *NEA,* App. A; Maxwell, "Professor Hinsdale," 186–88.
16. Butler and Gaynor, "Should New York Have a Paid Board of Education?" 204–10; W. Mowry, "Powers and Duties of School Superintendents," 49–50; Mosely Educational Commission, *Reports.*
17. Harper, as quoted in McCaul, "Dewey's Chicago," 265; Chicago Merchant's Club, *Public Schools and Their Administration,* 45; Thwing, "New Profession," 33.
18. J. B. Sears and Henderson, *Cubberley,* 63–73; Callahan, *Education and Cult of Efficiency,* ch. viii.
19. The clearest index of these new values are the dozens of theses on administration published under the auspices of Teachers College, Columbia University, especially those sponsored by George Strayer. A number of theses are cited in this chapter.
20. DeWeese, "Better School Administration," 61; Herney, "Movement to

Reform Boston School Committee," 7; Berrol, "Maxwell"; J. B. Sears, *School Survey*.

21. The Montague correspondence with leading educators is deposited in the Oregon Historical Society; Drost, *Snedden*, 145; Hanus, *Adventuring in Education*.

22. Scott, "Conference," 396; PEA president, as quoted in S. Cohen, *Progressives and Urban School Reform*, 27.

23. *Addresses Delivered at a Joint Meeting*, 29, 15–16; S. Cohen, *Progressives and Urban School Reform*, 4.

24. The speeches in Chicago Merchants' Club, *Public Schools and Their Administration*, give a good idea of the educational ideology of leading businessmen in Boston, New York, Chicago, and St. Louis.

25. Hays, "Politics of Reform," 165.

26. Cubberley, *Public School Administration*, 93–94; W. T. Harris, "City School Supervision," 168–69; Moore, "The Modern City Superintendent."

27. Cubberley, "Organization of Public Education," 97; Chancellor, *Our Schools*, 12–13.

28. Counts, *Social Composition*, 96.

29. Nearing, "Who's Who," 89–90; Struble, "School Board Personnel," 48–49, 137–38; Counts, *Social Composition*. For some cautions in the use of such data see Charters, "Social Class Analysis."

30. *Boston School Report for 1874*, 25; Butler and Gaynor, "Should New York Have a Paid Board of Education?" 205–206.

31. *Boston School Report for 1874*, 27; W. Mowry, "Powers and Duties of School Superintendents," 41–42; Wetmore, "Boston School Administration," 107; Chicago Merchants' Club, *Public Schools and Their Administration*, 26.

32. Nearing, "Workings of a Large Board of Education," 44–46; Gilland, *Powers and Duties of the City-School Superintendent*, ch. vi.

33. Hubbert, "Centralization," 968.

34. Toulmin Smith, *Local Self-Government*, 12; Olin, "Public School Reform in New York," 5–6; Forcey, *Crossroads of Liberalism*, ch. xiv.

35. Cubberley, *Public School Administration*.

36. Bobbitt, *Denver Survey*, 116; Claxton et al., *San Francisco Survey*, 83–88; Theisen, *City Superintendent*, 99–100; Mack, "Relation of a Board," 980, 984; Committee of Fifteen, "Report," 307.

37. Prince, "School Supervision," 155; Douglass, *Status of the City Superintendent*, 124; Morrison, *Legal Status*, 102; Mendenhall, *City School Board Member*, 2–4, 50–52.

38. Yeager, "School Boards," 978–79; Cubberley, *Public School Administration*, 12; Chicago City Council, *Recommendations*, 22; Rollins, *School Administration*, 33, 37.

39. Lowell, "Professional and Non-Professional," 1001–1002; Ayres, *Cleveland Education Survey*, 125.

40. Sayre, "Additional Observations," 74–75.

41. Hays, "Political Parties," 170; for a perceptive discussion of school politics as a "closed system" see Iannaccone, *Politics in Education*.

42. For some parallel applications of the corporate model in other institutions of government, see Weinstein, *Corporate Ideal*.

43. On urban reform strategies generally, see Banfield and Wilson, *City Politics*, ch. xi.

44. S. Cohen, *Progressives and Urban School Reform*, ch. i.

45. Hammack, "Centralization of New York City's Public School System," 27; Olin, "Public School Reform in New York."

46. Hammack, "Centralization of New York City's Public School System," 51–71.

47. Ibid., 71–78.

48. Butler, "Editorial"; letter from Jacob W. Mack to Mayor Strong, April 16, 1896, Box 6147.

49. Letter from Edward D. Page to Mayor Strong, April 11, 1896, Box 6147.

50. Letter of Riis to Mayor Strong, April 17, 1896, Box 6063; senator, as quoted in Hammack, "Centralization of New York City's School System," 85.

51. Butler, as quoted in Hammack, "Centralization of New York City's Public School System," 91, 92, 95.

52. Letter from Lucy A. Yendes to Mayor Strong, April 9, 1896, Box 6147; letter from E. Slight to Mayor Strong, April 10, 1896, Box 6147; letter from G. W. Arnold to Mayor Strong, April 21, 1896, Box 6147.

53. Butler, "Editorial."

54. Berrol, "Immigrants at School"; Berrol, "Maxwell."

55. A. Shaw, "Public Schools of Boss-Ridden City," 4460–62, 4465; Woodruff, "Corrupt School System," 433–39.

56. Issel, "Modernization in Philadelphia School Reform," 363, 359–60; Warner, *Private City: Philadelphia*, 214–15, chs. ix–xi; Fox, "Philadelphia Progressives."

57. Issel, "Modernization in Philadelphia School Reform," 365.

58. Taggart, as quoted in ibid., 371–72; Woodruff, "Corrupt School System," 439.

59. Issel, "Modernization in Philadelphia School Reform," 359–60; Nash, *Philadelphia Public Schools*, 62–67.

60. Issel, "Modernization in Philadelphia School Reform," 378–80; Nash, *Philadelphia Public Schools*, 52, 58–61.

61. Issel, "Modernization in Philadelphia School Reform," 379–82; the later problems of the Philadelphia schools are documented in Odell, *Educational Survey for Philadelphia*.

62. E. C. Eliot, "School Administration: St. Louis," 465; Gersman, "Progressive Reform," 5–6.

63. Gersman, "Progressive Reform," 8–10.

64. E. C. Eliot, "School Administration: St. Louis," 466–67; E. C. Eliot, "Nonpartisan School Law," 226.

65. Gersman, "Progressive Reform," 8, 15; E. C. Eliot, "Nonpartisan School Law," 228; Chicago Merchants' Club, *Public Schools and Their Administration*, 21.

66. *St. Louis School Report for 1913*, 254–55; E. C. Eliot, "Nonpartisan School Law," 226–27; E. C. Eliot, "School Administration: St. Louis," 465.

67. E. C. Eliot, "Nonpartisan School Law," 321; Callahan, *Superintendent*, ch. iii; Iannaccone and Lutz, *Politics, Power, and Policy*.

68. Commonwealth Club of California, *Transactions*, 456, 467, 457. When Roncovieri spoke, no one applauded, according to the stenographic report, although almost all others speaking won applause.

69. Dolson, "San Francisco Public Schools," 224, 295, 724–25; Cubberley, "School Situation in San Francisco," 366–68, 372.

70. Cubberley, "School Situation in San Francisco," 379, 381.

71. Collegiate Alumnae, *Conditions in Schools of San Francisco*, 6, 2, 48.

72. Claxton et al., *San Francisco Survey,* 76; Commonwealth Club of California, *Transactions,* 379, 446.

73. Claxton et al., *San Francisco Survey,* 76, 79; Commonwealth Club of California, *Transactions,* 455, 457.

74. Claxton et al., *San Francisco Survey,* 83, 88; Commonwealth Club of California, *Transactions,* 432.

75. Commonwealth Club of California, *Transactions,* 470–71; Dolson, "San Francisco Public Schools," 356.

76. Dolson, "San Francisco Public Schools," 414n; *Monitor,* as quoted in Senkewicz, "Catholics and Amendment 37," 4.

77. Commonwealth Club of California, *Transactions,* 469.

78. Shradar, "Amenders"; Bosche, "Administration of San Francisco Schools."

79. *San Francisco School Bulletin,* as quoted in Bosche, "Administration of San Francisco Schools," 16–17; *Organized Labor* and *Monitor,* as quoted in Senkewicz, "Catholics and Amendment 37," 1, 5.

80. Dolson, "San Francisco Public Schools," 442; Bosche, "Administration of San Francisco Schools," 19–21; Tyack, "Perils of Pluralism."

81. Shradar, "Amenders," 14–24; Bosche, "Administration of San Francisco Schools," 24–25; Dolson, "San Francisco Public Schools," 443–44.

82. Draper, "Plans of Organization," 1; E. C. Eliot, "Nonpartisan School Law," 229; Cubberley, *Changing Conceptions of Education,* 56–57.

83. Committee on City School Systems, "School Superintendence in Cities"; Committee of Fifteen, "Report."

84. *The Shorter Oxford English Dictionary,* 3rd ed., 235; Hinsdale, "American School Superintendent," 50; Paul Hanus, in Committee on School Inquiry, *Report,* I, 183; C. W. Eliot, "Undesirable and Desirable Uniformity," 82.

85. For differences between public bureaucracies and market-oriented large organizations, see Downs, *Inside Bureaucracy;* on bureaucratic dysfunctions, see Merton, *Social Theory,* and Crozie. *Bureaucratic Phenomenon.*

86. Reid, "Professionalization of Public School Teachers," 44–46; *Harper Commission Report,* 1–20; Chicago Merchants' Club, *Public Schools and Their Administration;* Chicago City Council, *Recommendations.*

87. Reid, "Professionalization of Public School Teachers," 188–95; Herrick, *Chicago Schools,* 83–92; Haley, "Why Teachers Should Organize," 148–51.

88. Chicago Merchants' Club. *Public Schools and Their Administration,* 45; Reid, "Professionalization of Public School Teachers," 54–55; Herrick, *Chicago Schools,* 80–81.

89. DeWeese, "Two Years' Progress in Chicago," 336, 326–27; Herrick, *Chicago Schools,* 81. In *Public Education in Detroit* (172–77) Moehlman tells how another astute superintendent, W. G. Martindale, achieved influence without structural reforms.

90. Herrick, *Chicago Schools,* 166, 137–39; Counts, *School and Society in Chicago,* 11–12, 251–56, 261–63, 280–82; Reid, "Professionalization of Public School Teachers," 182–83; Herrick, "Negro Employees," ch. ii; for the later history of Chicago school politics see Hazlett, "Crisis in School Government."

91. Vare, *My Forty Years in Politics,* 31, 63–64; Z. L. Miller, *Boss Cox's Cincinnati,* 93; Cronin, "Centralization of the Boston Public Schools," 6; Reid, "Professionalization of Public School Teachers," 182–83.

92. Lowi, *Patronage and Power in New York,* 30–34; Cronin, "Centralization of the Boston Public Schools," 9.

93. Schrag, *Village School Downtown*, 57–59.
94. Gompers, "Teachers' Right to Organize Affirmed," 1083–84; Counts, *School and Society in Chicago*, chs. vi, xiv.
95. Strayer, "Baltimore School Situation," 340, 337, 341–42; Brown et al., *Education in Baltimore*, 9, 61; Crooks, *Politics and Progress: Baltimore*, 93–99.
96. Callahan, *Superintendent*, 103–106; "Why Superintendents Lose Their Jobs," 18; "The Cleveland Plan," 10–11; "The 'Czar' Movement," 8; "The Cleveland Meeting," 9. See also the following cartoons in the *American School Board Journal*: "Julius Caesar Educationalized: Modern Roman Senate 'Committee of Fifteen,' " 10 (April 1895), 1; "The Play of Hamlet 'Correlated': An Episode in the Great Educational Controversy," 10 (March 1895), 1; "The Modern Feast of Herod: The Cleveland Plan, Or the Sacrifice of Sensible School Board Representation," 11 (Dec. 1895), 1.
97. Commonwealth Club of California, *Transactions*, 455; Higgins, "School Reform in Los Angeles," 6–9.
98. S. Cohen, *Progressives and Urban School Reform*, ch. iv, illustrates the frustrations of elite reformers with the persistence of old-style politics after structural reforms. For subsequent studies of decision-making in city systems, see Rogers, *110 Livingston Street*, and Gittell, *Participants and Participation*.

PART V. Inside the System: The Character of Urban Schools, 1890–1940

1. Todd, "Why Children Work," 73–78.
2. Dewey, *School and Society*, 33; Herrick, *Chicago Schools*, 114–15, 74; McCaul, "Dewey's Chicago."
3. Maxwell, "Teachers," 11878–79.
4. Ibid., 11877–80; A. Shaw, "Spread of Vacation Schools."
5. Cremin, *Cubberley;* Krug, *High School.*
6. Lazerson, *Urban Schools*, ch. ix; Katz, *Class, Bureaucracy, and Schools*, 114–18.
7. Hartmann, *Movement to Americanize the Immigrant.*
8. Lubove, *Professional Altruist*, chs. iv, vii; H. Miller and Smiley, eds., *Education in the Metropolis*, 1–13; Mills, *Sociological Imagination*, 9.
9. The study of Thorndike by Geraldine Joncich Clifford, *The Sane Positivist*, gives a detailed and sympathetic view of educational scientists as they saw themselves and their world.
10. Strachan, *Equal Pay;* Reid, "Professionalization of Public School Teachers."
11. Strayer, "Progress in City School Administration," 375–78.
12. U.S. Commissioner of Education, *Report for 1889*, II, 709; Counts, *Selective Character of American Education*, 1; U.S. Bureau of the Census, *Historical Statistics*, 207, 214; Stambler, "Effect of Compulsory Education and Child Labor Laws"; Haney, *Registration of City School Children;* Ensign, *Compulsory School Attendance.*
13. Lynd and Lynd, *Middletown*, 210; U.S. Commissioner of Education, *Report for 1889*, II, 772; *Report for 1890*, II, 1318–48; *Biennial Survey, 1920–22*, II, 94–114.
14. Wesley, *NEA*, 278–79; Kinney, *Certification in Education*, ch. vi; Martens, "Organization of Research Bureaus."

15. Lazerson, *Urban School*, ch. ii; A. G. Wirth, *Education in Technological Society*, chs. ii, v; Riis, *Children of the Poor.*

16. Letter from Charles Judd to members of the Cleveland Conference, Jan. 14, 1918, Edward C. Elliott Papers, Purdue University, courtesy of Dr. Walter Drost.

17. Krug, *High School;* Spring, *Education and the Corporate State.*

18.. Cubberley, *Changing Conceptions of Education,* 56–57; Karier, Violas, and Spring, *Roots of Crisis,* ch. vi. I am indebted to Professor Karier and to Russell Marks for their powerful insights into the social philosophy of some of the testers.

19. Cubberley, *Public School Administration,* 338.

20. Wirth, *Education in Technological Society,* ch. i; Curti, *Social Ideas of American Educators,* chs. vi, viii; Chicago City Council, *Recommendations,* 107–12.

21. Grubb and Lazerson, *Education and Industrialism,* "Introduction"; S. Cohen, "Industrial Education Movement."

22. Dooley, *Ne'er-Do-Well,* 8, 13–14, 16–18, 21, 27–28.

23. Snedden, *Reform Schools,* ch. xii.

24. Caswell, *City School Surveys,* 26.

25. Committee on School Inquiry, *Report,* I, 57; Hanus, *Adventuring in Education,* ch. xii.

26. Cubberley, *Portland Survey,* 125, 40, 128, 41–42, 46; Cubberley's colleagues were education professors and school administrators, including Edward C. Elliott, Frank E. Spaulding, J.·H. Francis, and Lewis Terman.

27. Koos, "School Surveys," 35–41.

28. U.S. Commissioner of Education, *Report for 1917,* I, 19–21; Pritchett, "Educational Surveys," 118–23; Caswell, *City School Surveys,* 32.

29. Moley, "Cleveland Surveys," 229–31; Caswell, *City School Surveys,* 60–72.

30. Bourne, "Portland Survey," 238.

31. Nearing, *New Education,* 128, 126, 165–69.

32. Cremin, *Transformation of the School,* ch. vi; Bowers, *Progressive Educator and the Depression.*

33. Swift, *Ideology and Change in the Public Schools.*

34. Dewey, *Educational Situation,* 22–23; Lynd and Lynd, *Middletown in Transition,* 241; Dewey, *Democracy and Education;* Katz, *Class, Bureaucracy, and Schools,* 113–25.

35. Kazin, *Walker in the City,* 17–22.

36. Dewey, "Individuality," 61–62.

37. For some recent studies of the·social role of educational psychologists see Church, "Educational Psychology and Social Reform"; D. K. Cohen and Lazerson, "Education and Corporate Order"; Sizer, "Testing."

38. Ayres, *Laggards,* 220.

39. Buckingham, "Child Accounting," 218–19.

40. Ayres, *Laggards,* 66, 38, 20, 4.

41. Ibid., 106–107, 103, 115.

42. Ibid., 7 (italics are in the original).

43. Ibid.

44. Ibid., 199, 170–71.

45. D. K. Cohen and Lazerson, "Education and the Corporate Order."

46. Richman, "Successful Experiment in Promoting Pupils," 23–26, 29; Richman, "What Can Be Done," 130–31.

47. Ettinger, "Facing the Facts," 505, 508–509, 512.

48. Woody and Sangren, *Administration of Testing*, 19–21; Kevles, "Testing the Army's Intelligence."

49. Spring, "Psychologists and the War," 5, 8–9.

50. For critical interpretations of the social philosophy of the testers see Karier, Violas, and Spring, *Roots of Crisis*, ch. vi, and Marks, "Testers, Trackers, and Trustees."

51. Brigham, *American Intelligence*, 197, 209; Marks, "Testers, Trackers, and Trustees."

52. Bond, *Education of the Negro*, 318; Dearborn, *Intelligence Tests*, 272–78.

53. Dearborn, *Intelligence Tests*, 279–80; Spring, "Psychologists and the War," 9–10; Terman, "Uses of Intelligence Tests," 30–31.

54. Pillsbury, "Selection," 64–65, 66–74.

55. Woody and Sangren, *Administration of Testing*, 21; Dickson, *Mental Tests and Classroom Teacher*, 28.

56. Haggerty, "Recent Developments," 242; Terman, "Problem," 3.

57. Chapman, "Intelligence Testing Movement"; I am much indebted to Mr. Chapman for sharing his sources on the testing movement. See also Terman, "Problem," 1, 3; Brooks, "Uses for Intelligence Tests," 219; Brooks, *Improving Schools*, ch. x; Pintner and Noble, "Classification of School Children," 726–27.

58. Davis, "Some Problems," 13–15.

59. Hines, "What Los Angeles Is Doing with Testing," 45; Brooks, *Improving Schools*, ch. x.

60. Terman, "Problem," 1–29; Deffenbaugh, "Uses of Intelligence and Achievement Tests"; "Cities Reporting the Use of Homogeneous Grouping"; D. K. Cohen and Lazerson, "Education and the Corporate Order," 54.

61. Layton, "Group Intelligence Testing Program of Detroit," 125–27.

62. Dickson, "Classification of School Children," 33–35.

63. Ibid., 48–52.

64. Dickson, "Relation of Mental Testing," 72, 75, 85; Dickson, "Use of Mental Tests," 609.

65. Tupper, "Use of Intelligence Tests," 97–98.

66. Ibid., 99–100, 101–102, 92.

67. Corning, *After Testing*, 12–147, 166–68, 189.

68. Young, *Mental Differences*, 3–4, ch. iii.

69. Ibid., 65–66.

70. Ibid., 68–69.

71. Ibid., 72.

72. Ibid., 16–17; Covello, *Social Background*.

73. W. S. Miller, "Administrative Use of Intelligence Tests," 190; Lippmann, "Abuse of Tests," 297; Department of Education, State of Ohio, *Classification of Pupils*.

74. Chicago Federation of Labor, as quoted in Counts, *School and Society in Chicago*, 185–88; Karier, Violas, and Spring, *Roots of Crisis*, ch. vi.

75. For an excellent, brief account of the early development of intelligence testing see Cronbach, *Essentials of Psychological Testing*, 197–206.

76. Terman, *Measurement of Intelligence*, 19.

77. Dickson, *Mental Tests and Classroom Teacher*, 129; Cubberley, *State and County Educational Reorganization*, 4.

78. Daniel, "Aims of Secondary Education," 467; Wilkerson, "Determination of Problems of Negroes."

79. Davison, "Educational Status of the Negro," 8, 10, 44–50.

80. Holloway, "Social Conditions," 1, 19, 30.

81. Boyer, *Adjustment of a School,* 3, 18–29, 65, 139–40.

82. Grace, "Effect of Negro Migration," 4, 141, 83–84.

83. Bulkley, "Industrial Condition," 590–96; G. Hayes, "Vocational Education," 71–74.

84. Blascoeur, *Colored Schoolchildren in New York,* 18; Speed, "Negro in New York," 1249–50; Osofsky, "Progressivism and the Negro."

85. Caliver, "Certain Significant Developments," 113–15; Caliver, "Negro High School Graduates and Nongraduates," 15.

86. Shamwell, "Vocational Choices," ch. i, 188–89. For comparable findings see Lawrence, "Vocational Aspirations."

87. V. Daniels, "Attitudes Affecting Occupational Affiliation," 45–49.

88. Ibid., 54–56, 57.

89. Ibid, 66–67.

90. Cofer, "We Face Reality in Detroit," 34–37; Wilkerson, 'Occupational Efficiency," 7; Committee of Teachers, *Negro Employment;* DuBois, "Northern Public Schools," 205–208.

91. Wilkerson, "Negro in American Education"; Herrick, "Negro Employees"; Porter, "Negro Education in Northern and Border Cities," 33–39.

92. Haney, *Registration,* 67; Hardin, *Negroes of Philadelphia,* 104.

93. Spaulding, *School Superintendents,* 617–19.

94. Grace, "Effect of Negro Migration," 68–69; Beckham, "Attendance," 18–29.

95. DuBois, "Pechstein," 313–14.

96. DuBois, "Does the Negro Need Separate Schools?" 328–29, 331; Sinette, "The Brownies' Book"; Woodson, "Negro Life and History."

97. Wilkerson, "The Status of Negro Education," 226.

98. Cole, "City's Responsibility to the Immigrant," 36; U.S. Immigration Commission, *Children of Immigrants,* I, 14–15; Covello, "High School and Its Immigrant Community," 331–32; Dixon, *Americanization;* Roberts, *Problem of Americanization;* Berry, "Problems of Americanization"; Loeb, "Compulsory English."

99. Berrol, "Immigrants at School," 85, 87, 55, 89; A. Shaw, "New York Public Schools," 4205.

100. A. Shaw, "New York Public Schools," 4205–207, 4210–15.

101. Ibid., 4205–206; Thomas, "American Education and the Immigrant"; Atzmon, "Educational Programs for Immigrants"; Berrol, "Immigrants at School," ch. iv.

102. Kallen, "Meaning of Americanization"; Gordon, *Assimilation;* Thernstrom, "Up from Slavery."

103. Buchanan, "Compulsory Education," 204–205; McDonald, *Adjustment of School Organization,* 68–69; *Twelfth Annual Report of the [New York] City Superintendent of Schools,* 227; Maxwell, *Quarter Century of Public School Development,* 58.

104. Bair, *Social Understandings of the Superintendent of Schools,* 77–78.

105. Horvath, "Plea of an Immigrant," 680; Miller, *School and the Immigrant,* 24, 55; Spaulding, *School Superintendents,* 616; U.S. Immigration Commission, *Children of Immigrants,* I, 134.

106. Inkeles, "Social Structure and the Socialization of Competence," 280–81; Strodtbeck, "Family Interaction, Values, and Achievement," 188;

Woodward, "Adjustment of the Non-English-Speaking Woman"; Holsinger, "Elementary School as Modernizer." For a stimulating essay on the assimilation of immigrants at work, see Gutman, "Work, Culture, and Society."

107. Chase, *Primer for Foreign-Speaking Women,* 12, 13, 17; O'Brien, *English for Foreigners,* 128–29, 149.

108. Duncan, *Immigration and Assimilation;* W. C. Smith, *Americans in the Making;* Novak, *Unmeltable Ethnics;* Schrag, *Decline of WASP;* Glazer and Moynihan, *Beyond the Melting Pot.* A number of groups—Greeks and Chinese come to mind—often established themselves in business by serving their own people or by providing ethnically specialized services to others. See Greer, *Great School Legend,* ch. v.

109. McDonald, *Adjustment of School Organization,* 69; Richman, "Immigrant Child," 119; Jenks, "Important Racial Information"; C. Shaw, *Brothers in Crime,* 135–37.

110. Richman, "Immigrant Child," 120; J. Daniels, *America via the Neighborhood,* 253–56; Mark, *Individuality,* 215; Todd, "Why Children Work," 74; Dixon, *Americanization,* 24; Mahoney and Herlihy, *First Steps in Americanization,* 1–13.

111. *Education of the Immigrant,* 6.

112. Covello, *Heart Is the Teacher,* 29–31, 43, 47, 129–30, 149–50.

113. Ibid., 197–98; Covello, "High School and Its Immigrant Community," 332; Covello, "School as the Center of Community Life"; Mills, "Community Control in Perspective," 7–9.

114. Galarza, *Barrio Boy,* 210–13. For a pioneer study in eliminating negative ethnic stereotypes, see Bogardus, *Essentials of Americanization.*

115. Todd, "Why Children Work," 78; Woolston, "Our Untrained Citizens."

116. Antin, *Promised Land,* 186, 271; observer, as quoted in W. C. Smith, *Americans in the Making,* 291; Bercovici, *On New Shores,* 156; Wytrwal, *America's Polish Heritage,* 161–62; Panunzio, *Soul of an Immigrant,* 255.

117. J. Daniels, *America via the Neighborhood,* 249–50; T. Smith, "Immigrant Social Aspirations"; Riis, *Children of the Poor,* 53; Berrol, "Immigrants at School," ch. iv.

118. Ayres, *Laggards in Our Schools,* ch. x; T. Smith, "Immigrant Social Aspirations," 523.

119. U.S. Immigration Commission, *Children of Immigrants,* I, 4–5, 31.

120. Ibid., 53, 32; D. K. Cohen, "Immigrants and the Schools," 19–20.

121. U.S. Immigration Commission, *Children of Immigrants,* I, 103, 108.

122. Van Denburg, *Causes of the Elimination of Students,* 36–37; D. K. Cohen, "Immigrants and the Schools," 22; Counts, *Selective Character,* ch. xii.

123. Hutchinson, *Immigrants and Their Children,* 202, 216.

124. Ibid., 220–21. As compared with Hutchinson, who studied occupations of *groups* at ten-year intervals, Stephan Thernstrom followed the career lines of *individual* immigrants in Boston. He also found important differences in mobility between groups. In the 1900–1909 cohort of immigrants he studied, 85 percent of Italians remained in blue-collar jobs for their lifetimes, whereas two thirds of the East European Jews reached the middle class. Within the second generation of young men born during the 1850's, only 15 percent of the Irish started work with white collars compared with 41 percent of all other children of immigrants (Thernstrom, "Immigrants and WASPs," 157–58, 150).

125. Blau and Duncan, *American Occupational Structure;* Coleman et al., *Equality of Educational Opportunity;* Jencks et al., *Inequality,* ch. vi.

126. A. Shaw, "New York Public Schools," 4215; Gold, *Jews without Money*, 23; Russell, "Coming of the Jews," 27–38; Johnson, *Discrimination against the Japanese in California*, 94–109; Mears, *Orientals on the American Pacific Coast*, 339–70; Spoehr, "Sambo and the Heathen Chinee"; Palmer, *Orientals in American Life*, 58–72; W. C. Smith, *Second Generation Oriental*.

127. Dushkin, *Jewish Education*, 182–207, 303–15; A. Levin, "Henrietta Szold"; LaViolette, *Americans of Japanese Ancestry*, 52–56, 84–90; Sone, *Nisei Daughter*.

128. Rischin, *Promised City*, 79; Van Denburg, *Causes of the Elimination of Students*, 79–81.

129. Levine and Levine, "Introduction," xxix–xxxvi; Berrol, "Immigrants at School," 64–66, 70–71. In *Immigrant Upraised*, Andrew Rolle has documented the striking achievements of Italian immigrants in the American West.

130. Jewish leader, as quoted in Rischin, *Promised City*, 39, 23–28, 61.

131. Ibid., 35; Berrol, "Immigrants at School," 68.

132. Howe, "Lower East Side," 13; Strodtbeck, "Family Interaction, Values, and Achievement," 151.

133. Rischin, *Promised City*, 200; Jewish parents, as quoted in Levine and Levine, "Introduction," xlii.

134. Educators, as quoted in Berrol, "Immigrants at School," 60–61; Richman, "Immigrant Child," 115.

135. Kazin, *Walker in the City*, 18–21; Metzker, ed., *Bintel Brief*.

136. Covello, *Social Background*, 277–78.

137. Ibid., 287–88.

138. Ibid., 291, 285, 288–90; Rolle, *Immigrant Upraised*, 279; Strodtbeck, "Family Interaction, Values, and Achievement," 150–51; Richman, "Immigrant Child," 115; Cinel, "Literacy versus Culture"; Addams, *Democracy and Social Ethics*, 181–85.

139. Richman, "Immigrant Child," 115; Covello, *Social Background*, 283; Berrol, "Immigrants at School," 55–57; M. Smith, "Raphael"; Dogherty, '*Scusa Me Teacher*.

140. Bromsen, "Maladaptation of the Italian Boy," 455–56, 458–61.

141. Todd, "Why Children Work," 76.

142. Dogherty, '*Scusa Me Teacher*, 24–27, 101, 35–38.

143. Patri, *Schoolmaster*, 24, 27, 29–31.

144. Gove, "Limitations of the Superintendents' Authority," 152–53.

145. Haley, "Why Teachers Should Organize," 147–48, 151–52; Reid, "Professionalization of Public School Teachers," 99.

146. *Report on Salaries*, 16, 146–48, 154; *Report on Teachers' Salaries and Cost of Living*, xi, xv–vi, xviii–ix, 158, 139, 53–58, 240–41.

147. Waller, *Sociology of Teaching*, 10; Addams, *Twenty Years at Hull-House*, 334; Burstall, *Impressions of American Education*, 11–12, 41, 290n; Young, *Isolation in the School*, 106; Schmid, "Organizational Structure of the National Education Association," 139.

148. Reid, "Professionalization of Public School Teachers."

149. Ibid., 177; Sandburg, as quoted in Herrick, *Chicago Schools*, 125.

150. Herrick, *Chicago Schools*, 94, 96; Counts, *School and Society in Chicago*, ch. vi; Wesley, *NEA*, 397; Schmid, "Organizational Structure of the National Education Association."

151. Herrick, *Chicago Schools*, 97, 99–101; Reid, "Professionalization of Public School Teachers," 42.

152. Herrick, *Chicago Schools*, 97, 100–102; Reid, "Professionalization of Public School Teachers," 55–63.

153. Haley, as quoted in Herrick, *Chicago Schools*, 107; Young, "A Reply," 358.

154. Huthmacher, "Urban Liberalism"; Ricker. "School-Teacher Unionized," 350–51; Herrick, *Chicago Schools*, 106–11; Reid, "Professionalization of Public School Teachers," 89–95.

155. Letter of labor leaders, Illinois Supreme Court decision, and Loeb comment, all as quoted in Reid, "Professionalization of Public School Teachers," 171, 192, 193; Gompers, "Teachers' Right to Organize Affirmed"; Gompers, "Teachers' Right to Organize."

156. Reid, "Professionalization of Public School Teachers," ch. vii; Herrick, *Chicago Schools*, 135–37; Counts, *School and Society in Chicago*. chs. vi–vii.

157. Ricker, "School-Teacher Unionized," 348.

158. Ibid., 348, 344–47.

159. McManis, *Ella Flagg Young*, 144; editor and Young, both as quoted in Alexander, *Teachers' Voluntary Associations*, 79, 95n, 69–70, 72; Wesley, *NEA*, 40, 325.

160. Reid, "Professionalization of Public School Teachers," 212, 214–16.

161. Haley, as quoted in ibid., 216–19; Schmid, "Organizational Structure of the National Education Association," 93.

162. Butler, *Across the Busy Years*, I, 188, 96; Haley, as quoted in Schmid, "Organizational Structure of the National Education Association," 100; Reid, "Professionalization of Public School Teachers," 221–23.

163. Reid, "Professionalization of Public School Teachers," 228–29, 232–33.

164. Strachan, *Equal Pay*, 16–17, 277–331, 545–68; Alexander, *Teachers' Voluntary Associations*, 84–92; Viggers, "The Women Teachers' Organization in the Equal Pay for Teachers Controversy," 16, ch. v.

165. McAndrew, "Matters of Moment," 554; Krug, *High School, 1920–41*, 149–51; Newlon, *Educational Administration as Social Policy*, chs. x–xi; Button, "Supervision in the Public Schools," ch. viii; Rudy, *Schools in an Age of Mass Culture*, 95–98; Schmid, "Organizational Structure of the National Education Association," 313–15; Deffenbaugh, "Smaller Cities," 27–37; Beale, *Are American Teachers Free?*

166. Dogherty, *'Scusa Me Teacher*, 35; Krug, *High School, 1920–41*, 147; Curtis, *Recreation for Teachers;* Simpson and Simpson, "Women and Bureaucracy in the Semi-Professions."

EPILOGUE. The One Best System Under Fire, 1940–1973

1. U.S. Bureau of the Census, *Statistical Abstract*, 112, 118, 128.

2. Brameld et al., "Battle for Free Schools"; "The Crisis in Education and the Changing Afro-American Community"; Jennings, "It Didn't Start with Sputnik."

3. Tyack, "Needed: The Reform of a Reform."

4. Karier, Violas, and Spring, *Roots of Crisis*.

5. Guthrie and Wynne, eds., *New Models for American Education*.

6. Hummel and Nagle, *Urban Education in America*, ch. i.

7. Edwards, *Equal Educational Opportunity for Youth*, 152.

8. H. M. Bell, *Matching Youth and Jobs*, 261–67; Thomas, *Occupational Struc-*

ture and Education, ch. xiv; Norton and Lawler, *Unfinished Business in American Education,* 3, 8–9, 24–25.

9. Norton and Lawler, *Unfinished Business in American Education;* Fine, *Our Children Are Cheated,* ix–xi, 1, 185–86.

10. Fine, *Our Children Are Cheated,* 14–15, 82–83, 6, 8, 25, 102, 67.

11. Ibid., 212–21.

12. *Biennial Survey of Education, 1950–52,* 17; *New York Times,* Aug. 10, 1953, 25; *Biennial Survey of Education, 1954–56,* 20; Sexton, *Education and Income;* James, Kelly, and Garms, *Determinants of Educational Expenditures.*

13. Norton and Lawler, *Unfinished Business in American Education,* 35; U.S. Bureau of the Census, *Statistical Abstract,* 390; U.S. Bureau of the Census, *Historical Statistics,* 209; Alison, *Searchlight,* chs. xix–xxi; Zitron, *New York City Teachers Union,* chs. xxxi–iv; Curti, *Roots of American Loyalty;* Brameld et al., "Battle for Free Schools."

14. Conant, *Slums and Suburbs,* 34, 2; Grissom, "Education and the Cold War."

15. Edwards, *Equal Educational Opportunity For Youth,* 151; Taeuber and Taeuber, "Negro Population in the United States," 125.

16. Hummel and Nagle, *Urban Education in America,* 76–77, 103; Harrington, *Other America.*

17. Hummel and Nagle, *Urban Education in America,* 115, 78–80.

18. Ibid., 215, 213, 216.

19. *Brown v. Board of Education; Report of the National Advisory Commission on Civil Disorders;* Newby and Tyack, "Victims without 'Crimes.'" I am deeply indebted to Robert Newby for sharing with me his insights into recent black history.

20. Lomax, *Negro Revolt,* 74; Bennett, *Before the Mayflower,* 318–19.

21. Drake, "Social and Economic Status of the Negro in the United States," 15; Rogers, *110 Livingston Street.* Meyer Weinberg has edited an excellent collection of studies in *Integrated Education.*

22. Harlem Parents Committee, *Education of Minority Group Children,* 34, 2, 17; U.S. Commission on Civil Rights, *Racial Isolation in the Public Schools,* II, 12–19.

23. Wilkerson, "Compensatory Education."

24. Boston assistant superintendent and school board chairman, as quoted in Ryan, *Blaming the Victim,* 32, 31.

25. K. Clark, *Black Ghetto,* 131; Wilkerson, "Blame the Negro Child!"; A. Mann, "Historical Overview."

26. D. K. Cohen, "Compensatory Education."

27. Jones, "The Issues at I. S. 201," 156; Goldberg, "I. S. 201."

28. For a variety of appraisals of reform in 1970, see "Education in America."

29. Coleman et al., *Equality of Educational Opportunity;* U.S. Commission on Civil Rights, *Racial Isolation in the Public Schools.* See also the discussions of the Coleman report and its implications for reform in "Equal Educational Opportunity."

30. Berg, *Education and Jobs.*

31. Luthin, *American Demagogues,* 61; "Alternative Schools"; "The Imperatives of Ethnic Education."

32. Bailey, "New Dimensions in School Board Leadership," 97.

33. Griffiths, *Human Relations,* 106; Cole, *Unionization of Teachers,* 8–33.

34. Cogen, as quoted in Rosenthal, *Pedagogues and Power*, 16, 8, 18.

35. West, "What's Bugging Teachers," 88; Rosenthal, *Pedagogues and Power*, 19, 23, 17; Glynn, "Blueprint for Power," 50, 46–49; Braun, *Teachers and Power*, 69–70, 85.

36. Demas, "School Elections," 4.

37. Braun, *Teachers and Power*, 150; Rosenthal, *Pedagogues and Power*, 128.

38. Popham, *Designing Teacher Evaluation Systems;* "Teacher Evaluation"; Elliott and Wigderson, "Fitting the Pieces."

39. Gallup, "Fifth Annual Gallup Poll"; Kleine, Nystrand, and Bridges, "Citizen Views of Big City Schools," 226; Illich, *Deschooling Society.*

Bibliography

Abbott, Edith, and Sophonisba Breckinridge. *Truancy and Non-Attendance in the Chicago Schools.* Chicago: University of Chicago Press, 1917.

Abelow, Samuel P. *Dr. William H. Maxwell, the First Superintendent of Schools of the City of New York.* Brooklyn: Schebor, 1934.

Adams, Charles Francis, Jr. "Scientific Common School Education." *Harper's New Monthly Magazine,* 61 (Oct. 1880), 935-40.

Addams, Jane. *Democracy and Social Ethics,* ed. Anne F. Scott. Cambridge, Mass.: Harvard University Press, 1964.

———— *Twenty Years at Hull-House, with Autobiographical Notes.* New York: Macmillan, 1939

Addresses Delivered at a Joint Meeting of the Civic Club, Department of Education and the Public Education Association, March 3, 1894. Philadelphia: n.p., 1894.

Alexander, Carter. *Some Present Aspects of the Work of Teachers' Voluntary Associations in the United States.* Contributions to Education, no. 36. New York: Teachers College, Columbia University, 1910.

Alford, Robert R. "School District Reorganization and Community Integration." *Harvard Educational Review,* 30 (Fall 1960), 350-71.

Alison, David. *Searchlight: An Exposé of New York City Schools.* New York: Teachers College Press, 1951.

Almack, John C. "Historical Development of School Administration." *School and Society,* 43 (May 9, 1936), 625–30.

"Alternative Schools." *Harvard Educational Review,* 42 (Aug. 1972).

"Alternative Schools." *Phi Delta Kappan,* 54 (March 1973).

Anderson, William E. "Qualification and Supply of Teachers for City Schools." *NEA Addresses and Proceedings,* 30th Annual Meeting, Toronto, 1891, 422–30.

Andersson, Theodore, and Mildred Boyer. *Bilingual Schooling in the U.S.* Washington, D.C.: GPO, 1970.

Andrews, Charles. *The History of the New York African Free-Schools.* New York: Negro Universities Press, 1969 [originally published in 1830].

Antin, Mary. *The Promised Land*. Boston: Houghton Mifflin, 1912.

Aptheker, Herbert, ed. *A Documentary History of the Negro People in the United States*. New York: Citadel Press, 1963 [originally published in 1951].

Ariès, Philippe. *Centuries of Childhood: A Social History of Family Life*. New York: Random House, 1962.

Arp, Julius B. *Rural Education and the Consolidated School*. Yonkers-on-Hudson: World Book, 1918.

Atzmon, Ezri. "The Educational Programs for Immigrants in the United States." *History of Education Journal*, 9 (Sept. 1958), 75–80.

Ayres, Leonard P. *Laggards in Our Schools: A Study of Retardation and Elimination in City School Systems*. New York: Charities Publication Committee, 1909.

——— *School Organization and Administration: Cleveland Education Survey*. Cleveland: Survey Committee of the Cleveland Foundation, 1916.

Bailey, Stephen K. "New Dimensions in School Board Leadership." In William E. Dickinson, ed., *New Dimensions in School Board Leadership: A Seminar Report and Woodbook*, 96–110. Evanston, Ill.: National School Boards Association, 1969.

Bair, Frederick Haigh. *The Social Understandings of the Superintendent of Schools*. Contributions to Education, no. 625. New York: Teachers College, Columbia University, 1934.

Baker, Ray Stannard. *Following the Color Line: An Account of Negro Citizenship in the American Democracy*. New York: Young People's Missionary Movement of the United States and Canada, 1908.

Banfield, Edward C., and James Q. Wilson. *City Politics*. Cambridge, Mass.: Harvard University Press, 1966.

Barber, Marshall. *The Schoolhouse at Prairie View*. Lawrence: University of Kansas Press, 1953.

Barnard, Henry. "Gradation of Public Schools, with Special Reference to Cities and Large Villages." *American Journal of Education*, 2 (Dec. 1856), 455–64.

Beach, Mark. "History of Education." *Review of Educational Research*, 39 (Dec. 1969), 561–76.

Beale, Howard K. *Are American Teachers Free? An Analysis of Restraints upon the Freedom of Teaching in American Schools*. New York: Charles Scribner's Sons, 1936.

——— *A History of Freedom of Teaching in American Schools*. New York: Charles Scribner's Sons, 1941.

Beckham, Albert. "A Study of Attendance in Negro Children of Adolescent Age." *Journal of Abnormal and Social Psychology*, 34 (April-June 1934), 18–29.

Bell, Daniel, ed. *The Radical Right: The New American Right*. Expanded and updated ed. Garden City, N.Y.: Anchor, 1964.

Bell, H. M. *Matching Youth and Jobs*. Washington, D.C.: American Council on Education, 1940.

Bell, Howard H. "Negroes in California, 1849–1859." *Phylon*, 28 (Summer 1967), 151–60.

Bennett, Lenore. *Before the Mayflower: A History of the Negro in America*. Chicago: Johnson, 1962.

Bercovici, Konrad. *On New Shores*. New York: Century, 1925.

Bere, May. *A Comparative Study of the Mental Capacity of Children of Foreign Par-*

entage. Contributions to Education, no. 154. New York: Teachers College, Columbia University, 1924.

Berg, Ivar E. *Education and Jobs: The Great Training Robbery*. New York: Praeger, 1970.

Berkowitz, Michael. "An Act to Enforce the Educational Rights of Children." Unpub. seminar paper, Stanford University, 1972.

Berrol, Selma Cantor. "Immigrants at School: New York City, 1898–1914." Unpub. Ph.D. diss., City University of New York, 1967.

—— "The Schools of New York in Transition, 1898–1914." *Urban Review*, 1 (Dec. 1966), 15–20.

—— "William Henry Maxwell and a New Educational New York." *History of Education Quarterly*, 8 (Summer 1968), 215–28.

Berry, Charles Scott. "Some Problems of Americanization as Seen by an Army Psychologist." *School and Society*, 13 (Jan. 22, 1921), 97–104.

The Bible in the Public Schools. Cincinnati: Robert Clarke, 1870.

Bidwell, Charles E. "The School as a Formal Organization." In James G. March, ed., *Handbook of Organizations*, 972–1022. Chicago: Rand McNally, 1965.

Biennial Survey of Education in the United States, 1950–52: Statistics of State School Systems. Washington, D.C.: GPO, 1955.

Biennial Survey of Education in the United States, 1954–56: Statistics of State School Systems. Washington, D.C.: GPO, 1959.

Billington, Ray. *The Protestant Crusade, 1800–1860: A Study of the Origins of American Nativism*. New York: Macmillan, 1938.

Blascoeur, Frances. *Colored Schoolchildren in New York*. New York: Public Education Association, 1915.

Blau, Peter M., and Otis Dudley Duncan. *The American Occupational Structure*. New York: Wiley, 1967.

Bobbitt, Franklin. "General Organization and Management, Part I." *Report of the School Survey of Denver*. Denver: School Survey Committee, 1916.

Bogardus, Emory S. *Essentials of Americanization*. Los Angeles: University of Southern California Press, 1919.

Bond, Horace Mann. *The Education of the Negro in the American Social Order*. Englewood Cliffs, N.J.: Prentice-Hall, 1934.

Bosche, Joanne. "The Administration of San Francisco Schools, 1910–1925." Unpub. seminar paper, Stanford University, 1970.

Bourne, Randolph. "The Portland School Survey." *New Republic*, 5 (Jan. 8, 1916), 238–39.

Bourne, William Olan. *History of the Public School Society of the City of New York*. New York: William Woodland, 1870.

Bowers, C. A. *The Progressive Educator and the Depression: The Radical Years*. New York: Random House, 1969.

Boyer, Philip A. *The Adjustment of a School to Individual and Community Needs*. Philadelphia: n.p., 1920.

Brameld, Theodore, et al. "The Battle for Free Schools." *Nation*, 173 (Oct. 27–Dec. 15, 1951).

Braun, Robert J. *Teachers and Power: The Story of the American Federation of Teachers*. New York: Simon and Schuster, 1972.

Brigham, Carl C. *A Study of American Intelligence*. Princeton: Princeton University Press, 1923.

Brim, Orville G. *Sociology and the Field of Education.* New York: Russell Sage Foundation, 1958.

Bromsen, Archie. "The Public School's Contribution to the Maladaptation of the Italian Boy." In Caroline C. Ware, *Greenwich Village, 1920–1930,* 455–61. Boston: Houghton Mifflin, 1935.

Brooks, Samuel S. *Improving Schools by Standardized Tests.* Boston: Houghton Mifflin, 1922.

——— "Some Uses for Intelligence Tests." *Journal of Educational Research,* 5 (March 1923), 217–38.

Brown, Elmer Ellsworth, et al. *Report of the Commission Appointed to Study the System of Education in the Public Schools of Baltimore.* Washington, D.C.: GPO, 1911.

Brown et al. v. Board of Education of Topeka et al., 347 U.S. 483 (1954).

Buchanan, John T. "Compulsory Education." In Winthrop Talbot and Julia E. Johnsen, eds., *Americanization,* 2nd ed., 204–205. New York: H. W. Wilson, 1920.

Buckingham, B. R. "Child Accounting." *Journal of Educational Research,* 3 (March 1921), 218–22.

Bulkley, William L. "The Industrial Condition of the Negro in New York City." *Annals of the American Academy of Political and Social Science,* 28 (May 1906), 590–96.

Bunker, Frank Forest. *Reorganization of the Public School System.* U.S. Bureau of Education, Bulletin no. 8. Washington, D.C.: GPO, 1916.

Burnett, Jacquetta Hill. "Ceremony, Rites, and Economy in the Student System of an American High School." *Human Organization,* 28 (Spring 1969), 1–10.

Burstall, Sara A. *Impressions of American Education in 1908.* London: Longmans, Green, 1909.

Burton, Warren. *The District School as It Was.* Boston: T. R. Marvin, 1852.

Butler, Nicholas Murray. *Across the Busy Years.* 2 vols. New York: Charles Scribner's Sons, 1939.

——— "Editorial." *Educational Review,* 12 (Sept. 1896), 196–207.

Butler, Nicholas Murray, and William Gaynor. "Should New York Have a Paid Board of Education?" *Educational Review,* 42 (Sept. 1911), 204–10.

Button, Henry Warren. "A History of Supervision in the Public Schools, 1870–1950." Unpub. Ph.D. diss., Washington University, 1961.

Caldwell, Otis W., and Stuart A. Courtis. *Then and Now in Education: 1845, 1923.* Yonkers-on-Hudson: World Book, 1925.

Caliver, Ambrose. "Certain Significant Developments in the Education of Negroes during the Past Generation." *Journal of Negro History,* 35 (April 1950), 111–34.

——— "Negro High School Graduates and Nongraduates: Relation of Their Occupational Status to Certain School Experiences." U.S. Office of Education, Pamphlet no. 87. Washington, D.C.: GPO, 1940.

Calkins, David L. "Black Education and the Nineteenth-Century City: Cincinnati's Colored Schools, 1850–87." Unpub. paper delivered at the American Educational Research Association Meeting, New York, 1972.

Callahan, Raymond E. *Education and the Cult of Efficiency.* Chicago: University of Chicago Press, 1962.

——— *The Superintendent of Schools: An Historical Analysis.* Report Résumé ED 010 410. Washington, D.C.: U.S. Office of Education, 1967.

Carney, Mabel. *Country Life and the Country School.* Chicago: Row, Peterson, 1912.

Carnoy, Martin, ed. *Schooling in a Corporate Society: The Political Economy of Education in America.* New York: McKay, 1972.

Caswell, Hollis L. *City School Surveys: An Interpretation and Appraisal.* Contributions to Education, no. 358. New York: Teachers College, Columbia University, 1929.

Chamberlain, Arthur H. "The Growth and Enlargement of the Power of the City School Superintendent." University of California, *Publications,* 3, no. 4 (May 15, 1913).

Chancellor, William E. *Our Schools: Their Administration and Supervision.* Boston: D. C. Heath, 1915.

Chapman, Paul D. "The Intelligence Testing Movement: Reorganizing the Schools for the Meritocracy." Unpub. seminar paper, Stanford University, 1972.

Charters, W. W., Jr. "Social Class Analysis and the Control of Public Education." *Harvard Educational Review,* 23 (Fall 1953), 268–83.

Chase, Amanda Matthews. *Primer for Foreign-Speaking Women: Part I.* Sacramento: Commission of Immigration and Housing of California, 1918.

Chicago City Council. *Recommendations for Reorganization of the Public School System of the City of Chicago: Report of an Investigation by the Committee on Schools, Fire, Police, and Civil Service of the City Council of the City of Chicago; Testimony of Educational Experts Who Appeared before the Committee.* Chicago: City of Chicago, 1917.

Chicago Merchants' Club. *Public Schools and Their Administration: Addresses Delivered at the Fifty-Ninth Meeting of the Merchants' Club of Chicago.* Chicago: Merchants' Club, 1906.

Church, Robert L. "Educational Psychology and Social Reform in the Progressive Era." *History of Education Quarterly,* 11 (Winter 1971), 390–405.

——— "History of Education as a Field of Study." In Lee C. Deighton, ed., *Encyclopedia of Education,* IV, 415–24. New York: Macmillan, 1971.

Cinel, Dino. "Literacy versus Culture: The Case of the Immigrants." Unpub. seminar paper, Stanford University, 1973.

"Cities Reporting the Use of Homogeneous Grouping and of the Winnetka Technique and the Dalton Plan." U.S. Bureau of Education, City School Leaflet no. 22. Washington, D.C.: GPO, 1926.

Clark, Kenneth. *Dark Ghetto.* New York: Harper & Row, 1965.

Claxton, Philander, et al. *The Public School System of San Francisco, California: A Report to the San Francisco Board of Education of a Survey Made under the Direction of the United States Commissioner of Education.* U.S. Bureau of Education, Bulletin no. 46. Washington, D.C.: GPO, 1917.

"The Cleveland Meeting." *American School Board Journal,* 10 (March 1895), 9.

"The Cleveland Plan." *American School Board Journal,* 11 (Dec. 1895), 10–11.

Clifford, Geraldine Joncich. *The Sane Positivist: A Biography of Edward L. Thorndike.* Middletown, Conn.: Wesleyan University Press, 1968.

Cofer, Lloyd M. "We Face Reality in Detroit." *National Educational Outlook among Negroes,* 1 (Nov. 1937), 34–37.

Coffman, Lotus Delta. *The Social Composition of the Teaching Population.* Contributions to Education, no. 41. New York: Teachers College, Columbia University, 1911.

Cohen, David K. "Compensatory Education." In Herbert J. Walberg and Andrew T. Kopan, eds., *Rethinking Urban Education*, 150–64. San Francisco: Jossey-Bass, 1972.
——— "Immigrants and the Schools." *Review of Educational Research*, 40 (Feb. 1970), 13–28.
Cohen, David K., and Marvin Lazerson. "Education and the Corporate Order." *Socialist Revolution*, 2 (March-April 1972), 47–72.
Cohen, Sol. "The Industrial Education Movement, 1906–17." *American Quarterly*, 20 (Spring 1968), 95–110.
——— *Progressives and Urban School Reform*. New York: Bureau of Publications, Teachers College, Columbia University, 1964.
Cole, Raymond E. "The City's Responsibility to the Immigrant." *Immigrants in America Review*, 1 (June 1915), 36–41.
Cole, Stephen. *The Unionization of Teachers: A Case Study of the UFT*. New York: Praeger, 1969.
Coleman, James S., et al. *Equality of Educational Opportunity*. Washington, D.C.: GPO, 1966.
Collegiate Alumnae Association. *Some Conditions in the Schools of San Francisco: A Report Made by the School Survey Class of the California Branch of the Association of Collegiate Alumnae, May 1, 1914*. San Francisco: n.p., 1914.
Committee of Fifteen. "Report of the Sub-Committee on the Organization of City School Systems." *Educational Review*, 9 (March 1895), 304–22.
Committee of Graduate School of Education, University of Nebraska. *The Rural Teacher of Nebraska*. U.S. Bureau of Education, Bulletin no. 20. Washington, D.C.: GPO, 1919.
Committee of Teachers of Philadelphia Public Schools. *Negro Employment: A Study of the Negro Employment Situation and Its Relation to School Programs*. Philadelphia: n.p., 1943.
Committee of Ten. *Report*. New York: Published for the National Education Association by American Book Co., 1894.
Committee of Twelve on Rural Schools, National Education Association. "Report." In *Report of the Commissioner of Education for the Year 1896–97*. Washington, D.C.: GPO, 1898.
Committee on City School Systems. "School Superintendence in Cities." *NEA Addresses and Proceedings*, 29th Annual Meeting, New York, 1890, 309–17.
Committee on School Inquiry, Board of Estimate and Apportionment, City of New York. *Report*. New York: City of New York, 1911–13.
Commonwealth Club of California. *Transactions*, 12 (Jan. 1917–Jan. 1918).
Conant, James Bryant. *Slums and Suburbs: A Commentary on Schools in Metropolitan Areas*. New York: McGraw-Hill, 1961.
"Confessions of Public School Teachers." *Atlantic Monthly*, 78 (July 1896), 97–110.
"Confessions of Three School Superintendents." *Atlantic Monthly*, 82 (Nov. 1898), 644–53.
Corning, Hobart M. *After Testing—What? The Practical Use of Test Results in One School System*. Chicago: Scott, Foresman, 1926.
Cornwell, Elmer E. "Bosses, Machines, and Ethnic Groups." *Annals of the American Academy of Political and Social Science*, 352 (March 1964), 27–39.
Counts, George S. *School and Society in Chicago*. New York: Harcourt, Brace, 1928.

—— *The Selective Character of American Secondary Education.* Chicago: University of Chicago Press, 1922.

—— *The Social Composition of Boards of Education.* Chicago: University of Chicago Press, 1927.

Covello, Leonard. *The Heart Is the Teacher.* New York: McGraw-Hill, 1958.

—— "A High School and Its Immigrant Community—A Challenge and an Opportunity." *Journal of Educational Sociology,* 9 (Feb. 1936), 331–46.

—— "The School as the Center of Community Life in an Immigrant Area." In Samuel Everett, ed., *The Community School,* 125–63. New York: D. Appleton-Century, 1938.

—— *The Social Background of the Italo-American School Child.* Leiden: E. J. Brill, 1967.

Cremin, Lawrence A. *The American Common School: An Historic Conception.* New York: Bureau of Publications, Teachers College, Columbia University, 1951.

—— "Curriculum-Making in the United States." *Teachers College Record,* 73 (Dec. 1971), 207–20.

—— *The Transformation of the School: Progressivism in American Education, 1876–1957.* New York: Knopf, 1961.

—— *The Wonderful World of Ellwood Patterson Cubberley: An Essay on the Historiography of American Education.* New York: Bureau of Publications, Teachers College, Columbia University, 1965.

"The Crisis in Education and the Changing Afro-American Community." *Freedomways,* 8 (Fall 1968).

Cronbach, Lee J. *Essentials of Psychological Testing.* New York: Harper & Row, 1970.

Cronin, Joseph M. "The Centralization of the Boston Public Schools." Unpub. paper delivered at the American Educational Research Association Meeting, Minneapolis, Feb. 1971.

—— *The Control of Urban Schools: Perspective on the Power of Educational Reformers.* New York: Free Press, 1973.

Crooks, James B. *Politics and Progress: The Rise of Urban Progressivism in Baltimore, 1895 to 1911.* Baton Rouge: Louisiana State University Press, 1968.

Crozier, Michael. *Bureaucratic Phenomenon.* Chicago: University of Chicago Press, 1964.

Cubberley, Ellwood P. *Changing Conceptions of Education.* Boston: Houghton Mifflin, 1909.

—— "Organization of Public Education." *NEA Addresses and Proceedings,* 53rd Annual Meeting, Oakland, 1915, 91–97.

—— *The Portland Survey.* Yonkers-on-Hudson: World Book, 1916.

—— *Public Education in the United States: A Study and Interpretation of American Educational History.* Rev. ed. Boston: Houghton Mifflin, 1934.

—— *Public School Administration: A Statement of the Fundamental Principles Underlying the Organization and Administration of Public Education.* Boston: Houghton Mifflin, 1916.

—— *Rural Life and Education: A Study of the Rural-School Problem as a Phase of the Rural-Life Problem.* Boston: Houghton Mifflin, 1914.

—— "The School Situation in San Francisco." *Educational Review,* 21 (April 1901), 364–81.

—— *State and County Educational Reorganization.* New York: Macmillan, 1914.

Curti, Merle. *The Roots of American Loyalty.* New York: Columbia University Press, 1946.

——— *The Social Ideas of American Educators.* Paterson, N.J.: Littlefield, Adams, 1959.

Curtis, Henry S. *Recreation for Teachers, or the Teacher's Leisure Time.* New York: Macmillan, 1918.

"The 'Czar' Movement." *American School Board Journal,* 10 (March 1895), 8.

Dabney, Charles W. *Universal Education in the South.* Chapel Hill: University of North Carolina Press, 1936.

Dabney, Lillian G. *The History of Schools for Negroes in the District of Columbia, 1807–1947.* Washington, D.C.: Catholic University of America Press, 1949.

Dalby, Michael T., and Michael Werthman, eds. *Bureaucracy in Historical Perspective.* Glenview, Ill.: Scott, Foresman, 1971.

Dallas, Neva, et al., comps. *Lamplighters: Leaders in Learning.* Portland, Ore.: Binfords and Mort, 1959.

Daniel, Walter G. "The Aims of Secondary Education and the Adequacy of the Curriculum of the Negro Secondary School." *Journal of Negro Education,* 9 (July 1940), 465–73.

Daniels, John. *America via the Neighborhood.* New York: Harper & Brothers, 1920.

Daniels, Virginia. "Attitudes Affecting the Occupational Affiliation of Negroes." Unpub. Ed.D. diss., University of Pittsburgh, 1938.

Darling, Arthur Burr. "Prior to Little Rock in American Education: The Roberts Case of 1849–1850." *Massachusetts Historical Society Proceedings,* 72 (Oct. 1957–Dec. 1960), 126–42.

Davis, Helen. "Some Problems Arising in the Administration of a Department of Measurements." *Journal of Educational Research,* 5 (Jan. 1922), 1–20.

Davison, Berlinda. "Educational Status of the Negro in the San Francisco Bay Region." Unpub. M.A. thesis, University of California, Berkeley, 1921.

Dearborn, Walter F. *Intelligence Tests: Their Significance for School and Society.* Boston: Houghton Mifflin, 1928.

Deffenbaugh, W. S. "The Smaller Cities." In U.S. Bureau of Education, Bulletin no. 48. Washington, D.C.: GPO, 1918.

——— "Uses of Intelligence and Achievement Tests in 215 Cities." U.S. Bureau of Education, City School Leaflet no. 20. Washington, D.C.: GPO, 1926.

DeFord, Miriam Allen. *They Were San Franciscans.* Caldwell, Idaho: Caxton, 1941.

Demas, Boulton H. "The School Elections: A Critique of the 1969 New York City School Decentralization." A Report of the Institute for Community Studies, Queens College, City University of New York, 1971.

Department of Education, State of Ohio. *The Classification of Pupils in Elementary Schools.* Columbus: Heer, 1925.

DeWeese, Truman A. "Better School Administration." *Educational Review,* 20 (June 1900), 61–71.

——— "Two Years' Progress in the Chicago Public Schools." *Educational Review,* 24 (Nov. 1902), 325–27.

Dewey, John. *Democracy and Education.* New York: Macmillan, 1916.

——— *The Educational Situation.* Chicago: University of Chicago Press, 1902.

——— "Individuality, Equality, and Superiority." *New Republic,* 33 (Dec. 13, 1922), 61–63.

—— *The School and Society.* Chicago: University of Chicago Press, 1899.

Dick, Everett. *The Sod-House Frontier.* New York: D. Appleton-Century, 1937.

Dickson, Virgil E. "Classification of School Children according to Mental Ability." In Lewis M. Terman, ed., *Intelligence Tests and School Reorganization,* 32–52. Yonkers-on-Hudson: World Book, 1922.

—— *Mental Tests and the Classroom Teacher.* Yonkers-on-Hudson: World Book, 1923.

—— "The Relation of Mental Testing to School Reorganization." Unpub. Ph.D. diss., Stanford University, 1919.

—— "The Use of Mental Tests in the Guidance of Eighth-Grade and High School Pupils." *Journal of Educational Research,* 2 (Oct. 1920), 601–10.

Dillon, Lee A. "The Portland Public Schools from 1873 to 1913." Unpub. M.A. thesis, University of Oregon, 1928.

Dixon, Robert S. "The Education of the Negro in the City of New York, 1853–1900." Unpub. M.S. thesis, College of the City of New York, 1935.

Dixon, Royal. *Americanization.* New York: Macmillan, 1916.

Dogherty, Marian A. *'Scusa Me Teacher.* Francestown, N.H.: Marshall Jones, 1943.

Dolson, Lee Stephen. "The Administration of the San Francisco Public Schools, 1847 to 1947." Unpub. Ph.D. diss., University of California, Berkeley, 1964.

Dooley, William H. *The Education of the Ne'er-Do-Well.* Cambridge, Mass.: Houghton Mifflin, 1916.

Dorchester, Daniel. *Romanism versus the Public School System.* New York: Phillips and Hunt, 1888.

Dorsett, Lyle W. *The Pendergast Machine.* New York: Oxford University Press, 1968.

Douglass, Bennet Cooper. *Professional and Economic Status of the City Superintendent of Schools in the United States.* New York: n.p., 1923.

Downs, Anthony. *Inside Bureaucracy.* Boston: Little, Brown, 1967.

Drake, St. Clair. "The Social and Economic Status of the Negro in the United States." In Talcott Parsons and Kenneth B. Clark, eds., *The Negro American,* 3–46. Boston: Beacon, 1967.

Draper, Andrew S. "Common Schools in the Larger Cities." *The Forum,* 27 (June 1899), 385–97.

—— *The Crucial Test of the Public School System.* Urbana, Ill.: published by the author, 1898.

—— "Plans of Organization for School Purposes in Large Cities." *Educational Review,* 6 (June 1893), 1–16.

Dreeben, Robert. *On What Is Learned in School.* Reading, Mass.: Addison-Wesley, 1968.

Drost, Walter. *David Snedden: Education for Social Efficiency.* Madison: University of Wisconsin Press, 1967.

DuBois, W. E. B. "Does the Negro Need Separate Schools?" *Journal of Negro Education,* 4 (July 1935), 328–35.

—— "Pechstein and Pecksniff." *The Crisis,* 36 (Sept. 1929), 313–14.

—— *The Philadelphia Negro: A Social Study.* New York: Schocken Books, 1969 [originally published in 1899].

Duncan, Hannibal G. *Immigration and Assimilation.* Boston: D. C. Heath, 1933.

Dunne, Finley Peter. *Mr. Dooley at His Best.* New York: Charles Scribner's Sons, 1938.

Dushkin, Alexander M. *Jewish Education in New York City.* New York: Bureau of Jewish Education, 1918.

Dutton, Samuel Train, and David Snedden. *The Administration of Public Education in the United States.* New York: Macmillan, 1912.

Dwight, Timothy. *Travels in New-England and New-York.* 4 vols. New Haven, Conn.: published by the author, 1821–22.

Eaton, John. *The Relation of Education to Labor.* Washington, D.C.: GPO, 1872.

"Education in America." *Saturday Review,* 53 (Sept. 19, 1970), 61–79.

Education of the Immigrant. U.S. Bureau of Education, Bulletin no. 51. Washington, D.C.: GPO, 1913.

Edwards, Newton. *Equal Educational Opportunity for Youth.* Washington, D.C.: American Council on Education, 1939.

Eggleston, Edward. *The Hoosier School-Master.* New York: Hill and Wang, 1965 [originally published in 1871].

Eggleston, J. D., and Robert Bruere. *The Work of the Rural School.* New York: Harper, 1913.

Eliot, Charles W. "Educational Reform and the Social Order." *School Review,* 17 (April 1909), 217–22.

———— "School Board Reform." *American School Board Journal,* 39 (July 1908), 3.

———— "Undesirable and Desirable Uniformity in Schools." *NEA Addresses and Proceedings,* 31st Annual Meeting, New York, 1892, 82–86.

Eliot, Edward C. "A Nonpartisan School Law." *NEA Addresses and Proceedings,* 44th Annual Meeting, Asbury Park, Ocean Grove, N.J., 1905, 223–31.

———— "School Administration: The St. Louis Method." *Educational Review,* 26 (Dec. 1903), 464–75.

Elliott, Frank, and Harry Wigderson. "Fitting the Pieces: PPBS and the Stull Bill." *California School Boards,* 31 (Sept. 1972), 8–10, 15–17.

Elsbree, Willard S. *The American Teacher: Evolution of a Profession in a Democracy.* New York: American Book, 1939.

Elson, Ruth. *Guardians of Tradition: American Schoolbooks of the Nineteenth Century.* Lincoln: University of Nebraska Press, 1964.

Ensign, Forest. *Compulsory School Attendance and Child Labor.* Iowa City: Athens Press, 1921.

"Equal Educational Opportunity." *Harvard Educational Review,* 38 (Winter 1968).

Ettinger, William L. "Facing the Facts." *School and Society,* 16 (Nov. 4, 1922), 505–12.

Everett, Edward. *Orations and Speeches: On Various Occasions.* Boston: Little, Brown, 1878.

Fantini, Mario D. "Options for Students, Parents, and Teachers: Public Schools of Choice." *Phi Delta Kappan,* 52 (May 1971), 541–43.

Fantini, Mario D., and Gerald Weinstein. *The Disadvantaged: Challenge to Education.* New York: Harper & Row, 1968.

Filene, Peter F. "An Obituary for 'the Progressive Movement.'" *American Quarterly,* 22 (Spring 1970), 20–34.

Fine, Benjamin. *Our Children Are Cheated: The Crisis in American Education.* New York: Henry Holt, 1947.

Finkelstein, Barbara Joan. "Governing the Young: Teacher Behavior in American Primary Schools, 1820–1880; A Documentary History." Unpub. Ed.D. diss., Teachers College, Columbia University, 1970.

Fishel, Leslie H. "The North and the Negro, 1865–1900: A Study in Race Discrimination." Unpub. Ph.D. diss., Harvard University, 1953.

Fishlow, Albert. "Levels of Nineteenth Century Investment in Education." *Journal of Economic History,* 26 (Dec. 1966), 418–36.

Fishman, Joshua. *Language Loyalty in the United States.* The Hague: Mouton, 1966.

Foner, Philip S., ed. *The Life and Writings of Frederick Douglass.* 4 vols. New York: International Publishers, 1950–55.

Forcey, Charles. *The Crossroads of Liberalism.* New York: Oxford University Press, 1961.

Fox, Bonnie R. "The Philadelphia Progressives: A Test of the Hofstadter-Hays Thesis." *Pennsylvania History,* 34 (Oct. 1967), 372–94.

Galarza, Ernesto. *Barrio Boy.* Notre Dame, Ind.: University of Notre Dame Press, 1971.

Gallup, George H. "Fifth Annual Gallup Poll of Public Attitudes toward Education." *Phi Delta Kappan,* 55 (Sept. 1973), 38–50.

Gans, Herbert J. *The Urban Villagers: Group and Class in the Life of Italian-Americans.* New York: Free Press of Glencoe, 1962.

Garland, Hamlin. *A Son of the Middle Border.* New York: Macmillan, 1941 [originally published in 1914].

Gear, Harold Lyman. "The Rise of City-School Superintendency as an Influence in Educational Policy." Unpub. Ed.D. diss., Harvard University, 1950.

Gersman, Elinor M. "Progressive Reform of the St. Louis School Board, 1897." *History of Education Quarterly,* 10 (Spring 1970), 3–21.

―――― "Separate but Equal: Negro Education in St. Louis, 1875–1900." Unpublished MS, Washington University, 1972.

Gilbert, Charles B. "The Freedom of the Teacher." *NEA Addresses and Proceedings,* 45th Annual Meeting, Winona, Minn., 1903, 164–77.

―――― *The School and Its Life: A Brief Discussion of the Principles of School Management and Organization.* New York: Silver, Burdett, 1906.

Gilland, Thomas M. *The Origins and Development of the Powers and Duties of the City-School Superintendent.* Chicago: University of Chicago Press, 1935.

Gittell, Marilyn. *Participants and Participation: A Study of School Policy in New York City.* New York: Praeger, 1967.

―――― "Urban School Reform in the 1970's." *Education and Urban Society,* 1 (Nov. 1968), 9–20.

Glazer, Nathan, and Daniel Patrick Moynihan. *Beyond the Melting Pot: The Negroes, Puerto Ricans, Jews, Italians, and Irish of New York City.* Cambridge, Mass.: M.I.T. Press, 1963.

Glynn, Lenny. "A Blueprint for Power: Unions." *Learning,* 1 (March 1973), 46–50.

Gold, Michael. *Jews without Money.* New York: Avon Books, 1965 [originally published in 1930].

Goldberg, G. S. "I.S. 201: An Educational Landmark." *IRCD Bulletin,* 2 (Winter 1966–67), 1–8.

Gompers, Samuel. "Teachers' Right to Organize." *American Federationist,* 22 (Oct. 1915), 857–60.

―――― "Teachers' Right to Organize Affirmed." *American Federationist,* 21 (Dec. 1914), 1083–85.

Goodlad, John I., and Robert H. Anderson. *The Nongraded Elementary School.* Rev. ed. New York: Harcourt, Brace, and World, 1963.

Goodwin, M. B. "History of Schools for the Colored Population in the District of Columbia." In Henry Barnard, ed., *Special Report of the Commissioner of Education on the Condition of Public Schools in the District of Columbia*, 192–300. House Executive Document 315, 41C, 2S. Washington, D.C.: GPO, 1869.

Gordon, Milton M. *Assimilation in American Life: The Role of Race, Religion, and National Origins*. New York: Oxford University Press, 1964.

Gove, Aaron. "Contributions to the History of American Teaching." *Educational Review*, 38 (Dec. 1909), 493–500.

———— "Duties of City Superintendents." *NEA Addresses and Proceedings*, 24th Annual Meeting, Madison, Wis., 1884, 26–33.

———— "Limitations of the Superintendents' Authority and of the Teacher's Independence." *NEA Addresses and Proceedings*, 43rd Annual Meeting, St. Louis, 1904, 152–57.

———— "The Trail of the City Superintendent." *NEA Addresses and Proceedings*, 39th Annual Meeting, Charleston, 1900, 214–22.

Grace, Alonzo G. "The Effect of Negro Migration on the Cleveland Public School System." Unpub. Ph.D. diss., Western Reserve University, 1932.

Greeley, Horace. *Hints toward Reforms*. New York: Harper & Brothers, 1853.

Green, Constance McLaughlin. *The Secret City: A History of Race Relations in the Nation's Capital*. Princeton: Princeton University Press, 1967.

Greer, Colin. *The Great School Legend: A Revisionist Interpretation of American Public Education*. New York: Basic Books, 1972.

Griffiths, Daniel E. *Human Relations in School Administration*. New York: Appleton-Century-Crofts, 1956.

Grissom, Thomas. "Education and the Cold War: The Role of James B. Conant." In Clarence J. Karier et al., *Roots of Crisis: American Education in the Twentieth Century*, 177–97. Chicago: Rand McNally, 1973.

Gross, Beatrice, and Ronald Gross, eds. *Radical School Reform*. New York: Simon and Schuster, 1970.

Grubb, Norton, and Marvin Lazerson. *Education and Industrialism: Documents in Vocational Education, 1870–1970*. Forthcoming in the Classics in Education series published by Teachers College, Columbia University.

Grund, Francis. *Aristocracy in America*. New York: Harper & Row, 1959 [originally published in 1839].

Gump, Paul V., and Roger Barker. *Big School, Small School: High School Size and Student Behavior*. Stanford, Calif.: Stanford University Press, 1964.

Gusfield, Joseph. *Symbolic Crusade: Status Politics and the American Temperance Movement*. Urbana, Ill.: University of Illinois Press, 1966.

Guthrie, James W., and Edward Wynne, eds. *New Models for American Education*. Englewood Cliffs, N.J.: Prentice-Hall, 1971.

Gutman, Herbert G. "Work, Culture, and Society in Industrializing America, 1815–1919." *American Historical Review*, 78 (June 1973), 531–88.

Haggerty, M. E. "Recent Developments in Measuring Human Capacities." *Journal of Educational Research*, 3 (April 1921), 241–53.

Haley, Margaret. "Why Teachers Should Organize." *NEA Addresses and Proceedings*, 43rd Annual Meeting, St. Louis, 1904, 145–52.

Hamilton, Gail [Mary Abigail Dodge]. *Our Common School System*. Boston: Estes and Lauriat, 1880.

Hammack, David C. "The Centralization of New York City's Public School System, 1896: A Social Analysis of a Decision." Unpub. M.A. thesis, Columbia University, 1969.

Handlin, Oscar. *John Dewey's Challenge to Education: Historical Perspectives on the Cultural Context*. New York: Harper and Brothers, 1959.

———— "The Modern City as a Field of Historical Study." In John Burchard and Oscar Handlin, eds., *The Historian and the City*, 1–26. Cambridge, Mass.: M.I.T. Press, 1963.

Haney, John D. *Registration of City School Children*. New York: Teachers College, Columbia University, 1910.

Hanus, Paul Henry. *Adventuring in Education*. Cambridge, Mass.: Harvard University Press, 1937.

Hardin, Clara A. *The Negroes of Philadelphia: The Cultural Adjustment of a Minority Group*. Philadelphia: n.p., 1945.

Harlem Parents Committee. *The Education of Minority Group Children in the New York City Public Schools, 1965*. New York: Harlem Parents Committee, n.d.

Harrington, Michael. *The Other America: Poverty in the United States*. New York: Macmillan, 1962.

Harris, Neil. Review of *The Irony of Early School Reform: Educational Innovation in Mid-Nineteenth Century Massachusetts*, by Michael B. Katz. *Harvard Educational Review*, 39 (Spring 1969), 383–89.

Harris, P. M. G. "The Social Origins of American Leaders: The Demographic Foundations." *Perspectives in American History*, 3 (1969), 159–344.

Harris, William T. "City School Supervision." *Educational Review*, 3 (Feb. 1892), 167–72.

———— "Elementary Education." In Nicholas M. Butler, ed., *Monographs on Education in the United States*, 79–139. Albany, N.Y.: J. B. Lyon, 1900.

Harris, William T., and Duane Doty. *A Statement of the Theory of Education in the United States as Approved by Many Leading Educators*. Washington, D.C.: GPO, 1874.

Hartmann, Edward G. *The Movement to Americanize the Immigrant*. New York: Columbia University Press, 1948.

Hayes, George. "Vocational Education and the Negro." In *Proceedings of National Society for the Promotion of Industrial Education*, 71–74. New York: National Society for the Promotion of Industrial Education, 1917.

Hays, Samuel P. "Political Parties and the Community-Society Continuum." In William Nisbet Chambers and Walter Dean Burnham, eds., *The American Party Systems: Stages of Political Development*, 152–81. New York: Oxford University Press, 1967.

———— "The Politics of Reform in Municipal Government in the Progressive Era." *Pacific Northwest Quarterly*, 55 (Oct. 1964), 157–69.

Hazard, Joseph T. *Pioneer Teachers of Washington*. Seattle: Seattle Retired Teachers Association, 1955.

Hazlett, James Stephen. "Crisis in School Government: An Administrative History of the Chicago Public Schools, 1933–1947." Unpub. Ph.D. diss., University of Chicago, 1968.

Heller, Herbert Lynn. "Negro Education in Indiana from 1816 to 1869." Unpub. Ph.D. diss., Indiana University, 1951.

Hentoff, Nat. *Our Children Are Dying*. New York: Viking, 1966.

Herney, John D. "The Movement to Reform the Boston School Committee in 1905." Unpub. MS, Harvard University, 1966.

Herrick, Mary J. *The Chicago Schools: A Social and Political History*. Beverly Hills, Calif.: Sage Publications, 1971.

Herrick, Mary J. "Negro Employees of the Chicago Board of Education." Unpub. M.A. thesis, University of Chicago, 1931.

Herriott, Robert E., and Benjamin J. Hodgkins. *The Environment of Schooling: Formal Education as an Open System.* Englewood Cliffs, N.J.: Prentice-Hall, 1973.

Higgins, Shelley. "School Reform in Los Angeles, 1903–1916." Unpub. seminar paper, Stanford University, 1970.

Higham, John. *From Boundlessness to Consolidation: The Transformation of American Culture, 1848–1860.* Ann Arbor: William L. Clements Library, 1969.

———— *Strangers in the Land: Patterns of American Nativism, 1860–1925.* New York: Atheneum, 1966.

Hines, Harlan C. "What Los Angeles is Doing with the Results of Testing." *Journal of Educational Research,* 5 (Jan. 1922), 45–57.

Hinsdale, B. A. "The American School Superintendent." *Educational Review,* 5 (Jan. 1894), 42–54.

———— *Our Common Schools.* Cleveland: published by the author, 1878.

Holli, Melvin G. *Reform in Detroit: Hazen S. Pingree and Urban Politics.* New York: Oxford University Press, 1969.

Holloway, Mary K. "A Study of Social Conditions Affecting Stowe Junior High School Girls with Suggestions for a Program of Guidance." Unpub. M.A. thesis, University of Cincinnati, 1928.

Holsinger, Donald B. "The Elementary School as Modernizer: A Brazilian Study." Unpublished MS, Stanford University, 1973.

Homel, Michael. "Black Education in Chicago." Unpub. preliminary draft of Ph.D. diss., University of Chicago, 1972.

Horvath, Helen. "The Plea of an Immigrant—Abstract." *NEA Addresses and Proceedings,* 61st Annual Meeting, Oakland-San Francisco, 1923, 680–82.

Howe, Irving. "The Lower East Side: Symbol and Fact." In Allon Schoener, ed., *The Lower East Side: Portal to American Life (1870–1924),* 11–14. New York: The Jewish Museum, 1966.

Hubbert, Harvey H. "What Kind of Centralization, If Any, Will Strengthen Our Local System?" *NEA Addresses and Proceedings,* 37th Annual Meeting, Washington, D.C., 1898, 986–89.

Hummel, Raymond C., and John M. Nagle. *Urban Education in America: Problems and Prospects.* New York: Oxford University Press, 1973.

Hutchinson, Edward P. *Immigrants and Their Children, 1850–1950.* New York: Wiley, 1956.

Huthmacher, J. Joseph. "Urban Liberalism and the Age of Reform." *Mississippi Valley Historical Review,* 49 (Sept. 1962), 231–41.

Iannaccone, Lawrence. *Politics in Education.* New York: Center for Applied Research in Education, 1967.

Iannaccone, Lawrence, and Frank W. Lutz. *Politics, Power, and Policy: The Governing of Local School Districts.* Columbus: Charles E. Merrill, 1970.

Illich, Ivan. *Deschooling Society.* New York: Harper & Row, 1970.

"Immigration." *Massachusetts Teacher,* 4 (Oct. 1851), 289–91.

"The Imperatives of Ethnic Education." *Phi Delta Kappan,* 53 (Jan. 1972).

Inkeles, Alex. "Social Structure and the Socialization of Competence." *Harvard Educational Review,* 36 (Summer 1966), 265–83.

Issel, William H. "Modernization in Philadelphia School Reform, 1882–1905." *Pennsylvania Magazine of History and Biography,* 94 (July 1970), 358–83.

———— "Teachers and Educational Reform during the Progressive Era: A Case

Study of the Pittsburgh Teachers Association." *History of Education Quarterly,* 7 (Summer 1967), 220–33.

Jackson, Kenneth T., and Stanley K. Schultz, eds. *Cities in American History.* New York: Knopf, 1972.

James, H. Thomas, James A. Kelly, and Walter I. Garms. *Determinants of Educational Expenditures in Large Cities of the United States.* Stanford, Calif.: School of Education, Stanford University, 1966.

Jay, John. "Public and Parochial Schools." *NEA Addresses and Proceedings,* 28th Annual Meeting, Nashville, 1889, 152–79.

Jencks, Christopher, et al. *Inequality: A Reassessment of the Effect of Family and Schooling in America.* New York: Basic Books, 1972.

Jenks, Albert E. "Types of Important Racial Information Which Teachers of Americanization Should Possess—Abstract." *NEA Addresses and Proceedings,* 62nd Annual Meeting, Washington, D.C., 1924, 569.

Jennings, Frank. "It Didn't Start with Sputnik." *Saturday Review,* 50 (Sept. 16, 1967), 77–79, 95–97.

Johnson, Clifton. *The Country School in New England.* New York: D. Appleton, 1895.

———— *Old Time Schools and School Books.* New York: Dover, 1963 [originally published in 1904].

Johnson, Herbert B. *Discrimination against the Japanese in California: A Review of the Real Situation.* Berkeley: Courier Publishing Co., 1907.

Johnson, Ronald Mabberry. "Captain of Education: An Intellectual Biography of Andrew S. Draper, 1848–1913." Unpub. Ph.D. diss., University of Illinois, 1970.

Joint Committee on Rural Schools, George A. Works, Chairman. *Rural School Survey of New York State.* Ithaca, N.Y.: William F. Fell, 1922.

Jones, Dorothy. "The Issues at I.S. 201: A View from the Parents' Committee." In Meyer Weinberg, ed., *Integrated Education: A Reader,* 154–63. Beverly Hills, Calif.: Glencoe, 1968.

Jones, L. H. "The Politician and the Public School: Indianapolis and Cleveland." *Atlantic Monthly,* 77 (June 1896), 810–22.

Kaestle, Carl F. "The Origins of an Urban School System: New York City, 1750–1850." Unpub. Ph.D. diss., Harvard University, 1970.

Kallen, Horace M. "The Meaning of Americanism." *Immigrants in America Review,* 1 (Jan. 1916), 12–19.

Karier, Clarence J., Paul Violas, and Joel Spring. *Roots of Crisis: American Education in the Twentieth Century.* Chicago: Rand McNally, 1973.

Katz, Michael B. *Class, Bureaucracy, and Schools: The Illusion of Educational Change in America.* New York: Praeger, 1971.

———— "The Emergence of Bureaucracy in Urban Education: The Boston Case, 1850–1884." *History of Education Quarterly,* 8 (Summer and Fall 1968), 155–88, 319–57.

———— *The Irony of Early School Reform: Educational Innovation in Mid-Nineteenth Century Massachusetts.* Cambridge, Mass.: Harvard University Press, 1968.

———— *School Reform: Past and Present.* Boston: Little, Brown, 1971.

Kazin, Alfred. *A Walker in the City.* New York: Harcourt, Brace, and World, 1951.

Keppel, Ann. "The Myth of Agrarianism in Rural Educational Reform, 1890–1914." *History of Education Quarterly,* 2 (June 1962), 100–109.

Kevles, Daniel J. "Testing the Army's Intelligence: Psychologists and the Military in World War I." *Journal of American History,* 55 (Dec. 1968), 565–81.

Kimball, Solon T., and James E. McClellan, Jr. *Education and the New America.* New York: Random House, 1962.

Kinney, Lucien B. *Certification in Education.* Englewood Cliffs, N.J.: Prentice-Hall, 1964.

Kirkpatrick, Marion G. *The Rural School from Within.* Philadelphia: Lippincott, 1917.

Kirst, Michael W., comp. *The Politics of Education at the Local, State, and Federal Levels.* Berkeley: McCutchan, 1970.

——— ed. *State, School, and Politics: Research Directions.* Lexington, Mass.: Heath, 1972.

Kleine, Paul F., Raphael O. Nystrand, and Edwin M. Bridges. "Citizen Views of Big City Schools." *Theory Into Practice,* 8 (Oct. 1969), 223–28.

Kleppner, Paul. *The Cross of Culture: A Social Analysis of Midwestern Politics, 1850–1900.* New York: Free Press, 1970.

Koos, Leonard V. "The Fruits of School Surveys." *School and Society,* 5 (Jan. 13, 1917), 35–41.

Korman, Gerd. *Industrialization, Immigrants, and Americanizers.* Madison, Wis.: State Historical Society of Wisconsin, 1967.

Kozol, Jonathan. *Death at an Early Age: The Destruction of the Hearts and Minds of Negro Children in the Boston Public Schools.* Boston: Houghton Mifflin, 1967.

——— *Free Schools.* Boston: Houghton Mifflin, 1972.

Krug, Edward A. *The Shaping of the American High School.* New York: Harper & Row, 1964.

——— *The Shaping of the American High School, 1920–1941.* Madison, Wis.: University of Wisconsin Press, 1972.

Lane, Roger. *Policing the City: Boston, 1822–1885.* Cambridge, Mass.: Harvard University Press, 1967.

Lannie, Vincent P. *Public Money and Parochial Education: Bishop Hughes, Governor Seward, and the New York School Controversy.* Cleveland: Press of Case Western Reserve University, 1968.

La Noue, George R. "Political Questions in the Next Decade of Urban Education." *The Record,* 69 (March 1968), 517–28.

LaViolette, Forrest E. *Americans of Japanese Ancestry: A Study of Assimilation in the American Community.* Toronto: Canadian Institute of International Affairs, 1945.

Lawrence, Paul F. "Vocational Aspirations of Negro Youth of California." *Journal of Negro Education,* 19 (Winter 1950), 47–56.

Layton, Warren K. "The Group Intelligence Testing Program of the Detroit Public Schools." In *Intelligence Tests and Their Use* (twenty-first yearbook of the National Society for the Study of Education), 123–90. Bloomington, Ill.: Public School Publishing, 1922.

Lazerson, Marvin. *Origins of the Urban School: Public Education in Massachusetts, 1870–1915.* Cambridge, Mass.: Harvard University Press, 1971.

Levin, Alexandra Lee. "Henrietta Szold and the Russian Immigrant School." *Maryland Historical Magazine,* 57 (March 1962), 1–15.

Levin, Henry, ed. *Community Control of Schools.* Washington, D.C.: Brookings Institution, 1970.

Levine, Adeline, and Murray Levine. "Introduction to the New Edition." In Randolph S. Bourne, *The Gary Schools,* xii–lv. Cambridge, Mass.: M.I.T. Press, 1970.

Lieberman, Myron. *The Future of Public Education.* Chicago: University of Chicago Press, 1960.

Lippmann, Walter. "The Abuse of the Tests." *New Republic,* 32 (Nov. 15, 1922), 297–98.

Litwack, Leon F. *North of Slavery: The Negro in the Free States, 1790–1860.* Chicago: University of Chicago Press, 1961.

Loeb, Max. "Compulsory English for Foreign-Born." *Survey,* 40 (July 13, 1918), 426–27.

Lomax, Louis. *The Negro Revolt.* New York: Harper & Row, 1962.

Lowell, A. Lawrence. "The Professional and Non-Professional Bodies in Our School System, and the Proper Function of Each." *NEA Addresses and Proceedings,* 34th Annual Meeting, Denver, 1895, 999–1004.

Lowi, Theodore J. *At the Pleasure of the Mayor: Patronage and Power in New York City, 1898–1958.* Glencoe, Ill.: Free Press, 1964.

Lubove, Roy. *The Professional Altruist: The Emergence of Social Work as a Career.* Cambridge, Mass.: Harvard University Press, 1965.

Luthin, Reinhard H. *American Demagogues: Twentieth Century.* Boston: Beacon, 1954.

Lynd, Robert S., and Helen M. Lynd. *Middletown: A Study in Contemporary American Culture.* New York: Harcourt, Brace, 1929.

—— *Middletown in Transition.* New York: Harcourt, Brace, 1937.

Mabee, Carleton. "A Negro Boycott to Integrate Boston Schools." *New England Quarterly,* 41 (Sept. 1968), 341–61.

Mack, William S. "The Relation of a Board to Its Superintendent." *NEA Addresses and Proceedings,* 35th Annual Meeting, Buffalo, 1896, 980–88.

MacRae, David. *The Americans at Home.* New York: Dutton, 1952 [originally published in 1875].

Mahoney, John J., and Charles M. Herlihy. *First Steps in Americanization: A Handbook for Teachers.* Boston: Houghton Mifflin, 1918.

Mandelbaum, Seymour J. *Boss Tweed's New York.* New York: Wiley, 1965.

Mann, Arthur. "A Historical Overview: The *Lumpenproletariat,* Education, and Compensatory Action." In Charles U. Daly, ed., *The Quality of Inequality: Urban and Suburban Public Schools,* 9–26. Chicago: University of Chicago Center for Policy Study, 1968.

Mann, George L. "The Development of Public Education for Negroes in Saint Louis, Missouri." Unpub. Ed.D. diss., Indiana University, 1949.

Mann, Horace. *Life and Works.* Boston: Walker, Fuller, 1865–1868.

Mann, Mary Peabody, and Elizabeth Peabody. *Moral Culture of Infancy and Kindergarten Guide.* Boston: T.O.H.P. Burnham, 1863.

Marble, Albert P. "City School Administration." *Educational Review,* 8 (Sept. 1894), 154–68.

Mark, H. Thiselton. *Individuality and the Moral Aim in American Education.* London: Longmans, Green, 1901.

Marks, Russell. "Testers, Trackers, and Trustees: The Ideology of the Intelligence Testing Movement in America, 1900–1954." Unpub. Ph.D. diss., University of Illinois at Urbana-Champaign, 1972.

Martens, Elsie H. "Organization of Research Bureaus in City School Systems." U.S. Bureau of Education, City School Leaflet no. 14. Washington, D.C.: GPO, 1931.

Masters, Edgar Lee. *Across Spoon River.* New York: Farrar and Rinehart, 1936.

Maxwell, William H. "Professor Hinsdale on the City School Superintendency." *Educational Review,* 7 (Feb. 1894), 186–88.

———— *A Quarter Century of Public School Development.* New York: American Book Co., 1912.

———— "Stories of the Lives of Real Teachers." *World's Work,* 13 (Aug. 1909), 11877–80.

Mayo, A. D. "Object Lessons in Moral Instruction in the Common School." *NEA Addresses and Proceedings,* 29th Annual Meeting, New York, 1880, 6–17.

McAndrew, William. "Matters of Moment." *School and Society,* 28 (Nov. 3, 1928), 551–58.

McCaul, Robert L. "Dewey's Chicago." *School Review,* 67 (Autumn 1959), 258–80.

McDonald, Robert A. F. *Adjustment of School Organization to Various Population Groups.* Contributions to Education, no. 75. New York: Teachers College, Columbia University, 1915.

McKitrick, Eric L. "The Study of Corruption." *Political Science Quarterly,* 72 (Dec. 1957), 502–514.

McManis, John T. *Ella Flagg Young and a Half-Century of the Chicago Public Schools.* Chicago: A. C. McClurg, 1916.

Mears, Elliott Grinnell. *Resident Orientals on the American Pacific Coast: Their Legal and Economic Status.* Chicago: University of Chicago Press, 1928.

Meier, August, and Elliot M. Rudwick. "Early Boycotts of Segregated Schools: The Alton, Illinois, Case, 1897–1908." *Journal of Negro Education,* 36 (Fall 1967), 394–402.

———— "Early Boycotts of Segregated Schools: The East Orange, New Jersey, Experience, 1899–1906." *History of Education Quarterly,* 7 (Spring 1967), 22–35.

Mendenhall, Edgar. *The City School Board Member and His Task: A Booklet for City School Board Members.* Pittsburg, Kans.: College Inn Book Store, 1929.

Merk, Lois Bannister. "Boston's Historic Public School Crisis." *New England Quarterly,* 31 (June 1958), 172–99.

Merton, Robert K. *Social Theory and Social Structure.* Rev. ed. Glencoe, Ill.: Free Press, 1957.

Metzker, Isaac, ed. *A Bintel Brief: Sixty Years of Letters from the Lower East Side to the "Jewish Daily Forward."* Garden City, N.Y.: Doubleday, 1971.

Miller, Harry, and Marjorie Smiley, eds. *Education in the Metropolis.* New York: Free Press, 1967.

Miller, Herbert Adolphus. *The School and the Immigrant.* Cleveland: Survey Committee of the Cleveland Foundation, 1916.

Miller, William, ed. *Men in Business.* New York: Harper Torchbooks, 1962.

Miller, W. S. "The Administrative Use of Intelligence Tests in the High School." In *Intelligence Tests and Their Use* (twenty-first yearbook of the National Society for the Study of Education), 189–222. Bloomington, Ill.: Public School Publishing, 1922.

Miller, Zane L. *Boss Cox's Cincinnati: Urban Politics in the Progressive Era.* New York: Oxford University Press, 1968.

Mills, C. Wright. *The Sociological Imagination.* New York: Oxford University Press, 1959.

Mills, Nicolaus C. "Community Control in Perspective." *IRCD Bulletin,* 8 (Nov. 1972), 3–11.

Moehlman, Arthur B. *Public Education in Detroit.* Bloomington, Ill.: Public School Publishing, 1925.

Moley, Raymond. "The Cleveland Surveys—Net." *The Survey,* 50 (May 15, 1923), 229–31.

Moore, Charles. "The Modern City Superintendent." *Education,* 21 (June 1901), 1–14.

Morehart, Grover Cleveland. *The Legal Status of City School Boards.* New York: Bureau of Publications, Teachers College, Columbia University, 1927.

Morrison, John Cayce. *The Legal Status of the City School Superintendent.* Baltimore: Warwick and York, 1922.

Mosely Educational Commission. *Reports of the Mosely Educational Commission to the United States of America, October–December 1903.* London: Co-Operative Printing Society, 1904.

Mowry, Duane. "The Milwaukee School System." *Educational Review,* 20 (Sept. 1900), 141–51.

Mowry, William A. "The Powers and Duties of School Superintendents." *Educational Review,* 9 (Jan. 1895), 38–51.

—— *Recollections of a New England Educator, 1838–1908.* New York: Silver, Burdett, 1908.

Nash, Charles R. *The History of Legislative and Administrative Changes Affecting the Philadelphia Public Schools, 1869–1921.* Philadelphia: published by the author, 1946.

Nearing, Scott. *The New Education: A Review of Progressive Educational Movements of the Day.* Chicago: Row, Peterson, 1915.

—— "Who's Who in Our Boards of Education?" *School and Society,* 5 (Jan. 20, 1917), 89–90.

—— "The Workings of a Large Board of Education." *Educational Review,* 38 (June 1909), 43–51.

Nelson, A. H. "The Little Red Schoolhouse." *Educational Review,* 23 (March 1902), 305.

Newby, Robert G., and David B. Tyack. "Victims without 'Crimes': Some Historical Perspectives on Black Education." *Journal of Negro Education,* 40 (Summer 1971), 192–206.

Newlon, Jesse H. *Educational Administration as Social Policy.* New York: Charles Scribner's Sons, 1934.

Northrup, B. G. *Report of the Secretary of the Board.* Annual Report of the Board of Education of the State of Connecticut, 1872.

Norton, John K., and Eugene S. Lawler. *Unfinished Business in American Education: An Inventory of Public School Expenditures in the United States.* Washington, D.C.: American Council on Education, 1946.

Novak, Michael. *The Rise of the Unmeltable Ethnics.* New York: Macmillan, 1972.

O'Brien, Sara R. *English for Foreigners.* Boston: Houghton Mifflin, 1909.

Odell, William Rockhold. *Educational Survey Report for the Philadelphia Board of Public Education.* Philadelphia: n.p., 1965.

Olin, Stephen H. "Public School Reform in New York." *Educational Review,* 8 (June 1894), 1–6.

Oregon Superintendent of Public Instruction. *Report for 1874.* Salem, Ore.: State Publishing Office, 1874.

Osofsky, Gilbert. "Progressivism and the Negro, New York, 1900–15." *American Quarterly,* 16 (Summer 1964), 153–68.

Palmer, A. Emerson. *The New York Public Schools.* New York: Macmillan, 1905.

Palmer, Albert W. *Orientals in American Life*. New York: Friendship Press, 1934.

Panunzio, Constantine M. *The Soul of an Immigrant*. New York: Macmillan, 1921.

Parks, Gordon. *The Learning Tree*. Greenwich, Conn.: Fawcett Books, 1963.

Patri, Angelo. *A Schoolmaster of the Great City*. New York: Macmillan, 1917.

Payne, William H. *Chapters on School Supervision: A Practical Treatise on Superintendence; Grading; Arranging Courses of Study; the Preparation and Use of Blanks, Records, and Reports; Examinations for Promotion, etc.* New York: American Book Co., 1903 [originally published in 1875].

Peil, Alice Applegate. "Old Oregon School Days." *Oregon Historical Quarterly*, 59 (Sept. 1958), 200.

Perkinson, Henry J. *The Imperfect Panacea: American Faith in Education, 1865–1965*. New York: Random House, 1968.

Perrin, John W. *The History of Compulsory Education in New England*. Meadville, Penn.: published by the author, 1896.

Philbrick, John D. *City School Systems in the United States*. U.S. Bureau of Education, Circular of Information no. 1. Washington, D.C.: GPO, 1885.

——— "Report of the Superintendent of Common Schools to the General Assembly [of Connecticut], May, 1856." *American Journal of Education*, 2 (Sept. 1856), 261–64.

Pierce, Bessie Louise. *A History of Chicago, 1871–1893*. Vol. III. New York: Knopf, 1957.

Pillsbury, W. B. "Selection—An Unnoticed Function of Education." *Scientific Monthly*, 12 (Jan. 1921), 62–74.

Pintner, Rudolph, and Helen Noble. "The Classification of School Children according to Mental Age." *Journal of Educational Research*, 2 (Nov. 1920), 713–28.

Popham, W. James. *Designing Teacher Evaluation Systems: A Series of Suggestions for Establishing Teacher Assessment Procedures as Required by the Stull Bill (AB 293), 1971 California Legislature*. Los Angeles: Instructional Objectives Exchange, 1971.

Porter, Jennie D. "The Problem of Negro Education in Northern and Border Cities." Unpub. Ph.D. diss., University of Cincinnati, 1928.

Powers, Alfred, and Howard M. Corning. "History of Education in Portland." Mimeo. Portland, Ore.: W.P.A. Adult Education Project, 1937.

Prince, John T. "The Evolution of School Supervision." *Educational Review*, 22 (Sept. 1901), 148–61.

Pritchett, Henry. "Educational Surveys." In Carnegie Foundation for the Advancement of Teaching, *Ninth Annual Report*, 1914, 118–23.

Raymer, Robert G. "A History of the Superintendency of Public Instruction in the State of Oregon, 1849–1925." Unpub. Ph.D. diss., University of Oregon, 1926.

Reid, Robert L. "The Professionalization of Public School Teachers: The Chicago Experience, 1895–1920." Unpub. Ph.D. diss., Northwestern University, 1968.

Reller, Theodore Lee. *The Development of the City Superintendency of Schools in the United States*. Philadelphia: published by the author, 1935.

Report of the Commission on Immigration on the Problem of Immigration in Massachusetts. Boston: Wright & Potter, 1914.

Report of a Committee of the National Education Association on Teachers' Salaries and Cost of Living. Ann Arbor: National Education Association, 1913.

Report of the Committee on Salaries, Tenure, and Pensions of Public School Teachers in the United States to the National Council of Education, July, 1905. N.p.: National Education Association, 1905.

Report of the National Advisory Commission on Civil Disorders. New York: New York Times Co., 1968.

Report to the Primary School Committee, June 15, 1846, on the Petition of Sundry Colored Persons, for the Abolition of the Schools for Colored Children. Boston: J. H. Eastburn, 1846.

Reports of the Annual Visiting Committees of the Public Schools of the City of Boston, 1845. Boston: J. H. Eastburn, 1845. Reproduced in Otis W. Caldwell and Stuart A. Courtis, *Then and Now in Education: 1845, 1923.* Yonkers-on-Hudson: World Book, 1925.

Rice, Joseph M. "A Plan to Free the Schools from Politics." *The Forum,* 16 (Dec. 1893), 500–507.

—— *The Public School System of the United States.* New York: Century, 1893.

Richardson, James F. *The New York Police: Colonial Times to 1901.* New York: Oxford University Press, 1970.

—— "To Control the City: The New York Police in Historical Perspective." In Kenneth T. Jackson and Stanley K. Schultz, eds., *Cities in American History,* 272–89. New York: Knopf, 1972.

Richman, Julia. "The Immigrant Child." *NEA Addresses and Proceedings,* 44th Annual Meeting, Asbury Park, N.J., 1905, 113–21.

—— "A Successful Experiment in Promoting Pupils." *Educational Review,* 18 (June 1899), 23–29.

—— "What Can Be Done in a Graded School for the Backward Child." *Survey,* 13 (Nov. 5, 1904), 129–31.

Ricker, David Swing. "The School-Teacher Unionized." *Educational Review,* 30 (Nov. 1905), 344–74.

Riis, Jacob. *The Children of the Poor.* New York: Charles Scribner's Sons, 1892.

Rischin, Moses. *The Promised City: New York's Jews, 1870–1914.* Cambridge, Mass.: Harvard University Press, 1962.

Roberts, Peter. *The Problem of Americanization.* New York: Macmillan, 1920.

Rogers, David. *110 Livingston Street: Politics and Bureaucracy in the New York City School System.* New York: Random House, 1968.

Rolle, Andrew. *The Immigrant Upraised: Italian Adventurers and Colonists in an Expanding America.* Norman, Okla.: University of Oklahoma Press, 1968.

Rollins, Frank. *School Administration in Municipal Government.* New York: Columbia University Press, 1902.

Rosenthal, Alan. *Pedagogues and Power: Teacher Groups in School Politics.* Syracuse: Syracuse University Press, 1969.

Rothman, David J. *The Discovery of the Asylum: Social Order and Disorder in the New Republic.* Boston: Little, Brown, 1971.

Rudy, Willis. *Schools in an Age of Mass Culture.* Englewood Cliffs, N.J.: Prentice-Hall, 1965.

Rules and Regulations and Course of Study of the Public Schools of District No. 1, Portland, Oregon. Portland, Ore., 1883.

Russell, Francis. "The Coming of the Jews." *Antioch Review,* 15 (March 1955), 19–38.

Ryan, William. *Blaming the Victim.* New York: Pantheon, 1971.

Salmon, Lucy. *Patronage in the Public Schools.* Boston: Women's Auxiliary of the Massachusetts Civil Service Reform Association, 1908.

Sayre, Wallace S. "Additional Observations on the Study of Administration: A Reply to 'Ferment in the Study of Organization.'" *Teachers College Record,* 60 (Oct. 1958), 73–76.

Schmid, Ralph Dickerson. "A Study of the Organizational Structure of the National Education Association, 1884–1921." Unpub. Ed.D. diss., Washington University, 1963.

School Directors of Milwaukee. *Proceedings, May 14, 1915.* Milwaukee: published by the Board, 1915.

"The School Mistress." *Harper's New Monthly Magazine,* 57 (Sept. 1878), 607–611.

Schrag, Peter. *The Decline of the WASP.* New York: Simon and Schuster, 1971.

———— *Village School Downtown: Politics and Education; A Boston Report.* Boston: Beacon, 1967.

Schultz, Stanley K. *The Culture Factory: Boston Public Schools, 1789–1860.* New York: Oxford University Press, 1973.

Scott, Marian Johonnot. "Conference of Eastern Public Education Association." *School Journal,* 74 (April 20, 1907), 396–97.

Sears, Barnabas. *Objections to the Public Schools Considered.* Boston: J. Wilson and Son, 1875.

Sears, Jesse B. *The School Survey: A Textbook on the Use of School Surveying in the Administration of Public Schooling.* New York: Houghton Mifflin, 1925.

Sears, Jesse B., and Adin D. Henderson. *Cubberley of Stanford and His Contribution to American Education.* Stanford, Calif.: Stanford University Press, 1957.

Selznick, Philip. *Leadership in Administration: A Sociological Interpretation.* Evanston, Ill.: Row Peterson, 1957.

Senkewicz, Robert. " 'To Punish Such Super-Patriotism': Catholics and Amendment 37." Unpub. seminar paper, Stanford University, 1971.

Seventh Annual Report of the Board of Education together with the Seventh Annual Report of the Secretary of the Board. Boston: Dutton and Wentworth, 1844.

Sexton, Patricia Cayo. *Education and Income: Inequalities of Opportunity in Our Public Schools.* New York: Viking, 1961.

Shamwell, Earl E. "The Vocational Choices of Negro Children Enrolled in the Minneapolis Public Schools with an Analysis of the Vocational Choices for the Children Made by Their Parents." Unpub. M.A. thesis, University of Minnesota, 1939.

Shatraw, Milton. "School Days." *American West,* 3 (Spring 1966), 68–71.

Shaw, Adele Marie. "Common Sense Country Schools." *World's Work,* 8 (June 1904), 4883–94.

———— "The Public Schools of a Boss-Ridden City." *World's Work,* 7 (Feb. 1904), 4460–66.

———— "The Spread of Vacation Schools." *World's Work,* 8 (Oct. 1904), 5405–14.

———— "The True Character of New York Public Schools." *World's Work,* 7 (Dec. 1903), 4204–21.

Shaw, Clifford, et al. *Brothers in Crime.* Chicago: University of Chicago Press, 1938.

Shearer, William J. *The Grading of Schools.* New York: H. P. Smith, 1898.

Shepard, Odell, ed. *The Heart of Thoreau's Journals.* Boston: Houghton Mifflin, 1927.

Shotwell, John B. *A History of the Schools of Cincinnati.* Cincinnati: School Life. Co., 1902.

Shradar, Victor L. "The Amenders and Appointees: The Changing of San

Francisco's Educational Establishment in 1921." Unpub. seminar paper, Stanford University, 1970.

Silberman, Charles E. *Crisis in the Classroom.* New York: Random House, 1970.

Silcox, Harry C. "The Pursuit of Black Education in Nineteenth-Century Boston and Philadelphia." Unpub. MS, 1972.

Simpson, Richard L., and Ida Harper Simpson. "Women and Bureaucracy in the Semi-Professions." In Amitai Etzioni, ed., *The Semi-Professions and Their Organization: Teachers, Nurses, Social Workers,* 196–265. New York: Free Press, 1969.

Sinette, Elinor D. "The Brownies' Book: A Pioneer Publication for Children." *Freedomways,* 5 (Winter 1965), 133–42.

Sizer, Theodore R. "Testing: Americans' Comfortable Panacea." Report for 1970 Invitational Conference on Educational Testing. Princeton: Educational Testing Service, 1971.

Skidmore, Thomas. *The Rights of Man to Property: Being a Proposition to Make It Equal among the Adults of the Present Generation.* New York: Alexander Ming, 1829.

Sloan, Douglas. "Historiography and the History of Education: Reflections on the Past Few Years." Unpub. MS, Dec. 1971.

Smith, Mary Gove. "Raphael in the Background: A Picture for Teachers of Aliens." *Education,* 39 (Jan. 1919), 270–79.

Smith, Olive M. "The Rural Social Center." *Oregon Teachers' Monthly,* 20 (Nov. 1915), 110.

Smith, Timothy L. "Immigrant Social Aspirations and American Education, 1880–1930." *American Quarterly,* 21 (Fall 1969), 523–43.

———— "Protestant Schooling and American Nationality, 1800–1850." *Journal of American History,* 53 (March 1967), 679–95.

Smith, Toulmin. *Local Self-Government and Centralization.* London: J. Chapman, 1851.

Smith, William Carlson. *Americans in the Making.* New York: D. Appleton-Century, 1939.

———— *The Second Generation Oriental in America.* Honolulu: Institute of Pacific Relations, 1927.

Snedden, David S. *Administration and Educational Work of American Juvenile Reform Schools.* New York: Teachers College, Columbia University, 1907.

Sone, Monica. *Nisei Daughter.* Boston: Little, Brown, 1953.

Spaulding, Frank E. *School Superintendents in Action in Five Cities.* Rindge, N.H.: Richard R. Smith, 1955.

Speed, Jonathan G. "The Negro in New York." *Harper's Weekly,* 44 (1901), 1249–50.

Spoehr, Luther W. "Sambo and the Heathen Chinee: Californians' Racial Stereotypes in the Late 1870's." *Pacific Historical Review,* 42 (May 1973), 185–204.

Spring, Joel H. *Education and the Rise of the Corporate State.* Boston: Beacon, 1972.

———— "Psychologists and the War: The Meaning of Intelligence in the Alpha and Beta Tests." *History of Education Quarterly,* 12 (Spring 1972), 3–14.

Stambler, Moses. "The Effect of Compulsory Education and Child Labor Laws on High School Attendance in New York City, 1898–1917." *History of Education Quarterly,* 8 (Summer 1968), 189–214.

Steffens, Lincoln. *The Autobiography of Lincoln Steffens.* New York: Harcourt, Brace, 1931.

Stephenson, Gilbert Thomas. *Race Distinctions in American Law.* New York: D. Appleton, 1910.

Still, Bayrd. *Milwaukee: The History of a City.* Madison, Wis.: State Historical Society of Wisconsin, 1948.

Strachan, Grace C. *Equal Pay for Equal Work: The Story of the Struggle for Justice Being Made by the Women Teachers of the City of New York.* New York: B. F. Buck, 1910.

Strayer, George D. "The Baltimore School Situation." *Educational Review,* 42 (Nov. 1911), 325–45.

——— "Progress in City School Administration during the Past Twenty-Five Years." *School and Society,* 32 (Sept. 1930), 375–78.

Strodtbeck, Fred L. "Family Interaction, Values, and Achievement." In David C. McClelland et al., *Talent and Society: New Perspectives in the Identification of Talent,* 135–91. Princeton: Van Nostrand, 1958.

Strong, Josiah. *Our Country,* ed. Jurgen Herbst. Cambridge, Mass.: Harvard University Press, 1963.

Struble, George. "A Study of School Board Personnel." *American School Board Journal,* 65 (Oct. 1922), 48–49.

Swett, John. *History of the Public School System of California.* San Francisco: A. L. Bancroft, 1876.

Swift, David. *Ideology and Change in the Public Schools: Latent Functions of Progressive Education.* Columbus: Merrill, 1971.

Taeuber, Karl E., and Alma F. Taeuber. "The Negro Population in the United States." In John P. Davis, ed., *The American Negro Reference Book,* 96–160. Englewood Cliffs, N.J.: Prentice-Hall, 1966.

"Teacher Evaluation." *California School Boards,* 31 (May 1972).

Terman, Lewis M. *The Measurement of Intelligence.* Boston: Houghton Mifflin, 1916.

——— "The Problem." In Lewis M. Terman, ed., *Intelligence Tests and School Reorganization,* 1–29. Yonkers-on-Hudson: World Book, 1922.

——— "The Use of Intelligence Tests in the Grading of School Children." *Journal of Educational Research,* 1 (Jan. 1920), 20–32.

Terrell, Mary Church. "History of the High School for Negroes in Washington." *Journal of Negro History,* 2 (July 1917), 252–65.

Theisen, William Walter. *The City Superintendent and the Board of Education.* New York: Teachers College, Columbia University, 1917.

Thernstrom, Stephan. "Immigrants and WASPs: Ethnic Differences in Occupational Mobility in Boston, 1890–1940." In Stephan Thernstrom and Richard Sennett, eds., *Nineteenth-Century Cities: Essays in the New Urban History,* 125–64. New Haven: Yale University Press, 1969.

——— "Up from Slavery." *Perspectives in American History,* 1 (1967), 434–39.

Thomas, Alan M., Jr. "American Education and the Immigrant." *Teachers College Record,* 55 (Feb. 1954), 253–67.

Thomas, Lawrence G. *The Occupational Structure and Education.* Englewood Cliffs, N.J.: Prentice-Hall, 1956.

Thompson, Frank. *The Schooling of the Immigrant.* New York: Harper & Row, 1920.

Thronbrough, Emma Lou. "The Negro in Indiana: A Study of a Minority." Indianapolis: Indiana Historical Bureau, 1957.

Thurston, Eve. "Ethiopia Unshackled: A Brief History of the Education of

Negro Children in New York City." *Bulletin of the New York Public Library,* 69 (April 1965), 211–31.

Thwing, Charles. "A New Profession." *Educational Review,* 15 (Jan. 1898), 26–33.

Ticknor, George. "Free Schools of New England." *North American Review,* 19 (1824), 448–57.

Todd, Helen M. "Why Children Work: The Children's Answer." *McClure's Magazine,* 40 (April 1913), 68–79.

Troen, Selwyn. "Popular Education in Nineteenth Century St. Louis." *History of Education Quarterly,* 13 (Spring 1973), 23–40.

——— "Public Education and the Negro: St. Louis, 1866–1880." Unpub. MS, 1972.

Tupper, C. R. "The Use of Intelligence Tests in the Schools of a Small City." In Lewis M. Terman, ed., *Intelligence Tests and School Reorganization,* 92–102. Yonkers-on-Hudson: World Book, 1922.

Twelfth Annual Report of the [New York] City Superintendent of Schools for the Year Ending July 31, 1910. New York: n.p., n.d.

Tyack, David B. "Bureaucracy and the Common School: The Example of Portland, Oregon, 1851–1913." *American Quarterly,* 19 (Fall 1967), 475–98.

——— "Catholic Power, Black Power, and the Schools." *Educational Forum,* 32 (Nov. 1967), 27–29.

——— "Education and Social Unrest, 1873–1878." *Harvard Educational Review,* 31 (Spring 1961), 194–212.

——— *George Ticknor and the Boston Brahmins.* Cambridge, Mass.: Harvard University Press, 1967.

——— "The Kingdom of God and the Common School: Protestant Ministers and the Educational Awakening in the West." *Harvard Educational Review,* 36 (Fall 1966), 447–69.

——— "Needed: The Reform of a Reform." In William E. Dickinson, ed., *New Dimensions in School Board Leadership: A Seminar Report and Workbook,* 29–51. Evanston, Ill.: National School Boards Association, 1969.

——— "New Perspectives on the History of American Education." In Herbert J. Bass, ed., *The State of American History,* 22–42. Chicago: Quadrangle Books, 1970.

——— "Onward Christian Soldiers: Religion in the American Common School." In Paul Nash, ed., *History and Education: The Educational Uses of the Past,* 212–55. New York: Random House, 1970.

——— "The Perils of Pluralism." *American Historical Review,* 74 (Oct. 1968), 74–98.

U.S. Bureau of the Census. *Historical Statistics of the United States: Colonial Times to 1957.* Washington, D.C.: GPO, 1960.

——— *Statistical Abstract of the United States: 1967.* Washington, D.C.: GPO, 1967.

U.S. Commission on Civil Rights. *Racial Isolation in the Public Schools.* 2 vols. Washington, D.C.: GPO, 1967.

U.S. Immigration Commission. *The Children of Immigrants in Schools.* Washington, D.C.: GPO, 1911.

U.S. Senate. *Abstracts of Reports of the Immigration Commission,* II, 1–86. Senate Document 747, 61st Cong., 3d sess., 1910.

Van Denburg, Joseph King. *Causes of the Elimination of Students in Public Secondary Schools of New York City.* Contributions to Education, no. 47. New York: Teachers College, Columbia University, 1911.

Vare, William S. *My Forty Years in Politics.* Philadelphia: Roland Swain, 1933.

Vidich, Arthur J., and Joseph Bensman. *Small Town in Mass Society: Class, Power, and Religion in a Rural Community.* Rev. ed. Princeton: Princeton University Press, 1968.

Viggers, Christine. "The Importance of the Women Teachers' Organization in the Equal Pay for Teachers Controversy." Unpub. M.A. thesis, University of Oregon, 1973.

Wade, Richard C. *The Urban Frontier.* Chicago: University of Chicago Press, 1964.

—— "Violence in the Cities: A Historical View." In Charles U. Daly, ed., *Urban Violence,* 7–26. Chicago: University of Chicago Center for Policy Study, 1969.

Waller, Willard. *The Sociology of Teaching.* New York: Wiley, 1965.

Warfield, W. C. "How to Test the Quality of a Teacher's Work." *NEA Addresses and Proceedings,* 34th Annual Meeting, St. Paul, Minn., 1895, 218–31.

Warner, Sam Bass, Jr. "If All the World Were Philadelphia: A Scaffolding for Urban History, 1774–1930." *American Historical Review,* 74 (Oct. 1968), 26–43.

—— *The Private City: Philadelphia in Three Periods of Its Growth.* Philadelphia: University of Pennsylvania Press, 1968.

Weinberg, Meyer, ed. *Integrated Education: A Reader.* Beverly Hills, Calif.: Glencoe, 1968.

—— *Race and Place: A Legal History of the Neighborhood School.* Washington, D.C.: GPO, 1967.

Weinstein, James. *The Corporate Ideal in the Liberal State, 1900–1918.* Boston: Beacon, 1968.

Wesley, Edgar B. *NEA, the First Hundred Years: The Building of the Teaching Profession.* New York: Harper & Brothers, 1957.

West, Allan M. "What's Bugging Teachers." *Saturday Review,* 48 (Oct. 16, 1965), 88.

West, James [Carl Withers]. *Plainville, U.S.A.* New York: Columbia University Press, 1945.

Wetmore, S. A. "Boston School Administration." *Educational Review,* 14 (Sept. 1897), 105–117.

White, Arthur O. "Jim Crow Education in Lockport." *New York State Association Proceedings,* 67 (Spring 1969), 265–82.

White, Dana F. "Education in the Turn-of-the-Century School." *Urban Education,* 1 (Spring 1969), 169–82.

White, E. B. "Letter from the East." *New Yorker,* March 27, 1971, 35–37.

White, E. E. "Religion in the School." *NEA Addresses and Proceedings,* 10th Annual Meeting, Trenton, N.J., 1869, 297.

"Why Superintendents Lose Their Jobs." *American School Board Journal,* 52 (May 1916), 18–19.

Wiebe, Robert H. *The Search for Order, 1877–1920.* New York: Hill and Wang, 1967.

—— "The Social Functions of Public Education." *American Quarterly,* 21 (Summer 1969), 147–64.

Wiley, Frank L. "The Layman in School Administration." *Teachers College Record,* 11 (Nov. 1910), 2–13.

Wilkerson, Doxey A. "Blame the Negro Child!" *Freedomways,* 8 (Fall 1968), 340–46.

———— "Compensatory Education." In Sheldon Marcus and Harry N. Rivlin, eds., *Conflicts in Urban Education*, 19–39. New York: Basic Books, 1970.

———— "A Determination of the Peculiar Problems of Negroes in Contemporary American Society." *Journal of Negro Education*, 5 (July 1936), 324–50.

———— "The Negro in American Education: A Research Memorandum for the Carnegie-Myrdal Study 'The Negro in America.' " 3 vols. New York, 1940. Unpub. MS in Schomburg Collection, New York Public Library.

Winship, A. E. "What the Superintendent Is Not." *NEA Addresses and Proceedings*, 38th Annual Meeting, Los Angeles, 1899, 307–309.

Wirth, Arthur G. *Education in the Technological Society: The Vocational-Liberal Studies Controversy in the Early Twentieth Century*. Scranton, Penn.: Intext Educational Publishers, 1972.

———— *John Dewey as Educator: His Design for Work in Education (1894–1904)*. New York: Wiley, 1966.

Wirth, Louis. "Urbanism as a Way of Life." *American Journal of Sociology*, 44 (July 1938), 1–24.

Wohl, R. Richard. "The 'Country Boy' Myth and Its Place in American Urban Culture: The Nineteenth-Century Contribution." *Perspectives in American History*, 3 (1969), 77–156.

Woodring, Paul. "The One-Room School." In Paul Woodring and John Scanlon, eds., *American Education Today*, 147–53. New York: McGraw-Hill, 1963.

Woodruff, Clinton R. "A Corrupt School System." *Educational Review*, 26 (Dec. 1903), 433–39.

Woodson, Carter G. *The Education of the Negro prior to 1861*. New York: G. P. Putnam's Sons, 1915.

———— "Negro Life and History in Our Schools." *Journal of Negro History*, 4 (July 1919), 273–80.

Woodward, C. Vann, ed. *The Comparative Approach to American History*. New York: Basic Books, 1968.

Woodward, Elizabeth A. "Subject Matter Most Vital for the Adjustment of the Non-English-Speaking Woman to American Life." *NEA Addresses and Proceedings*, 62nd Annual Meeting, Washington, D.C., 1924, 573–76.

Woody, Clifford, and Paul V. Sangren. *Administration of the Testing Program*. Yonkers-on-Hudson: World Book, 1933.

Woolston, Florence. "Our Untrained Citizens." *Survey*, 23 (Oct. 2, 1909), 21–35.

Wyllie, Irwin G. *The Self-Made Man in America*. New Brunswick, N.J.: Rutgers University Press, 1954.

Wytrwal, Joseph A. *America's Polish Heritage: A Social History of the Poles in America*. Detroit: Endurance Press, 1961.

Yeager, R. L. "School Boards, What and Why?" *NEA Addresses and Proceedings*, 35th Annual Meeting, Buffalo, 1896, 973–79.

Young, Ella Flagg. *Isolation in the School*. Chicago: University of Chicago Press, 1901.

———— "A Reply." *NEA Addresses and Proceedings*, 54th Annual Meeting, New York, 1916, 356–59.

Young, Kimball. *Mental Differences in Certain Immigrant Groups*. Eugene, Ore.: University of Oregon Press, 1923.

Zeigler, Harmon. *The Political Life of American Teachers*. Englewood Cliffs, N.J.: Prentice-Hall, 1967.

Zitron, Celia Lewis. *The New York City Teachers Union, 1916–1964: A Story of Educational and Social Commitment*. New York: Humanities Press, 1968.

Index